Synthesis Lectures on Distributed Computing Theory

Series Editor

Michel Raynal, Rennes, France

The series publishes short books on topics pertaining to distributed computing theory. The scope largely follows the purview of premier information and computer science conference. Potential topics include, but not are limited to: distributed algorithms and lower bounds, algorithm design methods, formal modeling and verification of distributed algorithms, and concurrent data structures.

Ashish Choudhury · Arpita Patra

Secure Multi-Party Computation Against Passive Adversaries

Ashish Choudhury
International Institute of Information
Technology
Bangalore, Karnataka, India

Arpita Patra
Department of Computer Science
and Automation
Indian Institute of Science Bangalore
Bangalore, Karnataka, India

ISSN 2155-1626   ISSN 2155-1634 (electronic)
Synthesis Lectures on Distributed Computing Theory
ISBN 978-3-031-12166-1   ISBN 978-3-031-12164-7 (eBook)
https://doi.org/10.1007/978-3-031-12164-7

This Springer imprint is published by the registered company Springer Nature Switzerland AG
The registered company address is: Gewerbestrasse 11, 6330 Cham, Switzerland

Preface

Ever since its inception, MPC is one of the most widely studied topics in secure distributed computing. There are two major categories of MPC protocols, the first category is that of MPC protocols against passive corruption, whereas the other category has maliciously-secure MPC protocols. While passive corruption deals with a benign adversary who simply eavesdrops on the state of the corrupt parties during the protocol execution, malicious corruption deals with a more powerful adversary, who can control and force the corrupt parties to behave in any arbitrary fashion during the protocol execution. Even though the passive corruption model may seem very weak, achieving security against such a benign form of adversary turns out to be non-trivial and demands sophisticated and highly advanced techniques. Moreover, very often, protocols secure against semi-honest corruptions serve as the basis for protocols secure against a malicious adversary. We strongly believe that the topic of passively-secure MPC protocols is in itself is a very vast and important topic to be covered in a single course.

The aim of this lecture series is to focus *only* on the passive corruption model and present all the seminal possibility and feasibility results of this model, ever since the inception of MPC, with formal security proofs. We present protocols both against computationally bounded as well as computationally unbounded adversaries. Detailed security proofs are provided for the seminal protocols. For a better understanding of the underlying concepts, pictorial illustrations are provided and several examples have been worked out. We also present the state-of-the-art efficiency improvement techniques in the domain of passively-secure MPC protocols. Our intention is to provide the readers a detailed and comprehensive explanation of all the important concepts and techniques in this domain with an aim to unfold the evolution of this topic since its inception to date.

This lecture series is intended to be self-contained enough to be read by anyone who has some background in Discrete Mathematics, Probability Theory and Algorithms. We assume *no* background regarding cryptography. The authors have used a large part of this lecture series for teaching graduate-level courses at their respective institutes. A companion online course with video lectures is freely available in the NPTEL course series at https://nptel.ac.in/courses/106108229.

Feedback and Errata

Our main aim in this lecture series was to provide a detailed introduction to this very important topic of secure multiparty computation and we hope that we will succeed in our mission. We will be very happy to receive feedback on this lecture series, especially constructive comments about how to further improve it. We tried to ensure that there are no typos and errors. However, if you do find any, then we will be very obliged if you can kindly let us know by emailing us at arpita@iisc.ac.in and ashish.choudhury@iiitb.ac.in. We plan to maintain a dedicated homepage for this lecture series with a complete list of known errata.

Bangalore, India   Ashish Choudhury
May 2022   Arpita Patra

Acknowledgments

Ashish Choudhury: I would like to thank all my beloved teachers at IIT Madras for teaching me, especially Prof. Kamala Krithivasn, Prof. C. Pandu Rangan and Prof. C. A. Choudum for teaching wonderful courses related to theoretical computer science, which sparked my love and interest for theoretical computer science. Special thanks to my Ph.D. supervisor Prof. C. Pandu Rangan, for being a great advisor, a great teacher, a great critic, a great friend and overall a great philosopher. My sincere thanks to Prof. Michel Raynal, who invited me to write a monogram on the topic of MPC, as part of the synthesis lecture series. I would also like to thank Prof. Palash Sarkar and Prof. Nigel Smart, for being wonderful hosts and advisors during my post-doctoral research. I am also thankful to all my past and present thesis students for all the wonderful discussions related to secure computation, which greatly enhanced my knowledge about this topic. Special thanks to the wonderful colleagues of IIIT Bangalore, for all their encouragement and well wishes ever since I joined the institute. I am grateful to my wonderful co-author of this book, Arpita, who is always a role model for me and for several aspiring young researchers in India in the domain of cryptography. Lastly, I would like to give a special thanks to my daughter Aparajita and to the all mighty for whatever I am today.

This project is an outcome of the R&D work undertaken in the project under the Visvesvaraya Ph.D. Scheme of Ministry of Electronics & Information Technology, Government of India, being implemented by Digital India Corporation.

Arpita Patra: First, I would like to thank my wonderful co-author of this book, Ashish, for being my constant companion in research since my Ph.D. days. He has been my continuous source of support in both academics and life. This book would not be possible without his sheer persuasion. It is he who felt that we must share and spread our excitement about secure computation, the topic we both love, cherish and relish most in cryptography. The love-factor apart, secure computation has hugely advanced the theory of computation. Towards the goal of spreading the joy of secure computation, he has offered courses on cryptography and secure computation with the support of NPTEL, a great online platform for learning in India. While we are blessed to have some great books on cryptography, the same is not true for secure computation. An accessible book on secure computation for curious students, who are about to be graduated or have just completed their graduation, seemed like the next apt step. This book will surely serve as a stepping stone to the vibrant and beautiful world of secure computation. I am thankful that he convinced me about the need and offered to jointly write the book. "I would also like to thank Prof. Michel Raynal", for providing me the opportunity, to be a part of this project.

I would like to thank my Ph.D. advisor, Prof. C. Pandu Rangan, for introducing me to the area of secure computation and for creating the most conducive environment for learning during my Ph.D. days.

I had the pleasure of working with many talented and hyper-active researchers who enriched my knowledge and deepened my understanding in cryptography and secure computation over the years. Special mention goes to Benny Applebaum, Yuval Ishai, Ivan Damgaard, Eliran Kachlon, Gilad Asharov, Carmit Hazay, Yehuda Lindell, Nigel Smart, Ittai Abraham and Akshayaram Srinivasan.

I am grateful to all my past and current students for the most dynamic and vibrant research ambience where we grew and continue to grow together. They are the ones who helped me to widen my knowledge spreading across the theory and practice of secure computation. I would like to thank Divya Ravi, Ajith Suresh, Swati Singla, Megha Byali, Varsha Bhat, Nishat Koti, Shravani Patil and Protik Paul for productive discussions over a multitude of topics and a memorable time.

My parents, Sima and Ahibhushan Patra, are my pillars of support. Thank you for being there for me always! Even today, they are the ones I look up to, in times of distress and moments of joy.

Lastly, I would like to thank my daughter Aparajita and my better half Ashish. All that I am, or hope to be, I owe to them. Without you, life has no meaning. Thank you for being part of my life!

May 2022   Ashish Choudhury
                                                                                           Arpita Patra

Contents

1 **Introduction** 1
   1.1 Real-World Applications of MPC 2
   1.2 Secure MPC: A Powerful Abstraction 4
   1.3 The Dimensions of Secure MPC 4
   1.4 Our Setting and Book Organization 7

2 **Relevant Topics from Abstract Algebra** 9
   2.1 Groups, Rings and Fields 9
   2.2 Properties of Polynomials over a Field 12

3 **Secret Sharing** 17
   3.1 Secret Sharing: Motivation and Definition 17
   3.2 A General Secret-Sharing Scheme 20
   3.3 Additive Secret-Sharing Scheme 23
   3.4 Efficient Threshold Secret-Sharing Scheme 24
      3.4.1 Advanced Properties of Polynomials over a Field 24
      3.4.2 The Shamir Secret-Sharing Scheme 27
   3.5 Application of Secret Sharing: Perfectly-Secure Message
      Transmission (PSMT) 29
   3.6 Secret Sharing Tolerating Malicious Adversaries 31

4 **A Toy MPC Protocol** 33
   4.1 Problem Definition and an Ideal Solution 33
   4.2 A Protocol to Securely Compute the Sum 34
   4.3 Possible Attacks Against Protocol Π_{Sum} 40

5 **The BGW Perfectly-Secure MPC Protocol for Linear Functions** 43
   5.1 Network Model and Adversary Setting 43
   5.2 The Principle Behind BGW Protocol: Shared Circuit-Evaluation 45
   5.3 Additional Properties of Shamir's Secret-Sharing Scheme 46
   5.4 BGW Protocol for Linear Functions 48
      5.4.1 The Protocol 49

　　　　5.4.2　Complexity Analysis of $\Pi_{\text{BGW-Linear}}$ 50
　　　　5.4.3　Security Analysis of $\Pi_{\text{BGW-Linear}}$ Through Example 50
　　　　5.4.4　Formal Security Definition of MPC 53
　　　　5.4.5　Formal Security Analysis of $\Pi_{\text{BGW-Linear}}$ 56
　　5.5　Securely Computing Product of a Public Matrix and a Secret
　　　　　Vector 61
　　5.6　Dealing with Malicious Adversaries 65

6　The BGW Perfectly-Secure MPC Protocol for Any Arbitrary Function ... 67
　　6.1　Challenges in Securely Evaluating Multiplication Gates 67
　　6.2　The Degree-Reduction Problem 70
　　6.3　The BGW Protocol for Any Function 71
　　　　6.3.1　The Sequential Modular Composition 71
　　　　6.3.2　The BGW Protocol in the $\mathcal{F}_{\text{Mult}}$-Hybrid Model 73
　　6.4　Securely Computing the $\mathcal{F}_{\text{Mult}}$ Function 75
　　　　6.4.1　The BGW Protocol for Degree-Reduction 76
　　　　6.4.2　The GRR Protocol for Degree-Reduction 78
　　　　6.4.3　The Complexity of the BGW Protocol 85
　　6.5　On the Necessity of the $t < n/2$ Condition 86
　　　　6.5.1　Impossibility of Perfectly-Secure 2-Party AND 86
　　6.6　Dealing with Malicious Adversaries 90

7　Perfectly-Secure MPC in the Pre-processing Model 91
　　7.1　MPC in the Pre-processing Model 91
　　7.2　Perfectly-Secure MPC Using Beaver's Multiplication-Triples 93
　　　　7.2.1　Securely Computing the Functionality $\mathcal{F}_{\text{Triple}}$ 97
　　7.3　Perfectly-Secure MPC Using Double-Shared Randomness 101
　　　　7.3.1　Securely Computing Function $\mathcal{F}_{\text{Double}}$ 104
　　7.4　On Lower Bounds for Optimally-Resilient Perfectly-Secure MPC 108
　　7.5　Dealing with Malicious Adversaries 109

8　Perfectly-Secure MPC Tolerating General Adversaries 111
　　8.1　Motivation for General Adversaries 111
　　8.2　Preliminaries and Definitions 112
　　　　8.2.1　Definitions 113
　　8.3　Necessary Condition for Perfectly-Secure MPC Against
　　　　　Non-threshold Adversaries 115
　　8.4　Various Building Blocks 116
　　　　8.4.1　The Secret-Sharing Protocol 117
　　　　8.4.2　The Reconstruction Protocol 117
　　　　8.4.3　Multiplication Protocol 118
　　8.5　A Perfectly-Secure MPC Protocol for Non-threshold Adversaries 120
　　8.6　Dealing with Malicious Adversaries 122

9   Perfectly-Secure MPC for Small Number of Parties 123
   9.1   MPC for Small Number of Parties: Motivation 123
   9.2   Secure 3PC Protocol of [9] 124
       9.2.1   The Secret-Sharing and Reconstruction Protocols 125
       9.2.2   The Multiplication Protocol 127
       9.2.3   Protocol for Securely Computing $\mathcal{F}_{\mathsf{Zero}}$ 128
       9.2.4   Putting Everything Together: The Secure 3PC Protocol 130
   9.3   ASTRA: Secure 3PC of [47] 131
       9.3.1   The Secret-Sharing and Reconstruction Protocols 133
       9.3.2   The Multiplication Protocol 135
       9.3.3   The ASTRA 3PC Protocol 137
   9.4   Dealing with Malicious Adversaries 137

10   The GMW MPC Protocol 139
   10.1   Cryptographically-Secure MPC: The Motivation 139
   10.2   Preliminaries and Definitions 141
   10.3   The GMW Protocol in the Pre-processing Model 143
       10.3.1   Additive Secret-Sharing and Related Protocols 143
       10.3.2   The GMW Protocol in the $\mathcal{F}_{\mathsf{Triple}}$-hybrid Model 145
       10.3.3   Protocol for $\mathcal{F}_{\mathsf{Triple}}$ in the $\mathcal{F}_{\mathsf{Mult}}$-hybrid Model 147
   10.4   Protocols for Computing $\mathcal{F}_{\mathsf{Mult}}$ in $\mathcal{F}_{\mathsf{OT}}$-hybrid Model 148
       10.4.1   Computing $\mathcal{F}_{\mathsf{Mult}}$ for 2-party Case over Boolean Ring 149
       10.4.2   Computing $\mathcal{F}_{\mathsf{Mult}}$ for n-party Case over Boolean Ring 152
       10.4.3   Computing $\mathcal{F}_{\mathsf{Mult}}$ over a General Ring 152
   10.5   Dealing with Malicious Adversaries 155

11   Oblivious Transfer 157
   11.1 $\mathcal{F}_{\mathsf{OT}}$ Cannot Be Computed Against Unbounded Adversaries 157
   11.2   Variants of OT 158
       11.2.1   1-out-of-2-OT $\Rightarrow$1-out-of-N-OT 159
   11.3   Securely Computing $\mathcal{F}_{\mathsf{OT}}$ 161
       11.3.1   Enhanced One-Way Trapdoor Permutation (OWTP)
              and Hard-core Predicates 162
       11.3.2   Protocol for Computing $\mathcal{F}_{\mathsf{OT}}$ from OWTP 165
   11.4   Efficiency of OT 168
       11.4.1   Domain Extension for OT 169
       11.4.2   Oblivious Transfer of a Matrix 171
       11.4.3   The OT-Extension Protocol 172
   11.5   Dealing with Malicious Adversaries 174

12   Yao's Protocol for Secure 2-party Computation 177
   12.1   Preliminaries and Definitions 178
      12.1.1   Garbling Scheme as a Primitive 179
   12.2   Yao's Garbling Scheme 180
      12.2.1   Informal Description of Yao's Garbling Scheme 180
      12.2.2   Special Symmetric-Key Encryption Used in Yao's
             Garbling 182
      12.2.3   Yao's Garbling Scheme: The Formal Details 188
   12.3   Yao's Protocol for Secure 2PC 205
   12.4   Optimizations of Yao's Garbling Scheme and Yao's Protocol 207
      12.4.1   The Point-and-Permute Technique or How to Garble
             from any CPA-secure Encryption Scheme 207
      12.4.2   The Free-XOR Optimization 212
      12.4.3   Other Optimizations of Yao's Garbling Scheme 215
      12.4.4   Yao's Protocol in 2 Rounds 216
      12.4.5   Yao's Protocol in the Pe-processing Model 216
   12.5   Tolerating Malicious Adversaries 218

13   Cryptographically-Secure 3PC 219
   13.1   Cryptographically-Secure 3PC Protocol of [9] 219
   13.2   Cryptographically Secure Variant of ASTRA 221
   13.3   Dealing with Malicious Adversaries 223

Bibliography 225

About the Authors

Dr. Ashish Choudhury is currently an associate professor at the International Institute of Information Technology (IIIT) Bangalore. He received his MS (by Research) and a Ph.D. degree from the Indian Institute of Technology, Madras. After his Ph.D., he worked as a visiting scientist at Indian Statistical Institute Kolkata and then as a research assistant at University of Bristol. His research interests include theoretical cryptography, with an emphasis on cryptographic protocols.

Arpita Patra is presently an associate professor at the Indian Institute of Science. Her area of interest is cryptography, focusing on theoretical and practical aspects of secure multiparty computation protocols. She received her Ph.D. from Indian Institute of Technology (IIT), Madras, and held post-doctoral positions at University of Bristol, UK, ETH Zurich, Switzerland, and Aarhus University, Denmark. Her research has been recognized with a Google Research Award, a NASI Young Scientist Platinum Jubilee Award, a SERB Women Excellence award, an INAE Young Engineer award and associateships with various scientific bodies such as the Indian Academy of Sciences (IAS), Indian National Academy of Engineering (INAE), The World Academy of Sciences (TWAS). She is a council member of the Indian Association for Research in Computing Science (IARCS) since December 2017.

Introduction

1

In today's digital era, we are living in the age of data. Data is everywhere around us. For example, every individual is associated with enormous amount of data, such as age, salary, citizenship, identity details (passport, PAN card, AADHAR etc.), income tax details, medical details, biometric traits (face, fingerprint, iris, speech), genome signature, bank account details, family member details, etc. Every profitable organization has details regarding its employees, profit, loss, turnover, salaries, etc. Similarly, educational organizations have details related to employees, students, awards, recognitions, patents, scientific publications, products, dropouts, drug addicts, suicide and sexual harassments cases, etc. Banks have details related to their employees, transactions etc. Hospitals have details related to their patients, doctors, nurses etc. Intelligence agencies (e.g., Research and Analysis Wing and Intelligence Bureau of India) have details regarding their employees, secret operations, etc. Military Organizations (e.g., army, air force, navy) have details related to their personals, operations, intercepted messages, etc. Countries have details about citizens, satellites, nuclear weapons, etc. The list goes on.

Though a lot of data are available freely in the public domain, certain data are very sensitive and may not be publicly available. For example, the data related to an individual's age, salary, Internet-banking details, biometric traits, genome signature are very sensitive. Educational institutions would prefer to keep private the details related to the suicide and sexual harassment cases. Patient database of any hospital is highly sensitive and cannot be made publicly available. Intelligence agencies will never prefer to make public the details of their employees and current secret operations. It is extremely dangerous for any country to publicly disclose the details related to its missile and nuclear programs.

Unauthorized access of sensitive data can be prevented via the use of various cryptographic primitives. Informally, cryptography is a mathematical science, which deals with constructing and analyzing algorithms, that prevent any unauthorized party from accessing sensitive data. One of the major goals of cryptography is to solve the problem of secure communication, which allows a *sender* and a *receiver* with *no* pre-shared information, to

A. Choudhury and A. Patra, *Secure Multi-Party Computation Against Passive Adversaries*,
Synthesis Lectures on Distributed Computing Theory,
https://doi.org/10.1007/978-3-031-12164-7_1

securely exchange messages over a public network, such as the Internet. However, today, cryptography is far beyond just secure communication. There are several real-world applications, where various mutually-distrusting parties with individual sensitive data are interested to perform some joint computation on their data, *without* disclosing their individual data to each other (we will soon see several examples of such applications). Secure *multi-party computation* (MPC) is a branch of cryptography, which deals with constructing and analyzing protocols to solve the above problem. Before we proceed, we give several examples of real-world applications which require mutually-distrusting parties to collaborate for performing some joint computation on sensitive data belonging to the individual parties.

1.1   Real-World Applications of MPC

In this section, we discuss several real-world applications to motivate the problem of secure MPC. The list is not comprehensive and there are tons of other applications.

Privacy-preserving data mining [114]: Consider a scenario where the local government authorities of a city are interested to find out various statistics about the patients registered across all the hospitals in the city. Examples of such statistics include but are not limited to finding the number of patients suffering from a particular disease (such as AIDS), finding the number of patients registered in more than one hospital, etc. One trivial way of solving this problem is to *trust* the government authorities and let each hospital share its entire patient database with the authorities. However, patient records are highly sensitive and there are various legal implications in sharing patient details. Instead, the hospitals would be interested to run a protocol among themselves, which allows them to compute the desired statistics without revealing any additional information about the individual patient databases of the hospitals.

Secure E-auction [36]: Consider a scenario where a group of bidders are interested to bid online for some antique, with the highest bid being the winning bid. Each bidder has a private bid-value which is a sensitive information. The bidders would like to run a protocol among themselves, which allows them to only learn the winning bid and nothing else.

Private Set Intersection (PSI) [73]: Let Alice and Bob be two mutually-distrusting parties with individual sets, who are interested to find out the elements common to both their sets, but would not like to reveal any information about the remaining elements in their individual sets to each other. An interesting use case of the PSI problem is the following: imagine Alice installs the Facebook messenger on her mobile and she is interested to let Facebook server notify all her friends who are also using Facebook messenger about this. However, Alice does not want the Facebook server to learn anything additional about Alice's contact list and at the same time, the privacy of the list of all Facebook users should be maintained. To solve this problem, Alice and Facebook server can run a PSI protocol, where the role of Bob is played by the Facebook server, thus allowing both Alice and Facebook to find out the list of people from Alice's contact list who are using Facebook messenger.

Yao's Millionaires' Problem [138]: The seminal work of Yao [138], which first formulated the secure MPC problem, presented the following toy application. There are two millionaires and they are interested to find out the richer between them, without disclosing the exact value of their individual assets to each other. Note that, the loosing millionaire will learn from the result, that its asset is less than the winner (and vice-versa), but that is allowed to be revealed.

Securely Preventing Satellite Collisions [90, 100]: Imagine two countries with mutually-conflicting interests launch their respective spy satellite, where the trajectory information of the individual satellite is known only to the respective country and which is a sensitive information. Since the satellites are launched without knowing each other's trajectory information, there is always a possibility of collision, which would result in a tremendous financial loss to both the countries. Indeed, several such collisions have been reported in the past. To prevent such a collision, the two countries might be interested to find out the chances of a possible collision, without disclosing their respective trajectory information to each other.

Privacy-preserving Machine Learning (PPML) [46, 121, 123, 130]: Machine learning (ML) is increasingly becoming one of the dominant research fields, with many real-world applications like smart keyboard predictions, self-driving cars, healthcare and medicine, etc. In order to be deployed in practice, ML models need to provide a high level of accuracy and robustness, which require availability of data from varied sources. Unfortunately, accumulating data from various sources is often not practical to realize for a single stakeholder. Moreover, there might be legal implications for any organization to share datasets with others without the prior consent of the customers. It is also possible that the companies providing ML services to clients end up leaking the model parameters, thus rendering its services redundant. The exciting area of PPML has emerged as a flourishing research area to deal with the above challenges. PPML techniques allow mutually-distrusting servers to collaborate and prepare an ML training model based on the training data across all the servers, without compromising the training data of the individual servers. This is referred as privacy-preserving training. The techniques also ensure that no information about a query or dataset is leaked other than what is permissible by the algorithm, which in some cases might be only the prediction output. This is referred as privacy-preserving inference.

1.2   Secure MPC: A Powerful Abstraction

All the applications discussed in the previous section can be abstracted by the problem of secure MPC as described below. There is a set of n mutually-distrusting parties, say $\mathcal{P} = \{P_1, \ldots, P_n\}$ where $n \geq 2$, with each party P_i having some private input x_i. The distrust in the system is modelled by a centralized entity, called *adversary*, who can "control" a subset of the parties in a varieties of ways, during the execution of a protocol. The parties not under the control of the adversary are called as *honest* parties, while the parties under adversary's control are called as *corrupt* parties. The honest parties may not know the identities of the corrupt parties. There is a *publicly-known n*-ary function f and the goal is to let every party learn the output $y \overset{def}{=} f(x_1, \ldots, x_n)$, such that the adversary does not learn any additional information, beyond what can be learnt from y and the inputs of the corrupt parties.

The MPC problem can be easily solved in the presence of a *trusted third party* (TTP). Each P_i can (securely) hand over its input x_i to the TTP, who then computes the output y and discloses y publicly. Since no interaction happens among the parties and the TTP is trusted to not disclose the individual inputs, the corrupt parties do not learn anything additional beyond the function output and the inputs of the corrupt parties. However, the problem with the above solution (which is often called as the *ideal* solution) is that it creates a *single point-of-failure*. Namely, if the TTP is compromised, then the security breaks down completely. Moreover, in practice it is not always possible to find such a TTP. The goal of a secure MPC protocol is to let the parties interact among themselves to emulate the role of the TTP in the above ideal solution.

It is not hard to see that the MPC problem captures all the real-world applications discussed in the previous section. For instance, consider the secure e-auction application. Here the set of bidders constitutes the parties, with x_i being the private bid of the individual parties and the function f is to compute the minimum among all the bids. For the PSI problem, Alice and Bob are the two parties, with their respective contact lists being their private inputs and the function which they want to securely compute is the set-intersection function.

A solution for the secure MPC problem will automatically imply a solution for all the applications discussed in the previous section. Due to its powerful abstraction, secure MPC holds a central importance, both in the regime of cryptography as well as distributed computing. The problem has been widely studied over the last three decades and several interesting and fundamental results have been achieved, concerning both theoretical possibility as well as practical deployability.

1.3   The Dimensions of Secure MPC

The MPC problem has been studied in varieties of dimensions. Here, we discuss some of them.

Dimension 1—Type of Function Abstraction: In the literature, MPC protocols have been proposed for specific tasks (for example, PSI, PPML, etc.), as well as for generic functions. Under the category of generic MPC protocols, we have two class of protocols, depending upon how the underlying function f is abstracted. The first class of protocols are for arithmetic functions [25, 49], where f is a function over some algebraic structure, such as a ring or a field and is represented by a corresponding arithmetic circuit. The second class of protocols are for Boolean functions [18, 138], where f is represented by a Boolean circuit.

While arithmetic circuits are suitable to represent linear functions, such as addition of two ℓ-bit numbers, non-linear operations such as comparing two ℓ-bit numbers can be compactly represented by Boolean circuits. To get best-of-the-both worlds for the purpose of practical efficiency, one may also design MPC protocols for a "mixed" circuit [66, 121, 129], where the linear operations in the function f are represented as an arithmetic circuit and non-linear operations are represented as a Boolean circuit.

Dimension 2—Type of Network: In any MPC protocol, the parties need to exchange messages (computed as per the protocol instructions) over the underlying communication network. Depending upon the level of synchronization in the underlying network, MPC protocols can be primarily categorized as *synchronous* or *asynchronous*. In the synchronous MPC protocols, it is assumed that the parties are synchronized through a global clock and there is a strict (publicly-known) upper bound on the message delays. Consequently, any expected message which does not arrive within the known timeout can be attributed to a *corrupt* sender. However, it is difficult to ensure such strict timeouts in real-world networks like the Internet, which is predominantly asynchronous.

In the asynchronous communication model [13, 20, 24, 26, 54, 127], the parties are not synchronized and the messages can be arbitrarily (but finitely) delayed. Moreover, the messages need not be delivered in the same order in which they were sent. However, every sent message is guaranteed to be *eventually delivered*. A major challenge in the asynchronous model is that a receiving party cannot distinguish between a *slow* sender party whose messages are delayed and a *corrupt* sender party who does not send messages at all. Due to this inherent phenomenon, asynchronous MPC (AMPC) protocols are more involved than their synchronous counterparts.

A third category of protocols are designed in the *hybrid* communication setting [128], which is a mix of the synchronous and asynchronous models. Namely, the protocol starts with a few initial synchronous communication rounds, followed by a completely asynchronous execution. The main motivation for considering a hybrid setting is to "bridge" the feasibility and efficiency gaps between completely synchronous and completely asynchronous protocols.

A recent line of work [3, 32, 33, 65, 124] consider protocols, which provide the best security guarantees, depending upon the type of the underlying network. Namely, in these protocols the parties will *not* be aware of whether the underlying network is synchronous or asynchronous. If the network is synchronous, then the protocol provides the same security guarantees as provided by a synchronous MPC protocol. Otherwise, the protocol provides the guarantees promised by an AMPC protocol.

Dimension 3—Corruption Capacity: Under this dimension, we have two categories of protocols. The more popular *threshold* protocols assume that the number of corrupt parties is bounded by a publicly-known threshold, say t, and the protocols are secure, as long as at most t parties are corrupt during the protocol execution. The other category of protocols consider a more generalized *non-threshold* adversary [57, 91, 120], whose corruption capacity is specified by a publicly-known *adversary structure*, which is a collection of potentially corrupt subset of parties. During the protocol execution, the adversary can choose any subset from the collection for corruption. A threshold adversary is a *special* type of non-threshold adversary, where the adversary structure consists of all subsets of $\mathcal{P}$ of size at most t.

Dimension 4—Corruption Power: If the adversary is *computationally bounded* (i.e. it is allowed to perform only polynomial amount of computation), then the notion of security achieved is *conditional/cryptographic* [80, 138], whereas *unconditionally-secure* protocols provide security even against a *computationally unbounded* adversary.[1] Unconditionally-secure protocols can be further categorized as *perfectly-secure* where all security guarantees are achieved in an error-free fashion [21, 25, 83], or *statistically-secure* where a negligible (but non-zero) error is permitted in the protocol outcomes [19, 27, 56, 85, 133].

Unconditionally-secure protocols require strong setup (for instance, guarantee of pairwise secure channels between every pair of parties), compared to conditionally-secure protocols. However, on the positive side, unconditionally-secure protocols are computationally very fast and provide ever-lasting security. The latter means that these protocols remain secure even if quantum computers become a reality.

Dimension 5—Type of Corruption: During the execution of an MPC protocol, the adversary can control the corrupt parties in different ways. The simplest form of corruption is the *passive* corruption, where the corrupt parties follow the instructions of the underlying protocol. However, the entire state (namely, the input, random coins and all the messages) of the corrupt parties during the protocol execution can be observed by the adversary. Passive corruption is often called as the *semi-honest* as well as *honest-but-curious* corruption model in the literature. A more powerful form of corruption is the *Byzantine* corruption (also known as the *malicious* or *active* corruption), where the adversary can influence the corrupt parties to deviate from the prescribed protocol instructions in any arbitrary fashion.

Often the semi-honest secure protocols act as the starting point of maliciously-secure MPC protocols and are several orders of magnitude faster than the latter.

Dimension 6—Timing of Corruption: Under this dimension, there are two categories of protocols. The first category of protocols are secure against a *static* adversary, who decides

---

[1] Unconditionally-secure protocols are also known as information-theoretically-secure protocols.

Table 1.1 The taxonomy for studying MPC in various dimensions

Circuit	Network	Corruption capacity	Corruption power	Type of corruption	Timing of corruption
Boolean	Synchronous	Threshold	Bounded	Passive	Static
Arithmetic	Asynchronous	Non-threshold	Unbounded	Byzantine	Adaptive

the set of corrupt parties at the onset of the protocol execution. The other category of protocols are secure against a more powerful *adaptive* adversary [43, 62, 89, 110], who can corrupt parties during the run time of the protocol.

Summary: We summarize the various dimensions of MPC in Table 1.1. A setting for MPC can be obtained by picking one attribute from each column.

Irrespective of the setting considered for studying the MPC problem, the following three inherent questions are fundamental.

- *Possibility*: What are the necessary and sufficient condition(s) for the existence of any MPC protocol in a given setting?
- *Feasibility*: Does there exist an efficient MPC protocol in a given setting (given that a protocol is already proven to be possible)?
- *Optimality*: What are the inherent lower bounds on the "resources" needed for an MPC protocol in a given setting? How can we design protocols that make "optimal" use of the resources? The common resources that are considered are:
  - *Communication complexity*: It is the number of bits to be communicated by the *honest* parties in the protocol.[2]
  - *Round complexity*: It is the maximum number of sequential interactions done by the *honest* parties with each other in the protocol.
  - *Computation complexity*: It is the measure of amount of computation done by the *honest* parties in the protocol.

1.4   Our Setting and Book Organization

In this book, we focus on generic *synchronous* MPC protocols in the *passive* (semi-honest/honest-but-curious) and static corruption model. We present protocols for both Boolean as well as arithmetic circuits. We consider threshold as well as non-threshold adversaries and both computationally-bounded as well as unbounded corruptions. Even though the passive corruption model may seem very weak, achieving security against such

---

[2] We do not focus on the amount of communication done by the *corrupt* parties, since they may not follow the protocol instructions and end up doing arbitrary communications.

a benign form of adversary is non-trivial and demands sophisticated techniques. Moreover, as mentioned earlier, very often protocols secure against semi-honest corruptions serve as the basis for protocols secure against a malicious adversary (this is at least true for *all* the protocols discussed in this book). Furthermore, in many realistic scenarios, it is sufficient to consider the semi-honest model. For instance, it is possible that the computing machines of the parties are strongly fortified and so it is extremely difficult for an adversary to corrupt those machines and load faulty programs in them. However, there is no guarantee that the storage used by the parties may not get compromised in the future. Here the threat model can be captured through the semi-honest corruption model. The setting of outsourced computation, where a computation is delegated to a set of cloud servers can be another scenario where semi-honest security seems sufficient. The cloud servers are expected to act honestly and perform the desired computation correctly, as otherwise their revenue generation may get affected due to bad repute. However, a subset of the servers may collude during the execution of a protocol in a bid to learn additional information about the information held by the other servers.

The book is organized as follows. In Chap. 2, we review some of the basic concepts from abstract algebra, which are used in the rest of the book. Chapter 3 focusses on the problem of secret-sharing, which is an important building block for several MPC protocols discussed later. Here, we present some of the heavily-used secret-sharing schemes, such as Shamir's secret-sharing scheme and additive secret-sharing scheme. In Chap. 4, we discuss an MPC protocol for a simple task of securely adding n values. This protocol will serve as a toy example and will pave way for the generic MPC protocols of later sections.

We devote Chaps. 5 to 9 to perfectly-secure MPC protocols. Chapter 5 presents the classic BGW MPC protocol for the case when the function to be securely computed is a linear function. The protocol is extended for any function in Chap. 6. This chapter also contains a formal proof of the necessary condition for the existence of any perfectly-secure MPC protocol against a threshold adversary. To improve its efficiency, the BGW protocol is then moulded in the pre-processing model in Chap. 7. Perfectly-secure MPC against non-threshold adversaries is discussed in Chap. 8. We conclude our discussion on perfectly-secure protocols in Chap. 9, with a practically-efficient protocol for the special case of 3 parties.

In Chap. 10, we start the tour of cryptographically-secure MPC protocols with the classic GMW protocol. Chapter 11 discusses about the fundamental primitive of oblivious transfer (OT) and OT-extension. The latter is a commonly used tool for practically instantiating the OTs. The classic Yao's protocol for secure 2-party computation and some of its popular optimizations are presented in Chap. 12. Finally, in Chap. 13, we present practically-efficient cryptographically-secure variants of the secure 3-party protocols presented in Chap. 9.

Relevant Topics from Abstract Algebra

2

In this chapter, we discuss the relevant topics from abstract algebra which are later used extensively.

2.1 Groups, Rings and Fields

We start with the definition of groups.

Definition 2.1 (*Group*) A set $\mathbb{G}$ with some binary operation o over $\mathbb{G}$, is called a group if all the following properties (also known as *group-axioms*) are satisfied:

- Closure (G_1): for every $a, b \in \mathbb{G}$, the element $a \, o \, b \in \mathbb{G}$.
- Associativity (G_2): for every a, b, c, the condition $(a \, o \, b) \, o \, c = a \, o \, (b \, o \, c)$ holds.
- Existence of identity (G_3): there exists a unique *identity* element $e \in \mathbb{G}$, such that for every $a \in \mathbb{G}$, the condition $(a \, o \, e) = (e \, o \, a) = a$ holds.
- Existence of inverse (G_4): for every $a \in \mathbb{G}$, there exists a unique element, say $a^{-1} \in \mathbb{G}$, such that the condition $(a \, o \, a^{-1}) = (a^{-1} \, o \, a) = e$ holds.

We note that in Definition 2.1, the operation o *need not* satisfy the commutative property. If apart from the axioms $G_1, \ldots, G_4$, the operation o satisfies the commutative property, then $\mathbb{G}$ along with the operation o is called as an *Abelian* group. We next present a couple of examples of groups, which will be useful later.

© The Author(s), under exclusive license to Springer Nature Switzerland AG 2022
A. Choudhury and A. Patra, *Secure Multi-Party Computation Against Passive Adversaries*,
Synthesis Lectures on Distributed Computing Theory,
https://doi.org/10.1007/978-3-031-12164-7_2

Example 2.2 (*Group based on addition modulo N*) Let N be a positive integer and let $\mathbb{Z}_N$ be the set $\mathbb{Z}_N \stackrel{def}{=} \{0, \ldots, N-1\}$. We define the operation *addition modulo N* over $\mathbb{Z}_N$, denoted by $+_N$, as follows:

$$a +_N b \stackrel{def}{=} (a+b) \mod N$$

Then the set $\mathbb{Z}_N$, along with the operation $+_N$ is an Abelian group. For this, we show that each of group-axioms for the Abelian group is satisfied.

- Closure: consider arbitrary $a, b \in \mathbb{Z}_N$ and let $r = a +_N b$. Then it is easy to see that $r \in \mathbb{Z}_N$.
- Associativity: consider arbitrary $a, b, c \in \mathbb{Z}_N$. Then it is easy to see that $(a +_N b) +_N c = a +_N (b +_N c) = (a+b+c) \mod N$ holds.
- Existence of identity: the integer $0 \in \mathbb{Z}_N$ is the identity element. This is because for any arbitrary $a \in \mathbb{Z}_N$, the condition $0 +_N a = a +_N 0 = a \mod N = a$ holds.
- Existence of inverse: consider an arbitrary $a \in \mathbb{Z}_N$. Then the element $-a \stackrel{def}{=} (N-a)$ is the *additive inverse* of a. This is because the condition $-a +_N a = a +_N -a = (a + N - a) \mod N = 0$ holds.
- Commutativity: consider arbitrary $a, b \in \mathbb{Z}_N$. Then the condition $a +_N b = b +_N a = (a+b) \mod N$ holds.

Example 2.3 (*Group based on multiplication modulo N*) Let N be a positive integer and let $\mathbb{Z}_N^\star$ be the set of integers from $\mathbb{Z}_N$ which are co-prime to N. That is,

$$\mathbb{Z}_N^\star \stackrel{def}{=} \{a \in \mathbb{Z}_N : \mathrm{GCD}(a, N) = 1\},$$

where $\mathrm{GCD}(a, N)$ denotes the *greatest common divisor* of a and N. We define the operation *multiplication modulo N* over $\mathbb{Z}_N^\star$, denoted by $\cdot_N$, as follows:

$$a \cdot_N b \stackrel{def}{=} (a \cdot b) \mod N.$$

Then the set $\mathbb{Z}_N^\star$, along with the operation $\cdot_N$ is an Abelian group. For this, we show that each of group-axioms for the Abelian group is satisfied.

- Closure: consider arbitrary $a, b \in \mathbb{Z}_N^\star$ and let $r = a \cdot_N b$. It is easy to see that $r \in \mathbb{Z}_N$. Since $a, b \in \mathbb{Z}_N^\star$, it implies that $\mathrm{GCD}(a, N) = \mathrm{GCD}(b, N) = 1$. This further implies that $\mathrm{GCD}(ab, N) = 1$. Also from the Division theorem, $r = ab - kN$ holds, for some integer k. This further implies that $\mathrm{GCD}(r, N) = 1$, as otherwise $\mathrm{GCD}(ab, N) \neq 1$, which is a contradiction. Hence from the definition of the set $\mathbb{Z}_N^\star$, we get that $r \in \mathbb{Z}_N^\star$.

- Associativity: consider arbitrary $a, b, c \in \mathbb{Z}_N^{\star}$. It is easy to see that $(a \cdot_N b) \cdot_N c = a \cdot_N (b \cdot_N c) = (a \cdot b \cdot c) \mod N$ holds.
- Existence of identity: the integer $1 \in \mathbb{Z}_N^{\star}$ is the identity element. This is because for any arbitrary $a \in \mathbb{Z}_N^{\star}$, the condition $1 \cdot_N a = a \cdot_N 1 = a \mod N = a$ holds.
- Existence of inverse: consider an arbitrary $a \in \mathbb{Z}_N^{\star}$. Note that $GCD(a, N) = 1$. Using the Extended-Euclid's GCD algorithm [30], one can find the integer $b \in \mathbb{Z}_N^{\star}$, such that $a \cdot_N b = b \cdot_N a = 1$ holds. The integer b is called the *multiplicative inverse* of a.
- Commutativity: consider arbitrary $a, b \in \mathbb{Z}_N^{\star}$. Then $a \cdot_N b = b \cdot_N a = (a \cdot b) \mod N$ holds.

If N is a prime number p, then $\mathbb{Z}_p = \{0, \ldots, p-1\}$ and $\mathbb{Z}_p^{\star} = \{1, \ldots, p-1\} = \mathbb{Z}_p - \{0\}$.

We next recall the definition of a ring, which is a set with two abstract binary operations, satisfying certain properties. More formally:

Definition 2.4 (*Ring*) A set $\mathbb{R}$ with abstract binary operations $+$ and $\cdot$ over $\mathbb{R}$, is called a ring if all the following properties (also known as *ring-axioms*) are satisfied:

- R_1: The set $\mathbb{R}$ along with the operation $+$ constitutes an Abelian group. We denote the identity element with respect to the $+$ operation (also called as the *additive identity*) as 0 and the inverse of an element a with respect to the $+$ operation (also called as the *additive inverse* of a) as $-a$. Hence for every $a \in \mathbb{R}$, we have $a + 0 = 0 + a = a$ and $a + (-a) = (-a) + a = 0$.
- R_2: The operation $\cdot$ satisfies the closure, associativity and existence of identity properties. Namely, all the following should be satisfied:
  - For every $a, b \in \mathbb{R}$, the element $a \cdot b \in \mathbb{R}$.
  - For every $a, b, c \in \mathbb{R}$, the condition $a \cdot (b \cdot c) = (a \cdot b) \cdot c$ holds.
  - There exists an element, say $1 \in \mathbb{R}$ (also called as the *multiplicative identity*), such that for every $a \in \mathbb{R}$, the condition $a \cdot 1 = 1 \cdot a = a$ holds.
- R_3: For all $a, b, c \in \mathbb{R}$, the following distributive laws hold:
  - $a \cdot (b + c) = (a \cdot b) + (a \cdot c)$.
  - $(a + b) \cdot c = (a \cdot c) + (b \cdot c)$.

Example 2.5 The set $\mathbb{Z}_N$, along with the operations $+_N$ and $\cdot_N$ over $\mathbb{Z}_N$ constitutes a ring. This is because as shown below, all the ring-axioms are satisfied.

- R_1: The set $\mathbb{Z}_N$ along with the operation $+_N$ constitutes an Abelian group.
- R_2: The operation $\cdot_N$ satisfies the closure, associativity and existence of the identity element.
- R_3: For every $a, b, c \in \mathbb{Z}_N$, the following distributive laws hold:

- $a \cdot_N (b +_N c) = (a \cdot_N b) +_N (a \cdot_N c)$.
- $(a +_N b) \cdot_N c = (a \cdot_N c) +_N (b \cdot_N c)$.

Note that the rings with $N = 2^{32}, 2^{64}, 2^{128}, 2^{256}$ constitute special case of integer arithmetic operations performed in computers.

We next recall the definition of a field, which is a special type of ring where *every* "non-zero" element is "invertible". More formally:

Definition 2.6 (*Field*) A set $\mathbb{F}$ with abstract binary operations $+$ and $\cdot$ over $\mathbb{F}$, is called a field if all the following properties (also known as *field-axioms*) are satisfied:

- F_1: The set $\mathbb{F}$ along with the operation $+$ constitutes an Abelian group.
- F_2: The set $\mathbb{F} - \{0\}$ along with the operation $\cdot$ constitutes an Abelian group, where the element $0 \in \mathbb{F}$ and denotes the *additive identity*. This implies that corresponding to every element $a \in \mathbb{F} - \{0\}$, there exists an element $a^{-1} \in \mathbb{F} - \{0\}$, which is called as the *multiplicative inverse* of a, such that the condition $a \cdot a^{-1} = a^{-1} \cdot a = 1$ holds.[1] Here $1 \in \mathbb{F} - \{0\}$ denotes the *multiplicative identity*.
- F_3: For all $a, b, c \in \mathbb{F}$, the following distributive laws hold:
  - $a \cdot (b + c) = (a \cdot b) + (a \cdot c)$.
  - $(a + b) \cdot c = (a \cdot c) + (b \cdot c)$.

Example 2.7 Let p be a prime number. Then the set $\mathbb{Z}_p = \{0, \ldots, p - 1\}$, along with the operations $+_p$ and $\cdot_p$ constitutes a field. Clearly the set $\mathbb{Z}_p$ constitutes an Abelian group with respect to the $+_p$ operation, with the integer 0 being the additive identity. The set $\mathbb{Z}_p - \{0\}$ is the same as the set $\mathbb{Z}_p^\star = \{1, \ldots, p - 1\}$, which constitutes an Abelian group with respect to the $\cdot_p$ operation. It is easy to see that the distributive laws hold.

We next discuss the properties of polynomials over a field.

2.2   Properties of Polynomials over a Field

We start with the definition of a d-degree polynomial over a field. Informally, it is similar to polynomials with integer/real-number coefficients, except that the coefficients are elements of a field and the addition and multiplication operations are performed over the field. More formally:

---

[1] Comparing the axiom F_2 with the ring-axiom R_2 in Definition 2.4, we find that for a ring $\mathbb{R}$, every element $a \in \mathbb{R} - \{0\}$ *need not* have a multiplicative inverse.

Definition 2.8 (*d-degree Polynomial Over a Field*) Let $(\mathbb{F}, +, \cdot)$ be a field. Then a d-degree polynomial in variable X over $\mathbb{F}$ is of the form

$$f(X) = a_0 + a_1 \cdot X + \ldots + a_d \cdot X^d,$$

where all the $+$ and $\cdot$ operations are performed over $\mathbb{F}$ and where $a_0, \ldots, a_d \in \mathbb{F}$ are called as the *coefficients* of the polynomial. Note that, as per the definition, the coefficient a_d of a d-degree polynomial can be 0.

Example 2.9 Consider the field $\mathbb{F} = \mathbb{Z}_7$, with the operations $+_7$ and $\cdot_7$ over $\mathbb{Z}_7$. Then the polynomial $f(X) = 6 + 2X + 3X^4$ is a 4-degree polynomial over $\mathbb{Z}_7$, with the coefficients $a_0 = 6, a_1 = 2, a_2 = 0, a_3 = 0$ and $a_4 = 3$. The polynomial takes the value $(6 + 2 + 3)$ mod $7 = 4$ at $X = 1$ (i.e. $f(1) = 4$). The value $f(8)$ is same as $f(8 \mod 7) = f(1)$, which is 4.

We next define the root of a polynomial over a field.

Definition 2.10 (*Root of a Polynomial*) Let $f(X)$ be a polynomial over some field $\mathbb{F}$. Then an element $v \in \mathbb{F}$ is called a *root* of $f(X)$ if $f(v) = 0$ holds, where 0 is the additive identity in $\mathbb{F}$.

We next state two fundamental facts about the roots of polynomials over a field and their proofs are available in any standard textbook on abstract algebra.

Theorem 2.11 ([30]) *Let $\mathbb{F}$ be a field. Then the following hold:*

- *Any d-degree polynomial over $\mathbb{F}$ has at most d roots.*
- *Two different d-degree polynomials over $\mathbb{F}$ can have at most d common values.*

Example 2.12 Consider the 0-degree polynomial $f(X) = 6$ over the field $(\mathbb{Z}_7, +_7, \cdot_7)$. Then there exists no root for $f(X)$, as none of the values $f(0), \ldots, f(6)$ is 0. On the other hand, the 4-degree polynomial $g(X) = X + 4X^2 + X^3 + X^4$ has four roots, since $g(0) = g(1) = g(2) = g(3) = 0$.

Consider the 2-degree polynomials $f(X) = 2 + 4X + X^2$ and $g(X) = 3 + 3X + X^2$ over $(\mathbb{Z}_7, +_7, \cdot_7)$. Then $f(X)$ and $g(X)$ have the same value at $X = 1$, as $f(1) = g(1) = 0$. So, the point $(1, 0)$ is common to both $f(X)$ and $g(X)$.

It is a well-known fact that given $d + 1$ distinct points on a two-dimensional plane, one can obtain a *unique d*-degree polynomial passing through the given points. The same result holds even over a finite field. More formally:

Theorem 2.13 ([30]) *Let $\mathbb{F}$ be a field and $(x_1, y_1), \ldots, (x_{d+1}, y_{d+1})$ be pairs of elements from $\mathbb{F}$, where $x_1, \ldots, x_{d+1}$ are distinct. Then there exists a unique d-degree polynomial over $\mathbb{F}$, say $f(X)$, such that $f(x_i) = y_i$ holds for $i = 1, \ldots, d + 1$.*

Lagrange's Polynomial Interpolation Over a Field: While there are several ways of computing the unique polynomial $f(X)$ passing through the points $(x_1, y_1), \ldots, (x_{d+1}, y_{d+1})$, we discuss the one based on Lagrange's polynomial interpolation. The idea is to express the *unknown* polynomial $f(X)$ as a linear combination of *publicly-known* polynomials $\delta_1(X), \ldots, \delta_{d+1}(X)$, using $y_1, \ldots, y_{d+1}$ as the linear combiners. The polynomials $\delta_1(X), \ldots, \delta_{d+1}(X)$ have the following properties:

- Each of them is a d-degree polynomial.
- For $i = 1, \ldots, d + 1$, the polynomial $\delta_i(X)$ takes the value 0 at $X = x_1, \ldots, x_{d+1}$ except at $X = x_i$. In other words, all the elements $x_1, \ldots, x_{d+1}$ are roots of $\delta_i(X)$, except x_i. At $X = x_i$, the polynomial $\delta_i(X)$ takes the value 1.

More specifically, the polynomial $\delta_i(X)$ is of the form:

$$\delta_i(X) = \frac{(X - x_1) \cdot \ldots \cdot (X - x_{i-1}) \cdot (X - x_{i+1}) \cdot \ldots \cdot (X - x_{d+1})}{(x_i - x_1) \cdot \ldots \cdot (x_i - x_{i-1}) \cdot (x_i - x_{i+1}) \cdot \ldots (x_i - x_{d+1})}.$$

Let $c_i \overset{def}{=} (x_i - x_1) \cdot \ldots \cdot (x_i - x_{i-1}) \cdot (x_i - x_{i+1}) \cdot \ldots (x_i - x_{d+1})$. Since $x_1, \ldots, x_{d+1}$ are *distinct*, it follows that $c_i \neq 0$ and c_i has a multiplicative-inverse, say c_i^{-1}. It then follows that

$$\delta_i(X) = c_i^{-1} \cdot (X - x_1) \cdot \ldots \cdot (X - x_{i-1}) \cdot (X - x_{i+1}) \cdot \ldots \cdot (X - x_{d+1})$$

Then the required polynomial $f(X)$ is computed as follows:

$$f(X) = y_1 \cdot \delta_1(X) + \cdots + y_{d+1} \cdot \delta_{d+1}(X). \tag{2.1}$$

It is easy to see that the $f(X)$ polynomial computed in Eq. 2.1 is a d-degree polynomial and for $i = 1, \ldots, d + 1$, the condition $f(x_i) = y_i$ holds.

From the above discussion, it follows that given $d + 1$ *distinct* points on an *unknown* d-degree polynomial, one can easily compute a *new* point on the same polynomial (without even computing the polynomial), as a *linear* function of the existing $d + 1$ points. Namely, given the points $(x_1, y_1), \ldots, (x_{d+1}, y_{d+1})$ where $x_1, \ldots, x_{d+1}$ are distinct, let $f(X)$ be the d-degree polynomial passing through these points. Then to compute the value of $f(X)$ at $X = x_{new}$ where x_{new} is *different* from $x_1, \ldots, x_{d+1}$, we note that from Eq. 2.1, the following holds:

$$f(x_{new}) = \delta_1(x_{new}) \cdot y_1 + \cdots + \delta_{d+1}(x_{new}) \cdot y_{d+1}.$$

The values $\delta_1(x_{new}), \ldots, \delta_{d+1}(x_{new})$ are called *Lagrange's interpolation-coefficients*.

Secret Sharing

3

In this chapter, we introduce the problem of secret-sharing. We present the generalized secret-sharing scheme of Ito et al. [98] and the threshold secret-sharing scheme of Shamir [135]. While secret-sharing schemes find extensive application in MPC, we showcase here another important application, namely perfectly-secure message transmission. We conclude with demonstrating what can go wrong in a secret-sharing scheme in the face of malicious adversaries.

3.1   Secret Sharing: Motivation and Definition

Consider the following application. There is a bank with three managers. There is a locker in the bank, which needs to be opened every day using the help of the managers. Each of the managers has got a password to operate the locker. However, no one trusts any single manager. So we want to design a system where the locker can be opened only if at least two of the managers enter their respective passwords, but the locker should remain inaccessible if only a single manager tries to open it. Similarly, consider a scenario where the passcode of a country's nuclear missile is shared among the top three entities of the country, say the president, vice-president and the prime-minister in such a way that the missile can be launched only when at least two of these three entities agree to do the same. Secret-sharing (SS) [31, 135] models several real-world scenarios as above.

Informally, any SS protocol for a set of n parties $\mathcal{P} = \{P_1, \ldots, P_n\}$ consists of two phases, a *sharing phase* realized by a protocol Sh and a *reconstruction phase* realized by a protocol Rec. While the goal of the sharing phase is to share a secret held by a designated *dealer* $D \in \mathcal{P}$, the aim of the reconstruction phase is to reconstruct back the shared secret. In a more detail, during the protocol Sh, the input of D is some secret $s \in \mathcal{S}$, where $\mathcal{S}$ is a publicly-known *secret-space* which is the set of all possible D's secrets. Additionally, the parties may have random inputs for the protocol. Let view_i denote the view of party P_i at the end of the protocol Sh, which consists of the local inputs of P_i, along with the messages sent and received by P_i. Based on view_i, each party P_i outputs a *share* s_i, which is a publicly-known function of view_i, as determined by the protocol Sh. During the reconstruction phase, each P_i may reveal a subset of its view view_i, as per the protocol Rec. Each party then applies a publicly-known reconstruction function on the revealed views, as determined by the protocol Rec and reconstructs some output.

Informally, we need two security properties from any SS protocol. The first property is the *correctness*, which demands that any "qualified subset" of parties should be able to reconstruct back the shared secret by executing the protocol Rec. The qualified subsets are also called as *access-sets* and the collection of all access-sets is called *access-structure*, denoted by Γ, where $\Gamma \subset 2^{\mathcal{P}}$. For example, if we consider the bank example with M_1, M_2, M_3 being the three managers, then Γ consists of the access-sets $\{M_1, M_2\}, \{M_2, M_3\}, \{M_1, M_3\}$ and $\{M_1, M_2, M_3\}$. Notice that explicitly stating $\{M_1, M_2, M_3\}$ to be a member of Γ is "redundant", since each of the remaining access-sets is a proper subset of this "larger" access-set. So, it is well-understood that if M_1 and M_2 can collectively access the locker, then the additional presence of M_3 will enable the same. Stated differently, we consider a *monotone* access-structure where the monotonicity means that if $A \in \Gamma$, then for any $A \subset A'$, the condition $A' \in \Gamma$ holds. A subset $A \in \Gamma$ is called a *minimal* access-set, if no subset of A is also an access-set. That is, there exists no set A', such that $A' \subset A$ and $A' \in \Gamma$. The set of minimal access-sets of Γ is denoted by Γ_0 and is called as the *basis* of Γ. From the definition, it follows that given the basis Γ_0, one can uniquely determine the corresponding access-structure Γ.

The second security property that we need from any SS protocol is that of *privacy*, which informally demands that the view of any "forbidden subset" of parties should not reveal any information about the shared secret. The collection of the forbidden subsets is called as *adversary-structure*, denoted by Σ, where $\Sigma \stackrel{def}{=} 2^{\mathcal{P}} \setminus \Gamma$. Similar to the case of access-structures, we consider a *monotone* adversary-structure, where if $B \in \Sigma$, then for any $B' \subset B$, the condition $B' \in \Sigma$ holds. That is, if a subset of parties B is *not* authorized to reconstruct the underlying shared secret, then any smaller subset of parties of B should also fail to learnt the secret. A subset $B \in \Sigma$ is called a *maximal* forbidden-set, if no superset of B is also a forbidden-set. That is, there exists no set B', such that $B \subset B'$ and $B' \in \Sigma$. The set of maximal forbidden-sets of Σ is denoted by Σ_0 and is called as the *basis* of Σ. From the definition, it follows that given the basis Σ_0, one can uniquely determine the corresponding adversary-structure Σ.

Before proceeding further, we give an example of access-structure and adversary-structure, along with the corresponding basis.

Example 3.1 Let $\mathcal{P} = \{P_1, \ldots, P_4\}$. Then consider the access-structure $\Gamma = \{\{P_1, P_2, P_4\}, \{P_1, P_3, P_4\}, \{P_2, P_3\}, \{P_1, P_2, P_3\}, \{P_2, P_3, P_4\}, \{P_1, P_2, P_3, P_4\}\}$. The basis of Γ, consisting of the minimal access-sets is $\Gamma_0 = \{\{P_1, P_2, P_4\}, \{P_1, P_3, P_4\}, \{P_2, P_3\}\}$.

The corresponding adversary-structure is $\Sigma = 2^{\mathcal{P}} \setminus \Gamma = \{\emptyset, \{P_1\}, \{P_2\}, \{P_3\}, \{P_4\},$
$\{P_1, P_2\}, \{P_1, P_3\}, \{P_1, P_4\}, \{P_2, P_4\}, \{P_3, P_4\}\}$. The basis of Σ consisting of the maximal
forbidden-sets is $\Sigma_0 = \{\{P_1, P_2\}, \{P_1, P_3\}, \{P_1, P_4\}, \{P_2, P_4\}, \{P_3, P_4\}\}$.

Depending upon whether the parties in the forbidden sets are computationally-bounded or
unbounded, we get *perfect* privacy and *cryptographic* privacy respectively. Unless explicitly
stated, we will focus on perfect-privacy. We next give the formal definition of a secret-sharing
scheme which consists of a share-generation function G and a recovery function R. While
G is probabilistic, the function R is deterministic. The function G generates shares for the
input secret, while R maps the shares back to the secret. The shares are generated in such a
way that the probability distribution of any set of shares corresponding to a forbidden set is
independent of the secret, while any set of shares corresponding to an access-set uniquely
determine the secret.

Definition 3.2 (*Secret-sharing*) Let $\mathcal{P} = \{P_1, \ldots, P_n\}$ and let Γ and Σ be an access-
structure and adversary-structure over $\mathcal{P}$ respectively. Then a secret-sharing scheme is a
pair of algorithms (G, R), such that

- **Syntax**: The *share-generation function* G takes input a secret s and some randomness r
  and outputs a vector of n shares $(s_1, \ldots, s_n)$, where the share s_i corresponds to party P_i.
  The *recovery* function R takes input a set of shares, corresponding to a subset of parties
  $Q \subseteq \mathcal{P}$ and outputs a value if Q belongs to Γ.
- **Correctness**: For any secret s and any vector of n shares $(s_1, \ldots, s_n)$ where $(s_1, \ldots, s_n) =$
  $G(s, r)$ for some randomness r, it holds that for every subset $A \in \Gamma$:

$$R(\{s_i\}_{P_i \in A}) = s.$$

- **Privacy**: For any subset $B \in \Sigma$, the probability distribution of the shares corresponding
  to the parties in B is independent of the underlying secret. That is, for any $B \subseteq \mathcal{P}$ where
  $B = \{P_{i_1}, \ldots, P_{i_t}\}$, let $g_B(s) \stackrel{def}{=} (s_{i_1}, \ldots, s_{i_t})$, where $(s_1, \ldots, s_n) = G(s, r)$ for some
  randomness r. Then we require that for *every* $B \in \Sigma$, the random variables $g_B(s)$ and
  $g_B(s')$ are identically distributed, for every pair (s, s') where $s \neq s'$.

A secret-sharing protocol from any secret-sharing scheme: Assume that there is
a secure channel between every pair of parties P_i, P_j such that no third party can
learn about the messages exchanged between P_i and P_j over this channel. Then given a
secret-sharing scheme (G, R) satisfying the properties of Definition 3.2, a corresponding
secret-sharing protocol (Sh, Rec) can be derived as follows. During the protocol Sh, on
having the input s, the dealer D picks some randomness r as per G and then generates
the shares $(s_1, \ldots, s_n) = G(s, r)$. It then sends the share s_i to party P_i.

> During the protocol Rec, if a set of parties Q want to reconstruct the shared secret, then the parties in Q can exchange their respective shares with each other. This is followed by the parties in Q applying the function R on the exchanged shares.
>
> The *correctness* property of R guarantees that if Q is an access-set, then the parties in Q recover the shared secret during Rec. On the other hand, the *privacy* property of G guarantees that any set of parties $B \in \Sigma$ does not learn any information about the shared secret during Sh.

We conclude this section with the properties of *threshold* t-out-of-n secret-sharing scheme, which is a special case of the general secret-sharing scheme. Here, the basis Σ_0 consists of all subsets of $\mathcal{P}$ of size t, where t is a *publicly-known* parameter. Hence, the adversary-structure Σ consists of all subsets of $\mathcal{P}$ of size *at most* t. This automatically implies that the basis Γ_0 for the access-structure consists of all subsets of $\mathcal{P}$ of size $t + 1$. Hence the access-structure Γ consists of all subsets of $\mathcal{P}$ of size *at least* $t + 1$. The threshold t determines the security guarantees of the secret-sharing scheme. Namely, any subset of t (or less number of) share-holders should learn no information about the secret, while any subset of $t + 1$ (or more) share-holders can reconstruct the shared secret.

3.2   A General Secret-Sharing Scheme

We discuss a general secret-sharing scheme due to Ito et al. [98]. In this scheme, the secret and shares are elements of some finite Abelian group $\mathbb{G}$ and all computations are done over $\mathbb{G}$.

Let Γ be a given monotone access-structure over $\mathcal{P}$ and let Σ be the corresponding monotone adversary-structure, with basis Σ_0. Moreover, let $\Sigma_0 = \{B_1, \ldots, B_k\}$. The scheme works as follows: to share a secret $s \in \mathbb{G}$, the share-generation algorithm G randomly "splits" s into k pieces $v_1, \ldots, v_k$. Then the piece v_i is assigned to all the parties in $\mathcal{P}$, except the parties in the set B_i. This ensures that the parties in each set $B_i \in \Gamma$ lacks at least one of the k pieces to determine s, thus guaranteeing privacy. On the other hand, we will show that the shares corresponding to any set $A \in \Gamma$ uniquely determine s. This is because these shares will have all the k pieces, which can be then "combined" to get back the shared secret. Note that the share of a party P_m consists of several pieces, one for each subset B_i in which P_m is *absent*. The formal details of the scheme are given in Fig. 3.1.[1]

Before we give the formal security proof of Π_{ISN}, we demonstrate the scheme with an example.

---

[1] The scheme presented here is taken from [120], which is a slight variation of the original scheme as presented in [98].

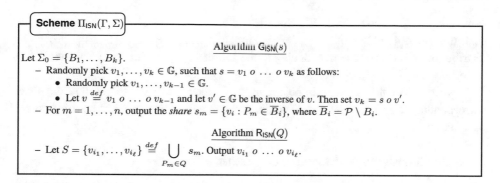

Scheme $\Pi_{\mathsf{ISN}}(\Gamma, \Sigma)$

Algorithm $\mathsf{G}_{\mathsf{ISN}}(s)$

Let $\Sigma_0 = \{B_1, \ldots, B_k\}$.

- Randomly pick $v_1, \ldots, v_k \in \mathbb{G}$, such that $s = v_1 \ o \ \ldots \ o \ v_k$ as follows:
  - Randomly pick $v_1, \ldots, v_{k-1} \in \mathbb{G}$.
  - Let $v \stackrel{def}{=} v_1 \ o \ \ldots \ o \ v_{k-1}$ and let $v' \in \mathbb{G}$ be the inverse of v. Then set $v_k = s \ o \ v'$.
- For $m = 1, \ldots, n$, output the *share* $s_m = \{v_i : P_m \in \overline{B_i}\}$, where $\overline{B_i} = \mathcal{P} \setminus B_i$.

Algorithm $\mathsf{R}_{\mathsf{ISN}}(Q)$

- Let $S = \{v_{i_1}, \ldots, v_{i_\ell}\} \stackrel{def}{=} \bigcup_{P_m \in Q} s_m$. Output $v_{i_1} \ o \ \ldots \ o \ v_{i_\ell}$.

Fig. 3.1 The secret-sharing scheme of Ito et al. [98]

Example 3.3 Consider the Abelian group $\mathbb{G} = (\mathbb{Z}_5, +_5)$ and the set of parties $\mathcal{P} = \{P_1, P_2, P_3, P_4\}$. Let the adversary-structure be $\Sigma = \{\emptyset, \{P_1\}, \{P_2\}, \{P_3\}, \{P_4\}, \{P_1, P_2\}, \{P_1, P_3\}, \{P_1, P_4\}, \{P_2, P_3\}, \{P_3, P_4\}, \{P_1, P_3, P_4\}\}$ with basis $\Sigma_0 = \{\{P_1, P_2\}, \{P_2, P_3\}, \{P_1, P_3, P_4\}\}$ and hence the the access-structure $\Gamma = \{\{P_2, P_4\}, \{P_1, P_2, P_3\}, \{P_1, P_2, P_4\}, \{P_2, P_3, P_4\}, \{P_1, P_2, P_3, P_4\}\}$. Let $s = 4$. Then to compute the shares of an input $s \in \mathbb{Z}_5$, the algorithm $\mathsf{G}_{\mathsf{ISN}}$ randomly selects $v_1, v_2, v_3 \in \mathbb{Z}_5$, such that $s = (v_1 + v_2 + v_3) \mod 5$ holds. Let v_1 and v_2 are selected as 4 and 4 respectively. Then $v_3 = 1$. The algorithm then outputs the shares as shown in the first table below.

Party	Share
P_1	$s_1 = \{v_2\} = \{4\}$
P_2	$s_2 = \{v_3\} = \{1\}$
P_3	$s_3 = \{v_1\} = \{4\}$
P_4	$s_4 = \{v_1, v_2\} = \{4, 4\}$

$s = ?$	v_1	v_2	$v_3 = ?$
0	4	4	2
1	4	4	3
2	4	4	4
3	4	4	0
4	4	4	1

$s = ?$	$v_1 = ?$	v_2	v_3
0	0	4	1
1	1	4	1
2	2	4	1
3	3	4	1
4	4	4	1

It is easy to see that each subset from Σ misses at least one v_i, ensuring that the probability distribution of the shares corresponding to each subset from Σ is independent of the underlying s. For instance, consider the subset $\{P_1, P_3, P_4\} \in \Sigma$ and the shares corresponding to these parties consist of $v_1 = 4$ and $v_2 = 4$, which are completely independent of the underlying s. Hence, any $s \in \mathbb{Z}_5$ could equally-likely lead to the shares $v_1 = 4$ and $v_2 = 4$. Namely, as shown in the second table above, for every candidate $s \in \mathbb{Z}_5$ (shown in bold), there exists a *unique* $v_3 \in \mathbb{Z}_5$ (also shown in bold), such that $(4 + 4 + v_3) \mod 5 = s$ holds.

On the other hand, if we consider the subset $\{P_1, P_2\} \in \Sigma$, then the shares corresponding to these parties consist of $v_2 = 4$ and $v_3 = 1$. However, the piece v_1 is missing, which is selected uniformly at random, independent of s. Hence, any $s \in \mathbb{Z}_5$ could equally-likely lead to the shares $v_2 = 4$ and $v_3 = 1$. Namely, as shown in the third table above, for every candidate $s \in \mathbb{Z}_5$ (shown in bold), there exists a *unique* $v_1 \in \mathbb{Z}_5$ (also shown in bold), such that $(v_1 + 4 + 1) \mod 5 = s$ holds. Similarly, it can be shown that the probability distribution of the shares corresponding to the subset $\{P_2, P_3\}$ will be independent of the underlying s.

If we consider the access-sets belonging to Γ, then it is easy to see that the shares corresponding to *every* subset $A \in \Sigma$ will have v_1, v_2 and v_3. Hence s can be reconstructed back uniquely.

We next formally prove the security of the scheme Π_{ISN}.

Theorem 3.4 *The scheme* $\Pi_{\mathsf{ISN}} = (\mathsf{G}_{\mathsf{ISN}}, \mathsf{R}_{\mathsf{ISN}})$ *is a valid secret-sharing scheme.*

Proof We first prove the *privacy* property. So consider an *arbitrary* subset $B \in \Sigma$ and let $B_i \in \Sigma_0$ be the corresponding maximal forbidden set such that $B \subseteq B_i$. We first note that the shares corresponding to the parties in B do not include at least one element among $v_1, \ldots, v_k$, as v_i is missing among the shares of the parties in B. We consider the *worst* case scenario, when the shares corresponding to the parties in B consists of $k - 1$ elements among $v_1, \ldots, v_k$. Now there are following two possible cases:

- *Shares of B do not include v_k:* In this case, the shares of the parties in B include $v_1, \ldots, v_{k-1}$. Since these elements are picked randomly in $\mathsf{G}_{\mathsf{ISN}}$, *independent* of the underlying secret, it follows easily that the random variables $g_B(s)$ and $g_B(s')$ are identically distributed, for every $s, s' \in \mathbb{G}$ where $s \neq s'$.
- *Shares of B include v_k:* In this case, there exists at least one $v_i \in \{v_1, \ldots, v_{k-1}\}$ missing from the shares of the parties in B. For simplicity and without loss of generality, let the missing $v_i = v_1$. So, the shares corresponding to the parties in B consist of $v_2, \ldots, v_k$. Let us fix these elements. The elements $v_2, \ldots, v_{k-1}$ are picked *independently* of the underlying secret. On the other hand, the element v_k is same as $v_k = s \; o \; v'$, where $v' \in \mathbb{G}$ is the inverse of the element $v \overset{def}{=} v_1 \; o \; (v_2 \; o \; \ldots \; o \; v_{k-1})$. Hence for every candidate $s \in \mathbb{G}$, there exists a *unique* $v_1 \in \mathbb{G}$, which along with the fixed $v_2, \ldots, v_{k-1}$, produces the fixed v_k. However, since the element v_1 is picked uniformly at random, *independent* of the underlying secret and since v_1 is not present among the shares corresponding to the parties in B, it follows that the probability distribution of v_k is *independent* of the underlying secret. Hence it follows that even in this case, the random variables $g_B(s)$ and $g_B(s')$ are identically distributed, for every $s \neq s'$.

We next prove the *correctness* property. So consider any *arbitrary* subset $A \in \Gamma$. Now from the definition of Γ, it follows that the subset A is *different* from all the subsets $B_1, \ldots, B_k$. This implies that for *every* $B_i \in \Sigma_0$, there exists some party $P_m \in A$, possessing the element v_i as part of the share s_m. This further implies that in algorithm $\mathsf{R}_{\mathsf{ISN}}$, the set $S = \{v_{i_1}, \ldots, v_{i_\ell}\} \stackrel{def}{=} \bigcup\limits_{P_m \in A} s_m$ will be same as $\{v_1, \ldots, v_k\}$ and hence $v_{i_1} \circ \ldots \circ v_{i_\ell}$ will be same as $v_1 \circ \ldots \circ v_k = s$. The last equality follows from how v_k was set and the fact that $\mathbb{G}$ is an Abelian group. □

We conclude with the complexity of the scheme Π_{ISN}. To share the secret s, it is divided into $k = |\Sigma_0|$ elements, where $|\Sigma_0| = \mathcal{O}(2^n)$, as $\Sigma_0 \subset 2^\mathcal{P}$. Hence in general, algorithm $\mathsf{G}_{\mathsf{ISN}}$ may divide the secret into exponentially many number of elements (and hence may be inefficient). Also the share of every party may consists of more than one element of $\mathbb{G}$ (see Example 3.3). In the next few sections, we consider some special kind of access-structures and show *efficient* secret-sharing schemes for such access-structures.

3.3 Additive Secret-Sharing Scheme

In this section, we discuss *additive* secret-sharing scheme, where the access-structure consists of a single subset which is the entire set of parties $\mathcal{P}$. That is, $\Gamma = \{\{P_1, \ldots, P_n\}\}$. Hence the shares of any subset of parties of size $n - 1$ or less should be independent of the shared secret. The adversary-structure Σ consists of all subsets of parties of size *at most* $n - 1$. Hence the corresponding basis Σ_0 will have all subsets of parties of size *exactly* $n - 1$ and will have $k = \binom{n}{n-1} = n$ such subsets. One can view this secret-sharing scheme as a special type of t-out-of-n secret-sharing scheme, where the threshold $t = n - 1$. By applying the algorithm $\mathsf{G}_{\mathsf{ISN}}$ for this access-structure, we see that the secret will be divided into n elements, where each of these n elements is owned by a distinct party. Moreover, the secret can be reconstructed back only when *all* the n elements are available and "combined" (hence the name additive secret-sharing). The scheme will be efficient for this particular case, with each party receiving a single element from $\mathbb{G}$ as share. For the sake of completeness, we present the formal details of the scheme in Fig. 3.2. The security guarantees of the scheme follow as a special case of Theorem 3.4.

Scheme Π_{Add}

Algorithm $\mathsf{G}_{\mathsf{Add}}(s)$
- Randomly pick $v_1, \ldots, v_n \in \mathbb{G}$, such that $s = v_1 \circ \ldots \circ v_n$.
- For $i = 1, \ldots, n$, output the *share* $s_i = v_i$.

Algorithm $\mathsf{R}_{\mathsf{Add}}(Q)$
- Let $Q = \{P_{i_1}, \ldots, P_{i_\ell}\}$. Output $v_{i_1} \circ \ldots \circ v_{i_\ell}$.

Fig. 3.2 The additive secret-sharing scheme

3.4   Efficient Threshold Secret-Sharing Scheme

In this section, we present an efficient t-out-of-n secret-sharing scheme for *any* given threshold $t < n$, attributed to Adi Shamir [135]. We first note one can readily obtain a t-out-of-n secret-sharing scheme from the general scheme of Ito et al. (Fig. 3.1), where the basis Σ_0 of the adversary-structure Σ consists of all subsets of $\mathcal{P}$ of size t. However, the scheme *need not* be efficient for every t. This is because the secret is divided into $k = |\Sigma_0| = \binom{n}{t}$ elements, which could be exponentially large. For instance if $t = \frac{n}{2}$, then $k = \Theta(2^n)$. To get an efficient scheme, we use advanced properties of polynomials over fields, which we discuss next.

3.4.1   Advanced Properties of Polynomials over a Field

Building on the properties of polynomials over fields discussed in Sect. 2.2, we derive additional useful properties.

Definition 3.5 Let $\mathbb{F}$ be a field. Then $\mathcal{P}^{s,d}$ denotes the set of all d-degree polynomials over $\mathbb{F}$, with s as the constant term. Namely, each $f(X) \in \mathcal{P}^{s,d}$ is of the form $f(X) = s + a_1 X + \cdots + a_d X^d$, where $a_1, \ldots, a_d \in \mathbb{F}$.

It is easy to see that $|\mathcal{P}^{s,d}| = |\mathbb{F}|^d$, since $a_1, \ldots, a_d$ can be any element from $\mathbb{F}$.

Example 3.6 Consider the field $\mathbb{F} = (\mathbb{Z}_3, +_3, \cdot_3)$. Let $s = 1$ and $d = 2$. Then the set $\mathcal{P}^{1,2}$ denotes the set of all 2-degree polynomials over $\mathbb{Z}_3$, with 1 as the constant term. The set consists of the following $|\mathbb{Z}_3|^2 = 9$ polynomials

1	$1 + X$	$1 + X^2$	$1 + X + X^2$	$1 + 2X + X^2$
	$1 + 2X$	$1 + 2X^2$	$1 + X + 2X^2$	$1 + 2X + 2X^2$

Let $\mathbb{F}$ be a field and let $(x_{i_1}, y_{i_1}), \ldots, (x_{i_d}, y_{i_d})$ be d *arbitrary* pairs of elements from $\mathbb{F}$, where $x_{i_1}, \ldots, x_{i_d}$ are all *distinct*, different from 0. Then for *any* $s \in \mathbb{F}$, there is a *unique* d-degree polynomial from $\mathcal{P}^{s,d}$, say $f(X)$, passing through the $d + 1$ distinct points $(x_{i_1}, y_{i_1}), \ldots, (x_{i_d}, y_{i_d})$ and $(0, s)$ (due to Theorem 2.13).

We next present a randomized experiment $\mathsf{Exp}_{\mathsf{Sha}}$ in Fig. 3.3. The input to the experiment is a *private* input $s \in \mathbb{F}$ and *publicly-known* n *evaluation-points* $\alpha_1, \ldots, \alpha_n \in \mathbb{F}$. Here $\mathbb{F}$ is some finite field with the constraint that $|\mathbb{F}| > n$. The experiment randomly picks a d-degree from $\mathcal{P}^{s,d}$ and outputs the value of the polynomial at the evaluation-points. Here d is some publicly-known parameter, such that $1 \le d < n$.

Experiment $\mathsf{Exp}_{\mathsf{Sha}}(s, d, \alpha_1, \ldots, \alpha_n)$

- Randomly pick $f(X)$ from $\mathcal{P}^{s,d}$. For $i = 1, \ldots, n$, output $y_i \overset{def}{=} f(\alpha_i)$.

Fig. 3.3 A randomized experiment

We next show that any subset of d output values *does not* reveal any information about the input s. Intuitively, this is because the polynomial $f(X)$ is a random d-degree polynomial and to uniquely determine $f(X)$, one needs $d + 1$ output values. We make this intuition formal by showing that the probability distribution of *any* subset of d output values is independent of s. This will imply that given any d output values, with equal probability the input could be s or s', where $s \neq s'$.

Lemma 3.7 ([11]) *In experiment* $\mathsf{Exp}_{\mathsf{Sha}}$, *for any set of distinct non-zero elements* $\alpha_1, \ldots, \alpha_n \in \mathbb{F}$, *any pair of values* $s, s' \in \mathbb{F}$, *any subset* $I \subset \{1, \ldots, n\}$ *where* $|I| = d$ *and every* $\vec{y} \in \mathbb{F}^d$, *it holds that*

$$\Pr_{f(X) \in_r \mathcal{P}^{s,d}}\left[\vec{y} = (\{f(\alpha_i)\}_{i \in I})\right] = \Pr_{g(X) \in_r \mathcal{P}^{s',d}}\left[\vec{y} = (\{g(\alpha_i)\}_{I \in I})\right],$$

where $f(X)$ *and* $g(X)$ *are chosen randomly from* $\mathcal{P}^{s,d}$ *and* $\mathcal{P}^{s',d}$, *respectively.*[2]

Proof For simplicity and without loss of generality, we consider the case when $I = \{1, \ldots, d\}$. Consider arbitrary $s, s' \in \mathbb{F}$ where $s \neq s'$ and arbitrary distinct non-zero elements $\alpha_1, \ldots, \alpha_n \in \mathbb{F}$ and an arbitrary $\vec{y} \in \mathbb{F}^d$, where $\vec{y} = (y_1, \ldots, y_d)$. We next show that:

$$\Pr_{f(X) \in_r \mathcal{P}^{s,d}}\left[(y_1 = f(\alpha_1)) \wedge \ldots \wedge (y_d = f(\alpha_d))\right] = \frac{1}{|\mathcal{P}^{s,d}|}.$$

For this, let $f'(X)$ be the unique d-degree polynomial, passing through the $d + 1$ distinct points $(0, s), (\alpha_1, y_1), \ldots, (\alpha_d, y_d)$. It is easy to see that $f'(X) \in \mathcal{P}^{s,d}$. Hence,

$$\Pr_{f(X) \in_r \mathcal{P}^{s,d}}\left[(y_1 = f(\alpha_1)) \wedge \ldots \wedge (y_d = f(\alpha_d))\right] = \Pr[f(X) = f'(X)] = \frac{1}{|\mathcal{P}^{s,d}|}.$$

This is because in the experiment, the polynomial $f(X)$ is picked uniformly at random from $\mathcal{P}^{s,d}$ (if s is the input) and $f'(X)$ is a fixed polynomial in $\mathcal{P}^{s,d}$.

---

[2] The notation $f(X) \in_r \mathcal{P}^{s,d}$ denotes that $f(X)$ is a random element of $\mathcal{P}^{s,d}$.

Using the same reasoning and letting $g'(X)$ be the unique d-degree polynomial passing through the $d + 1$ distinct points $(0, s'), (\alpha_1, y_1), \ldots, (\alpha_d, y_d)$, we get that

$$\Pr_{g(X) \in_r \mathcal{P}^{s',d}} \Big[(y_1 = f(\alpha_1)) \wedge \ldots \wedge (y_d = f(\alpha_d)) \Big] = \Pr[g(X) = g'(X)] = \frac{1}{|\mathcal{P}^{s',d}|}.$$

The proof now follows from the fact that $|\mathcal{P}^{s,d}| = |\mathcal{P}^{s',d}| = \frac{1}{|\mathbb{F}|^d}$.   □

We next demonstrate Lemma 3.7 with an example.

Example 3.8 Consider the field $\mathbb{F} = (\mathbb{Z}_{17}, +_{17}, \cdot_{17})$. Let $n = 5$, $d = 2$ with $\alpha_1 = 1$, $\alpha_2 = 2$, $\alpha_3 = 3$, $\alpha_4 = 4$ and $\alpha_5 = 5$. Consider an instance of the experiment $\mathsf{Exp}_{\mathsf{Sha}}$ with input $s = 13$, where the polynomial $f(X)$ picked during the experiment is $f(X) = 13 + 10X + 2X^2$. Consequently, the experiment outputs $y_1 = 8$, $y_2 = 7$, $y_3 = 10$, $y_4 = 0$ and $y_5 = 11$.

Now consider the subset $I = \{1, 3\}$ and corresponding $\vec{y} = (y_1, y_3) = (8, 10)$. Then the probability distribution of $\vec{y}$ is independent of s. For this, in the following table we show that for every candidate $s \in \mathbb{Z}_{17}$, there is a unique 2-degree polynomial $f(X)$ over $\mathbb{Z}_{17}$ with s as the constant term, resulting in $y_1 = 8$ and $y_3 = 10$. Since the polynomial $f(X)$ is randomly selected in the experiment, the outputs $y_1 = 8$ and $y_3 = 10$ can result from *any* input $s \in \mathbb{Z}_{17}$.

Candidate s	Candidate $f(X)$	$y_1 = f(1)$	$y_3 = f(3)$
0	$0 + 16X + 9X^2$	8	10
1	$1 + 9X + 15X^2$	8	10
2	$2 + 2X + 4X^2$	8	10
3	$3 + 12X + 10X^2$	8	10
4	$4 + 5X + 16X^2$	8	10
5	$5 + 15X + 5X^2$	8	10
6	$6 + 8X + 11X^2$	8	10
7	$7 + X + 0X^2$	8	10
8	$8 + 11X + 6X^2$	8	10
9	$9 + 4X + 12X^2$	8	10
10	$10 + 14X + X^2$	8	10
11	$11 + 7X + 7X^2$	8	10
12	$12 + 0X + 13X^2$	8	10
13	$13 + 10X + 2X^2$	8	10
14	$14 + 3X + 8X^2$	8	10
15	$15 + 13X + 14X^2$	8	10
16	$16 + 6X + 3X^2$	8	10

3.4.2 The Shamir Secret-Sharing Scheme

In the Shamir's scheme, all computations are performed over a *finite* field $\mathbb{F}$, where $|\mathbb{F}| > n$. The secret as well as the shares are elements of $\mathbb{F}$. The scheme considers publicly-known, distinct, non-zero elements $\alpha_1, \ldots, \alpha_n \in \mathbb{F}$ called *evaluation-points*, where α_i is associated with party P_i. The share-generation algorithm $\mathsf{G}_{\mathsf{Sha}}$ of the Shamir's secret-sharing scheme takes input a secret $s \in \mathbb{F}$. To compute the shares, a polynomial $f(X)$ is picked uniformly at random from the set $\mathcal{P}^{s,t}$ of all t-degree polynomials over $\mathbb{F}$ whose constant term is s, where $|\mathcal{P}^{s,t}| = |\mathbb{F}|^t$.[3] The output of the algorithm is the vector of *shares* $(s_1, \ldots, s_n)$, where $s_i = q(\alpha_i)$. As the polynomial is chosen randomly and is a t-degree polynomial, the probability distribution of any subset of t shares will be independent of the underlying secret, which follows from Lemma 3.7 by substituting $d = t$.[4] Since $\mathsf{G}_{\mathsf{Sha}}$ is a randomized algorithm, we use the notation $(s_1, \ldots, s_n) \leftarrow \mathsf{G}_{\mathsf{Sha}}(s)$ to denote the random vector of shares, produced by $\mathsf{G}_{\mathsf{Sha}}$.

Let $I \subset \{1, \ldots, n\}$, where $|I| = t + 1$. Then the recovery function $\mathsf{R}_{\mathsf{Sha}}$ takes input the shares $\{s_i\}_{i \in I}$ and outputs s. The standard instantiation of $\mathsf{R}_{\mathsf{Sha}}$ is the Lagrange's interpolation formula, which interpolates $f(X)$ through the points $\{(\alpha_i, s_i)\}_{i \in I}$ (see Sect. 2.2). If $|I| > t + 1$, then the function $\mathsf{R}_{\mathsf{Sha}}$ can interpolate $f(X)$ by considering *any* subset of $t + 1$ shares. We use the notation $s = \mathsf{R}_{\mathsf{Sha}}(I, \{s_i\}_{i \in I})$ for using the function $\mathsf{R}_{\mathsf{Sha}}$.

From the above discussion, it follows easily that the pair of algorithms $(\mathsf{G}_{\mathsf{Sha}}, \mathsf{R}_{\mathsf{Sha}})$ satisfies the privacy and correctness properties of t-out-of-n secret-sharing scheme. The scheme is efficient, as the share of each party consists of just a single element from $\mathbb{F}$. We conclude this section by highlighting the importance of a field for the security of the Shamir's secret-sharing scheme.

Role of a Finite Field in Shamir's Secret-Sharing Scheme: Suppose instead of performing the operations over a field, we perform operations over the set of Integers $\mathbb{Z}$ (which is not a field). Namely, the polynomials are selected with coefficients from $\mathbb{Z}$ and the $+$ and $\cdot$ operations are the integer addition and multiplication. We show that in this case, the resultant scheme may not satisfy the properties of a secret-sharing scheme.

Example 3.9 Consider the case when $t = 1$ and the evaluation-point α_i associated with P_i is the integer i. Now suppose that to share an integer $s \in \mathbb{Z}$, the sharing algorithm $\mathsf{G}_{\mathsf{Sha}}$ picks a random 1-degree polynomial $f(X) = s + (v - s)X$, where v is a randomly chosen integer, which ensures that the coefficient $v - s$ is also a random integer. Then $\mathsf{G}_{\mathsf{Sha}}$ outputs the shares $y_1 = f(1) = v$, $y_2 = f(2) = 2v - s$, $y_3 = \ldots$ and so on. Since $t = 1$, for *privacy*, the probability distribution of any single share y_i should be independent of s. However, it is easy to see that this is not the case, as the probability distribution of the share y_2 is *dependent*

---

[3] Let $f(X) = s + f_1 X + \ldots + f_t X^t$. To ensure that $f(X)$ is a random polynomial from the set $\mathcal{P}^{s,t}$, it is sufficient to select the coefficients $f_1, \ldots, f_t$ uniformly at random from $\mathbb{F}$.

[4] We often use the term Shamir-sharing polynomial to denote the t-degree polynomial used in the algorithm.

on s. Namely, since the share y_2 is now an integer, it follows that y_2 is an even number, if and only if s is an even number. Hence depending upon the parity of y_2, one can determine the parity of the shared secret.

Note that the above problem does not arise if the operations are performed over a field, say $\mathbb{Z}_p$ (where p is a prime). This is because the *field* element $2v - s$ will be any field element (odd as well as even) with equal probability, irrespective of the value of s. Namely, for every candidate s belonging to the field, there exists a unique field element $v \overset{def}{=} (s + y_2) \cdot 2^{-1}$ resulting in y_2, where 2^{-1} denotes the multiplicative-inverse of 2 in the field. Since v is now a random field element, it implies that y_2 is also a random field element.

We note that the above issue resurfaces if a ring is used instead of a field. Continuing with the same example, y_2 may no longer be a random ring element. This is because the ring element 2 may not have a multiplicative inverse. And hence one cannot claim the one-to-one mapping between the unknown v and unknown s over the ring, for the fixed $y_2 = 2v - s$.

In addition to privacy, correctness may not hold too when the operations are *not* performed over a field, as demonstrated in the following example, taken from [1].

Example 3.10 Consider the case when $t = 2$ and the evaluation-point α_i associated with P_i is the integer i and all operations are performed over the set of integers $\mathbb{Z}$. Let $s = 1234$ and algorithm G_{Sha} picks the sharing-polynomial $f(X) = 1234 + 166X + 94X^2$. Let $n = 5$ and so the algorithm outputs the shares $y_1 = f(1) = 1494$, $y_2 = f(2) = 1942$, $y_3 = f(3) = 2578$, $y_4 = f(4) = 3402$ and $y_5 = f(5) = 4414$.

Since $t = 2$, the algorithm R_{Sha} should correctly output s, if the input to R_{Sha} are the shares $\{y_2, y_4, y_5\}$. Suppose R_{Sha} uses the Lagrange's interpolation to interpolate $f(X)$ through the points $\{(2, 1942), (4, 3402), (5, 4414)\}$. Now as a part of the interpolation, the following polynomials will be computed:

$$\delta_1(X) = \frac{(X - 4)(X - 5)}{(2 - 4)(2 - 5)}, \quad \delta_2(X) = \frac{(X - 2)(X - 5)}{(4 - 2)(4 - 5)} \quad \text{and} \quad \delta_3(X) = \frac{(X - 2)(X - 4)}{(5 - 2)(5 - 4)},$$

which are same as

$$\delta_1(X) = \frac{1}{6}X^2 - \frac{3}{2}X + \frac{10}{3}, \quad \delta_2(X) = -\frac{1}{2}X^2 + \frac{7}{2}X - 5 \quad \text{and} \quad \delta_3(X) = \frac{1}{3}X^2 - 2X + \frac{8}{3}.$$

Since all the above operations are performed over $\mathbb{Z}$, when implemented in computers they are implemented as floating-point operations and hence the reconstruction may be error-prone. This issue does not occur if the operations are instead performed over a field. This is because in this case, the division operations are interpreted as multiplication with the multiplicative-inverse of the denominators, which are guaranteed to exist since all the denominators in the formula for Lagrange's interpolation will be non-zero elements of the field.

We note that a *finite* field is preferred in the Shamir's secret-sharing scheme, as sampling random field elements (required to select the random sharing-polynomial during G_{Sha}) is relatively easier in a finite field. We also note that none of the evaluation-points $\alpha_1, \ldots, \alpha_n$ is allowed to be 0, as otherwise the *privacy* is violated. For instance, if $\alpha_i = 0$, then the share $\alpha_i = f(\alpha_i)$ will be the same as the secret s itself and hence the probability distribution of the single share s_i will no longer be independent of s. Finally, we require the evaluation-points to be *distinct* (which further implies that $|\mathbb{F}| > n$ should hold), as otherwise the correctness property will be violated. For instance, if $\alpha_1 = \alpha_{t+1} = \alpha$, then the shares y_1 and y_{t+1} will be the same as $f(\alpha)$. Hence the algorithm R_{Sha} will fail to uniquely interpolate the sharing-polynomial $f(X)$, if it is provided with the input shares $\{(\alpha_1, y_1), \ldots, (\alpha_{t+1}, y_{t+1})\}$, which now constitute *only* t distinct points on the unknown t-degree sharing-polynomial, since (α_1, y_1) and (α_{t+1}, y_{t+1}) are the same.

We further note that in the scheme, the size of each share is the same as the size of the secret itself (namely, the secret is a field element and so is each share). In fact, using arguments from information theory, one can prove a generic statement that: in *any* secret-sharing scheme with *perfect* privacy, the size of each share should be at least as large, as the secret itself. This means that Shamir's secret-sharing is *optimal* in this sense. At a high-level the idea is as follows. Assume that there is a share smaller in size than the secret, say the first one without loss of generality. Consider a subset of $t + 1$ shares from the set of n shares including the first share. From the privacy property, the set of t shares in this subset excluding the first share is independent of the underlying secret and carries no information about the latter. This implies that the first share should completely determine the shared secret and must carry as much "information" as the secret itself, as otherwise it would be impossible to reconstruct the secret using the subset of $t + 1$ shares. This puts a bound on the size of the first share which must be as large as the secret. The argument extends for any share.

The large share-size is one of the limitations of Shamir's secret-sharing scheme (and any secret-sharing scheme with perfect privacy). Another limitation is that enormous amount of randomness is required in the sharing algorithm. Namely, to share a single field element, algorithm G_{Sha} needs to pick t uniformly random field elements. However, this limitation is also attributed to the perfect privacy of the scheme.

3.5   Application of Secret Sharing: Perfectly-Secure Message Transmission (PSMT)

In this section, we discuss a powerful application of secret-sharing, namely *perfectly-secure message transmission* (PSMT) [53, 67, 109, 137]. In the PSMT problem, a *sender* S and a *receiver* R with *no* pre-shared information are a part of a distributed communication network, modelled as a connected graph. A part of the network is "compromised", meaning that a subset of the intermediate nodes in the network (excluding S and R) could be under the control of a *computationally-unbounded passive* adversary, which can see all the information

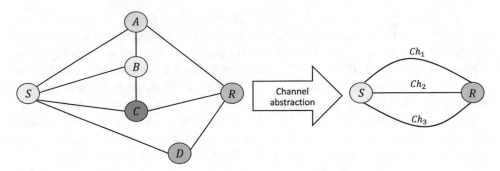

Fig. 3.4 Example of the channel abstraction of the intermediate network between S and R

passing through the nodes under its control. However, the exact identity of the adversarial nodes are unknown to S and R. The goal is to design a protocol, which allows S to send some message held by it to R with *perfect privacy*, so that the adversary does not learn any information about S's message. Note that since adversary is computationally-unbounded, we are not allowed to use any cryptographic mechanisms, such as encryption to solve the problem, the security of which holds only against a computationally-bounded adversary.

The communication network between S and R is abstracted to form n distinct channels $Ch_1, \ldots, Ch_n$ between S and R, with the adversary eavesdropping a *proper subset* of these channels. Note that if adversary is allowed to eavesdrop all the n channels, then clearly the problem is unsolvable. The motivation for the channel abstraction is that if some intermediate node is under the adversary's control, then *all* the paths between S and R passing through that intermediate node is compromised. Hence the communication network is simplified to the set of vertex-disjoint paths between S and R. For instance, for the network shown in Fig. 3.4, the two paths (S, B, C, R) and (S, C, R) can be abstracted as a single channel between S and R. This is because if the node C is under the adversary's control, then any information sent over the path (S, B, C, R) or (S, C, R) will be completely learnt by the adversary.

One can consider two different kinds of adversaries. In the *non-threshold* setting, the adversary is modelled by a *publicly-known* adversary-structure $\Sigma \subset 2^{\{Ch_1, \ldots, Ch_n\}}$, where the adversary can control any subset of channels belonging to Σ. As said earlier, the exact identity of the subset under adversary's control will be unknown to S and R. On the other hand, in a *threshold* setting, the adversary can control any subset of t channels (again the exact identity of these t channels will be unknown). It is easy to note that the threshold setting is a special case of the non-threshold setting, where the size of each subset of potentially corrupt channels in Σ is exactly t.

An obvious necessary condition to solve the PSMT problem is that every subset in Σ should be a proper subset of $\{Ch_1, \ldots, Ch_n\}$; i.e. the adversary should not be able to control all the n channels. Following the terminology of [91], this condition is often called as the $\mathcal{Q}^{(1)}$ condition. For the threshold setting, this necessary condition translates to $t < n$.

PSMT Protocol from Any Secret-Sharing Scheme: We now discuss how one can design a PSMT protocol from *any* given secret-sharing scheme. For simplicity, we consider a *threshold* adversary setting. A similar idea can be used to get a PSMT protocol against a non-threshold adversary. Let (G, R) be a t-out-of-n secret-sharing scheme with *perfect* privacy and correctness. In the PSMT protocol, the sender on having an input message m executes the algorithm $G(m)$ and generates the shares $m_1, \ldots, m_n$. It then sends the share m_i over the channel Ch_i. To recover the message m, the receiver applies the algorithm R on any subset of $t + 1$ received shares.

The (perfect) *privacy* of G guarantees that an adversary controlling any subset of t channels fails to learn m, as it learns only t shares, whose probability distribution is independent of the underlying m. The recovery of m by the receiver is guaranteed, which follows from the *correctness* property of the secret-sharing scheme.

3.6   Secret Sharing Tolerating Malicious Adversaries

We note that the idea of obtaining a secret-sharing protocol from any secret-sharing scheme *fails* completely if we consider a *malicious* (Byzantine) adversary, who can control a subset of parties in a malicious fashion and forces them to deviate from the protocol instructions in any *arbitrary* fashion. For instance, if in the Shamir's secret-sharing protocol we consider t malicious corruptions (potentially including the dealer D itself), then we face the following problems. A potentially *corrupt* D may not execute the algorithm G_{Sha} correctly and hence the shares distributed to the parties may not be "consistent" (i.e. the shares may not lie on a single t-degree polynomial, as required). On the other hand, even if it is ensured that the distributed shares are consistent, at the time of reconstruction, even if a single *corrupt* party produces an *incorrect* share (different from the one as obtained from D), then the reconstructed polynomial and hence the secret may be different from the one shared.

By enhancing the secret-sharing protocol with a *public* "verification" mechanism, the above issues can be tackled. The verification ensures that the shared secret is shared consistently, maintaining the privacy of the secret (if the dealer is not under the control of the adversary). Moreover, at the time of reconstruction, incorrect shares can be identified and discarded. Such protocols are referred as *verifiable secret-sharing* (VSS) [44, 52] and their discussion is out of scope of the current lecture series focusing on semi-honest adversaries.

A Toy MPC Protocol

4

In this chapter, we discuss a simple MPC protocol, which allows a set of n mutually-distrusting parties to compute the sum of their private bits "securely", without revealing anything beyond the sum. This is a simple case study for a specific function before we plunge into the more involved general case. We will also introduce a powerful proof mechanism based on the simulation-paradigm, which is used extensively throughout this book. We conclude with a few possible breaks for the MPC protocol in the face of stronger adversarial setting, including malicious adversaries.

4.1 Problem Definition and an Ideal Solution

Consider a set of n mutually-distrusting parties $\mathcal{P} = \{P_1, \ldots, P_n\}$, where each party P_i has a *private* bit $b_i \in \{0, 1\}$. The parties are interested to learn the sum $S \overset{def}{=} b_1 + \cdots + b_n$ and nothing beyond. Specifically, each P_i should learn only S and whatever it can infer about the inputs of the other parties from its own input b_i and the sum S. For instance, once S is learnt by P_i, an obvious inference that P_i can make is that the sum of the remaining inputs, namely $b_1 + \cdots + b_{i-1} + b_{i+1} + \cdots + b_n$, is $S - b_i$. Such an inference is allowed and is not considered as a "breach" of privacy.

An Ideal Solution: We can construct an ideally-secure protocol assuming the presence of a *trusted third party* (TTP) as discussed in Sect. 1.2. Assume further that there is a mechanism for each party P_i to *privately* interact with the TTP, such that no other party in $\mathcal{P}$ learns the messages exchanged between the TTP and P_i. Given such a setup, the parties can securely compute the sum S as follows. Every party P_i privately sends its input b_i to the TTP, who upon receiving $b_1, \ldots, b_n$ computes $S = b_1 + \cdots + b_n$ and then sends S to each P_i. Clearly, this protocol achieves our desired goal. We call the above protocol as the *ideal protocol*.

© The Author(s), under exclusive license to Springer Nature Switzerland AG 2022
A. Choudhury and A. Patra, *Secure Multi-Party Computation Against Passive Adversaries*,
Synthesis Lectures on Distributed Computing Theory,
https://doi.org/10.1007/978-3-031-12164-7_4

The ideal protocol suffers from a single point-of-failure. That is, if the TTP (the single point) gets compromised by an adversary, then the privacy of the inputs of all the parties is lost. Hence, a solution where the parties should be able to securely compute S, without assuming any sort of TTP, is desired. It may sound impossible at the first sight, but it is otherwise possible in reality.

4.2   A Protocol to Securely Compute the Sum

Suppose there exists a secure channel between every pair of parties P_i, P_j which allows them to interact securely. Then we present a protocol, which allows the parties to securely compute S. In the protocol all operations are performed over $\mathbb{Z}_M$, where $M > n$. The idea behind the protocol is very simple. We start with any designated party, say P_1, masking its input b_1 with some random mask and sending the masked input to P_2. This does not reveal any information about b_1 to P_2, since the random mask is known only to P_1. Party P_2 then adds its own input to the received value (which is masked b_1) and sends it to P_3. Thus P_3 receives the partial sum $b_1 + b_2$ in a masked fashion. And since the mask is unknown to P_3, it does not reveal b_1, b_2 and their sum to P_3. This process is repeated for n rounds, where in round r, party P_r upon receiving the partial sum $b_1 + \cdots + b_{r-1}$ in a masked form from its "predecessor" P_{r-1}, adds b_r and sends the resultant partial masked sum to its "successor" P_{r+1}. Finally in round n, party P_n upon adding its input b_n sends the final masked sum to P_1. Since the mask has been selected by P_1, it can now unmask it and declare the result S to all the parties.

It is easy to note that any $P_i \in \{P_2, \ldots, P_n\}$ does not learn any additional information beyond S and b_i, due to the masked evaluation. On the other hand, P_1 also does not learn any additional information beyond S and b_1. The protocol is formally presented in Fig. 4.1. We next analyze the protocol Π_{Sum}. We start with the complexity analysis.

Protocol Π_{Sum}

– Round 1:
  – Party P_1 picks a random element $k \in \mathbb{Z}_M$ and sends $c_1 \overset{def}{=} (b_1 + k) \mod M$ to party P_2.
– Round $r \in \{2, \ldots, n-1\}$:
  – Party P_r upon receiving c_{r-1} from party P_{r-1}, sends $c_r \overset{def}{=} (c_{r-1} + b_r) \mod M$ to party P_{r+1}.
– Round n:
  – Party P_n upon receiving c_{n-1} from party P_{n-1}, sends $c_n \overset{def}{=} (c_{n-1} + b_n) \mod M$ to party P_1.
– Round $n+1$:
  – Party P_1 upon receiving c_n from party P_n, sends $S \overset{def}{=} (c_n - k) \mod M$ to all the parties in $\mathcal{P}$.

Fig. 4.1 A protocol for securely computing the sum of n bits

Lemma 4.1 *Protocol* Π_{Sum} *requires* $n + 1$ *communication rounds and communication of* $\mathcal{O}(n)$ *elements from* $\mathbb{Z}_M$.

Proof The round complexity follows from the protocol inspection. During rounds $1, \ldots, n$, a single party sends a single element from $\mathbb{Z}_M$ to another party. During round $n + 1$, party P_1 sends S to all the parties. So overall the protocol incurs a communication of $\mathcal{O}(n)$ elements from $\mathbb{Z}_M$. $\square$

We next prove the correctness of the protocol.

Lemma 4.2 *In protocol* Π_{Sum}, *the condition* $S = b_1 + \cdots + b_n$ *holds.*

Proof The value S is same as $(c_n - k) \mod M$, where $c_n = (b_1 + \cdots + b_n + k) \mod M$. Hence S is the same as $(b_1 + \cdots + b_n) \mod M$. Since each $b_i \in \{0, 1\}$ and $M > n$ holds, it follows that $(b_1 + \cdots + b_n) \mod M$ will be the same as $b_1 + \cdots + b_n$. $\square$

We next proceed to prove the privacy of the protocol by showing that the information learnt by any P_i does not allow it to learn anything beyond what it can learn from the final output S and its own input b_i. Interestingly, this holds even if P_i is *computationally unbounded*. The only additional information learnt by P_i (apart from S and b_i) is the value c_i, which P_i receives from P_{i-1}. We first demonstrate through an example that for any legitimate pair (S, b_i) allowed as per the protocol, c_i is consistent with every candidate $(b_1, \ldots, b_{i-1}, b_{i+1}, \ldots, b_n) \in \{0, 1\}^{n-1}$, such that $b_1 + \cdots + b_{i-1} + b_i + b_{i+1} + \cdots + b_n = S$ holds.

Example 4.3 Let $\mathcal{P} = \{P_1, \ldots, P_4\}$ and let all the computations be performed over $\mathbb{Z}_5$. Let the inputs of the parties be $b_1 = 1$, $b_2 = 0$, $b_3 = 1$ and $b_4 = 0$. Then consider the following execution of the protocol Π_{Sum}. Party P_1 picks $k = 4$ and sends $c_1 = (b_1 + k) \mod 5 = 0$ to P_2. Party P_2 sends $c_2 = (c_1 + b_2) \mod 5 = 0$ to P_3. Party P_3 sends $c_3 = (c_2 + b_3) \mod 5 = 1$ to P_4. Party P_4 sends $c_4 = (c_3 + 0) \mod 5 = 1$ to P_1. Finally party P_1 computes $S = (c_4 - k) \mod 5 = 2$ and sends S to all the parties. The inputs of the respective parties and the values received by the various parties during the execution are shown in the first table below.

	P_1	P_2	P_3	P_4
b_1	1			
b_2		0		
b_3			1	
b_4				0
k	4			
c_1		0		
c_2			0	
c_3				1
c_4	1			
S	2	2	2	2

	P_1	P_2	P_3	P_4
b_1	?			
b_2		?		
b_3			**1**	
b_4				?
k	?			
c_1		?		
c_2			**0**	
c_3				1
c_4	?			
S	2	2	**2**	2

Now assume that party P_3, with the goal to learn more information than allowed, analyzes the information learnt during the execution. In the second table above, the values known to P_3 are shown in bold and the values unknown to P_3 are marked with ? Based on its input $b_3 = 1$ and the final sum $S = 2$, P_3 can infer that *exactly* one of the inputs b_1 or b_2 or b_4 could be 1. However, as we demonstrate below, P_3 cannot tell apart amongst the three possible cases satisfying its inference: $(b_1 = 1, b_2 = 0, b_4 = 0)$, $(b_1 = 0, b_2 = 1, b_4 = 0)$ and $(b_1 = 0, b_2 = 0, b_4 = 1)$. For each case, there is a matching value of k, that makes the execution possible.

Suppose P_3 makes the hypothesis that $b_1 = 0, b_2 = 0$ and $b_4 = 1$, which is consistent with the sum S being 2. Since $c_2 = 0$ (which is part of P_3's view) and b_2 is assumed to be 0, P_2 sends $c_2 = 0$ to P_3 only when it receives $c_1 = 0$ from P_1. Since b_1 is assumed to be 0, P_1 sends $c_1 = 0$ to P_2, when k is selected as 0. Finally, since $c_3 = 1$ and b_4 is assumed to be 1, P_1 finds the final sum to be 2, when P_4 sends $c_4 = 2$ to P_1. So if indeed $b_1 = 0, b_2 = 0$ and $b_4 = 1$, the parties should exchange values, as per the third table below. Similarly, the remaining two tables showcase the executions for the hypothesis $(b_1 = 1, b_2 = 0, b_4 = 0)$ and $(b_1 = 0, b_2 = 1, b_4 = 0)$ respectively. The tables show that the view of P_3 is the same in all the three scenarios $(b_1 = 1, b_2 = 0, b_4 = 0)$, $(b_1 = 0, b_2 = 1, b_4 = 0)$ and $(b_1 = 0, b_2 = 0, b_4 = 1)$ and so each is equally possible from P_3s point of view.

	P_1	P_2	P_3	P_4
b_1	1			
b_2		0		
b_3			**1**	
b_4				0
k	4			
c_1		0		
c_2			**0**	
c_3				1
c_4	1			
S	2	2	**2**	2

	P_1	P_2	P_3	P_4
b_1	0			
b_2		1		
b_3			**1**	
b_4				0
k	4			
c_1		4		
c_2			**0**	
c_3				1
c_4	1			
S	2	2	**2**	2

	P_1	P_2	P_3	P_4
b_1	0			
b_2		0		
b_3			**1**	
b_4				1
k	0			
c_1		0		
c_2			**0**	
c_3				1
c_4	2			
S	2	2	**2**	2

A similar analysis confirms our claim that for any $P_i \in \{P_2, \ldots, P_4\}$, the value c_{i-1} learnt by P_i does not allow it to infer any additional information about the inputs of the other parties, beyond what can be revealed from the input b_i and the final sum S.

We now analyse the view of P_1. It receives c_4 from party P_4, which is same as $S + k$. With the knowledge of k, P_1 obtains $c_4 - k = S$ alone. Stated differently, given the final output S (the desired output to be learnt by all the parties) and the value k selected by P_1 itself, P_1 knows that c_4 that it receives from P_3 will be the same as $S + k$. So, c_4 does not reveal any additional information about the inputs of the other parties. We demonstrate this in the following tables, where P_1 makes the hypothesis that ($b_2 = 1$, $b_3 = 0$, $b_4 = 0$), ($b_2 = 0$, $b_3 = 1$, $b_4 = 0$) and ($b_2 = 0$, $b_3 = 0$, $b_4 = 1$) respectively (which are consistent with $b_1 = 1$ and $S = 2$). As can be noted, each of these three hypothesis is equally likely to occur from the point of view of P_1.

	P_1	P_2	P_3	P_4
b_1	**1**			
b_2		1		
b_3			0	
b_4				0
k	**4**			
c_1		**0**		
c_2			0	
c_3				1
c_4	**1**			
S	**2**	2	2	2

	P_1	P_2	P_3	P_4
b_1	**1**			
b_2		0		
b_3			1	
b_4				0
k	**4**			
c_1		**0**		
c_2			0	
c_3				1
c_4	**1**			
S	**2**	2	2	2

	P_1	P_2	P_3	P_4
b_1	**1**			
b_2		0		
b_3			0	
b_4				1
k	**4**			
c_1		**0**		
c_2			0	
c_3				0
c_4	**1**			
S	**2**	2	2	2

Before formally proving the privacy, we prove that for any $i \in \{2, \ldots, n\}$, the value c_i in the protocol is a random element from $\mathbb{Z}_M$. Intuitively, this follows from the fact that c_i is the sum of $b_1, \ldots, b_i, k$, and k is randomly chosen from $\mathbb{Z}_M$.

Lemma 4.4 *In protocol Π_{Sum}, for each $i \in \{2, \ldots, n\}$ and each $S \in \{0, \ldots, n\}$, as the choice of the inputs $b_1, \ldots, b_n$ varies, subject to each $b_j \in \{0, 1\}$ and $S = b_1 + \cdots + b_n$, the probability distribution of c_i is the uniform distribution over $\mathbb{Z}_M$.*

Proof Consider an arbitrary $S \in \{0, \ldots, n\}$ and an arbitrary vector $(b_1, \ldots, b_n) \in \{0, 1\}^n$, subject to the condition that $S = b_1 + \cdots + b_n$. Let $L_i \stackrel{def}{=} (b_1 + \cdots + b_i)$ and $R_i \stackrel{def}{=} (b_{i+1} + \cdots + b_n)$. Hence $S = (L_i + R_i)$, which further implies that $L_i = S - R_i$. From the protocol steps, $c_i = k + (b_1 + \cdots + b_i) \mod M$, which is the same as $(k + L_i) \mod M$. Substituting the value of L_i, we get that $c_i = (k + S - R_i) \mod M$. Let x be an arbitrary element of $\mathbb{Z}_M$. Then it follows that:

$$\Pr[c_i = x] = \Pr[k = (x + R_i - S) \mod M] = \frac{1}{M}.$$

The last equality follows from the fact that k is picked uniformly at random from $\mathbb{Z}_M$. $\square$

We now formally prove the privacy that means that by participating in Π_{Sum}, every P_i learns nothing beyond (S, b_i), irrespective of the computing power of P_i. The formalization that certain information, say Y, does not allow to learn anything beyond certain other information, say X, in itself is challenging. Here, Y indicates the view of P_i in Π_{Sum} and X indicates (S, b_i). The *simulation-paradigm* introduced in [82] in the context of formally defining the security of encryption schemes, formulates the idea by showing that Y can be "efficiently" recreated or simulated from X.

For a proof of Π_{Sum} based on the simulation-paradigm, we next define the view view_i of party P_i, which consists of all the values seen by P_i during the execution of Π_{Sum}. Hence view_i consists of the input b_i, the final output S, c_{i-1} and c_i for every $i \in \{2, \ldots, n\}$. Whereas view_1 consists of b_1, S, k, c_1 and c_n. We note that view_1 is a random variable, for k is chosen randomly. Since each c_i depends upon k, each view_i where $i \in \{2, \ldots, n\}$ is also a random variable. Now formally privacy means that there exists an efficient probabilistic algorithm, namely a *simulator* $\mathcal{S}_{\mathsf{Sum}}$, which can take the input (S, b_i) corresponding to any P_i and can produce an output whose probability distribution is identical to that of view_i. That is,

$$\left\{ \mathcal{S}_{\mathsf{Sum}}(S, b_i) \right\} \equiv \left\{ \mathsf{view}_i \right\}$$

holds, where $\equiv$ denotes that the two probability distributions are identical. In essence, the existence of a $\mathcal{S}_{\mathsf{Sum}}$ with the above property implies that view_i does not "contain" any additional information beyond S and b_i. Further, what P_i can learn about the inputs of the

---

Simulator S_{Sum}

Upon input (S, b_i) corresponding to party P_i, the simulator does the following.
- If $P_i = P_1$:
  - Pick a random element $\widetilde{k} \in \mathbb{Z}_M$ and compute $\widetilde{c}_1 = (b_1 + \widetilde{k}) \mod M$.
  - Output $\widetilde{\text{view}}_1 = (b_1, S, \widetilde{k}, \widetilde{c}_1, \widetilde{c}_n)$, where $\widetilde{c}_n = (S + \widetilde{k}) \mod M$.
- If $P_i \in \{P_2, \ldots, P_n\}$:
  - Pick a random element $\widetilde{c}_{i-1} \in \mathbb{Z}_M$ and compute $\widetilde{c}_i = \widetilde{c}_{i-1} + b_i$.
  - Output $\widetilde{\text{view}}_i = (b_i, S, \widetilde{c}_{i-1}, \widetilde{c}_i)$.

Fig. 4.2 Simulator to simulate the view of P_i for the protocol Π_{Sum}

other parties by participating in the protocol Π_{Sum}, can be effectively computed by P_i by running the algorithm S_{Sum} and *without* participating in the protocol Π_{Sum}.

We now present the steps of the simulator S_{Sum} (see Fig. 4.2). The steps will be different, depending upon whether $P_i = P_1$ or $P_i \in \{P_2, \ldots, P_n\}$. If $P_i = P_1$, then the simulator picks a random mask on the behalf of P_1 and generates the corresponding masked b_1 and masked sum S. On the other hand, if $P_i \neq P_1$, then the simulator sets the value of c_{i-1} as a random element from $\mathbb{Z}_M$ and generates the corresponding c_i on the behalf of P_i. In the steps of the simulator, to differentiate the values generated by the simulator from the ones generated in Π_{Sum}, we use variables of the form $\widetilde{k}, \widetilde{c}$ etc.

To complete the proof of the privacy, we show that the probability distribution of the simulated view generated by the simulator is identical to the actual view of party P_i in Π_{Sum}.

Lemma 4.5 *The probability distributions $\{\text{view}_i\}$ and $\{\widetilde{\text{view}}_i\}$ are identical, corresponding to any $P_i \in \mathcal{P}$.*

Proof If $P_i = P_1$, then $\text{view}_1 = (b_1, S, k, c_1, c_n)$ and $\widetilde{\text{view}}_1 = (b_1, S, \widetilde{k}, \widetilde{c}_1, \widetilde{c}_n)$. The components b_1 and S are identical in both the views and hence have the same distribution. So fix b_1 and S. Conditioned on b_1 and S, the variables k and $\widetilde{k}$ are identically distributed, since both of them are uniformly random elements from $\mathbb{Z}_M$, so fix k. Next conditioned on b_1, S and k, both c_1 and $\widetilde{c}_1$ are identically distributed, since $c_1 = b_1 + k$ and $\widetilde{c}_1 = b_1 + \widetilde{k}$. Since k and $\widetilde{k}$ are identically distributed, it follows that c_1 and $\widetilde{c}_1$ have the same distribution, namely uniform distribution over $\mathbb{Z}_M$. Next fix c_1 and $\widetilde{c}_1$ to some arbitrary value in $\mathbb{Z}_M$, say x. It is now easy to see that conditioned on b_1, S, k and c_1 which are identically distributed both in view_1 and $\widetilde{\text{view}}_1$, the values c_n and $\widetilde{c}_n$ are also identically distributed. Namely, $c_n = S + k$ and $\widetilde{c}_n = S + \widetilde{k}$. Since k and $\widetilde{k}$ are identically distributed, it follows that c_n and $\widetilde{c}_n$ have the same distribution, namely uniform distribution over $\mathbb{Z}_M$.

If $P_i \in \{P_2, \ldots, P_n\}$, then $\text{view}_i = (b_i, S, c_{i-1}, c_i)$ and $\widetilde{\text{view}}_i = (b_i, S, \widetilde{c}_{i-1}, \widetilde{c}_i)$. The components b_i and S are identical in both the views and hence have the same distribution. So fix b_i and S. Conditioned on b_i and S, the variables c_{i-1} and $\widetilde{c}_{i-1}$ are identically distributed.

This is because from Lemma 4.4, c_{i-1} is uniformly distributed over $\mathbb{Z}_M$ and from the steps of $\mathcal{S}_{\mathsf{Sum}}$, the element $\widetilde{c}_{i-1}$ is also a uniformly random element from $\mathbb{Z}_M$. Next fix c_{i-1} and $\widetilde{c}_{i-1}$ to some arbitrary value in $\mathbb{Z}_M$, say x. It is now easy to see that conditioned on b_i, S and c_{i-1} which are identically distributed both in view_i and $\widetilde{\mathsf{view}}_i$, the values c_i and $\widetilde{c}_i$ are also identically distributed. Namely, $c_i = c_{i-1} + b_i$ and $\widetilde{c}_i = \widetilde{c}_{i-1} + b_i$. Since c_{i-1} and $\widetilde{c}_{i-1}$ are identically distributed, it follows that c_i and $\widetilde{c}_i$ have the same distribution, namely uniform distribution over $\mathbb{Z}_M$. $\square$

We conclude this section with a discussion on the "equivalence" of the protocol Π_{Sum} and the ideal solution in terms of the privacy guarantees, as implied by the simulation-paradigm.

Equivalence of the Ideal protocol and Protocol Π_{Sum}: Recall the ideal protocol for computing the sum of $b_1, \ldots, b_n$ in the presence of a TTP, where every P_i learns exactly (b_i, S). By proving that the view of the party P_i in the protocol Π_{Sum} can be efficiently simulated solely based on the knowledge of (b_i, S) (see Lemma 4.5), we have shown that P_i's knowledge about the inputs of the other parties during Π_{Sum} remains the same as that in the ideal protocol. Since in the ideal solution P_i does not learn anything additional about the inputs of the other parties other than what can be inferred from S and b_i, it follows that the same holds even in the protocol Π_{Sum}. This shows that the protocol Π_{Sum} (where there is *no* TTP) has the *same* security guarantees as that of the ideal protocol. In this lecture series, we will use this paradigm to prove the privacy of the protocols. So, we recommend the readers to understand the subtleties of this paradigm as illustrated in this chapter.

4.3   Possible Attacks Against Protocol Π_{Sum}

While protocol Π_{Sum} does not allow any *single* party to learn anything additional about the inputs of the other parties, any *two* parties colluding together can do so. Specifically, parties P_i and P_{i+2} together can recover the input b_{i+1} as $c_{i+1} - c_i$, given the knowledge of c_i and c_{i+1}. Note that in the ideal solution, even if P_i and P_{i+2} collude together, they collectively learn (S, b_i, b_{i+2}), which does not allow them to learn the exact value of b_{i+1}. Hence the equivalence between Π_{Sum} and the ideal solution does not hold for a collusion between any two parties, implying a privacy breach in the protocol Π_{Sum}. Later we will see how to maintain the privacy of the inputs of the parties, if multiple parties collude together.

Finally, we note that the correctness guarantees of the protocol Π_{Sum} are ensured only if all the parties follow the protocol instructions correctly. The correctness breaks down completely, if the parties start deviating from the protocol instructions and behave *maliciously*. For instance, if P_1 behaves maliciously, then it may decide to publicly declare an incorrect sum S in the last round. Worse, it may decide not to reveal any result at the first place after learning the final sum S itself. There are ways to deal with such malicious behaviour and discussing those mechanisms is out of scope of this lecture series.

The BGW Perfectly-Secure MPC Protocol for Linear Functions

5

In this chapter, we present the classic perfectly-secure MPC protocol due to Ben-Or, Goldwasser and Wigderson [25], popularly known as the BGW MPC protocol. Here our focus will be on secure computation of linear functions. We present the formal security definition of MPC and prove the security in the simulation paradigm. Using the secure linear function evaluation method, we then construct protocol for a special linear function involving the product of a public matrix and a secret vector. This special linear function will then be used for building the BGW protocol for *any* function in the next chapter. We conclude the chapter mentioning the issues that BGW protocol for linear functions may have while facing a malicious adversary.

5.1   Network Model and Adversary Setting

The BGW MPC protocol is a generic MPC protocol, which allows the parties to securely compute any finite function. The set of mutually-distrusting parties is denoted by $\mathcal{P} = \{P_1, \ldots, P_n\}$. The distrust in the system is modelled by a centralized entity called *adversary*, denoted by Adv, who can control any subset of at most t parties out of the n parties during the protocol execution. The adversary is *passive*, meaning that the parties under Adv's control (also called as the *corrupt* parties) do not deviate from the prescribed protocol instructions. However, the adversary will have full access to the entire state of the corrupt parties during the protocol execution. For simplicity, the adversary is assumed to be *static*, who decides the set of corrupt parties at the onset of the protocol. However, we note that the security of the BGW protocol can be proved even against a more powerful *adaptive* adversary, who may decide the set of corrupt parties during the run time; for details, we refer to [11]. Also, for simplicity, we consider the case when a single instance of the protocol is executed. However, the security can be proved even for the case when multiple instances of the protocol are executed in parallel; for the details we refer to [11].

© The Author(s), under exclusive license to Springer Nature Switzerland AG 2022   43
A. Choudhury and A. Patra, *Secure Multi-Party Computation Against Passive Adversaries*,
Synthesis Lectures on Distributed Computing Theory,
https://doi.org/10.1007/978-3-031-12164-7_5

The BGW protocol assumes the *secure-channel* model, where a secure channel for communication between every pair of parties (P_i, P_j) is assumed. The communication network is modelled by an undirected complete graph over the set of nodes $\{P_1, \ldots, P_n\}$. One can consider various mechanisms to securely emulate such a virtual complete graph over an incomplete graph. For instance, we may run a PSMT protocol between every pair of sender P_i and receiver P_j, provided the underlying graph is t-connected (see Sect. 3.5). More specifically, any value v which P_i may want to securely send to P_j in the BGW protocol can be securely communicated by executing a PSMT protocol, considering P_i as the sender S with input v and P_j as the receiver R.

The underlying communication network is assumed to be *synchronous* where the parties are synchronized by a global clock and there exists a strict *publicly-known* upper bound Δ on the message delays. So, a protocol over such a network operates as a sequence of communication *rounds*. In each round, a party performs some computation and then sends some messages to the other parties, followed by receiving the messages sent by the other parties to it in that round. Messages sent by a party at the beginning of a round are guaranteed to be delivered in the same order to the designated receiver by the end of the round, where each round spans for Δ clock cycles.

The function f to be securely computed by the parties is represented by a *publicly-known* arithmetic circuit cir over some finite field $(\mathbb{F}, +, \cdot)$, where $|\mathbb{F}| > n$ holds. Looking ahead, the restriction on the size of the field comes from the fact that the BGW protocol is based on Shamir's t-out-of-n secret-sharing scheme, which demands a finite field $\mathbb{F}$ with $|\mathbb{F}| > n$. For simplicity and without loss of generality, we assume that every party P_i has a single input $x_i \in \mathbb{F}$ for the function f and all the parties are supposed to learn the function output $y \stackrel{def}{=} f(x_1, \ldots, x_n)$. Hence the function f is an n-ary function $f : \mathbb{F}^n \to \mathbb{F}$ over $\mathbb{F}$. The protocol can be easily modified to handle the case when a party may have more than one input for f and where the function output consists of multiple values, each meant for a designated party.

The circuit cir consists of various gates over $\mathbb{F}$. For an example of arithmetic circuit over $\mathbb{F}$, see Fig. 5.1. Apart from the input gates and the output gate, cir consists of following types of gates.

Fig. 5.1 Arithmetic circuit for the function
$y = f(x_1, x_2, x_3, x_4)$ over $\mathbb{F}$, where
$y = c \cdot (x_1 + x_2) \cdot (x_3 \cdot x_4)$

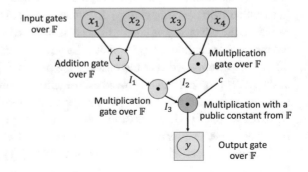

- *Addition Gates*: These gates are of the form $c = g_{\mathsf{Add}}(a, b)$, where $a, b \in \mathbb{F}$ are the gate inputs and $c = a + b$ is the gate output.
- *Multiplication with a Public Constant*: These gates are of the form $b = g_{\mathsf{ConsMult}}(c, a)$, where $a \in \mathbb{F}$ is the gate input, $c \in \mathbb{F}$ is some *publicly-known* constant and $b = c \cdot a$ is the gate output.
- *Addition with a Public Constant*: These gates are of the form $b = g_{\mathsf{ConsAdd}}(c, a)$, where $a \in \mathbb{F}$ is the gate input, $c \in \mathbb{F}$ is some *publicly-known* constant and $b = c + a$ is the gate output.
- *Multiplication Gates*: These gates are of the form $c = g_{\mathsf{Mult}}(a, b)$, where $a, b \in \mathbb{F}$ are the gate inputs and $c = a \cdot b$ is the gate output.

On the Arithmetic Circuit Representation: The arithmetic circuit representation of the function f is without loss of generality. It is a well-known fact that *any* efficient algorithm/computation can be represented by a polynomial-sized Boolean circuit, consisting of just AND and NOT gates. The Boolean circuit can be simulated by an equivalent polynomial-sized arithmetic circuit over $(\mathbb{F}, +, \cdot)$ as follows: the bit 0 and 1 can be mapped to the elements "0" and "1" respectively of $\mathbb{F}$. Then the NOT operation $\neg b$ (where b is a bit) can be simulated by the field operation $1 - "b"$, while the Binary operation $a \wedge b$ can be simulated by the field operation $"a" \cdot "b"$. While this approach shows the feasibility of representing any function through an arithmetic circuit, often smaller arithmetic representation is found using heuristics.

5.2   The Principle Behind BGW Protocol: Shared Circuit-Evaluation

To evaluate a circuit for a function f, given the inputs $x_1, \ldots, x_n$, one can evaluate each gate of the circuit in a topological order. The BGW protocol (and the followup generic MPC protocols with perfect security) follows the principle of *shared circuit-evaluation* where the inputs are secret-shared and the evaluation takes place topologically on the shared data. Elaborately, the parties first evaluate the input gates, where each party P_i acts as a dealer and secret-shares its input x_i amongst all the parties (including itself) using an instance of a t-out-of-n secret-sharing scheme with *perfect* privacy. This ensures that if P_i is *honest*, then x_i remains private from the adversary Adv who may learn only t shares of x_i. Recall that the probability distribution of these t shares seen by Adv is independent of the shared secret. Denoting these steps as *input stage*, we note that all the inputs for the function f are available in a secret-shared fashion after the completion of this stage.

In the next stage denoted as the *computation stage*, the parties collectively evaluate each gate in the circuit topologically, in a secret-shared fashion. To achieve this goal, the parties maintain the following invariant for each gate: given the input(s) of gate in a secret-shared fashion, the gate evaluation produces the output in a secret-shared fashion. Note that the invariant ensures that if the inputs of a gate are unknown to Adv, the output of the gate maintains the same status. Maintaining the invariant requires distinct techniques for a linear gate and a non-linear gate. If the underlying secret-sharing scheme is *linear*, a non-interactive technique suffices for a linear gate. On the other hand, for a non-linear (multiplication) gate, the parties need to interact.

Lastly, the computation stage is followed by an *output stage* to enable *public* reconstruction of the function output y from its secret-sharing. For this, the parties exchange their respective shares of y, followed by applying the R function of the underlying secret-sharing scheme on the received shares.

Intuitively, the fact that Adv learns only t shares for each gate input and the final output, allows us to argue about the privacy goal of the protocol. In the remaining sections, we discuss the techniques needed to maintain the invariant in the BGW protocol for linear gates. Prior to that, we present some additional useful properties of the Shamir's secret-sharing scheme (see Sect. 3.4).

5.3   Additional Properties of Shamir's Secret-Sharing Scheme

Informally, a value s is said to be d-Shamir-shared, if it is secret-shared as per an instance of Shamir's secret-sharing scheme, through some d-degree sharing-polynomial. Formally:

Definition 5.1 (*d-Shamir-sharing*) A value $s \in \mathbb{F}$ is said to be d-Shamir-shared where $d < n$, if there exists some d-degree polynomial $f(X)$ over $\mathbb{F}$ with $f(0) = s$, such that each party $P_i \in \mathcal{P}$ holds the share $s_i \overset{def}{=} f(\alpha_i)$. Here $\alpha_1, \ldots, \alpha_n$ are publicly-known, non-zero distinct elements from $\mathbb{F}$, where α_i is the *evaluation-point* associated with P_i.

We use the notation $[s]_d$ to denote the vector of n shares corresponding to a d-Shamir-sharing of s. That is, $[s]_d \overset{def}{=} (s_1, \ldots, s_n)$. A d-Shamir-sharing of a value s is said to be *random*, if the underlying sharing-polynomial, say $f(X)$, is a random d-degree polynomial from the set $\mathcal{P}^{s,d}$. That is, all the coefficients of $f(X)$ are random elements from $\mathbb{F}$, except the constant term, which is s.

Linearity of d-Shamir-Sharing: From the definition of d-Shamir-sharing, it follows that it satisfies the following *linearity* properties:

- *Multiplication of a secret-shared value with a public constant*: Let s be a value which is d-Shamir-shared through a d-degree polynomial, say $f(X)$, and let $[s]_d = (s_1, \ldots, s_n)$ be the vector of shares, where $s_i = f(\alpha_i)$. Moreover, let $c \in \mathbb{F}$ be a *publicly-known* constant. Then it follows that the vector $(c \cdot s_1, \ldots, c \cdot s_n)$ constitutes a vector of shares, corresponding to d-Shamir-sharing of the value $c \cdot s$, with P_i holding the share $c \cdot s_i$. This is because the shares $(c \cdot s_1, \ldots, c \cdot s_n)$ lie on the d-degree polynomial $g(X) \overset{def}{=} c \cdot f(X)$, where $g(\alpha_i) = c \cdot s_i$ holds. Moreover, the constant term $g(0)$ of the polynomial $g(X)$ is same as $c \cdot f(0) = c \cdot s$.

We write $[c \cdot s]_d = c \cdot [s]_d$ to mean that the parties can *non-interactively* compute their respective shares of $c \cdot s$, given the publicly-known c and their respective shares of s.

- *Addition of a secret-shared value with a public constant*: From the above discussion, it follows that the vector $(c + s_1, \ldots, c + s_n)$ constitutes a vector of shares, corresponding to d-Shamir-sharing of the value $c + s$, with party P_i holding the share $c + s_i$. This is because the shares $(c + s_1, \ldots, c + s_n)$ lie on the d-degree polynomial $h(X) \stackrel{def}{=} c + f(X)$, where $h(\alpha_i) = c + s_i$ holds. Moreover, the constant term $h(0)$ of $h(X)$ is same as $c + f(0) = c + s$.

  We write $[c + s]_d = c + [s]_d$ to mean that the parties can *non-interactively* compute their respective shares of $c + s$, given the publicly-known c and their respective shares of s.

- *Addition of Two Secret-Shared Values*: Let a and b be two values which are d-Shamir-shared through d-degree polynomials, say $f_a(X)$ and $f_b(X)$ respectively. Moreover, let $[a]_d = (a_1, \ldots, a_n)$ and $[b]_d = (b_1, \ldots, b_n)$ be the respective vector of shares, where $a_i = f_a(\alpha_i)$ and $b_i = f_b(\alpha_i)$ holds for each P_i. Then it follows that the vector $(a_1 + b_1, \ldots, a_n + b_n)$ constitutes a vector of shares, corresponding to d-Shamir-sharing of the value $a + b$, with P_i holding the share $a_i + b_i$. This is because the shares $(a_1 + b_1, \ldots, a_n + b_n)$ lie on the d-degree polynomial $f_c(X) \stackrel{def}{=} f_a(X) + f_b(X)$, where $f_c(\alpha_i) = a_i + b_i$ holds. Moreover, the constant term $f_c(0)$ of the polynomial $f_c(X)$ is same as $f_a(0) + f_b(0) = a + b$.

  We write $[a + b]_d = [a]_d + [b]_d$ to mean that the parties can *non-interactively* compute their respective shares of $a + b$, given their respective shares of a and b.

From the above discussion, it follows that the parties can non-interactively compute any *linear* function of d-Shamir-shared values. Namely, given d-Shamir-shared values $x^{(1)}, \ldots, x^{(\ell)}$ and a *publicly-known* linear function $g : \mathbb{F}^\ell \to \mathbb{F}^m$, where $g(x^{(1)}, \ldots, x^{(\ell)}) = (y^{(1)}, \ldots, y^{(m)})$, the parties can non-interactively compute their respective shares, corresponding to d-Shamir-sharing of $y^{(1)}, \ldots, y^{(m)}$. For this, the parties have to apply the linear function g on their respective shares of $x^{(1)}, \ldots, x^{(\ell)}$. We use the term *parties locally compute* $([y^{(1)}]_d, \ldots, [y^{(m)}]_d) = g([x^{(1)}]_d, \ldots, [x^{(\ell)}]_d)$ to denote the above computation.

We next demonstrate the linearity property of Shamir secret-sharing with an example.

Example 5.2 Let $\mathcal{P} = \{P_1, P_2, P_3\}$ and the computation is performed over field $\mathbb{F} = (\mathbb{Z}_5, +_5, \cdot_5)$. In all the instances of Shamir secret-sharing, the evaluations-points α_1, α_2 and α_3 are set to 1, 2 and 3 respectively. Moreover, let the instances of secret-sharing have threshold $d = 1$. Consider the following function: given distinct points $(x_1, y_1) = (4, 4)$ and $(x_2, y_2) = (3, 1)$, let $g(X)$ be the unique 1-degree polynomial passing through these points. The goal is to compute the value $y = g(2)$. Recall that y is a *publicly-known* linear function of y_1 and y_2, where the linear combiners are called Lagrange's interpolation coefficients (see Sect. 2.2). We calculate these coefficients using the Lagrange's interpolation formula:

$$g(X) = \frac{(X-3)}{(4-3)} \cdot 4 + \frac{(X-4)}{(3-4)} \cdot 1 = (X-3) \cdot 4 + 4(X-4) \cdot 1$$

Hence,

$$y = g(2) = 4 \cdot 4 + 2 \cdot 1 = 4 \cdot y_1 + 2 \cdot y_2 \tag{5.1}$$

So the Lagrange's interpolation coefficients are $c_1 = 4$ and $c_2 = 2$ and hence $y = 3$.

Next imagine that the values $y_1 = 4$ and $y_2 = 1$ are not known in the clear, and instead, they are 1-Shamir-shared through 1-degree polynomials, say $f_{y_1}(X) = 4 + 0X$ and $f_{y_2}(X) = 1 + 3X$ respectively. This leads to the vector of shares $[y_1]_1 = [4]_1 = (4, 4, 4)$ and $[y_2]_1 = [1]_1 = (4, 2, 0)$ respectively, obtained by evaluating the corresponding sharing-polynomials at $\alpha_1 = 1, \alpha_2 = 2$ and $\alpha_3 = 3$. The shares corresponding to the respective parties are shown in the following table. It then follows that by applying the linear function as shown in the previous equation, the parties can obtain their respective shares of the value y, corresponding to a 1-Shamir-sharing of the value y. That is, the parties can locally compute $[y]_1 = 4 \cdot [y_1]_1 + 2 \cdot [y_2]_1$. The shares of the respective parties, corresponding to $[y]_1$ are also shown in the following table. For instance, the share of y for P_3 is obtained as $4 \cdot 4 + 2 \cdot 0 = 1$, while the share of y for P_1 is obtained as $4 \cdot 4 + 2 \cdot 4 = 4$.

	Sharing-Polynomial	P_1s Share	P_2s Share	P_3s Share
$y_1 = 4$	$4 + 0X$	4	4	4
$y_2 = 1$	$1 + 3X$	4	2	0
$y = 3$	$3 + X$	4	0	1

It is easy to verify that the vector of shares $(4, 0, 1)$ indeed constitutes a 1-Shamir-sharing of the value $y = 3$, since the corresponding 1-degree Shamir-sharing polynomial interpolating through the shares $(1, 4), (2, 0)$ and $(3, 1)$ is $f_y(X) = 3 + X$, whose constant term is 3.

5.4   BGW Protocol for Linear Functions

In this section, we assume that the function f is a *deterministic* linear function.[1] Consequently, the corresponding arithmetic circuit cir consists of only linear gates over $\mathbb{F}$. The statement of the BGW protocol, that will be proved in this section is stated below.

Let $\mathcal{P} = \{P_1, \ldots, P_n\}$ be connected by pair-wise secure channels and let $f(x_1, \ldots, x_n)$ be a publicly-known linear function over a field $(\mathbb{F}, +, \cdot)$ where $|\mathbb{F}| > n$, with P_i having the input x_i and where

---

[1] We will soon discuss that this is without loss of generality.

$$y = f(x_1, \ldots, x_n) \overset{def}{=} c_1 \cdot x_1 + \cdots + c_n \cdot x_n.$$

Then there exists a perfectly-secure MPC protocol for computing y, tolerating a computationally-unbounded adversary Adv, who can corrupt any t out of the n parties in a passive fashion, where $t < n$.

We note that the *resilience* $t < n$ of the BGW protocol for linear functions as stated above is *optimal* in the sense that the protocol tolerates the *maximum* number of allowed corruptions. Indeed, if $t = n$, then the circuit-evaluation in clear can be used for computing f where each party makes its input public.

5.4.1   The Protocol

The high level idea of the protocol is very simple. Each party P_i secret-shares its input x_i through an instance of t-out-of-n Shamir's secret-sharing. This ensures that each x_i is t-Shamir-shared. The parties then *non-interactively* compute the function f over the t-Shamir-shared inputs, owing to the linearity property of the Shamir's secret-sharing. Finally, the parties exchange their respective shares of the function output and interpolate the function output. The privacy of the inputs of the honest parties is preserved due to the *perfect-privacy* of Shamir's secret-sharing. And since $t < n$ holds, the *correctness* property of the secret-sharing scheme guarantees that each party receives sufficient number of shares to reconstruct the function output. For the formal details, see Fig. 5.2. In the protocol, $\mathsf{G}_{\mathsf{Sha}}$ and $\mathsf{R}_{\mathsf{Sha}}$ denote the share-generation and recovery algorithm respectively of the Shamir's secret-sharing scheme (see Sect. 3.4 for their formal details).

We next proceed to the complexity analysis and security analysis of the protocol $\Pi_{\mathsf{BGW\text{-}Linear}}$.

Protocol $\Pi_{\mathsf{BGW\text{-}Linear}}$

- *Input Stage*:
    - On having the input x_i, compute the shares $(x_{i1}, \ldots, x_{in}) \leftarrow \mathsf{G}_{\mathsf{Sha}}(x_i)$.
    - For $j = 1, \ldots, n$, send the share x_{ij} to party $P_j \in \mathcal{P}$.
    For $k = 1, \ldots, n$, let x_{ki} denote the share, received from the party $P_k \in \mathcal{P}$ at the end of the input stage.
- *Computation Stage*: Compute $y_i = c_1 \cdot x_{1i} + \ldots + c_n \cdot x_{ni}$.
- *Output Stage*:
    - Send the share y_i to every party in $\mathcal{P}$.
    - Upon receiving the shares $y_1, \ldots, y_n$, output $y = \mathsf{R}_{\mathsf{Sha}}(\mathcal{P}, \{y_1, \ldots, y_n\})$.

Fig. 5.2 BGW protocol for securely computing linear functions. The above steps are executed by each $P_i \in \mathcal{P}$

5.4.2 Complexity Analysis of $\Pi_{\text{BGW-Linear}}$

The round complexity and communication complexity of the protocol are stated in Lemma 5.3, which follows from the protocol inspection.

Lemma 5.3 *The round complexity and communication complexity of the protocol* $\Pi_{\text{BGW-Linear}}$ *are as follows:*

- *Round Complexity: The number of communication rounds required during the various stages are as follows.*
  - *Input stage: one round.*
  - *Computation stage: nil*
  - *Output stage: one round.*
- *Communication Complexity: The total number of field elements communicated during the various stages are as follows.*
  - *Input stage:* $\mathcal{O}(n^2)$ *field elements.*
  - *Computation stage: nil*
  - *Output stage:* $\mathcal{O}(n^2)$ *field elements.*

Trading Rounds for Communication Complexity: A closer look into the protocol $\Pi_{\text{BGW-Linear}}$ shows that one can reduce the communication complexity of the *output stage* to $\mathcal{O}(n)$ field elements by increasing the number of rounds to 2. Namely, to publicly reconstruct the secret-shared output y, the parties can first enable a *single* designated party, say P_1, to reconstruct y. For this, the parties send their respective shares of y *only* to the party P_1, who then applies the function $\mathsf{R_{Sha}}$ on the received shares to reconstruct y. This requires one communication round and a communication of $\mathcal{O}(n)$ field elements. Party P_1 then sends the value y to every other party, which requires one more round and a communication of $\mathcal{O}(n)$ field elements.

5.4.3 Security Analysis of $\Pi_{\text{BGW-Linear}}$ Through Example

We begin with the security analysis through an example run of the protocol $\Pi_{\text{BGW-Linear}}$.

Example 5.4 Let $\mathcal{P} = \{P_1, P_2, P_3, P_4\}$, $t = 2$ and suppose that the parties want to securely compute the function $y = x_1 + x_2 + x_3 + x_4$ over the field $\mathbb{F} = (\mathbb{Z}_5, +_5, \cdot_5)$, where each P_i has the input x_i. Let the evaluation-points associated with the various parties be $\alpha_1 = 1$, $\alpha_2 = 2$, $\alpha_3 = 3$ and $\alpha_4 = 4$. Let the inputs of the parties be $x_1 = 2$, $x_2 = 1$, $x_3 = 1$ and $x_4 = 0$ and let the sharing-polynomials selected by P_1, P_2, P_3 and P_4 to share their respective inputs be $A(Z) = 2 + 0Z + 0Z^2$, $B(Z) = 1 + 0Z + 1Z^2$, $C(Z) = 1 + 2Z + 0Z^2$ and $D(Z) = 0 +$

$3Z + 2Z^2$ respectively. Note that all the polynomials are 2-degree polynomials over $\mathbb{F}$. This leads to the vector of shares $[x_1]_2 = (2, 2, 2, 2)$, $[x_2]_2 = (2, 0, 0, 2)$, $[x_3]_2 = (3, 0, 2, 4)$ and $[x_4]_2 = (0, 4, 2, 4)$ corresponding to x_1, x_2, x_3 and x_4 respectively. The shares are then distributed to the respective parties, as shown in the following table. For instance, P_2's share of x_1, x_2, x_3 and x_4 are obtained by evaluating the sharing-polynomials at $\alpha_2 = 2$. Each party then locally adds its share of x_1, x_2, x_3 and x_4, resulting in its share of the output y. Finally, the parties exchange their shares of y and then reconstruct y by interpolating $E(Z) = 4 + 0Z + 3Z^2$ through the points $(1, 2)$, $(2, 1)$, $(3, 1)$ and $(4, 2)$.

Variable	Value	Sharing-Polynomial	P_1	P_2	P_3	P_4
x_1	2	$A(Z) = 2 + 0Z + 0Z^2$	2	2	2	2
x_2	1	$B(Z) = 1 + 0Z + 1Z^2$	2	0	0	2
x_3	1	$C(Z) = 1 + 2Z + 0Z^2$	3	0	2	4
x_4	0	$D(Z) = 0 + 3Z + 2Z^2$	0	4	2	4
y	4	$E(Z) = 4 + 0Z + 3Z^2$	2	1	1	2

Next imagine that P_1 and P_4 are under Adv's control. The values seen by Adv during the execution are shown in bold in the following table, while the values marked as "?" denote the values unknown to Adv.

Variable	Value	Sharing-Polynomial	P_1	P_2	P_3	P_4
x_1	**2**	**$A(Z) = 2 + 0Z + 0Z^2$**	**2**	**2**	**2**	**2**
x_2	?	$B(Z) =$?	**2**	?	?	**2**
x_3	?	$C(Z) =$?	**3**	?	?	**4**
x_4	**0**	**$D(Z) = 0 + 3Z + 2Z^2$**	**0**	**4**	**2**	**4**
y	**4**	**$E(Z) = 4 + 0Z + 3Z^2$**	**2**	**1**	**1**	**2**

Now based on the values learnt by Adv, it can conclude that (x_2, x_3) can take the possible values $(0, 2)$, $(1, 1)$, $(2, 0)$, $(3, 4)$ and $(4, 3)$. Suppose it makes the hypothesis that $x_2 = 0$ and $x_3 = 2$ and checks whether it is consistent with the information seen by Adv during the execution. As shown in the following table, it turns out that the hypothesis $x_2 = 0$ and $x_3 = 2$ is indeed consistent with the information learnt by Adv. Namely, for $x_2 = 0$ to be true, the 2-degree $B(Z)$ polynomial used by P_2 must have 0 as the constant term and must evaluate to 2 and 2 at $Z = \alpha_1 = 1$ and $Z = \alpha_4 = 4$ respectively. That is, P_2 must have used the *unique* 2-degree sharing-polynomial $B(Z) = 0 + 0Z + 2Z^2$ passing through the points $(0, 0)$, $(1, 2)$ and $(4, 2)$, which leads to the vector of shares $[x_2]_2 = (\mathbf{2}, 3, 3, \mathbf{2})$. Similarly, for $x_3 = 2$ to be true, P_3 must have used the *unique* 2-degree sharing-polynomial $C(Z) = 2 + 2Z + 4Z^2$ passing through the points $(0, 2)$, $(1, 3)$ and $(4, 4)$, which leads to the vector of shares $[x_3]_2 = (\mathbf{3}, 2, 4, \mathbf{4})$. Hence, Adv cannot rule out the possibility of $x_2 = 0$ and $x_3 = 2$.

Variable	Value	Sharing-Polynomial	P_1	P_2	P_3	P_4
x_1	2	$A(Z) = 2 + 0Z + 0Z^2$	2	2	2	2
x_2	0	$B(Z) = 0 + 0Z + 2Z^2$	2	3	3	2
x_3	2	$C(Z) = 2 + 2Z + 4Z^2$	3	2	4	4
x_4	0	$D(Z) = 0 + 3Z + 2Z^2$	0	4	2	4
y	4	$E(Z) = 4 + 0Z + 3Z^2$	2	1	1	2

Next suppose that Adv makes the hypothesis that $x_2 = 1$ and $x_3 = 1$. Now, as shown in the following table, this hypothesis is also consistent with the information learnt by Adv during the protocol execution. And hence Adv cannot rule out the possibility that x_2 was 1 and x_3 was 1.

Variable	Value	Sharing-Polynomial	P_1	P_2	P_3	P_4
x_1	2	$A(Z) = 2 + 0Z + 0Z^2$	2	2	2	2
x_2	1	$B(Z) = 1 + 0Z + 1Z^2$	2	0	0	2
x_3	1	$C(Z) = 1 + 2Z + 0Z^2$	3	0	2	4
x_4	0	$D(Z) = 0 + 3Z + 2Z^2$	0	4	2	4
y	4	$E(Z) = 4 + 0Z + 3Z^2$	2	1	1	2

In a similar vein, it can be shown that the information learnt by Adv during the protocol execution will be consistent with every candidate $x_2, x_3 \in \mathbb{Z}_5$, such that $2 + x_2 + x_3 + \mathbf{4} = \mathbf{4}$ holds. This implies that the information seen by Adv does not help it to learn anything additional, beyond what can be inferred by the function output y and the inputs x_1 and x_4 of the corrupt parties.

5.4.4   Formal Security Definition of MPC

In this section, we present the formal definition of secure MPC, which is used to formally prove the security of the protocol $\Pi_{\text{BGW-Linear}}$ and all the protocols presented in this lecture series. Intuitively, an n-party protocol for computing a given function will be considered as a secure protocol, if the parties obtain the correct output at the end of the protocol (often called as the *correctness* property) and adversary learns nothing beyond the function output and the inputs of the corrupt parties (often called as the *privacy* property). Privacy is formally captured though *simulation-paradigm*, introduced in Chap. 4. Namely, we show that whatever Adv learns by participating in the protocol, can be efficiently recreated/simulated solely based on the function output and the inputs of the corrupt parties. To formalize this intuition, we define the *view* of a party, which consists of all the information seen by the party during a protocol execution.

Formally, the view of the party P_i during the execution of a protocol Π with inputs $\vec{x} = (x_1, \ldots, x_n)$, denoted by $\text{view}_i^\Pi(\vec{x})$, is defined to be $(x_i, r_i, m_{i_1}, \ldots, m_{i_k})$. Here x_i is the private input of P_i, while r_i denotes P_i's internal coin tosses and m_{i_j} denotes the jth message *received* by P_i during the protocol execution. We note that the messages *sent* by P_i are not explicitly added to $\text{view}_i^\Pi(\vec{x})$, as these can be computed from $\text{view}_i^\Pi(\vec{x})$, using publicly-known functions, determined by the protocol steps of Π.

For every $I = \{i_1, \ldots, i_\ell\} \subseteq \{1, \ldots, n\}$, the notation $\text{view}_I^\Pi(\vec{x})$ denotes the view of the parties $P_{i_1}, \ldots, P_{i_\ell}$. That is, $\text{view}_I^\Pi(\vec{x}) = (\text{view}_{i_1}^\Pi(\vec{x}), \ldots, \text{view}_{i_\ell}^\Pi(\vec{x}))$. Finally, the output of all the parties from an execution of Π on inputs $\vec{x}$ is denoted by $\text{output}^\Pi(\vec{x})$. Notice that the output of each party can be computed from its own (private) view of the execution. The formal definition of securely computing any *deterministic* function f is given as follows.

Definition 5.5 (*Perfect Security of n-party Protocols for Deterministic Functions* [78]) Let $f : (\{0, 1\}^\star)^n \rightarrow (\{0, 1\}^\star)^n$ be a *deterministic n-ary* function and let Π be an n-party protocol. We say that Π is a t-*perfectly-secure* protocol for f, if for every $\vec{x} = (x_1, \ldots, x_n) \in (\{0, 1\}^\star)^n$ where $|x_1| = |x_2| = \cdots = |x_n|$ and for every adversary Adv controlling a subset of at most t parties with indices in $I \subset \{1, \ldots, n\}$ where $|I| \leq t$, the following two conditions hold:

- *Correctness*:

$$\text{output}^\Pi(\vec{x}) = f(x_1, \ldots, x_n).$$

- *Privacy*: there exists a probabilistic polynomial-time algorithm $\mathcal{S}$, called *simulator*, such that the probability distribution of the output generated by $\mathcal{S}$ is identical to the view of the adversary. That is:

$$\left\{ \mathcal{S}(I, \vec{x}_I, f_I(x_1, \ldots, x_n)) \right\} \equiv \left\{ \text{view}_I^\Pi(\vec{x}) \right\}.$$

Here $\vec{x}_I$ denotes the inputs corresponding to the parties with indices in I and $f_I(x_1, \ldots, x_n)$ denotes the function output, restricted to the parties with index in I.

Remark 5.6 We note that Definition 5.5 is for general n-ary functions, where the inputs of the parties can be binary strings and where each party has a *dedicated* function output. In the context of the BGW protocol, we will be focussing on the case where the inputs of the parties are from $\mathbb{F}$ and there is a *single* function output meant for everyone (recall that this is without loss of generality).

Definition 5.5 *separately* considers the issues of correctness and privacy for a *deterministic* function. However, for *probabilistic* functions, it is necessary to "combine" these two requirements and instead consider the joint distribution of the simulator and the parties (we will demonstrate the underlying subtlety with an example); the interested readers are referred to [78] for more discussion on this fact. Thus for probabilistic functions, we use the following security definition.

Definition 5.7 (*Perfect Security of n-party Protocols for any function* [78]) Let $f : (\{0, 1\}^\star)^n \rightarrow (\{0, 1\}^\star)^n$ be a *randomized n*-ary function and let Π be an n-party protocol. We say that Π is a t-*perfectly-secure* protocol for f, if for every $\vec{x} = (x_1, \ldots, x_n) \in (\{0, 1\}^\star)^n$ where $|x_1| = |x_2| = \cdots = |x_n|$ and for every adversary Adv controlling a subset of at most t parties with indices in $I \subset \{1, \ldots, n\}$ where $|I| \leq t$, there exists a probabilistic polynomial-time algorithm $\mathcal{S}$ called *simulator*, such that the following holds:

$$\left\{ (\mathcal{S}(I, \vec{x}_I, f_I(x_1, \ldots, x_n)), f(x_1, \ldots, x_n)) \right\} \equiv \left\{ (\text{view}_I^\Pi(\vec{x}), \text{output}^\Pi(\vec{x})) \right\}.$$

We note that Definition 5.5 is a special case of the Definition 5.7. This is because if f is a deterministic function, then the function output $f(x_1, \ldots, x_n)$ is a single value for any fixed $\vec{x} = (x_1, \ldots, x_n)$, instead of a probability distribution. Hence the separate requirements of correctness and privacy actually imply the joint distribution of Definition 5.7.

Why Separate Definition for Randomized Functions? We consider the following example to understand the need of a different definition for randomized functions.

Example 5.8 Let $\mathcal{P} = \{P_1, P_2\}$ and $t = 1$ and consider the 2-party randomized function $f(x_1, x_2) = (r, \perp)$, where r is a uniformly random bit. The function outputs a uniform random bit, only for party P_1, irrespective of the inputs of the parties, while P_2 has no output. Thus P_2 does not learn the output of f. It is easy to note that the function is a randomized function, since even for the same x_1, x_2, the output r can take the value 0 with probability $\frac{1}{2}$ and value 1 with probability $\frac{1}{2}$. The function, in fact, abstracts the requirement of a 2-party secure coin-tossing functionality, which outputs a random bit for one of the parties.

Consider a protocol Π to securely compute the function f where P_1 picks a uniformly random bit r, sends r to P_2 and outputs r. Party P_2 simply outputs $\bot$.

Though the output of P_1 is a random bit, clearly, the protocol Π is *not* a secure protocol. This is because if P_2 is under adversary's control, then the adversary learns the output r of P_1, which is not allowed as per the function f. We will next show that the protocol Π can be shown to be secure under Definition 5.5, In contrast, it can not be proven secure under Definition 5.7. This justifies the need for a distinct definition, namely Definition 5.7, for randomized functions.

We now show that Π is secure as per Definition 5.5. As per this definition, we have to consider the correctness and privacy *separately*. A quick look into the protocol Π tells that the *correctness* property is satisfied, since the output of P_1 and P_2 are r and $\bot$ respectively, where r is a uniform random bit. We next consider the *privacy* when P_2 is *corrupt*. We need to design a simulator, which takes as input x_2 and $\bot$ (the input and output of P_2), and produces the messages received by P_2 from P_1 in the protocol Π. The simulator $\mathcal{S}$ simply outputs a random bit $\tilde{r}$ as the message being received by P_2 from P_1. Now it is easy to see that the output of the simulator has the same probability distribution, as the message received by P_2 in Π. Namely, in Π, party P_2 receives a random bit from P_1. Where as, the output of $\mathcal{S}$ is also a random bit. Hence, we can conclude that Π is a secure protocol as per Definition 5.5.

The same simulator $\mathcal{S}$ does not prove the privacy under Definition 5.7. The *joint* probability distribution of the output of $\mathcal{S}$ and the output of f is $\left\{ (\tilde{r}, r) \right\}$, where $\tilde{r}$ and r are *independent* bits. This is because $\mathcal{S}$ is *not* aware of the output of f. On the other hand, the *joint* probability distribution of the view of P_2 (namely the message received by P_2 from P_1) and the output of P_1 in the protocol Π is $\left\{ (r, r) \right\}$. This is because in the protocol Π, the message received by P_2 from P_1 is nothing but the output of P_1. Now clearly, the probability distributions $\left\{ (\tilde{r}, r) \right\}$ and $\left\{ (r, r) \right\}$ are *not* identical. For instance, the samples $(0, 1)$ and $(1, 0)$ can be present in the former distribution with *non-zero* probabilities, where as they occur with *zero* probability in the latter distribution. While we analysed one simulator $\mathcal{S}$ to showcase the violation as per Definition 5.7, there is no way to come up with any simulator that can prove the privacy of the protocol under Definition 5.7. This arises from the fact that, the simulator will not learn the random bit picked by P_1. The best it can do is guess, but that may lead to failing the simulation with $1/2$ probability. Hence, we can conclude that Π is not private as per Definition 5.7.

Deterministic Functions are Sufficient: In [78] it is shown that it is possible to compute any *probabilistic* function with t-perfect-security, using any generic protocol for computing any *deterministic* function with t-perfect-security (in fact, the result holds even for cryptographic-security). To understand this relation, consider the case where $n = 2$ and $t = 1$.[2] Let the parties wish to securely compute the randomized functionality $g(x_1, x_2)$, which picks some uniform randomness r from some appropriate domain and computes the function $g(x_1, x_2; r)$. Note that once the randomness r is fixed (along with the inputs x_1 and x_2), the output of g is computed *deterministically*, as a function of x_1, x_2 and r.

Now consider another 2-ary function $f((x_1, r_1), (x_2, r_2))$, where the inputs of P_1 and P_2 are (x_1, r_1) and (x_2, r_2) respectively. Here r_1 and r_2 are uniformly random inputs of P_1 and P_2 respectively. Moreover, we have $f((x_1, r_1), (x_2, r_2)) \stackrel{def}{=} g(x_1, x_2; r_1 + r_2)$. That is, the output of f for inputs (x_1, r_1) and (x_2, r_2) is same as the output of the function g for inputs x_1 and x_2, with respect to the randomness $r \stackrel{def}{=} r_1 + r_2$. Note that the function f is a *deterministic* function and the randomness $r_1 + r_2$ is uniformly distributed, since the honest party's (either P_1 or P_2) contribution is distributed uniformly at random from the randomness-space. Hence, g can be emulated by the deterministic function f and computing g is "equivalent" to computing f (see [78] for the formal details). Based on the above discussion, we analyze the BGW protocol only for *deterministic* functions, as it makes the proofs simpler.

5.4.5 Formal Security Analysis of $\Pi_{\text{BGW-Linear}}$

We next prove the security of the protocol $\Pi_{\text{BGW-Linear}}$ as per Definition 5.5.

Theorem 5.9 (BGW Protocol for Linear Functions [11]) *Let $y = f(x_1, \ldots, x_n)$ be an n-ary function over $\mathbb{F}$ where $y \stackrel{def}{=} c_1 \cdot x_1 + \cdots + c_n \cdot x_n$, with P_i holding the private input x_i and where $c_1, \ldots, c_n$ are publicly-known constants belonging to $\mathbb{F}$. Moreover, let $t < n$. Then protocol $\Pi_{\text{BGW-Linear}}$ is t-perfectly-secure for f.*

Proof From the linearity property of the Shamir's secret-sharing, it follows that the vector of shares $(y_1, \ldots, y_n)$ corresponds to a t-Shamir-sharing of the value y. It then follows from the correctness of $\mathsf{R_{Sha}}$ that the parties correctly obtain y by applying $\mathsf{R_{Sha}}$ on the shares $y_1, \ldots, y_n$. This guarantees that $\mathsf{output}^{\Pi_{\text{BGW-Linear}}}(\vec{x}) = f(x_1, \ldots, x_n)$ holds.

To prove the privacy, we present a simulator for simulating the view of the corrupt parties. We make a simplifying assumption that the adversary corrupts the *maximum* number of parties allowed, namely t parties. However, this is without loss of generality and the proof can be extended for the case when adversary corrupts less than t parties (see the remark after the proof). We first define the view $\mathsf{view}_I^{\Pi_{\text{BGW-Linear}}}$ of the adversary Adv during the protocol

---

[2] The argument can be generalized to any n and t, where $t < n$.

$\Pi_{\text{BGW-Linear}}$, controlling a subset of t parties with indices in $I \subset \{1, \ldots, n\}$, where $|I| = t$. The view consists of the following information from various stages[3]:

- *Input stage*—In this stage, the view consists of the following information:
  - The inputs $\{x_i\}_{i \in I}$.
  - The t-degree sharing-polynomials $\{f_{x_i}(Z)\}_{i \in I}$, where each polynomial $f_{x_i}(Z)$ is selected uniformly at random from the set $\mathcal{P}^{x_i, t}$ of t-degree polynomials over $\mathbb{F}$ with x_i as the constant term. Note that the polynomials $\{f_{x_i}(Z)\}_{i \in I}$ completely determine the vectors of shares $\{[x_i]_t = (x_{i1}, \ldots, x_{in})\}_{i \in I}$, generated by the corrupt parties in the protocol.
  - The shares $\{x_{ji}\}_{j \notin I, i \in I}$ corresponding to the input x_j, received from the party P_j. Note that these shares are uniformly distributed over $\mathbb{F}$, independent of x_j, which follows from the perfect-privacy of the Shamir's secret-sharing scheme. Let $f_{x_j}(Z)$ be the t-degree sharing-polynomial selected uniformly at random by P_j from the set $\mathcal{P}^{x_j, t}$ of t-degree polynomials over $\mathbb{F}$ with x_j as the constant term.
- *Computation Stage*—In this stage, the view consists of the shares $\{y_i\}_{i \in I}$. Note that these shares are uniformly distributed over $\mathbb{F}$. This is because the shares $\{x_{ji}\}_{j \in \{1, \ldots, n\}, i \in I}$ are uniformly distributed over $\mathbb{F}$ and $y_i = c_1 \cdot x_{1i} + \cdots + c_n \cdot x_{ni}$.
- *Output Stage*—In this stage, the view consists of the vector of shares $[y]_t = (y_1, \ldots, y_n)$, lying on a t-degree polynomial, say $f_y(Z)$, with y as the constant term. Note that $f_y(Z)$ is a random element from the set $\mathcal{P}^{y, t}$ of t-degree polynomials over $\mathbb{F}$ with y as the constant term. This follows from the fact that $f_y(Z) = c_1 \cdot f_{x_1}(Z) + \cdots + c_n \cdot f_{x_n}(Z)$ holds, where each polynomial $f_{x_i}(Z)$ is a random element from the respective set $\mathcal{P}^{x_i, t}$.

Now the formal details of the simulator $\mathcal{S}$ are given in Fig. 5.3. Informally, the simulator works by selecting random Shamir-shares of *arbitrary* values on the behalf of the honest parties during the input stage. And during the output stage, the simulator selects shares on the behalf of the honest parties, which along with the shares of the corrupt parties, yield the actual function output.

We next show that the view of Adv during the protocol $\Pi_{\text{BGW-Linear}}$ and the view of Adv as generated by $\mathcal{S}$ have the same probability distributions.

- *Input Stage*: The inputs $\{x_i\}_{i \in I}$ of the corrupt parties are *exactly same* in both the distributions. Let $\{\widetilde{f}_{x_i}(Z)\}_{i \in I}$ be the random t-degree sharing-polynomials used by the simulator to generate the vector of shares $\{[x_i]_t = (\widetilde{x}_{i1}, \ldots, \widetilde{x}_{in})\}_{i \in I}$, corresponding to the inputs of the corrupt parties. It is easy to see that the probability distribution of the sharing-polynomials $\{f_{x_i}(Z)\}_{i \in I}$ used by the corrupt parties in the protocol and the sharing-polynomials $\{\widetilde{f}_{x_i}(Z)\}_{i \in I}$ used by the simulator are identical. More specifi-

---

[3] Recall that from the definition, the view of a party consists of its private input, its random choices in the protocol and all the messages received by the party. However, for the sake of clarity, we include all the information available with the adversary from the corrupt parties during the protocol execution.

Simulator S

The input of the simulator is the index set $I \subset \{1, \ldots, n\}$ of the corrupt parties where $|I| = t$, the inputs $\{x_i\}_{i \in I}$ of the corrupt parties and the function output y.

- *Simulating the Input Stage*:
    - For every $i \in I$, S computes the shares $(\widetilde{x}_{i1}, \ldots, \widetilde{x}_{in}) \leftarrow \mathsf{G}_{\mathsf{Sha}}(x_i)$.
    - For every $j \notin I$, S sets $\widetilde{x}_j = 0$ and computes the shares $(\widetilde{x}_{j1}, \ldots, \widetilde{x}_{jn}) \leftarrow \mathsf{G}_{\mathsf{Sha}}(\widetilde{x}_j)$.
    For every $i \in I$, the view of P_i for this stage is then set by S to be $\{x_i, (\widetilde{x}_{i1}, \ldots, \widetilde{x}_{in}), \{\widetilde{x}_{ji}\}_{j \notin I, i \in I}\}$. The view of Adv for this stage consists of the view of P_i for this stage, for every $i \in I$.
- *Simulating the Computation Stage*: For every $i \in I$, S computes $\widetilde{y}_i = c_1 \cdot \widetilde{x}_{1i} + \ldots + c_n \cdot \widetilde{x}_{ni}$.
    For every $i \in I$, the view of the party P_i for this stage is then set by S to be $\widetilde{y}_i$. The view of Adv for this stage consists of the view of P_i for this stage, for every $i \in I$.
- *Simulating the Output Stage*: S computes the unique t-degree polynomial $\widetilde{f}_y(Z)$, such that $\widetilde{f}_y(0) = y$ and $\widetilde{f}_y(\alpha_i) = \widetilde{y}_i$, for every $i \in I$.[a]
    The view of Adv for this stage is then set by S to be $(\widetilde{f}_y(\alpha_1), \ldots, \widetilde{f}_y(\alpha_n))$.

S outputs the view of Adv across all the stages.

---

[a]The polynomial $\widetilde{f}_y(Z)$ is well-defined, since $|I| = t$ and there exists a unique t-degree polynomial, passing through the $t + 1$ distinct points $(0, y), \{(\alpha_i, \widetilde{y}_i)\}_{i \in I}$.

Fig. 5.3 Simulator for simulating the view of the corrupt parties in the protocol $\Pi_{\mathsf{BGW\text{-}Linear}}$

cally, both $f_{x_i}(Z)$ as well as $\widetilde{f}_{x_i}(Z)$ are random t-degree polynomials, belonging to the set $\mathcal{P}^{x_i, t}$ of t-degree polynomials over $\mathbb{F}$, with x_i as the constant term. This automatically implies that the probability distribution of $\{[x_i]_t = (x_{i1}, \ldots, x_{in})\}_{i \in I}$ is identical to $\{[x_i]_t = (\widetilde{x}_{i1}, \ldots, \widetilde{x}_{in})\}_{i \in I}$.

Next, the probability distribution of the shares $\{x_{ji}\}_{j \notin I, i \in I}$ seen by the corrupt parties in the protocol, is identical to the probability distribution of the shares $\{\widetilde{x}_{ji}\}_{j \notin I, i \in I}$ produced by the simulator. While for every $j \notin I$, the shares $\{x_{ji}\}_{i \in I}$ used in the protocol are derived from a random t-degree polynomial $f_{x_j}(Z) \in \mathcal{P}^{x_j, t}$, the simulated shares $\{\widetilde{x}_{ji}\}_{i \in I}$ are derived from a random t-degree polynomial, say $\widetilde{f}_{\widetilde{x}_j}(Z) \in \mathcal{P}^{\widetilde{x}_j, t}$, where $\widetilde{x}_j = 0$. However, since $|I| = t$ and both $f_{x_j}(Z)$ as well as $\widetilde{f}_{\widetilde{x}_j}(Z)$ are random t-degree polynomials, it follows from Lemma 3.7 that the shares $\{x_{ji}\}_{i \in I}$ and $\{\widetilde{x}_{ji}\}_{i \in I}$ are identically distributed. Hence, we have shown that the partial view of Adv in $\mathsf{view}_I^{\Pi_{\mathsf{BGW\text{-}Linear}}}$ and in the output of S are identically distributed, till the end of the input stage. Since the shares of the corrupt parties during the input stage in $\mathsf{view}_I^{\Pi_{\mathsf{BGW\text{-}Linear}}}$ and in the output of S are identically distributed and are random elements of $\mathbb{F}$, let us fix these shares to $\{\beta_{ji}\}_{j \in \{1, \ldots, n\}, i \in I}$, where each β_{ji} is an arbitrary element of $\mathbb{F}$.

- *Computation Stage*: Conditioned on the partial view till the end of the input stage (which we have shown to be identically distributed in both the probability distributions), the probability distribution of the shares $\{y_i\}_{i \in I}$ during the computation stage of the protocol, is identical to the distribution of the shares $\{\widetilde{y}_i\}_{i \in I}$ generated by the simulator. This is because $y_i = c_1 \cdot x_{1i} + \cdots + c_n \cdot x_{ni}$ and $\widetilde{y}_i = c_1 \cdot \widetilde{x}_{1i} + \cdots + c_n \cdot \widetilde{x}_{ni}$. And since we are conditioning on the views till the end of the input stage, we have fixed $\{x_{ji}\}_{j \in \{1, \ldots, n\}, i \in I}$ and $\{\widetilde{x}_{ji}\}_{j \in \{1, \ldots, n\}, i \in I}$ to $\{\beta_{ji}\}_{j \in \{1, \ldots, n\}, i \in I}$. Hence, we have shown that the partial view of Adv in view$_I^{\Pi_{\text{BGW-Linear}}}$ and in the output produced by S are identically distributed, till computation stage.

Since the shares $\{y_i\}_{i \in I}$ and $\{\widetilde{y}_i\}_{i \in I}$ are identically distributed and are random elements of $\mathbb{F}$, let us fix these shares to $\{\gamma_i\}_{i \in I}$, where each γ_i is an arbitrary element of $\mathbb{F}$.

- *Output Stage*: Finally, conditioned on the views till the end of the computation stage (which we have shown to be identically distributed), we show that the view of Adv in view$_I^{\Pi_{\text{BGW-Linear}}}$ as well as in the output generated by S are identically distributed. To achieve this goal, we abstract out the process of generating the output by the protocol $\Pi_{\text{BGW-Linear}}$ and S through corresponding randomized experiments and show that the outputs generated in both the experiments have the same probability distribution.

Experiment $A(y)$	Experiment $B(y)$
(1) Randomly select $f_y(Z) \in \mathcal{P}^{y,t}$	(1) $\forall i \in I$, randomly select $\widetilde{y}_i \in \mathbb{F}$
(2) $\forall i \in I$, set $y_i = f_y(\alpha_i)$	(2) Select $\widetilde{f}_y(Z) \in \mathcal{P}^{y,t}$, s.t. $\forall i \in I$, $\widetilde{f}_y(\alpha_i) = \widetilde{y}_i$
(3) Output $f_y(Z)$	(3) Output $\widetilde{f}_y(Z)$

Before we proceed, we note that the experiment $A(y)$ abstracts the process of generating the output in the protocol $\Pi_{\text{BGW-Linear}}$. Namely, the t-degree polynomial $f_y(Z)$ reconstructed during the output stage is a random polynomial from the set of polynomials $\mathcal{P}^{y,t}$, where the shares $\{y_i\}_{i \in I}$ of the corrupt parties are randomly distributed over $\mathbb{F}$. On the other hand, the experiment $B(y)$ abstracts the process of generating the output by S. Namely, at the end of the computation stage, the shares $\{\widetilde{y}_i\}_{i \in I}$ generated by the simulator are random elements from $\mathbb{F}$. And to produce the output for the output stage, S picks the t-degree polynomial $\widetilde{f}_y(Z)$ from $\mathcal{P}^{y,t}$, agreeing with the shares $\{\widetilde{y}_i\}_{i \in I}$. We note that the polynomial $\widetilde{f}_y(Z)$ is also a random element from $\mathcal{P}^{y,t}$, since $|I| = t$ and the points $\{(\alpha_i, \widetilde{y}_i)\}_{i \in I}$ are randomly distributed, since the shares $\{\widetilde{y}_i\}_{i \in I}$ are randomly distributed.

Let the random variables $\mathbf{A}(y)$ and $\mathbf{B}(y)$ denote the output of the experiments $A(y)$ and $B(y)$ respectively. To show that the view of Adv during the output stage of $\Pi_{\text{BGW-Linear}}$ and the view generated by S during the output stage are identically distributed, it is sufficient to show that the variable $\mathbf{A}(y)$ and $\mathbf{B}(y)$ are identically distributed, for every $y \in \mathbb{F}$. $\qquad\square$

Claim 1 *For every $y \in \mathbb{F}$, the probability distributions $\left\{\mathbf{A}(y)\right\}$ and $\left\{\mathbf{B}(y)\right\}$ are identical.*

Proof Let $\mathbf{A}(y) = (\mathbf{A}_1, \mathbf{A}_2(Z))$, where $\mathbf{A}_1$ denotes the values $\{y_i\}_{i \in I}$ and $\mathbf{A}_2(Z)$ denotes the output polynomial $f_y(Z)$ in the experiment $A(y)$. Similarly, let $\mathbf{B}(y) = (\mathbf{B}_1, \mathbf{B}_2(Z))$, where $\mathbf{B}_1$ denotes the values $\{\widetilde{y}_i\}_{i \in I}$ and $\mathbf{B}_2(Z)$ denotes the output polynomial $\widetilde{f}_y(Z)$ in the experiment $B(y)$. From Lemma 3.7, it follows that the probability distributions $\left\{\mathbf{A}_1\right\}$ and $\left\{\mathbf{B}_1\right\}$ are identical. Therefore, to prove the claim, it is sufficient to show that the probability distributions $\left\{\mathbf{A}_2(Z)|\mathbf{A}_1\right\}$ and $\left\{\mathbf{B}_2(Z)|\mathbf{B}_1\right\}$ are identical. For this, we have to show that for every set of field elements $\{\gamma_i\}_{i \in I}$ and every polynomial $h(Z) \in \mathcal{P}^{y,t}$, the following condition holds.

$$\Pr\left[\mathbf{A}_2(Z) = h(Z) | (\forall i \in I) : \mathbf{A}_2(\alpha_i) = \gamma_i\right] = \Pr\left[\mathbf{B}_2(Z) = h(Z) | (\forall i \in I) : \mathbf{B}_2(\alpha_i) = \gamma_i\right]$$

Here $\{\gamma_i\}_{i \in I}$ are the conditioned values in $\mathbf{A}_1$ and $\mathbf{B}_1$.[4] There are two possible cases. If there exists an $i \in I$, such that $h(\alpha_i) \neq \gamma_i$, then both the probabilities in the above condition turn out to be zero and so the condition holds trivially. So we consider the other case, when indeed $h(\alpha_i) = \gamma_i$ for every $i \in I$. We first claim that

$$\Pr\left[\mathbf{B}_2(Z) = h(Z) | (\forall i \in I) : \mathbf{B}_2(\alpha_i) = \gamma_i\right] = 1,$$

which immediately follows from the process of generating the random variable $\mathbf{B}(y)$. This is because $\mathbf{B}_2(Z) = \widetilde{f}_y(Z)$ is selected under the constraint that $\widetilde{f}_y(Z) \in \mathcal{P}^{y,t}$, such that $\widetilde{f}_y(\alpha_i) = \gamma_i$ holds for every $i \in I$. Since $|I| + 1 = t + 1$ points are already fixed, there is exactly one polynomial from $\mathcal{P}^{y,t}$ satisfying the above constraints, which will be selected in the experiment $B(y)$. We next claim that

$$\Pr\left[\mathbf{A}_2(Z) = h(Z) | (\forall i \in I) : \mathbf{A}_2(\alpha_i) = \gamma_i\right] = 1.$$

For this, we first observe that

$$\Pr\left[\mathbf{A}_2(Z) = h(Z) \quad \wedge \quad (\forall i \in I) : \mathbf{A}_2(\alpha_i) = \gamma_i\right] = \Pr\left[\mathbf{A}_2(Z) = h(Z)\right].$$

This is because

$$\Pr\left[(\forall i \in I) : \mathbf{A}_2(\alpha_i) = \gamma_i | \mathbf{A}_2(Z) = h(Z)\right] = 1,$$

which follows from the fact that we are considering the case where the output $\mathbf{A}_2(Z) = h(Z)$ satisfies the condition $h(\alpha_i) = \gamma_i$ for each $i \in I$. Hence,

$$\Pr\left[\mathbf{A}_2(Z) = h(Z) \wedge (\forall i \in I) : \mathbf{A}_2(\alpha_i) = \gamma_i\right] = \Pr\left[\mathbf{A}_2(Z) = h(Z)\right]$$
$$\cdot \Pr\left[(\forall i \in I) : \mathbf{A}_2(\alpha_i) = \gamma_i | \mathbf{A}_2(Z) = h(Z)\right],$$

which will be same as $\Pr\left[\mathbf{A}_2(Z) = h(Z)\right]$. Therefore, we can conclude that

---

[4] The same γ_i are used for both $\mathbf{A}_1$ and $\mathbf{B}_1$, since they are identically distributed and we are now conditioning on them. We caution the reader that even though both the probability expressions look similar, they have different interpretations, since the output of the experiments $A(y)$ and $B(y)$ are generated differently. Namely, $\mathbf{A}_2(Z)$ denotes the output polynomial selected randomly from $\mathcal{P}^{y,t}$, *independent* of the values $\mathbf{A}_1 = \{\gamma_i\}_{i \in I}$. On the other hand, $\mathbf{B}_2(Z)$ denotes the output polynomial selected from $\mathcal{P}^{s,y}$, *depending* upon the values $\mathbf{B}_1 = \{\gamma_i\}_{i \in I}$.

$$\Pr\Big[\mathbf{A}_2(Z) = h(Z) | (\forall i \in I) : \mathbf{A}_2(\alpha_i) = \gamma_i\Big] = \frac{\Pr\Big[\mathbf{A}_2(Z) = h(Z) \quad \wedge \quad (\forall i \in I) : \mathbf{A}_2(\alpha_i) = \gamma_i\Big]}{\Pr\Big[(\forall i \in I) : \mathbf{A}_2(\alpha_i) = \gamma_i\Big]}$$

$$= \frac{\Pr\Big[\mathbf{A}_2(Z) = h(Z)\Big]}{\Pr\Big[(\forall i \in I) : \mathbf{A}_2(\alpha_i) = \gamma_i\Big]}$$

$$= \frac{1}{|\mathbb{F}|^t} \cdot |\mathbb{F}|^t = 1.$$

The last equality follows from the fact that $\mathbf{A}_2(Z) = h(Z)$ is selected uniformly from $\mathcal{P}^{y,t}$, where $|\mathcal{P}^{y,t}| = |\mathbb{F}|^t$. And from Lemma 3.7, the probability that $\mathbf{A}_2(\alpha_i) = \gamma_i$ for each $i \in I$ is $\frac{1}{|\mathbb{F}|^t}$. $\square$

The theorem now follows easily from the above claim. $\square$

Remark 5.10   In the proof of Theorem 5.9, we made the assumption that adversary corrupts a set of exactly t parties (i.e. $|I| = t$). However, the proof can be modified even for the case when adversary corrupts less than t parties (i.e. $|I| \le t$). First of all, the proof of the Lemma 3.7 has to be modified for the case when $|I| \le d$, instead of $|I| = d$. The steps of $\mathcal{S}$ need to be modified for generating the view for the output stage. Now the simulated polynomial $\widetilde{f}_y(Z)$ during the output stage will not be a unique polynomial from $\mathcal{P}^{y,t}$ and hence simulator has to pick $(t + 1) - (|I| + 1) = t - |I|$ random elements from $\mathbb{F}$ to compute the polynomial $\widetilde{f}_y(Z)$. Correspondingly, the experiments $A(y)$ and $B(y)$ need to be modified and the follow-up probability arguments will be different. We leave the details as an exercise for the interested readers and defer them to [11] for the details.

5.5   Securely Computing Product of a Public Matrix and a Secret Vector

Consider a vector of values $\vec{x} = (x_1, \dots, x_n) \in \mathbb{F}^n$, with party P_i holding the input x_i. Moreover, let $A \in \mathbb{F}^{n,n}$ be a *publicly-known* matrix. Then consider the matrix-multiplication function $\mathcal{F}^A_{\mathsf{MatMult}}$, where $(\vec{y})^T = \mathcal{F}^A_{\mathsf{MatMult}}(\vec{x}) \overset{def}{=} A \cdot (\vec{x})^T$ and party P_i holds the output y_i, where $\vec{y} = (y_1, \dots, y_n)$. Here the notations $(\vec{y})^T$ and $(\vec{x})^T$ denote the transpose of the vectors y and x respectively. It is easy to see that $\mathcal{F}_{\mathsf{MatMult}}$ is a linear function over $\mathbb{F}$. In a more detail, let $A = [a_{ij}]_{i,j \in \{1,\dots,n\}}$, where a_{ij} denotes the (i, j)th value of the matrix A. Then it is easy to see that the following holds, for every $j = 1, \dots, n$.

$$y_j = a_{j1} \cdot x_1 + \cdots + a_{jn} \cdot x_n.$$

Hence, each output y_j is a *publicly-known* linear function of $\vec{x}$. It then follows from Theorem 5.9 that the parties can compute the function $\mathcal{F}^A_{\mathsf{MatMult}}$ in a t-perfectly-secure fashion. Namely, each P_i can generate a t-Shamir-sharing of its input x_i and then each

---

Protocol $\Pi^A_{\mathsf{MatrixMult}}$

Input: Each party $P_i \in \mathcal{P}$ has a private input $x_i \in \mathbb{F}$. Moreover, $A = [a_{ij}]_{i,j \in \{1,\dots,n\}} \in \mathbb{F}^{n,n}$ is a publicly-known matrix.

Output: Each party $P_i \in \mathcal{P}$ obtains the output y_i, where $(y_1, \dots, y_n) = \mathcal{F}^A_{\mathsf{MatMult}}(x_1, \dots, x_n)$.

- *Input Stage*:
  - Compute the shares $(x_{i1}, \dots, x_{in}) \leftarrow \mathsf{G}_{\mathsf{Sha}}(x_i)$.
  - For $j = 1, \dots, n$, send the share x_{ij} to party $P_j \in \mathcal{P}$.
  For $k = 1, \dots, n$, let x_{ki} denote the share, received from the party $P_k \in \mathcal{P}$ at the end of the input stage.
- *Computation Stage*: For $j = 1, \dots, n$, compute the share $y_{ji} = a_{j1} \cdot x_{1i} + \dots + a_{jn} \cdot x_{ni}$.
- *Output Stage*:
  - For $j = 1, \dots, n$, send the share y_{ji} only to party P_j.
  - Upon receiving $y_{i1}, \dots, y_{in}$ from $P_1, \dots, P_n$ respectively, output $y_i = \mathsf{R}_{\mathsf{Sha}}(\mathcal{P}, \{y_{i1}, \dots, y_{in}\})$.

Fig. 5.4 Protocol for securely computing the function $\mathcal{F}^A_{\mathsf{MatMult}}$. The above steps are executed by each $P_i \in \mathcal{P}$

output y_j can be computed by the parties *non-interactively*, in a t-Shamir-shared fashion. Finally, the secret-shared output y_j is reconstructed, *only* towards the party P_j. For this, the parties send their shares of y_j only to P_j, who can then reconstruct y_j using the Lagrange's interpolation. We call the protocol as $\Pi^A_{\mathsf{MatrixMult}}$ and present it in Fig. 5.4. Looking ahead, the protocol will be useful in the next chapter, for securely evaluating multiplication gates in the BGW protocol.

The properties of the protocol $\Pi^A_{\mathsf{MatrixMult}}$ are stated in Lemma 5.11, which follows easily from the above discussion, the protocol steps (of $\Pi^A_{\mathsf{MatrixMult}}$) and Theorem 5.9. The protocol needs two rounds of communication, one during the input stage for sharing $\vec{x}$ and one during the output stage for reconstructing $\vec{y}$. Moreover, $\mathcal{O}(n^2)$ field elements are communicated during both these stages.

Lemma 5.11 *Let* $(y_1, \dots, y_n)^T = \mathcal{F}^A_{\mathsf{MatMult}}(x_1, \dots, x_n)^T$ *be an n-ary function over $\mathbb{F}$ where P_i holds the private input x_i and where P_i receives the output y_i, with $A \in \mathbb{F}^{n,n}$ being a publicly-known matrix over $\mathbb{F}$. Moreover, let $t < n$. Then protocol $\Pi^A_{\mathsf{MatrixMult}}$ is t-perfectly-secure for $\mathcal{F}^A_{\mathsf{MatMult}}$.*

The protocol requires 2 rounds and communication of $\mathcal{O}(n^2)$ field elements.

Securely Truncating a $2t$-degree Polynomial to a t-degree Polynomial: We now discuss a special use case of the protocol $\Pi^A_{\mathsf{MatrixMult}}$, which will be used in the next chapter when we discuss the BGW protocol for evaluating multiplication gates. Consider the following n-party *degree-reduction* function $\mathcal{F}_{\mathsf{DegRed}}$:

$$\mathcal{F}_{\mathsf{DegRed}}\Big(h(\alpha_1), \dots, h(\alpha_n)\Big) = \Big(\hat{h}(\alpha_1), \dots, \hat{h}(\alpha_n)\Big)$$

with the following inputs and outputs:

- *Input*: Party P_i has the input $h(\alpha_i)$, where $h(Z)$ is some $2t$-degree polynomial, with coefficient-vector $(h_0, \ldots, h_{2t})$. That is, $h(Z) = h_0 + h_1 Z + \cdots + h_t Z^t + \cdots + h_{2t} Z^{2t}$
- *Output*: Party P_i has the output $\hat{h}(\alpha_i)$, where $\hat{h}(Z)$ is the polynomial $h(Z)$, *truncated* to degree t. That is, $\hat{h}(Z) = h_0 + h_1 Z + \cdots + h_t Z^t$.

We next show that securely computing the function $\mathcal{F}_{\mathsf{DegRed}}$ is equivalent to multiplying the the vector of values $(h(\alpha_1), \ldots, h(\alpha_n))$ with a *publicly-known* matrix.

Claim 2 *([11, 25]) Let $t < n/2$. Then there exists a matrix $A \in \mathbb{F}^{n \times n}$, such that for every $2t$-degree polynomial $h(Z) = h_0 + h_1 Z + \cdots + h_t Z^t + \cdots + h_{2t} Z^{2t}$ and the corresponding truncated polynomial $\hat{h}(Z) = h_0 + h_1 Z + \cdots + h_t Z^t$, it holds that:*

$$\left(\hat{h}(\alpha_1), \ldots, \hat{h}(\alpha_n)\right)^T = A \cdot \left(h(\alpha_1), \ldots, h(\alpha_n)\right)^T.$$

Proof Let V denote the $n \times n$ *Vandermonde matrix* where the ith row is $(\alpha_i^0, \ldots, \alpha_i^{n-1})$. Since $\alpha_1, \ldots, \alpha_n$ are distinct and non-zero elements from $\mathbb{F}$, it follows that the matrix V is invertible. Consider the n-length vector $\vec{h} = (h_0, \ldots, h_t, \ldots, h_{2t}, 0, \ldots, 0)$. It then follows that the following holds:

$$\left(h(\alpha_1), \ldots, h(\alpha_n)\right)^T = V \cdot \vec{h}^T$$

Since V is invertible, we get that the following holds:

$$\vec{h}^T = V^{-1} \cdot \left(h(\alpha_1), \ldots, h(\alpha_n)\right)^T$$

Similarly, by letting $\vec{\hat{h}}$ to denote the vector $(h_0, \ldots, h_t, 0, \ldots, 0)$ of length n, we get that the following holds:

$$\left(\hat{h}(\alpha_1), \ldots, \hat{h}(\alpha_n)\right)^T = V \cdot \vec{\hat{h}}^T$$

Next consider the $n \times n$ matrix P, where $P(i, j) = 1$, if and only if $i = j \in \{1, \ldots, t\}$ and 0 otherwise. It then follows that the following holds:

$$P \cdot \vec{h}^T = \vec{\hat{h}}^T$$

Now combining all the above relations together, we get that

$$
\begin{aligned}
\left(\hat{h}(\alpha_1), \dots, \hat{h}(\alpha_n) \right)^T &= V \cdot \vec{\hat{h}}^T \\
&= V \cdot (P \cdot \vec{h}^T) \\
&= V \cdot P \cdot V^{-1} \cdot \left(h(\alpha_1), \dots, h(\alpha_n) \right)^T \\
&= A \cdot \left(h(\alpha_1), \dots, h(\alpha_n) \right)^T
\end{aligned}
$$

holds, where $A \overset{def}{=} V \cdot P \cdot V^{-1}$ is the desired constant matrix (see Fig. 5.5 for the matrix-multiplications involved in the computation of $\mathcal{F}_{\mathsf{DegRed}}$). $\square$

$$
\begin{bmatrix} \hat{h}(\alpha_1) \\ \vdots \\ \hat{h}(\alpha_i) \\ \vdots \\ \hat{h}(\alpha_n) \end{bmatrix}
=
\begin{bmatrix}
\alpha_1^0 & \dots & \alpha_1^t & 0 & \dots & 0 \\
\vdots & \dots & \vdots & \vdots & \dots & \vdots \\
\alpha_i^0 & \dots & \alpha_i^t & 0 & \dots & 0 \\
\vdots & \dots & \vdots & \vdots & \dots & \vdots \\
\alpha_n^0 & \dots & \alpha_n^t & 0 & \dots & 0
\end{bmatrix}
\cdot
\begin{bmatrix} h_0 \\ \vdots \\ h_t \\ \vdots \\ h_{2t} \\ 0 \\ \vdots \\ 0 \end{bmatrix}
$$

$$
=
\begin{bmatrix}
\alpha_1^0 & \dots & \alpha_1^t & \alpha_1^{t+1} & \dots & \alpha_1^{n-1} \\
\vdots & \dots & \vdots & \vdots & \dots & \vdots \\
\alpha_i^0 & \dots & \alpha_i^t & \alpha_i^{t+1} & \dots & \alpha_i^{n-1} \\
\vdots & \dots & \vdots & \vdots & \dots & \vdots \\
\alpha_n^0 & \dots & \alpha_n^t & \alpha_n^{t+1} & \dots & \alpha_n^{n-1}
\end{bmatrix}
\cdot
\begin{bmatrix}
1 & 0 & \dots & 0 & 0 & \dots & 0 \\
0 & 1 & \dots & 0 & 0 & \dots & 0 \\
\vdots & \vdots & \dots & \vdots & \vdots & \dots & \vdots \\
0 & 0 & \dots & 1 & 0 & \dots & 0 \\
0 & 0 & \dots & 0 & 0 & \dots & 0 \\
\vdots & \vdots & \dots & \vdots & \vdots & \dots & \vdots \\
0 & 0 & \dots & 0 & 0 & \dots & 0
\end{bmatrix}
\cdot V^{-1} \cdot
\begin{bmatrix} h(\alpha_1) \\ \vdots \\ h(\alpha_i) \\ \vdots \\ h(\alpha_n) \\ 0 \\ \vdots \\ 0 \end{bmatrix}
$$

$$
= A \cdot
\begin{bmatrix} h(\alpha_1) \\ \vdots \\ h(\alpha_i) \\ \vdots \\ h(\alpha_n) \\ 0 \\ \vdots \\ 0 \end{bmatrix}
$$

Fig. 5.5 The matrix multiplications involved in the computation of $\mathcal{F}_{\mathsf{DegRed}}$

From Claim 2 and the description of the the functionality $\mathcal{F}_{\text{DegRed}}$, we get that the following holds.

$$\left(\hat{h}(\alpha_1), \ldots, \hat{h}(\alpha_n)\right)^T = \mathcal{F}_{\text{DegRed}}\left(h(\alpha_1), \ldots, h(\alpha_n)\right) = A \cdot \left(h(\alpha_1), \ldots, h(\alpha_n)\right)^T$$

Since A is a constant matrix and known-publicly, it then follows from Lemma 5.11 that the parties can use an instance of the protocol $\Pi^A_{\text{MatrixMult}}$ to securely compute the functionality $\mathcal{F}_{\text{DegRed}}$. Namely, in the protocol $\Pi^A_{\text{MatrixMult}}$, the input of P_i will be $h(\alpha_i)$ and the protocol will generate the output $\hat{h}(\alpha_i)$ for P_i. We capture the above discussion in the following lemma.

Lemma 5.12 *There exists a t-perfectly-secure protocol for $\mathcal{F}_{\text{DegRed}}$, which requires 2 rounds of interaction and communication of $\mathcal{O}(n^2)$ field elements.*

5.6 Dealing with Malicious Adversaries

We conclude this chapter by noting that the security properties of the protocol $\Pi_{\text{BGW-Linear}}$ (and the follow-up protocol $\Pi^A_{\text{MatrixMult}}$ and the protocol for computing $\mathcal{F}_{\text{DegRed}}$) are guaranteed *only* if all the parties (including the corrupt parties) follow the protocol instructions correctly. However, if the corrupt parties start behaving *maliciously* then security breaks down. Two ways a maliciously corrupt party can misbehave are: (a) it *may not* share its input using a t-degree sharing-polynomial; (b) it may produce an *incorrect* share of y during the output stage, leading to the honest parties reconstructing an *incorrect* output. Both these misbehaviours are associated with the underlying secret sharing scheme. Therefore, both these problems can be tackled using a maliciously-secure secret-sharing scheme, aka, VSS, as mentioned in Sect. 3.6.

The BGW Perfectly-Secure MPC Protocol for Any Arbitrary Function

6

In this chapter, we discuss the BGW protocol for securely evaluating *any* function. We first discuss the challenges associated with evaluating the multiplication gates, leading to the degree-reduction problem. We then present two different protocols for solving the degree-reduction problem. Finally, we discuss the necessary condition for *any* generic t-perfectly-secure MPC protocol. We conclude the chapter mentioning the issues that BGW protocol (and related sub-protocols) may have while facing a malicious adversary.

We follow the same network model and adversarial setting, as used in Chap. 5. That is, we assume that the parties want to securely compute a *deterministic* function $f : \mathbb{F}^n \to \mathbb{F}$ over the field $\mathbb{F}$, where $y = f(x_1, \ldots, x_n)$. The function f is abstracted as a publicly-known arithmetic circuit cir over $\mathbb{F}$. However, unlike the previous chapter (where cir consists of *only* linear gates over $\mathbb{F}$), we do not put any restriction on the types of gates present in cir.

6.1 Challenges in Securely Evaluating Multiplication Gates

Recall that the BGW protocol is based on the principle of shared circuit-evaluation, wherein each value during the evaluation of the circuit cir is available to the parties in a random t-Shamir-shared fashion and the circuit output alone is *publicly* reconstructed from its the secret-sharing.[1] Since for every value in the circuit (except the output value), adversary sees at most t randomly distributed shares, this paradigm preserves privacy of all the intermediate values. To follow this principle, the parties maintain the following *gate-invariant* for each gate in the circuit:

---

[1] See Definition 5.1 for the definition of t-Shamir-sharing. A t-Shamir-sharing of a value s is called *random*, if the underlying sharing-polynomial is a *random* t-degree polynomial from $\mathcal{P}^{s,t}$.

© The Author(s), under exclusive license to Springer Nature Switzerland AG 2022
A. Choudhury and A. Patra, *Secure Multi-Party Computation Against Passive Adversaries*,
Synthesis Lectures on Distributed Computing Theory,
https://doi.org/10.1007/978-3-031-12164-7_6

Given the gate input(s) in a random t-Shamir-shared fashion, the gate-output is randomly t-Shamir-shared among the parties.

In the previous chapter, we have seen that maintaining the above invariant is "free" for the *linear* gates and *does not* require any interaction among the parties. Unfortunately, maintaining the invariant for the *non-linear* (multiplication) gates is not free and *requires* interaction among the parties. Consider a multiplication gate in cir with inputs a, b and output c (hence $c = a \cdot b$), where the inputs a and b are randomly t-Shamir-shared. That is, there exists a random vector of shares $[a]_t = (a_1, \ldots, a_n)$ and similarly, a random vector of shares $[b]_t = (b_1, \ldots, b_n)$, where each party P_i holds the shares a_i and b_i. Let $f_a(Z) \in \mathcal{P}^{a,t}$ and $f_b(Z) \in \mathcal{P}^{b,t}$ be the underlying random t-degree sharing polynomials, where $a_i = f_a(\alpha_i)$ and $b_i = f_b(\alpha_i)$.

Imagine that the parties locally multiply their respective shares of a and b, with party P_i computing $k_i = a_i \cdot b_i$. Then the vector of shares $(k_1, \ldots, k_n)$ *no* longer constitutes a t-Shamir-sharing of the product c. This is because the shares $k_1, \ldots, k_n$ lie on the $2t$-degree polynomial $K(Z) \overset{def}{=} f_a(Z) \cdot f_b(Z)$, where $K(0) = c$, $K(\alpha_i) = k_i$. If the parties simply proceed with the shares $(k_1, \ldots, k_n)$ of c to evaluate the remaining gates, then this could lead to two security problems. Below, we elaborate on each problem and illustrate them using concrete examples.

The *first* problem is that if the output c of the multiplication gate serves as the input to other multiplication gates in cir, then by following the above procedure, the degree of Shamir-sharing of the final output may be more than n and hence the robust reconstruction of the final shared circuit output may not be possible. To understand this security problem, we consider the following example.

Example 6.1 Let $\mathcal{P} = \{P_1, P_2, P_3, P_4\}$, $t = 2$ and let the parties want to securely compute the function $y = x_1 \cdot x_2$ over the field $(\mathbb{Z}_5, +_5, \cdot_5)$, where P_1 and P_2 have the inputs x_1 and x_2 respectively.[2] Hence the circuit cir consists of just a single multiplication gate, with inputs x_1 and x_2. Let the evaluation-points be $\alpha_1 = 1$, $\alpha_2 = 2$, $\alpha_3 = 3$ and $\alpha_4 = 4$. Let x_1 be 0 and secret-shared among the parties through the 2-degree polynomial $0 + 0Z + Z^2$. And let x_2 be 1 and secret-shared through the 2-degree polynomial $1 + 0Z + Z^2$. Then the shares available with the respective parties are shown in the following table.

Variable	Value	Sharing-Polynomial	P_1's Share	P_2's Share	P_3's Share	P_4's Share
x_1	0	$0 + 0Z + Z^2$	1	4	4	1
x_2	1	$1 + 0Z + Z^2$	2	0	0	2
y	1	$1 + 0Z + Z^2$	2	0	0	2

---

[2] We can imagine that the inputs x_3 and x_4 of P_3 and P_4 are 1 and 1 respectively.

If the parties locally multiply their respective shares of x_1 and x_2, then it leads to the vector of shares $(2, 0, 0, 2)$, shown in red color. Notice that these shares lie on the $2t = 4$-degree polynomial $f_y(Z) = (0 + 0Z + Z^2) \cdot (1 + 0Z + Z^2)$. To robustly reconstruct the polynomial $f_y(Z)$, one requires at least *five* distinct points (shares), where as there are only 4 parties. If the parties exchange their respective shares obtained after multiplying the respective shares of x_1 and x_2, then by interpolating the points $(1, 2), (2, 0), (3, 0)$ and $(4, 2)$, the parties will reconstruct the polynomial $1 + 0Z + Z^2$ (shown in red color). Hence, the parties will conclude that the function output is $y = 1$, which is incorrect (shown in red color), since the correct output $x_1 \cdot x_2 = 1 \cdot 0$ is 0.

For a moment, assume that $n > 2t$ and there are no other multiplication gates in cir after the multiplication gate with inputs a, b and output c. In this case, one may feel that it is "safe" to proceed evaluating the circuit with the vector of shares $(k_1, \ldots k_n)$ which constitute a $2t$-Shamir-sharing of c. This is because any $2t$-Shamir-shared secret can be robustly reconstructed as long as $n > 2t$ due to the availability of sufficient number of shares. The *second* security issue in continuing evaluating the circuit with the vector of shares $(k_1, \ldots k_n)$ is that these shares *do not* constitute a *random* $2t$-Shamir-sharing of c. That is, the underlying sharing-polynomial $K(Z)$ is *not* a random $2t$-degree polynomial from the set $\mathcal{P}^{s,2t}$ of $2t$-degree polynomials over $\mathbb{F}$. For instance, the polynomial $K(Z)$ is *not* an *irreducible* polynomial, since it can be factored into the t-degree polynomials $f_a(Z)$ and $f_b(Z)$. The adversary can exploit this fact to breach the privacy of a and b beyond what is permitted. We demonstrate this problem with an example.

Example 6.2 Let us consider the same setting as in the previous example, except that now $t = 1$. Let $x_1 = 1$ and secret-shared among the parties through the 1-degree polynomial $1 + 2Z$. And let $x_2 = 4$ and secret-shared through the 1-degree polynomial $4 + 0Z$. Then the shares of x_1 and x_2 available with the respective parties are shown in the following table.

Variable	Value	Sharing-Polynomial	P_1's Share	P_2's Share	P_3's Share	P_4's Share
x_1	1	$1 + 2Z$	3	0	2	4
x_2	4	$4 + 0Z$	4	4	4	4
y	4	$4 + 3Z + 0Z^2$	2	0	3	1

Suppose the parties locally multiply their respective shares of x_1 and x_2, followed by exchanging the resultant shares and reconstructing the underlying secret-shared output y. This leads to the parties reconstructing the sharing-polynomial $4 + 3Z + 0Z^2$ and the resultant function output $y = 4$. Now imagine that P_3 is corrupt, then the values learnt by P_3 are shown in bold in the following table. Namely, P_3 learns one share each for x_1 and x_2 and all the shares for the output y. Moreover, the values being marked with "?" are unknown to P_3 (shown in red colour). Now based on its view, the adversary can conclude that the pair (x_1, x_2) can take the values $(1, 4), (2, 2), (3, 3)$ or $(4, 1)$.

Variable	Sharing-Polynomial	P_1's Share	P_2's Share	P_3's Share	P_4's Share
$x_1 = ?$	?	?	?	2	?
$x_2 = ?$	?	?	?	4	?
$y = 4$	$4 + 3Z + 0Z^2$	2	0	3	1

If the above protocol is secure, then the adversary's view should be consistent with all the above four possibilities. However, we show that this is not the case. For instance, as shown in the following table, the adversary's view is *not* consistent with $x_1 = 4$ and $x_2 = 1$, implying that the protocol *is not* perfectly-secure.[3] More specifically, if adversary makes the hypothesis that $x_1 = 4$ and $x_2 = 1$, then that is possible provided x_1 and x_2 are shared through the 1-degree polynomials $4 + Z$ and $1 + Z$ respectively. This is because there is a *unique* 1-degree polynomial belonging to $\mathcal{P}^{4,1}$ (namely $4 + Z$) which evaluates to 2 at $Z = \alpha_3$. And similarly, there is a *unique* 1-degree polynomial belonging to $\mathcal{P}^{1,1}$ (namely $1 + Z$) which evaluates to 4 at $Z = \alpha_3$. But this configuration does not lead to the shares $2, 0, 3$ and 1 respectively for P_1, P_2, P_3 and P_4, corresponding to $y = 4$. For instance, if P_1's shares for $x_1 = 4$ and $x_2 = 1$ are 0 and 2 respectively, then P_1's share for y should have been $0 \cdot 2 = 0$, where as in the protocol execution, adversary has received the share 2 from P_1, corresponding to y. Hence adversary can rule out the possibility of $x_1 = 4$ and $x_2 = 1$. In the same way, it can be shown that adversary can rule out the possibility of $x_1 = 3$ and $x_2 = 3$, whereas adversary's view will be consistent with $x_1 = 2$ and $x_2 = 2$.

Variable	Sharing-Polynomial	P_1's Share	P_2's Share	P_3's Share	P_4's Share
$x_1 = 4$	$4 + Z$	0	1	2	3
$x_2 = 1$	$1 + Z$	2	3	4	0
$y = 4$	$4 + 3Z + 0Z^2$	2	0	3	1

6.2   The Degree-Reduction Problem

From the discussion in the previous section, we can conclude that in order to maintain the BGW gate-invariant for a multiplication gate, the parties have to interact and jointly "reduce" the degree of sharing of the gate output to t. Loosely speaking, the parties need an n-party "secure" sub-protocol, say Π_{Mult}, with the following inputs and output:

– *Inputs*: The inputs of the protocol are vector of shares $[a]_t = (a_1, \ldots, a_n)$ and $[b]_t = (b_1, \ldots, b_n)$, corresponding to t-Shamir-sharing of a and b respectively, where the shares a_i and b_i are held by the party P_i.

---

[3] In a perfectly-secure protocol, all possible inputs, consistent with the adversary's view should be equally likely.

– *Output*: The output of the protocol is a vector of shares $(c_1, \ldots, c_n)$, corresponding to a *random* t-Shamir-sharing of $c \overset{def}{=} ab$. Namely, each share $c_i = f_c(\alpha_i)$, where $f_c(Z)$ is some *random* polynomial, belonging to the set of the t-degree polynomials $\mathcal{P}^{c,t}$. And each share c_i is available with P_i.

Informally, the security of Π_{Mult} means that Adv does not learn any additional information about a, b and c, except that $c = ab$ holds. To formally capture the security requirements of the protocol Π_{Mult}, we envision an n-party function $\mathcal{F}_{\mathsf{Mult}}$, where:

$$\mathcal{F}_{\mathsf{Mult}}\Big((a_1, b_1), \ldots, (a_n, b_n)\Big) = (c_1, \ldots, c_n).$$

Here P_i has the input (a_i, b_i) and the output for P_i is the share c_i. The security of the protocol Π_{Mult} then means that it is a t-*perfectly-secure* protocol for computing $\mathcal{F}_{\mathsf{Mult}}$ (see Sect. 5.4.4).

6.3 The BGW Protocol for Any Function

We will now proceed to discuss the BGW protocol for securely computing *any deterministic* function, *assuming* we have an instantiation of the protocol Π_{Mult} to securely compute $\mathcal{F}_{\mathsf{Mult}}$.[4] To prove the security of the resultant protocol in a modular fashion, we use the *sequential-composition theorem* of [41]. Hence we pause for a moment and discuss about the theorem.

6.3.1 The Sequential Modular Composition

Let Π_f be a protocol for securely computing some given function f and suppose Π_f uses a subprotocol Π_g for securely computing another function, say g (for instance, Π_f could be the BGW MPC protocol, which uses the subprotocol Π_{Mult}). Then the composition theorem states that it is sufficient to consider the execution of Π_f in a *hybrid* model, where some *trusted third party* (TTP) is designated with the task of ideally computing g, instead of the parties running the subprotocol Π_g. This model is denoted as the *g-hybrid model*, since it involves both interaction among the parties, as well as interaction between the parties and the TTP for computing g. The composition theorem allows to do a modular security analysis of Π_f as follows.

– First, prove that the protocol Π_g securely computes the function g.
– Then, prove that the "bigger" protocol Π_f securely computes f in the g-hybrid model.

---

[4] Recall that in the previous chapter, we have discussed that it is sufficient to consider only deterministic functions.

In a more detail, in the protocol Π_f, if in some round r the parties are supposed to run the sub-protocol Π_g with inputs, say $u_1, \ldots, u_n$ (where P_i owns the input u_i), then in the *g-hybrid model* the parties jointly "call" the TTP, with each P_i securely sending u_i to the TTP. Recall that in an ideal solution, it is assumed that there is a secure channel between every party and the TTP. The TTP then computes $v \stackrel{def}{=} g(u_1, \ldots, u_n)$ and securely sends v to every party in the round $r + 1$.

Using the composition theorem, one can then prove that if Π_f is a protocol for securely computing f in the *g-hybrid model* and if Π_g is a protocol for securely computing g, then the protocol Π_f with every call to the TTP being replaced by an instance of the sub-protocol Π_g, is also a secure protocol for computing the functionality f (see Fig. 6.1). At a high level, this follows from the following argument. Since Π_g is a secure protocol for computing g, there exists some simulator, say $\mathcal{S}_g$, which can simulate the view of the corrupt parties in the protocol Π_g. To prove the security of the protocol Π_f, one needs to show the existence of a simulator, say $\mathcal{S}_f$, which can simulate the view of the corrupt parties in Π_f, including the instances of the subprotocol Π_g. Now to simulate the view of the corrupt parties for the instances of Π_g, the simulator $\mathcal{S}_f$ can run the steps of the simulator $\mathcal{S}_g$. We refer the readers to [41] for the complete formal details.

To differentiate the hybrid model from the model where the parties are just assumed to have access to pair-wise secure channels, we call the latter model as *plain model*. We stress that our ultimate goal is to design protocols in the plain model, but for the sake of simpler presentations and modular security analysis, we will be presenting protocols in the hybrid models wherever applicable.

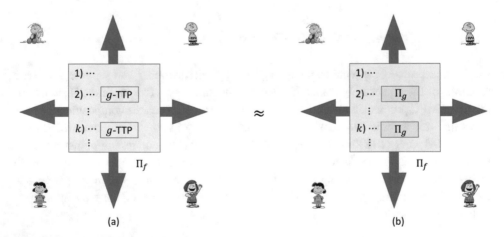

Fig. 6.1 Pictorial depiction of the sequential-composition theorem. Figure **a** denotes the protocol Π_f being executed in the g-hybrid model, where it is assumed that parties have a secure access to g-TTP, who can ideally compute the functionality g. Figure **b** denotes the protocol Π_f, where each call to the g-TTP is replaced by an instance of the sub-protocol Π_g. According to sequential-composition theorem, if Π_g securely computes g, then the protocol in Fig. **b** achieves the same security as the protocol in Fig. **a**

6.3.2   The BGW Protocol in the $\mathcal{F}_{\mathsf{Mult}}$-Hybrid Model

In this section, we present the formal details of the BGW protocol in a hybrid model, where we assume the existence of a TTP for ideally computing the function $\mathcal{F}_{\mathsf{Mult}}$. We abuse the notation and use $\mathcal{F}_{\mathsf{Mult}}$ to denote the TTP itself and assume that there is a secure channel between every party and the TTP $\mathcal{F}_{\mathsf{Mult}}$, through which the parties can send inputs to $\mathcal{F}_{\mathsf{Mult}}$ and receive output from $\mathcal{F}_{\mathsf{Mult}}$. Later to complete the security proof, we will show various protocols for securely computing the function $\mathcal{F}_{\mathsf{Mult}}$.

The high level idea of the protocol Π_{BGW} (see Fig. 6.2) is similar to the protocol $\Pi_{\mathsf{BGW\text{-}Linear}}$. The parties secret-share their respective inputs for the function. They then jointly and securely evaluate each gate of the underlying circuit in a t-Shamir-shared fashion. For this, the parties maintain the BGW-invariant for each gate in the circuit, where given the gate-inputs in a random t-Shamir-shared fashion, the parties jointly and securely compute a random t-Shamir-sharing of the gate-output. As already seen in the protocol $\Pi_{\mathsf{BGW\text{-}Linear}}$, maintaining the invariant for *linear* gates is free and does not require any interaction among the parties, owing to the linearity of t-Shamir-sharing. For multiplication gates, the parties take the "help" of the TTP $\mathcal{F}_{\mathsf{Mult}}$ to maintain the invariant. Namely, to evaluate a multiplication gate, the parties provide their respective shares of the multiplication-gate input to $\mathcal{F}_{\mathsf{Mult}}$, who in return provides shares corresponding to a random t-Shamir-sharing of the multiplication-gate output. Finally, once all the gates are evaluated and the function

---

Protocol Π_{BGW}

- *Input Stage*:
    - On having the input x_i, compute the shares $(x_{i1}, \ldots, x_{in}) \leftarrow \mathsf{G}_{\mathsf{Sha}}(x_i)$.
    - For $j = 1, \ldots, n$, send the share x_{ij} to party $P_j \in \mathcal{P}$.
    For $k = 1, \ldots, n$, let x_{ki} denote the share, received from the party $P_k \in \mathcal{P}$ at the end of the input stage.
- *Computation Stage*: Let $G_1, \ldots, G_\ell$ be a publicly-known topological ordering of the gates of cir. For $k = 1, \ldots, \ell$, do the following for gate G_k:
    - If G_k *is an addition gate*: Let $a_i^{(k)}$ and $b_i^{(k)}$ be the shares held by P_i, corresponding to the gate-inputs. Set $a_i^{(k)} + b_i^{(k)}$ to be the share, corresponding to the gate-output.
    - If G_k *is a multiplication-with-a-constant gate with constant* c: Let $a_i^{(k)}$ be the share held by P_i, corresponding to the gate-input. Set $c \cdot a_i^{(k)}$ to be the share, corresponding to the gate-output.
    - If G_k *is an addition-with-a-constant gate with constant* c: Let $a_i^{(k)}$ be the share held by P_i, corresponding to the gate-input. Set $c + a_i^{(k)}$ to be the share, corresponding to the gate-output.
    - If G_k *is a multiplication gate*: Let $a_i^{(k)}$ and $b_i^{(k)}$ be the shares held by P_i, corresponding to the gate-inputs. Invoke $\mathcal{F}_{\mathsf{Mult}}$ with inputs $(a_i^{(k)}, b_i^{(k)})$. Set $c_i^{(k)}$ to be the share, corresponding to the gate-output, where $c_i^{(k)}$ is the share returned back by $\mathcal{F}_{\mathsf{Mult}}$.
- *Output Stage*:
    - Send the share y_i to every party in $\mathcal{P}$.
    - Upon receiving the shares $y_1, \ldots, y_n$, output $y = \mathsf{R}_{\mathsf{Sha}}(\mathcal{P}, \{y_1, \ldots, y_n\})$.

Fig. 6.2 BGW protocol for securely computing any deterministic function in the $\mathcal{F}_{\mathsf{Mult}}$-hybrid model. The above steps are executed by each $P_i \in \mathcal{P}$

output is available in a secret-shared fashion, the parties proceed to publicly reconstruct the secret-shared output.

The intuitive argument for the privacy goes as follows. Throughout the protocol the parties interact during the input stage and during the output stage (to evaluate the multiplication gates, the parties do not interact among themselves, but rather with $\mathcal{F}_{\mathsf{Mult}}$, through secure channels). Hence, for every value during the circuit-evaluation (except for the final output), Adv sees at most t shares, which are randomly distributed and independent of the underlying value.

The complexity analysis of the protocol Π_{BGW} remains the same as in Lemma 5.3, except that for each multiplication gate, the parties need to interact with the TTP $\mathcal{F}_{\mathsf{Mult}}$.

Theorem 6.3 (BGW Protocol for Any Deterministic Function [11]) *Let $y = f(x_1, \ldots, x_n)$ be an n-ary deterministic function over $\mathbb{F}$ with P_i holding the private input x_i. Moreover, let $t < n$. Then protocol Π_{BGW} is t-perfectly-secure for f in the $\mathcal{F}_{\mathsf{Mult}}$-hybrid model.*

The protocol requires 2 rounds and communication of $\mathcal{O}(n^2)$ field elements for the input and output stage. In addition, c_M calls to $\mathcal{F}_{\mathsf{Mult}}$ are made to evaluate the multiplication gates, where c_M denotes the number of multiplication gates in the circuit cir representing the function f.

Proof Since we are considering deterministic functions, we prove the security as per Definition 5.5. The *correctness* property follows immediately from the linearity property of the Shamir's secret-sharing and from the fact that $\mathcal{F}_{\mathsf{Mult}}$ outputs a t-Shamir-sharing for each multiplication gate in cir. This guarantees that $\mathsf{output}^{\Pi_{\mathsf{BGW}}}(\vec{x}) = f(x_1, \ldots, x_n)$ holds.

To prove the *privacy*, we present a simulator, which simulates the view of the corrupt parties. We make a simplifying assumption that the adversary corrupts the *maximum* number of parties allowed, namely t parties. We stress that this is solely for simplicity and the proof can be extended to the case of less than t corruptions. The high level idea of the simulator remains the same as in the proof of Theorem 5.9. That is, the simulator selects random Shamir-shares of arbitrary values on the behalf of the honest parties during the input stage. And during the output stage, the simulator selects shares on the behalf of the honest parties, which along with the shares of the corrupt parties, yield the actual function output. During the computation stage, the simulator has to simulate the shares returned by $\mathcal{F}_{\mathsf{Mult}}$ to the corrupt parties, corresponding to the evaluation of the multiplication gates. For this, we observe that from the description of $\mathcal{F}_{\mathsf{Mult}}$, the shares returned by $\mathcal{F}_{\mathsf{Mult}}$ to the t corrupt parties correspond to a *random* t-Shamir-sharing and hence they are uniformly distributed over $\mathbb{F}$ (follows from Lemma 3.7). Hence, to simulate these shares, the simulator can just pick any t random values from $\mathbb{F}$, which generates the same probability distribution, as the shares returned by $\mathcal{F}_{\mathsf{Mult}}$. For the formal details of the simulator, see Fig. 6.3.

To complete the proof, we now show that probability distribution of the view generated by $\mathcal{S}$ is identical to the view of Adv during the execution of the protocol Π_{BGW}. If the circuit consists of only *linear* gates, then the proof is the same as the proof of Theorem 5.9.

> ### Simulator $\mathcal{S}$
>
> The input of the simulator is the index set $I \subset \{1, \ldots, n\}$ of the corrupt parties where $|I| = t$, the inputs $\{x_i\}_{i \in I}$ of the corrupt parties and the function output y.
> - *Simulating the Input Stage*: The steps remain the same as in Fig 5.3.
> - *Simulating the Computation Stage:* For every gate $G_k \in \{G_1, \ldots, G_\ell\}$, the simulator does the following:
>   - If G_k *is an addition gate*: Let $\{\widetilde{a}_i^{(k)}\}_{i \in I}$ and $\{\widetilde{b}_i^{(k)}\}_{i \in I}$ be the shares of the corrupt parties, corresponding to the gate-inputs. For every $i \in I$, set $\widetilde{a}_i^{(k)} + \widetilde{b}_i^{(k)}$ to be the share of P_i, corresponding to the gate-output.
>   - If G_k *is a multiplication-with-a-constant gate with constant* c: Let $\{\widetilde{a}_i^{(k)}\}_{i \in I}$ be the shares of the corrupt parties, corresponding to the gate-input. For every $i \in I$, set $c \cdot \widetilde{a}_i^{(k)}$ to be the share of P_i, corresponding to the gate-output.
>   - If G_k *is an addition-with-a-constant gate with constant* c: Let $\{\widetilde{a}_i^{(k)}\}_{i \in I}$ be the shares of the corrupt parties, corresponding to the gate-input. For every $i \in I$, set $c + \widetilde{a}_i^{(k)}$ to be the share of P_i, corresponding to the gate-output.
>   - If G_k *is a multiplication gate*: The simulator computes a random t-Shamir-sharing $(\widetilde{c}_1^{(k)}, \ldots, \widetilde{c}_n^{(k)})$ of 0 by picking a random polynomial, say $f_0^{(k)}(Z)$, from the set $\mathcal{P}^{0,t}$ of t-degree polynomials over $\mathbb{F}$ with 0 as the constant term and setting $\widetilde{c}_i^{(k)} \stackrel{def}{=} f_0^{(k)}(\alpha_i)$, for $i = 1, \ldots, n$. For every $i \in I$, the simulator sets $\widetilde{c}_i^{(k)}$ to be the share returned by $\mathcal{F}_{\mathsf{Mult}}$ to P_i.
>   The simulator then adds the shares as generated above to Adv's view.
> - *Simulating the Output Stage*: The steps remain the same as in Fig 5.3.
> $\mathcal{S}$ outputs the combined view of Adv for all the stages.

Fig. 6.3 Simulator for simulating the view of the corrupt parties in the protocol Π_{BGW}

So we consider the case when there are multiplication gates in cir. Let G_k be an arbitrary multiplication gate.

During the execution of Π_{BGW}, the view of Adv for the output of G_k consists of the shares $\{c_i^{(k)}\}_{i \in I}$ returned by $\mathcal{F}_{\mathsf{Mult}}$. On the other hand, the simulated shares generated by the simulator are $\{\widetilde{c}_i^{(k)}\}_{i \in I}$. The difference between these shares is that the shares $\{c_i^{(k)}\}_{i \in I}$ lie on a random t-degree polynomial, say $f_c^{(k)}(Z)$, with $c^{(k)}$ as the constant term, where $c^{(k)} = a^{(k)} \cdot b^{(k)}$ and $a^{(k)}$ and $b^{(k)}$ are the gate-inputs. On the other hand, the shares $\{\widetilde{c}_i^{(k)}\}_{i \in I}$ lie on a random t-degree polynomial, say $f_0^{(k)}(Z)$, with 0 as the constant term. However, since $|I| = t$, it follows from Lemma 3.7 that the probability distributions of the shares $\{c_i^{(k)}\}_{i \in I}$ will be identical to the probability distribution of the shares $\{\widetilde{c}_i^{(k)}\}_{i \in I}$. The rest of the proof remains the same as in Theorem 5.9. We do not work out the complete formal details to avoid repetition and refer the interested readers to [11]. $\square$

6.4   Securely Computing the $\mathcal{F}_{\mathsf{Mult}}$ Function

We have shown how the parties can securely compute any given function in the $\mathcal{F}_{\mathsf{Mult}}$-hybrid model. We now design protocols that securely compute $\mathcal{F}_{\mathsf{Mult}}$. We note that the threshold required for securely computing $\mathcal{F}_{\mathsf{Mult}}$ is $t < n/2$ and hence the threshold for the BGW protocol Π_{BGW} for securely computing an *arbitrary* function is $t < n/2$. Later, we will prove that the bound $t < n/2$ is necessary for securely computing certain functions, implying the optimality of the threshold. We will discuss two different protocols for securely computing the $\mathcal{F}_{\mathsf{Mult}}$ function: the original BGW protocol [25] and a more efficient protocol due to [75].

6.4.1   The BGW Protocol for Degree-Reduction

Recall that the $\mathcal{F}_{\mathsf{Mult}}$ function is defined as follows:

$$\mathcal{F}_{\mathsf{Mult}}\Big((f_a(\alpha_1), f_b(\alpha_1)), \dots, (f_a(\alpha_n), f_b(\alpha_n))\Big) = \Big(f_{ab}(\alpha_1), \dots, f_{ab}(\alpha_n)\Big),$$

where $f_a(Z)$ and $f_b(Z)$ are *random* polynomials from the sets $\mathcal{P}^{a,t}$ and $\mathcal{P}^{b,t}$ respectively and $f_{ab}(Z)$ is a *random* polynomial from the set $\mathcal{P}^{ab,t}$.[5]

The BGW protocol securely computes the function $\mathcal{F}_{\mathsf{Mult}}$ as follows. Each party P_i first *locally* multiplies its shares $f_a(\alpha_i)$ and $f_b(\alpha_i)$. As discussed earlier, this simple approach is not sufficient for securely computing $\mathcal{F}_{\mathsf{Mult}}$ due to two reasons. First, the resulting vector of values lie on a $2t$-degree polynomial, instead of a t-degree polynomial. Second, the resulting $2t$-degree polynomial is not a random $2t$-degree polynomial with ab as the constant term. In a more detail, let the vector of values $\{f_a(\alpha_i) \cdot f_b(\alpha_i)\}_{i \in \{1,\dots,n\}}$ lie on the $2t$-degree polynomial $K(Z)$, belonging to the set $\mathcal{P}^{ab,2t}$ of $2t$-degree polynomials with ab as the constant term. It is easy to see that $K(0) = f_a(0) \cdot f_b(0) = ab$ and $K(\alpha_i) = f_a(\alpha_i) \cdot f_b(\alpha_i)$. Moreover, $K(Z)$ is not a random polynomial from the set $\mathcal{P}^{ab,2t}$, since $K(Z) = f_a(Z) \cdot f_b(Z)$.

The above two problems are sorted out using a 2-stage approach. The first stage randomizes the underlying $2t$-degree polynomial, which is taken as the input by the second stage to produce a "truncated" random t-degree polynomial. The details follow.

Stage I – Randomizing the $2t$-degree Polynomial In this stage, the parties jointly and securely randomize the vector of values $\{f_a(\alpha_i) \cdot f_b(\alpha_i)\}_{i \in \{1,\dots,n\}}$ and compute a vector of shares, say $(S(\alpha_1), \dots, S(\alpha_n))$, with P_i holding the share $S(\alpha_i)$, where the shares lie on a *random* $2t$-degree polynomial, say $S(Z)$, belonging to the set $\mathcal{P}^{ab,2t}$. Moreover in the process, no additional information is revealed to the adversary.

To achieve the above goal, the parties first jointly and securely generate a *random* polynomial from the set $\mathcal{P}^{0,2t}$, say $R(Z)$, with every P_i holding the share $R(\alpha_i)$ lying on this polynomial. Party P_i can then set $S(\alpha_i)$ to be $R(\alpha_i) + K(\alpha_i)$. Thus, $S(Z) = K(Z) + R(Z)$ and so $S(0) = K(0) + R(0) = ab + 0 = ab$. Moreover, $S(\alpha_i) = K(\alpha_i) + R(\alpha_i)$ will hold. Note that $S(Z)$ will be a *random* $2t$-degree polynomial from $\mathcal{P}^{ab,2t}$, owing to the fact that $R(Z)$ is a random polynomial from $\mathcal{P}^{0,2t}$.

---

[5] We note that while we have presented the $\mathcal{F}_{\mathsf{Mult}}$ function earlier in terms of input and output shares, an equivalent formulation could be in terms of the corresponding input and output sharing-polynomials, as presented here.

To jointly generate the random polynomial $R(Z)$, each party P_i "contributes" by picking a *random* polynomial $R_i(Z)$ from the set $\mathcal{P}^{0,2t}$ and distributing shares lying on this polynomial. The polynomial $R(Z)$ is then set to $R(Z) \stackrel{def}{=} R_1(Z) + \ldots + R_n(Z)$. Since $t < n/2$, the polynomial $R(Z)$ is a well-defined $2t$-degree polynomial. Moreover, $R(Z)$ will be a random polynomial from the set $\mathcal{P}^{0,2t}$, owing to the fact that the $R_i(Z)$ polynomial used by an *honest* party P_i is a random polynomial and there is at least one honest party in $\mathcal{P}$. Hence this stage requires one round of interaction among the parties to distribute the shares lying on the $R_i(Z)$ polynomials and a communication of $\mathcal{O}(n^2)$ field elements.

Stage II – Degree Reduction In this stage, the parties reduce the degree of the polynomial $S(Z)$ from $2t$ to t. That is, they securely transform the vector of shares $(S(\alpha_1), \ldots, S(\alpha_n))$ into vector of shares $(f_{ab}(\alpha_1), \ldots, f_{ab}(\alpha_n))$, with P_i holding the share $f_{ab}(\alpha_i)$.

A closer look into the above requirement reveals that the task can be achieved by securely evaluating the function $\mathcal{F}_{\text{DegRed}}$ (see Sect. 5.5 and Lemma 5.12). Specifically, let $S(Z) = ab + s_1 Z + \ldots + s_t Z^t + s_{t+1} Z^{t+1} + \ldots + s_{2t} Z^{2t}$. Since $S(Z)$ is a random polynomial from the set $\mathcal{P}^{ab,2t}$, each of the coefficients s_i is a *random* element from $\mathbb{F}$. Hence the polynomial $ab + s_1 Z + \ldots + s_t Z^t$ will be a *random* polynomial from the set $\mathcal{P}^{ab,t}$ and can be considered as the polynomial $f_{ab}(Z)$, the output of the function $\mathcal{F}_{\text{Mult}}$.

To achieve the above goal, the parties proceed to securely evaluate the function $\mathcal{F}_{\text{DegRed}}$, where the input of P_i will be the value $S(\alpha_i)$ and at the end of the evaluation, the output of the party P_i will be $f_{ab}(\alpha_i)$. From Lemma 5.12, this stage requires one round of communication and a communication of $\mathcal{O}(n^2)$ field elements.

Based on the above discussion, we now formally present the steps of the protocol Π_{BGWMult} (see Fig. 6.4) to securely compute the function $\mathcal{F}_{\text{Mult}}$. We present the protocol in the $\mathcal{F}_{\text{DegRed}}$-hybrid model, where we assume that parties have secure access to a TTP for ideally computing the functionality $\mathcal{F}_{\text{DegRed}}$ (we refer the TTP as well by $\mathcal{F}_{\text{DegRed}}$). To securely compute the function $\mathcal{F}_{\text{DegRed}}$, we can use Lemma 5.12.

Protocol Π_{BGWMult}

Input: Each party P_i has input $f_a(\alpha_i)$ and $f_b(\alpha_i)$, where $f_a(Z) \in \mathcal{P}^{a,t}$ and $f_b(Z) \in \mathcal{P}^{b,t}$.

– *Stage I – Randomizing $2t$-degree Polynomial*:
  • Randomly pick a polynomial $R_i(Z) \in \mathcal{P}^{0,2t}$ and send the share $R_i(\alpha_j)$ to every party $P_j \in \mathcal{P}$.
  • Compute $S(\alpha_i) = f_a(\alpha_i) \cdot f_b(\alpha_i) + R_1(\alpha_i) + \ldots + R_n(\alpha_i)$, where $R_j(\alpha_i)$ is received from party P_j, for $j = 1, \ldots, n$.
– *Stage II – Degree Reduction*:
  • Invoke the TTP $\mathcal{F}_{\text{DegRed}}$, with input $S(\alpha_i)$.
  • Output the share $\hat{S}(\alpha_i)$ received from $\mathcal{F}_{\text{DegRed}}$.

Fig. 6.4 BGW protocol for securely computing $\mathcal{F}_{\text{Mult}}$ in the $\mathcal{F}_{\text{DegRed}}$-hybrid model. The above steps are executed by each $P_i \in \mathcal{P}$

The security of of the protocol Π_{BGWMult} follows easily from the detailed informal discussion. We leave the formal security proof of the protocol Π_{BGWMult} (stated in Lemma 6.4) as an exercise; the interested readers can refer to [11] for more details.

Lemma 6.4 ([11]) *Let $t < n/2$. Then protocol Π_{BGWMult} is a t-perfectly-secure protocol for $\mathcal{F}_{\text{Mult}}$ in the $\mathcal{F}_{\text{DegRed}}$-hybrid model.*

The protocol requires one round during Stage I and communication of $\mathcal{O}(n^2)$ field elements. During Stage II, one call to $\mathcal{F}_{\text{DegRed}}$ is made.

6.4.2   The GRR Protocol for Degree-Reduction

We now discuss a simpler, direct and more efficient method of securely computing the function $\mathcal{F}_{\text{Mult}}$, called as the Genarro-Rabin-Rabin (GRR) method [75]. On a very high level, the method "replaces" the two stages of the BGW method with a single step. Here, each party P_i generates a *random t-Shamir-sharing* of its "product-share" $f_a(\alpha_i) \cdot f_b(\alpha_i)$. Then a specific (*publicly-known*) linear combination of these shared product-shares leads to a *random t-Shamir-sharing* of the value ab. For a pictorial comparison between the BGW and GRR methods, see Fig. 6.5.

The high-level idea behind the GRR method is as follows: let $k_i = f_a(\alpha_i) \cdot f_b(\alpha_i)$ be the *product-share* available with P_i. These product-shares lie on the $2t$-degree polyno-

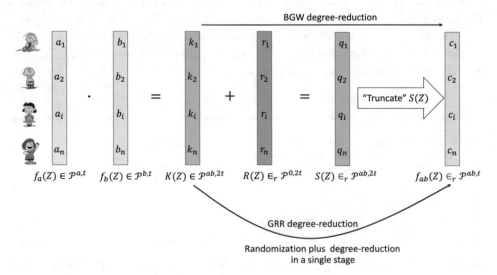

Fig. 6.5 Pictorial comparison of the BGW and GRR methods of securely computing $\mathcal{F}_{\text{Mult}}$. For the BGW method, the transformation from the polynomial $K(Z)$ to $f_{ab}(Z)$ is a 2-stage process, whereas for the GRR method, the transformation requires a single stage. The notation $\in_r$ denotes that the corresponding element is a random element from its underlying domain

mial $K(Z) \in \mathcal{P}^{ab,2t}$, where $K(\alpha_i) = k_i$ and $K(0) = ab$. Since $t < n/2$, it follows from the properties of the Lagrange's interpolation that $K(0)$ is a *publicly-known linear function* of the product-shares $k_1, \ldots, k_n$ (see Sect. 2.2). In a more detail, there are publicly-known *Lagrange's interpolation-coefficients*, say $c_1, \ldots, c_n$, such that the following holds:

$$K(0) = ab = c_1 \cdot k_1 + \ldots + c_n \cdot k_n.$$

Hence from the linearity property of Shamir's secret-sharing, it follows that a t-Shamir-sharing of ab can be computed *non-interactively*, provided parties have access to t-Shamir-sharing of each of the product-shares $k_1, \ldots, k_n$, owing to the following relationship:

$$[ab]_t = c_1 \cdot [k_1]_t + \ldots + c_n \cdot [k_n]_t.$$

To implement the above idea, each party P_i is required to generate a *random t-Shamir-sharing* of its product-share k_i. The randomness used by the parties to generate t-Shamir-sharing of the product-shares will ensure that the resultant t-Shamir-sharing of ab is also random. In a more detail, let $f_{k_i}(Z)$ be the t-degree polynomial, used by P_i to generate a random t-Shamir-sharing of k_i, where $f_{k_i}(Z)$ is a *random* polynomial from the set $\mathcal{P}^{k_i,t}$. Then the final t-Shamir-sharing of ab is generated through the t-degree polynomial $f_{ab}(Z) \stackrel{def}{=} c_1 \cdot f_{k_1}(Z) + \ldots + c_n \cdot f_{k_n}(Z)$, where $f_{ab}(Z)$ is a random polynomial from the set $\mathcal{P}^{ab,t}$, with each coefficient being a random element from $\mathbb{F}$, except the constant term. This follows from the fact that the coefficients of each of the polynomials $f_{k_i}(Z)$ (except their constant terms) are random elements from $\mathbb{F}$.

No additional information is revealed to Adv in the above method, since for each *honest* P_i, adversary receives at most t shares corresponding to the product-share k_i, which are distributed randomly, independent of k_i. The protocol needs one round of interaction for sharing the product-shares, which requires a total communication of $\mathcal{O}(n^2)$ field elements. The resultant protocol called Π_{GRRMult} is formally presented in Fig. 6.7. For a pictorial depiction of the protocol, see Fig. 6.6.

Before we formally prove the security of the protocol Π_{GRRMult}, we demonstrate its working through an example.

Example 6.5 Consider the same setting as in Example 6.2, where $n = 4, t = 1$ and the parties want to securely compute the function $y = f(x_1, x_2, \bot, \bot) = x_1 x_2$. Suppose the parties use the protocol Π_{BGW} to securely compute this function, where the calls to the functionality $\mathcal{F}_{\text{Mult}}$ are replaced by instances of the protocol Π_{GRRMult}. Let $x_1 = 1, x_2 = 4$, and they are secret-shared through sharing-polynomials $1 + 2Z$ and $4 + 0Z$ respectively. Thus the parties obtain shares of x_1 and x_2, as shown in the following table. Once the inputs x_1 and x_2 are secret-shared, the parties proceed to evaluate the gates in the circuit in a shared fashion. In this case, there is only a single gate, which is a multiplication gate with inputs x_1 and x_2.

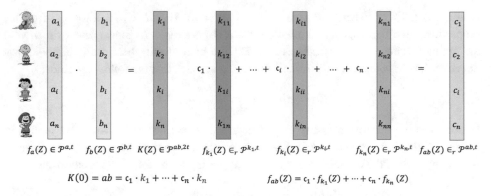

$$K(0) = ab = \mathfrak{c}_1 \cdot k_1 + \cdots + \mathfrak{c}_n \cdot k_n \qquad\qquad f_{ab}(Z) = \mathfrak{c}_1 \cdot f_{k_1}(Z) + \cdots + \mathfrak{c}_n \cdot f_{k_n}(Z)$$

Fig. 6.6 Pictorial depiction of the GRR protocol for computing $\mathcal{F}_{\mathsf{Mult}}$. The private input for each party P_i is its product-share $k_i = a_i b_i$. Each P_i secret-shares its k_i and a secret-sharing of ab is generated as a publicly-known linear combination of these secret-shared product-shares

---

Protocol Π_{GRRMult}

Private Input: The inputs for each P_i are $a_i = f_a(\alpha_i)$ and $b_i = f_b(\alpha_i)$, where $f_a(Z) \in \mathcal{P}^{a,t}$ and $f_b(Z) \in \mathcal{P}^{b,t}$.
Public Input: Lagrange's interpolation-coefficients $\mathfrak{c}_1, \ldots, \mathfrak{c}_n$, such that the following holds:

$$f_a(0) \cdot f_b(0) = \mathfrak{c}_1 \cdot (a_1 b_1) + \ldots + \mathfrak{c}_n \cdot (a_n b_n).$$

– *Secret-sharing the product-shares*:
  • Compute the *product-share* $k_i \stackrel{def}{=} a_i b_i$.
  • Randomly select a polynomial $f_{k_i}(Z) \in \mathcal{P}^{k_i,t}$ and send the share $k_{ij} \stackrel{def}{=} f_{k_i}(\alpha_j)$ to each $P_j \in \mathcal{P}$.
    Let $k_{1i}, \ldots, k_{ni}$ be the shares of the product-shares received from $P_1, \ldots, P_n$ respectively.
– *Computing the output*: Output $c_i \stackrel{def}{=} \mathfrak{c}_1 \cdot k_{1i} + \ldots + \mathfrak{c}_n \cdot k_{ni}$.

Fig. 6.7 GRR protocol for securely computing $\mathcal{F}_{\mathsf{Mult}}$. The above steps are executed by each $P_i \in \mathcal{P}$

To evaluate the multiplication gate using the protocol Π_{GRRMult}, each party randomly secret-shares its product-share. For instance, the product-share k_1 of P_1 will be $(3 \cdot 4)$ mod $5 = 2$, which is secret-shared by P_1. The sharing-polynomials used to secret-share the product-shares and the various shares of the product-shares received by the parties are also shown in the table.

Variable	Value	Sharing-Polynomial	P_1's Share	P_2's Share	P_3's Share	P_4's Share
x_1	1	$1 + 2Z$	3	0	2	4
x_2	4	$4 + 0Z$	4	4	4	4
k_1	2	$2 + 0Z$	2	2	2	2
k_2	0	$0 + 4Z$	4	3	2	1
k_3	3	$3 + 2Z$	0	2	4	1
k_4	1	$1 + 3Z$	4	2	0	3
y	4	$4 + Z$	0	1	2	3

Let us next calculate the Lagrange's interpolation-coefficients. Let $K(Z) = f_{x_1}(Z) f_{x_2}(Z)$ $= (1 + 2Z)(4 + 0Z)$. From Lagrange's interpolation formula, the polynomial $K(Z)$ is uniquely defined through the product-shares, by interpolating the distinct points (α_1, k_1), (α_2, k_2), (α_3, k_3) and (α_4, k_4), which in this case are $(1, 2)$, $(2, 0)$, $(3, 3)$ and $(4, 1)$. More specifically, the following holds:

$$K(Z) = \delta_1(Z) \cdot 2 + \delta_2(Z) \cdot 0 + \delta_3(Z) \cdot 3 + \delta_4(Z) \cdot 1,$$

where the *publicly-known* interpolating-polynomials $\delta_1(Z), \ldots, \delta_4(Z)$ are as follows:

$$\delta_1(Z) = \frac{(Z-2)(Z-3)(Z-4)}{(1-2)(1-3)(1-4)} \qquad \delta_2(Z) = \frac{(Z-1)(Z-3)(Z-4)}{(2-1)(2-3)(2-4)},$$

$$\delta_3(Z) = \frac{(Z-1)(Z-2)(Z-4)}{(3-1)(3-2)(3-4)} \qquad \delta_4(Z) = \frac{(Z-1)(Z-2)(Z-3)}{(4-1)(4-2)(4-3)}$$

Hence the Lagrange's interpolation-coefficients are $c_1 = \delta_1(0) = 4$, $c_2 = \delta_2(0) = 4$, $c_3 = \delta_3(0) = 4$ and $c_4 = \delta_4(0) = 4$.

Next the parties apply the linear combination on their shares of product-shares with respect to the linear-combiners $c_1, \ldots, c_4$, which leads to their respective shares of the output of the multiplication gate, namely y. For instance, the resultant share of y for P_2 will be $(4 \cdot 2 + 4 \cdot 3 + 4 \cdot 2 + 4 \cdot 2) \mod 5 = 1$. These shares are shown in the table above.

Since there are no more gates left in the circuit for evaluation, the parties proceed to the output stage to publicly reconstruct the output y. For this, the parties exchange their respective shares of y and then by applying the recovery function R_{Sha} on the received shares, they reconstruct the polynomial $4 + Z$. The constant term of this polynomial, which is 4, is the final output.

Now as in Example 6.2, we consider the case when P_3 is corrupt during the protocol execution. Then the view of the adversary is shown in bold in the following table, while the values being marked as "?" denote the values unknown to the adversary.

Variable	Value	Sharing-Polynomial	P_1's Share	P_2's Share	P_3's Share	P_4's Share
x_1	?	?	?	?	**2**	?
x_2	?	?	?	?	**4**	?
k_1	?	?	?	?	**2**	?
k_2	?	?	?	?	**2**	?
k_3	**3**	**3 + 2Z**	**0**	**2**	**4**	**1**
k_4	?	?	?	?	**0**	?
y	**4**	**4 + Z**	**0**	**1**	**2**	**3**

Based on its view, the adversary can conclude that (x_1, x_2) can take the values $(1, 4)$, $(2, 2)$, $(3, 3)$ or $(4, 1)$. We now show that *unlike* Example 6.2, the view of the adversary will be consistent with all these possibilities, implying that the adversary does not learn anything additional about x_1 and x_2, except that $x_1, x_2 \in \{0, \ldots, 4\}$ with $x_1 x_2 = 4$. For instance, let adversary make the hypothesis that $x_1 = 4$ and $x_2 = 1$. For x_1 to be 4 with P_3's share being 2, P_1 must have shared x_1 using the 1-degree sharing-polynomial $4 + Z$, passing through the points $(0, 4)$ and $(3, 2)$. Similarly, for x_2 to be 1 with P_3's share being 4, P_2 must have shared x_2 using the 1-degree sharing-polynomial $1 + Z$ passing through the points $(0, 1)$ and $(3, 4)$. This leads to the product-shares $k_1 = 0$, $k_2 = 3$ and $k_4 = 0$ for P_1, P_2 and P_4 respectively, as shown in the following table.

Variable	Value	Sharing-Polynomial	P_1's Share	P_2's Share	P_3's Share	P_4's Share
x_1	4	$4 + Z$	0	1	**2**	3
x_2	1	$1 + Z$	2	3	**4**	0
k_1	0	$0 + 4Z$	4	3	**2**	1
k_2	3	$3 + 3Z$	1	4	**2**	0
k_3	3	$\mathbf{3 + 2Z}$	**0**	**2**	**4**	**1**
k_4	0	$0 + 0Z$	0	0	**0**	0
y	**4**	$\mathbf{4 + Z}$	**0**	**1**	**2**	**3**

Since P_3's share for k_1 is 2, for k_1 to be 0, P_1 must have shared k_1 using the 1-degree polynomial $0 + 4Z$, passing through the points $(0, 0)$ and $(3, 2)$. Using similar logic, for k_2 to be 3 with P_3's share being 2, P_2 must have shared k_2 through the 1-degree polynomial $3 + 3Z$. And for k_4 to be 0 with P_3's share being 0, P_4 must have shared k_4 through the 1-degree polynomial $0 + 0Z$.

Since the Lagrange's interpolation-coefficients are $c_1 = 4$, $c_2 = 4$, $c_3 = 4$ and $c_4 = 4$, as shown before, the above configuration leads to the shares $0, 1, 2$ and 3 and the sharing-polynomial $4 + Z$, corresponding to the function output y. This is consistent with the view of the adversary in the output stage of the protocol.

Similarly, one can verify that adversary's view will be consistent with each of the other possibilities $(1, 4)$, $(2, 2)$ and $(3, 3)$ for (x_1, x_2).

We now formally prove the security of the protocol Π_{GRRMult}.

Lemma 6.6 *Let $t < n/2$. Then protocol Π_{GRRMult} is a t-perfectly-secure protocol for $\mathcal{F}_{\mathsf{Mult}}$. The protocol requires one round and has communication of $\mathcal{O}(n^2)$ field elements.*

Proof The number of communication rounds and communication complexity follow from the protocol inspection. Since $\mathcal{F}_{\mathsf{Mult}}$ is a *randomized* function, we prove the security of the protocol Π_{GRRMult} as per Definition 5.7.[6] Towards that, we present a simulator $\mathcal{S}$ which

---

[6] As discussed in Sect. 5.4.4, one can formulate an n-party *deterministic* function, say $\mathcal{F}'_{\mathsf{Mult}}$, where each party P_i has some additional random inputs (apart from (a_i, b_i)), such that computing $\mathcal{F}_{\mathsf{Mult}}$ is equivalent to computing $\mathcal{F}'_{\mathsf{Mult}}$. This will then allow us to prove that Π_{GRRMult} securely computes $\mathcal{F}'_{\mathsf{Mult}}$ (and hence $\mathcal{F}_{\mathsf{Mult}}$), as per Definition 5.5. We avoid doing this and instead directly prove that Π_{GRRMult} securely computes $\mathcal{F}_{\mathsf{Mult}}$ as per Definition 5.7.

Simulator $\mathcal{S}$

The input of the simulator is the index set $I \subset \{1, \ldots, n\}$ of the corrupt parties where $|I| = t$, the inputs $\{a_i = f_a(\alpha_i), b_i = f_b(\alpha_i)\}_{i \in I}$ of the corrupt parties and their outputs $\{c_i\}_{i \in I}$. The simulator does the following.

- Corresponding to every $i \in I$, compute the product-share $k_i = a_i b_i$, select a random polynomial $\widetilde{f}_{k_i}(Z) \in \mathcal{P}^{k_i, t}$ and compute the shares $\widetilde{k}_{ij} = \widetilde{f}_{k_i}(\alpha_j)$, for $j = 1, \ldots, n$.
- Corresponding to every $j \notin I$ and every $i \in I$, randomly select $\widetilde{k}_{ji}$ from $\mathbb{F}$, subject to the condition that the following holds for every $i \in I$:
$$c_i = \mathfrak{c}_1 \cdot \widetilde{k}_{1i} + \ldots + \mathfrak{c}_n \cdot \widetilde{k}_{ni}.$$
- **Output**: For every $i \in I$, the simulator outputs $((a_i, b_i), c_i, (\widetilde{k}_{i1}, \ldots, \widetilde{k}_{in}), \{\widetilde{k}_{ji}\}_{j \notin I})$ as the simulated view, where (a_i, b_i) denotes P_i's input, c_i denotes P_i's output, $(\widetilde{k}_{i1}, \ldots, \widetilde{k}_{in})$ denotes the shares of P_i's product-share and $\{\widetilde{k}_{ji}\}_{j \notin I}$ denotes the shares of the product-shares received by P_i from the honest parties P_j where $j \notin I$.

Fig. 6.8 Simulator for simulating the view of the corrupt parties in the protocol Π_{GRRMult}

simulates the view of the corrupt parties. For simplicity, we assume that the adversary corrupts exactly t parties during the execution of the protocol Π_{GRRMult}, with $I \subset \{1, \ldots, n\}$ denoting the indices of the corrupt parties.

By inspecting the protocol Π_{GRRMult}, we note that in Π_{GRRMult}, the corrupt parties receive shares of the product-shares of the honest parties. These shares are randomly distributed, subject to the condition that their linear combination (as per the Lagrange's interpolation-coefficients) results in the output-shares of the corrupt parties. Since simulator will be knowing the output-shares of the corrupt parties as part of the simulation, the shares received by the corrupt parties can be easily simulated. More formally, the steps of the simulator are shown in Fig. 6.8.

We next show that the joint distribution of the output of all the parties together with the view of the corrupt parties in Π_{GRRMult}, is distributed identically to the joint distribution of the output of all the parties as computed by the function $\mathcal{F}_{\mathsf{Mult}}$ and the output of the simulator $\mathcal{S}$. Since our goal is to prove the equivalence of two joint distributions, each of which has two components (namely the output of the parties and the view of the corrupt parties), we first show that the outputs of all the parties are identically distributed in both the distributions. Then conditioned on this, we show that the view of the corrupt parties are identically distributed in both the distributions.

The Outputs of the Parties: From the definition of the function $\mathcal{F}_{\mathsf{Mult}}$, the output of $\mathcal{F}_{\mathsf{Mult}}$ is a random polynomial $f_{ab}(Z)$ from the set $\mathcal{P}^{ab, t}$, with P_i holding the share $f_{ab}(\alpha_i)$. We next show that in the protocol Π_{GRRMult}, the shares $\{c_i\}_{i \in \{1, \ldots, n\}}$ also lie on a random polynomial from the set $\mathcal{P}^{ab, t}$, thus proving that the outputs of the parties are identically distributed in both the distributions. From the steps of Π_{GRRMult}, it follows that the shares $\{c_i\}_{i \in \{1, \ldots, n\}}$ lie on the polynomial $f(Z) \stackrel{def}{=} \mathfrak{c}_1 \cdot f_{k_1}(Z) + \ldots + \mathfrak{c}_{n} \cdot f_{k_n}(Z)$, that is $c_i = f(\alpha_i)$ holds. We wish to show that $f(Z)$ is a random polynomial from the set $\mathcal{P}^{ab, t}$.

First, note that $f(Z)$ is a t-degree polynomial, since each of the polynomials $f_{k_1}(Z), \ldots, f_{k_n}(Z)$ is a t-degree polynomial. Next, $f(0) = ab$ holds, since $f_{k_i}(0) = k_i = a_i b_i$ and the condition $ab = c_1 \cdot k_1 + \ldots + c_n \cdot k_n$ holds. Finally, $f(Z)$ is a random t-degree polynomial with all its coefficients except the constant term (which is ab) being random. This follows from the fact that each polynomial $f_{k_i}(Z)$ is a random t-degree polynomial with all its coefficients being random, except the constant term (which is k_i).

Thus the outputs of the parties are identically distributed in both the distributions. Since we are next going to condition on them, let us fix the output t-degree polynomial of $\mathcal{F}_{\text{Mult}}$ and the protocol Π_{GRRMult} to $f(Z)$, which is some *arbitrary* polynomial belonging to the set $\mathcal{P}^{ab,t}$.

The View of the Corrupt Parties: We show that conditioned on the event that the output of the parties during the protocol Π_{GRRMult} and from the computation of the function $\mathcal{F}_{\text{Mult}}$ lie on the polynomial $f(Z) \in \mathcal{P}^{ab,t}$, the view of the corrupt parties in Π_{GRRMult} is identically distributed as the output of the simulator. It is easy to see that the view of the corrupt parties in Π_{GRRMult} is

$$\left\{ \{(a_i, b_i), c_i, (k_{i1}, \ldots, k_{in}), \{k_{ji}\}_{j \notin I}\}_{i \in I} \right\}$$

On the other hand, the view of the corrupt parties as generated by $\mathcal{S}$ is

$$\left\{ \{(a_i, b_i), c_i, (\widetilde{k}_{i1}, \ldots, \widetilde{k}_{in}), \{\widetilde{k}_{ji}\}_{j \notin I}\}_{i \in I} \right\}$$

The components (a_i, b_i) and c_i are identical in both the distributions. Moreover, since we have fixed the output polynomial to $f(Z)$, the condition $c_i = f(\alpha_i)$ holds for each $i \in I$. Next, for every $i \in I$, the probability distribution of the shares $(k_{i1}, \ldots, k_{in})$ and $(\widetilde{k}_{i1}, \ldots, \widetilde{k}_{in})$ are identical. This follows from the fact that the shares $(k_{i1}, \ldots, k_{in})$, as per the protocol, lie on a random t-degree polynomial from the set $\mathcal{P}^{k_i,t}$. On the other hand, the shares $(\widetilde{k}_{i1}, \ldots, \widetilde{k}_{in})$ also lie on a random t-degree polynomial from the set $\mathcal{P}^{k_i,t}$. Finally, consider the shares $\{k_{ji}\}_{j \notin I}\}_{i \in I}$ received by the corrupt parties from the honest parties in the protocol. From the properties of the Shamir's secret-sharing (see Lemma 3.7), these shares are randomly distributed over $\mathbb{F}$, subject to the condition that the following holds for every $i \in I$:

$$c_i = c_1 \cdot k_{1i} + \ldots + c_n \cdot k_{ni}.$$

From the steps of the simulator, the simulated shares $\{\widetilde{k}_{ji}\}_{j \notin I}\}_{i \in I}$ are also uniformly random elements from $\mathbb{F}$, subject to the condition that the following holds for every $i \in I$:

$$c_i = c_1 \cdot \widetilde{k}_{1i} + \ldots + c_n \cdot \widetilde{k}_{ni}.$$

This shows that the probability distribution of the shares $\{k_{ji}\}_{j \notin I}\}_{i \in I}$ and $\{\widetilde{k}_{ji}\}_{j \notin I}\}_{i \in I}$ are identical, thus completing the proof. $\qquad\qquad\square$

6.4.3   The Complexity of the BGW Protocol

In Theorem 6.3 we have shown that protocol Π_{BGW} is perfectly-secure in the $\mathcal{F}_{\mathsf{Mult}}$-hybrid model for *any* $t < n$. Next, we have shown two different perfectly-secure protocols for securely computing the functionality $\mathcal{F}_{\mathsf{Mult}}$, the BGW protocol Π_{BGWMult} and the more efficient GRR protocol Π_{GRRMult}, both of which requires $t < n/2$. While the communication complexity of both these protocols is $\mathcal{O}(n^2)$ field elements, protocol Π_{GRRMult} requires one round less than Π_{BGWMult}. Using any of these protocols for replacing the calls to $\mathcal{F}_{\mathsf{Mult}}$ in the protocol Π_{BGW} leads to a communication complexity of $\mathcal{O}(c_M n^2)$ field elements during the computation stage of the protocol Π_{BGW}, where c_M is the number of multiplication gates in the circuit cir.

   One may think that the number of communication rounds required during the computation stage of Π_{BGW} is also $\mathcal{O}(c_M)$, as there are c_M instances of the protocol Π_{BGWMult} or Π_{GRRMult} corresponding to the c_M multiplication gates and each such instance requires 1 and 2 rounds respectively. However, the multiplication gates in cir *need not* be evaluated *sequentially*. *Independent* multiplication gates can be evaluated in parallel, where two multiplication gates are independent of each other, if the output of one gate does not serve as the input of the other. If there are such independent gates in the circuit, they can be evaluated in parallel in the protocol Π_{BGW}, by invoking the corresponding instances of $\Pi_{\mathsf{BGWMult}}/\Pi_{\mathsf{GRRMult}}$ in parallel.[7] Hence, the number of communication rounds required in the computation stage of the protocol Π_{BGW} will be proportional to the *multiplicative depth D_M* of the circuit cir. Intuitively, D_M denotes the number of layers of multiplication gates in cir, where all the multiplication gates in a given layer are independent. Hence we assume that the gates in cir are arranged in some pre-determined topological ordering with D_M independent layers of multiplication gates. Then during the shared circuit-evaluation, the multiplication gates are evaluated layer by layer, where all the multiplication gates in a layer are evaluated in parallel. Consequently, the number of communication rounds required during the computation stage of Π_{BGW} is $\mathcal{O}(D_M)$.

   Based on the above discussion, we get the following theorem.

Theorem 6.7 (BGW Protocol for Any Deterministic Function) *Let $y = f(x_1, \ldots, x_n)$ be an n-ary deterministic function over $\mathbb{F}$ with P_i holding the private input x_i and where f is represented by an arithmetic circuit cir over $\mathbb{F}$, with c_M number of multiplication gates and a multiplicative-depth of D_M. Moreover, let $t < n/2$. Then there exists a t-perfectly-secure for f. The protocol requires $\mathcal{O}(D_M)$ rounds and communication of $\mathcal{O}(c_M n^2)$ field elements.*

---

[7] Though the security of the protocols Π_{GRRMult} and Π_{BGWMult} is argued in the "stand-alone" setting where a single instance of the protocol is executed, it can be shown that security can be achieved even when multiple instances of these protocols are executed in parallel with any secure protocol; see [11, 42, 110] for more details.

6.5   On the Necessity of the $t < n/2$ Condition

Recall that we have assumed the condition $t < n/2$ to hold, both during the protocol Π_{BGWMult} as well as in the protocol Π_{GRRMult}. We urge the interested readers to find how both these protocols fail, if instead $t \geq n/2$ is assumed. In this section, we show that the condition $t < n/2$ is necessary, by showing that for certain functions perfect security is impossible to achieve with $t \geq n/2$. This allows to conclude that the protocol stated in Theorem 6.7 has *optimal* resilience in the sense that it tolerates the maximum number of allowed corruptions.[8]

In more detail, we first show that there is *no* perfectly-secure protocol that allows two mutually-distrusting parties to securely compute the Boolean AND of their private bits.[9] We will then introduce an interesting proof mechanism called the *player-partitioning* technique and then extend this result to show that there exists no t-perfectly-secure protocol which allows n parties to securely compute the AND of their private bits, if $t \geq n/2$ holds.

6.5.1   Impossibility of Perfectly-Secure 2-Party AND

Let $n = 2$, $\mathcal{P} = \{P_1, P_2\}$ and $t = 1$ and consider the 2-party function $\mathcal{F}_{\text{2AND}}$ defined as follows:

$$\mathcal{F}_{\text{2AND}}(b_1, b_2) = (b_1 \wedge b_2, b_1 \wedge b_2),$$

where P_i has the private input $b_i \in \{0, 1\}$ and the output for both the parties is $b_1 \wedge b_2$. We want to show that there exists *no* 1-perfectly-secure protocol for $\mathcal{F}_{\text{2AND}}$. We stress that we want to rule out the possibility of *any* perfectly-secure protocol for computing $\mathcal{F}_{\text{2AND}}$ and not just the protocol Π_{BGW}.[10] The proof is done by contradiction. That is, we will assume that there exists some *arbitrary* 1-perfectly-secure protocol Π_{2AND} for $\mathcal{F}_{\text{2AND}}$. We will then conclude that there always exists a strategy for a *corrupt* P_1 in the protocol Π_{2AND} which allows it to find out the bit b_2 of the *honest* P_2 if the input b_1 of P_1 is 0. This will be a contradiction because in any perfectly-secure protocol for $\mathcal{F}_{\text{2AND}}$, a corrupt P_1 should not learn the *exact* value of b_2 when the input $b_1 = 0$. This follows from the fact that in this case the output will be 0, irrespective of any input of P_2.

Since the protocol Π_{2AND} is an arbitrary 2-party protocol, before we proceed, we make certain assumptions about the general structure of the protocol Π_{2AND}. Without loss of generality, we assume that there are s *phases* of interaction between P_1 and P_2 in the

---

[8] We caution the readers that Theorem 6.7 does not contradict the result stated in Theorem 5.9, since the protocol $\Pi_{\text{BGW-Linear}}$ is for securely computing only *linear* functions.

[9] Looking ahead, later we will show that this result does not hold, if one settles for *cryptographic* security tolerating *computationally-bounded* adversaries, instead of perfect security.

[10] Nonetheless one can quickly verify that Π_{BGW} is not a 1-perfectly-secure protocol for $\mathcal{F}_{\text{2AND}}$. But we alert that this conclusion does not rule out the possibility of *any other* perfectly-secure protocol for $\mathcal{F}_{\text{2AND}}$.

protocol Π_{2AND}, where in each phase, P_1 first sends some message to P_2 followed by P_2 responding back to P_1. In more detail, protocol Π_{2AND} has the following form:

- Each party P_i has a private bit b_i. Before the protocol execution starts, P_i selects a private random string $r_i \in \{0, 1\}^*$ of some appropriate length, as determined by the protocol. The rest of the actions of both the parties are then *uniquely* determined by these initial choices, based on the steps of the protocol Π_{2AND}.
- The parties then interact for s phases, where for $i = 1, \ldots, s$, party P_1 first sends a message m_{1i} to P_2, which is determined as per the steps of the protocol Π_{2AND}, based on b_1, r_1 and all the messages sent and received by P_1 till now. This is followed by P_2 sending a message m_{2i} to P_1, which is determined as per the steps of the protocol Π_{2AND}, based on b_2, r_2 and all the messages sent and received by P_2 till now.
- At the end of s phases, each party P_i computes the function output y, based on the messages exchanged during the s phases, as determined by the protocol Π_{2AND}.

The *transcript* $\mathcal{T}$ of the protocol execution is defined to be:

$$\mathcal{T} = (m_{11}, m_{21}, \ldots, m_{1s}, m_{2s}, y).$$

For $i = 1, 2$, the view of P_i is defined to be:

$$\mathsf{view}_i = (b_i, r_i, \mathcal{T}).$$

We next prove the following theorem.

Theorem 6.8 *There exists no 1-perfectly-secure protocol for $\mathcal{F}_{2AND}$.*

Proof On contrary, let there exist a 1-perfectly-secure protocol Π_{2AND} for $\mathcal{F}_{2AND}$. We assume that Π_{2AND} involves s phases of interaction as per the structure discussed earlier, where $s \geq 1$. From the definition of 1-perfect-security, protocol Π_{2AND} should satisfy the *correctness* property, implying that the protocol should output $b_1 \wedge b_2$ and *perfect-privacy* property, implying that if P_i is corrupt then view_i depends only upon b_i and y and it should be independent of the input of the other party.

Let $\mathcal{T}(a, b)$ be the set of all transcripts which can be produced during the execution of Π_{2AND} when $b_1 = a$ and $b_2 = b$. That is, a transcript $\mathcal{T} = (m_{11}, m_{21}, \ldots, m_{1s}, m_{2s}, y)$ belongs to the set $\mathcal{T}(a, b)$, if there exist some randomness $r_1, r_2 \in \{0, 1\}^*$, such that the transcript $\mathcal{T}$ is generated if P_1 and P_2 execute the protocol Π_{2AND} with inputs a and b and randomness r_1 and r_2 respectively. We now claim that there exists no transcript common to the set of transcripts $\mathcal{T}(0, 1)$ and $\mathcal{T}(1, 1)$.

Claim 3 *In protocol Π_{2AND}, the condition $\mathcal{T}(0, 1) \cap \mathcal{T}(1, 1) = \emptyset$ holds.*

Proof This simply follows the from the fact that the function output y (which is also a part of transcript) will be different for the case when $(b_1 = 0, b_2 = 1)$ and when $(b_1 = 1, b_2 = 1)$. Namely, in the former case, $y = 0$ and in the latter case, $y = 1$. $\qquad\square$

We next show that the set of transcripts $\mathcal{T}(0, 0)$ and $\mathcal{T}(1, 0)$ are identical.

Claim 4 *In protocol* $\Pi_{2\text{AND}}$, *the condition* $\mathcal{T}(0, 0) = \mathcal{T}(1, 0)$ *holds*.

Proof On the contrary, let there exist a transcript $\mathcal{T}'$, such that $\mathcal{T}' \in \mathcal{T}(0, 0)$, but $\mathcal{T}' \notin \mathcal{T}(1, 0)$. Let during the execution of $\Pi_{2\text{AND}}$, the parties have the inputs $b_1 = 0$ and $b_2 = 0$ and suppose a *corrupt* P_2 sees the transcript $\mathcal{T}'$ being generated during the execution.[11] Then it can conclude that $b_1 \neq 1$, as $\mathcal{T}'$ is not an element of $\mathcal{T}(1, 0)$. This allows the corrupt P_2 to learn the exact value of the bit b_1, which is a breach of the *privacy* of $\Pi_{2\text{AND}}$.[12] Hence the claim holds. $\qquad\square$

Now based on the above two claims, we present an adversarial strategy which *always* allows a *corrupt* P_1 to learn b_2 during the execution of $\Pi_{2\text{AND}}$ when $b_1 = 0$, implying a violation of the *privacy* property of $\Pi_{2\text{AND}}$. So consider an *arbitrary* execution of $\Pi_{2\text{AND}}$ where P_1 is *corrupt* and its input $b_1 = 0$, resulting in the transcript $\mathcal{T} = (m_{11}, m_{21}, \ldots, m_{1s}, m_{2s}, y)$, where $y = 0$. Party P_1 then uses the following strategy to find out the exact value of b_2 by analyzing the transcript $\mathcal{T}$.

- P_1 checks if $\mathcal{T}$ is *consistent* with $b_1 = 1$ as well. Namely, it fixes the messages received from P_2 during the s phases to be $m_{21}, \ldots, m_{2s}$ respectively. Then it checks if there exists some randomness, say $r \in \{0, 1\}^\star$, such that if P_1 executes its steps of the protocol $\Pi_{2\text{AND}}$ with input $b_1 = 1$ and randomness r, it leads to messages $m_{11}, \ldots, m_{1s}$ when P_2's sent messages are $m_{21}, \ldots, m_{2s}$. We note that this step may require an infinite amount of time, since P_1 may have to explore the entire randomness-space, but that is allowed since the perfect-security of $\Pi_{2\text{AND}}$ should hold even against computationally-unbounded adversaries.
- If P_1 finds that $\mathcal{T}$ is consistent with $b_1 = 1$ as well, then it concludes that $b_2 = 0$, else it concludes that $b_2 = 1$.

To complete the proof, we show that using the above strategy, a corrupt P_1 can always find out the bit b_2 by analyzing $\mathcal{T}$. Indeed if $b_2 = 0$, then from Claim 4, the transcript $\mathcal{T}$ belongs to the set $\mathcal{T}(1, 0)$ as well and hence P_1 will find that $\mathcal{T}$ is consistent with $b_1 = 1$. On the other hand, from Claim 3, if $b_2 = 1$, then $\mathcal{T}$ cannot belong to the set $\mathcal{T}(1, 1)$ and hence P_1 will find that $\mathcal{T}$ is *not* consistent with $b_1 = 1$. $\qquad\square$

---

[11] The probability of this event may be negligible, but it is *non-zero*.

[12] Recall that any perfectly-secure protocol for $\mathcal{F}_{2\text{AND}}$ should not reveal the exact value of b_1 to a *corrupt* P_2, if $b_2 = 0$.

We next generalize Theorem 6.8 and show that there exists no t-perfectly-secure protocol for securely computing the n-party AND function for any $t \geq n/2$.

Theorem 6.9 *Let $f : \{0, 1\}^n \rightarrow \{0, 1\}$ be the n-party Boolean AND function where $f(B_1, \ldots, B_n) \overset{def}{=} B_1 \wedge \ldots \wedge B_n$, with each party P_i having the private input-bit B_i. Then there exists no t-perfectly-secure protocol for f, if $t \geq n/2$.*

Proof Let $t = n/2$ and let there exist a t-perfectly-secure protocol, say Π_{nAND}, for f. Since Π_{nAND} is t-perfectly-secure, it has the *correctness* property (implying that the parties obtain the output $B_1 \wedge \ldots \wedge B_n$ at the end of the protocol) and *privacy* property (implying that the view of any t corrupt parties under adversary's control is independent of the input-bits of the remaining t parties). We next show that protocol Π_{nAND} can be used to get a 1-perfectly-secure protocol Π_{2AND}, which allows two mutually-distrusting parties P_A and P_B to securely compute $a \wedge b$, where P_A and P_B have the private input bits a and b respectively. However, from Theorem 6.8 we know that there exists no such protocol Π_{2AND}, which nullifies the existence of Π_{nAND} as well. The derivation of Π_{2AND} from Π_{nAND} is through the *player-partitioning* technique (see Fig. 6.9 for a pictorial depiction).

The steps of the protocol Π_{2AND} are as follows:

– Party P_A plays the role of the parties $P_1, \ldots, P_t$ as per the protocol Π_{nAND} with inputs $B_1 = \ldots = B_t = a$ respectively. While P_B plays the role of the parties $P_{t+1}, \ldots, P_{2t}$ as per the protocol Π_{nAND} with inputs $B_{t+1} = \ldots = B_{2t} = b$ respectively.
– If in the protocol Π_{nAND}, any party $P_i \in \{P_1, \ldots, P_t\}$ needs to send some message m to any party $P_j \in \{P_{t+1}, \ldots, P_{2t}\}$, then in the protocol Π_{2AND}, party P_A sends m to P_B.
– If in the protocol Π_{nAND}, any party $P_k \in \{P_{t+1}, \ldots, P_{2t}\}$ needs to send some message m' to any party $P_\ell \in \{P_1, \ldots, P_t\}$, then in the protocol Π_{2AND}, party P_B sends m' to P_A.
– If in the protocol Π_{nAND}, any party $P_i \in \{P_1, \ldots, P_t\}$ needs to send some message to any party $P_j \in \{P_1, \ldots, P_t\}$, then in the protocol Π_{2AND}, party P_A keeps the message with itself. In the same way, if in the protocol Π_{nAND}, any party $P_i \in \{P_{t+1}, \ldots, P_{2t}\}$ needs

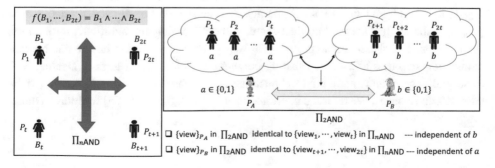

Fig. 6.9 Pictorial depiction of the transformation of Π_{nAND} into Π_{2AND}

to send some message to any party $P_j \in \{P_{t+1}, \ldots, P_{2t}\}$, then in the protocol $\Pi_{2\text{AND}}$, party P_B keeps the message with itself.

- P_A outputs whatever P_1 outputs during the execution of $\Pi_{n\text{AND}}$, while P_B outputs whatever P_{t+1} outputs during the execution of $\Pi_{n\text{AND}}$.

The *correctness* property of $\Pi_{n\text{AND}}$ ensures that in the protocol $\Pi_{2\text{AND}}$, parties P_A and P_B obtain the output $a \wedge b$. In the protocol $\Pi_{2\text{AND}}$, if P_A is *corrupt*, then its view will be the same as the view of the parties $P_1, \ldots, P_t$ in the protocol $\Pi_{n\text{AND}}$. And from the *privacy* property of the protocol $\Pi_{n\text{AND}}$, the view of corrupt $P_1, \ldots, P_t$ will be independent of the inputs $B_{t+1}, \ldots, B_{2t}$. Since $B_{t+1}, \ldots, B_{2t}$ are set to b inside the protocol $\Pi_{2\text{AND}}$, it follows that the view of the corrupt P_A will be independent of b. Using a similar argument, if P_B is *corrupt* in the protocol $\Pi_{2\text{AND}}$, then its view will be the same as the view of the parties $P_{t+1}, \ldots, P_{2t}$ in the protocol $\Pi_{n\text{AND}}$. And from the *privacy* property of the protocol $\Pi_{n\text{AND}}$, it follows that the view of the corrupt P_B will be independent of a. Thus the privacy property of $\Pi_{n\text{AND}}$ translates to the privacy property of $\Pi_{2\text{AND}}$.   □

6.6   Dealing with Malicious Adversaries

We conclude this chapter with the issues that may occur if the protocol Π_{BGW} (and the associated sub-protocols Π_{BGWMult} and Π_{GRRMult}) are executed in the presence of a malicious adversary. The issues that we mention in the previous chapter for $\Pi_{\text{BGW-Linear}}$ in the face of a malicious adversary hold for Π_{BGW} as well: i.e. the corrupt parties *not* sharing their inputs using a t-degree sharing-polynomial and corrupt parties producing incorrect shares during the output stage. As mentioned, these can be taken care of by using a maliciously-secure secret-sharing scheme, aka, VSS [44, 52].

However, VSS alone is *not* sufficient to deal with malicious adversaries during the evaluation of multiplication gates (for securely computing $\mathcal{F}_{\text{Mult}}$) in the computation stage. For instance, in the protocol Π_{GRRMult}, a maliciously-corrupt party *may not* participate with the correct product-share and instead secret-share an arbitrary value as its product share. This will result in an incorrect evaluation of multiplication gates, thus breaching correctness of Π_{BGW}. So, apart from using a VSS, the parties also need to additionally verify whether each party has shared the "correct" product-share, without learning any additional information about the product-shares. In the protocol Π_{BGWMult}, the parties need to ensure that the randomization step uses a $2t$-degree sharing-polynomial with constant term 0. Dealing with these challenges require additional technicalities and discussing them is out of scope of the current lecture series. We refer the interested readers to [2, 8, 11, 25, 75] for more details.

Perfectly-Secure MPC in the Pre-processing Model 7

In this chapter, we discuss how one can improve the efficiency of the BGW protocol in the pre-processing model, where parties are allowed to generate correlated randomness in advance, independent of the circuit-evaluation. We discuss two classes of protocols in the pre-processing model, one based on Beaver's random multiplication-triples and another based on random double-shared values. We conclude the chapter by discussing the issues that the presented protocols may have while facing a malicious adversary.

7.1   MPC in the Pre-processing Model

Recall that in the BGW MPC protocol (protocol Π_{BGW} in the previous chapter), interaction happens due to three reasons:

- for secret-sharing the function-inputs during the *input* stage,
- for reconstructing the secret-shared function-output during the *output* stage,
- for the evaluation of each multiplication gate in the *computation* stage (to solve the degree-reduction problem, by securely computing an instance of $\mathcal{F}_{\mathsf{Mult}}$ functionality).

The complexity of any *generic* (perfectly-secure) MPC protocol is typically measured in terms of the amortized complexity for securely evaluating the multiplication gates in the circuit to be evaluated. The amortized complexity is derived under the assumption that the circuit cir representing the function f is large enough, so that the complexity of the input and output stage is subsumed by the complexity for evaluating the multiplication gates in cir.

A powerful paradigm used to improve the complexity of MPC protocols is to design protocols in the *correlated randomness* model, also popularly known as the *pre-processing* model. The paradigm was pioneered in the seminal work of Beaver [16] and is

© The Author(s), under exclusive license to Springer Nature Switzerland AG 2022   91
A. Choudhury and A. Patra, *Secure Multi-Party Computation Against Passive Adversaries*,
Synthesis Lectures on Distributed Computing Theory,
https://doi.org/10.1007/978-3-031-12164-7_7

widely-used for designing MPC protocols. In this paradigm, an MPC protocol is divided into two *independent* phases. The first phase is a *function-independent, pre-processing* phase which is independent of cir; this phase is often called as the *offline* phase. The second phase follows the first phase, which is a *function-dependent, circuit-evaluation* phase, and depends upon cir; this phase is often called as the *online* phase (more on these terminologies later).

In the pre-processing phase, the parties jointly and securely generate some secret-shared "correlated randomness", which can be viewed as some form of "raw data".[1] Later, in the circuit-evaluation phase, the raw data is used for the evaluation of cir. The pre-processing phase helps to pre-pone all "expensive" operations to the pre-processing phase, allowing for a more efficient and faster shared circuit-evaluation.

The above approach makes a lot of sense when the *same* set of n parties would like to securely compute the *same* function f (and hence evaluate the *same* cir) over multiple sets of inputs over a period of time. Specifically, suppose the parties $\mathcal{P} = \{P_1, \ldots, P_n\}$ would like to compute the same function f, say k number of times. Since the pre-processing phase is *independent* of the function f (and the inputs of the parties for f), the correlated randomness for all the k instances of the circuit-evaluation can be generated in *parallel* in advance during the pre-processing phase. Later, as and when the function inputs are available with the parties, they can consume the data generated during the pre-processing phase and quickly evaluate the circuit.

The repeated function evaluation is typical in a privacy-preserving *Machine-Learning as a service* (MLaaS) application, where a group of mutually-distrusting cloud service-providers jointly provide ML as a service. On a very high level, the service-providers hold a secret-shared training-model. To query the model, a client secret-shares its query amongst the service-providers and gets the results of the query with respect to the trained model. This process ensures that the client does not learn anything additional about the model and similarly, the service-providers does not learn anything about the query. Note that the client *does not* need to run the computation to get the result of the query, instead the entire computation is performed by the service-providers themselves in a secret-shared fashion. Here, thousands of clients may be interested to get the results of their respective queries either at the same time or at different point of time. Clearly, we need a super-fast MPC protocol to generate the results of the queries. Since the *same* set of service-providers are involved in running the computation of inference (but over different inputs or queries), it is possible to pre-compute a lot of correlated randomness in advance to allow for a super-fast real-time processing of the queries as and when they arrive.

Another motivation for MPC in the pre-processing model is that the parties can deploy a *trusted third-party* (TTP), say a trusted cloud service-provider, to execute the pre-processing phase, for generating the required shared pre-processing data. In fact, later in this chapter we show that if such a possibility is available, then it can significantly help to improve the resilience of generic MPC protocols. One may argue that if the deployability of a TTP is possible then why the parties cannot deploy the TTP to compute the function f. We stress

---

[1] There can be various forms of correlated randomness and in this chapter, we discuss two of them.

that we are envisioning a scenario where the TTP (if available) will be deployed only during the pre-processing phase and the actual circuit-evaluation will be carried out by the parties themselves.

On the Terms Offline and Online Phase: Some texts use the terms offline and online phase for the pre-processing and the circuit-evaluation phase respectively. The term "offline" signifies that the parties execute this phase when they are "free" and not involved in the shared circuit-evaluation. It also signifies that if a TTP is deployed to run the pre-processing phase, then the parties need not be running the protocol and hence they can be considered as being offline. On the other hand, the term "online" signifies that the parties are actually running the corresponding protocol code to do the shared circuit-evaluation. We prefer to use the terms pre-processing and circuit-evaluation phase, which will be retained for the rest of the discussion.

Before we proceed, we note that if an MPC protocol is designed in the pre-processing model, then its overall complexity is stated separately for the pre-processing phase and the circuit-evaluation phase.

7.2   Perfectly-Secure MPC Using Beaver's Multiplication-Triples

In this section, we recast the BGW MPC protocol in the pre-processing model, where the pre-processing phase securely generates t-Shamir-shared random *multiplication-triples* (also called as Beaver's multiplication-triples). In more detail, a triplet $(a, b, c) \in \mathbb{F}^3$ is called a *multiplication-triple*, if $c = ab$ holds. The multiplication-triple is called a *random* multiplication-triple, provided a, b and c are randomly distributed over $\mathbb{F}$, subject to the constraint that $c = ab$ holds. Let c_M be the number of multiplication gates in the circuit cir. Then the pre-processing phase generates c_M number of t-Shamir-shared random multiplication-triples, with adversary learning at most t shares corresponding to each multiplication-triple. Hence, the view of the adversary will be independent of the underlying multiplication-triples.

The requirements of the pre-processing phase is abstracted by a function $\mathcal{F}_{\text{Triple}}$, which generates random t-Shamir-sharing of c_M random multiplication-triples $\{(a^{(\ell)}, b^{(\ell)}, c^{(\ell)})\}_{\ell=1,\ldots,c_M}$ and distributes the shares to the respective parties. More formally, the function $\mathcal{F}_{\text{Triple}}$ is as follows:

$$\mathcal{F}_{\text{Triple}}(\lambda, \ldots, \lambda) = (O_1, \ldots, O_n),$$

where λ denotes the empty string and where for $i = 1, \ldots, n$,

$$O_i = \left(\{(f_{a^{(\ell)}}(\alpha_i), f_{b^{(\ell)}}(\alpha_i), f_{c^{(\ell)}}(\alpha_i))\}_{\ell=1,\ldots,c_M} \right).$$

Here for $\ell = 1, \ldots, c_M$, the polynomials $f_{a^{(\ell)}}(Z)$, $f_{b^{(\ell)}}(Z)$ and $f_{c^{(\ell)}}(Z)$ are random polynomials from the set of t-degree polynomials $\mathcal{P}^{a^{(\ell)},t}$, $\mathcal{P}^{b^{(\ell)},t}$ and $\mathcal{P}^{c^{(\ell)},t}$ respectively, where $c^{(\ell)} = a^{(\ell)} b^{(\ell)}$.

The idea behind the shared circuit-evaluation using the shared multiplication-triples is as follows. Consider a multiplication gate in the circuit cir, with inputs x, y and output z, where $z = xy$. Let the inputs x and y be t-Shamir-shared among the parties and the goal is to securely compute a random t-Shamir-sharing of z. Let (a, b, c) be a random multiplication-triple from the pre-processing phase, which is randomly t-Shamir-shared among the parties. The crucial observation used to evaluate the multiplication gate using the multiplication-triple is that the following relationship holds:

$$
\begin{aligned}
z &= xy \\
&= (x - a + a)(y - b + b) \\
&= (x - a)(y - b) + (x - a)b + (y - b)a + ab \\
&= de + db + ea + c, \quad \text{where } d \stackrel{def}{=} (x - a) \quad \text{and} \quad e \stackrel{def}{=} (y - b)
\end{aligned}
$$

The observation that z can be expressed as a *publicly-known linear* function of the multiplication-triple (a, b, c), provided d and e are known publicly, constitutes the crux of the Beaver's method. Consequently, provided d and e are known publicly, the linearity of t-Shamir-sharing allows the parties to *non-interactively* compute a t-Shamir-sharing of z from t-Shamir-sharing of (a, b, c) as follows :

$$
[z]_t = de + d[b]_t + e[a]_t + [c]_t.
$$

To implement the above idea, the parties first *non-interactively* compute a t-Shamir-sharing of d and e, since the following hold:

$$
[d]_t = [x]_t - [a]_t, \quad [e]_t = [y]_t - [b]_t.
$$

The parties then *publicly* reconstruct the secret-shared values d and e by exchanging the shares of d and e with each other. The only communication involved among the parties during the evaluation of the multiplication gate is for reconstructing the values d and e. We observe that the public values d and e do not give out any additional information about the secret-shared gate-inputs x and y, owing to the random multiplication-triple (a, b, c). The values d and e can be interpreted as the *one-time pad* (OTP) encryptions [102] of gate-inputs x and y respectively, with respect to the pads a and b. Since the pads are uniformly random for the adversary, learning d and e does not add any new information to the view of the adversary. The resultant t-Shamir-sharing of z generated by the above method will be a *random* t-Shamir-sharing (i.e., the corresponding t-degree sharing-polynomial will be a random polynomial from the set $\mathcal{P}^{z,t}$). This follows from the fact that it is a linear combination of the random t-Shamir-sharing of a, b and c. For a pictorial depiction of the Beaver's method for evaluating multiplication gates, see Fig. 7.1.

We note that in the Beaver's method to evaluate the multiplication-gates in the circuit, an *independent* and uniformly random multiplication-triple is required for evaluating each

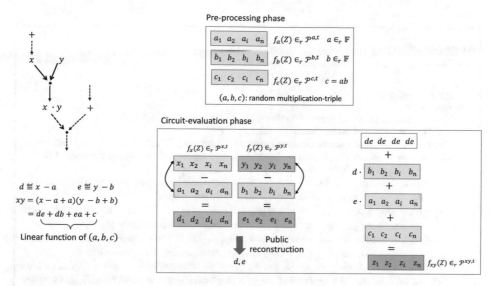

Fig. 7.1 Pictorial depiction of evaluating a multiplication gate in the circuit, using a pre-processed Beaver's random multiplication-triple

multiplication-gate in the circuit cir. For example, the shared triple (a, b, c) can not be used for evaluating two multiplication gates with inputs x, y and x', y'. Such double-usage allows the adversary to learn $d \stackrel{def}{=} (x - a)$ and $d' \stackrel{def}{=} (x' - a)$ and so $x - x'$ via $d - d'$, leading to breaching the privacy (i.e., the view of the adversary will no longer be independent of x and x').

We now formally present the t-perfectly-secure protocol Π_{Beaver} (see Fig. 7.2), based on the BGW approach of shared circuit-evaluation, in the pre-processing model. The protocol is presented in the $\mathcal{F}_{\text{Triple}}$-hybrid model, assuming that the parties have a secure access to a TTP, who ideally computes the function $\mathcal{F}_{\text{Triple}}$ for the parties (for simplicity, the TTP itself is referred by $\mathcal{F}_{\text{Triple}}$). In the protocol, we use the index ℓ to refer to the ℓth multiplication gate in cir, where $\ell \in \{1, \ldots, c_M\}$. To evaluate this multiplication gate, the parties use the ℓth shared multiplication-triple generated in the pre-processing phase. Recall that during the evaluation of each multiplication gate, the parties need to *publicly* reconstruct two secret-shared values. Naively the parties can exchange their shares with each other to reconstruct these values. This process will require a communication complexity of $\mathcal{O}(n^2)$ per multiplication gate. A more efficient way of reconstruction goes as follows. We first let a *designated* party, say P_1, to reconstruct these values, who can then relay the reconstructed values to every other party, which leads to an overall communication complexity of $\mathcal{O}(n)$ per multiplication gate. We follow the latter approach in the protocol Π_{Beaver}.

The properties of the protocol Π_{Beaver} are stated in Lemma 7.1.

Protocol Π_{Beaver}

The Pre-processing Phase

 – Invoke the TTP $\mathcal{F}_{\text{Triple}}$ with input λ. In response, let $\{(a_i^{(\ell)}, b_i^{(\ell)}, c_i^{(\ell)})\}_{\ell \in 1,\ldots,c_M}$ be the shares received.

The Circuit-evaluation Phase
 – *Input Stage*:
   • On having the input x_i, compute the shares $(x_{i1}, \ldots, x_{in}) \leftarrow \mathsf{G}_{\text{Sha}}(x_i)$.
   • For $j = 1, \ldots, n$, send the share x_{ij} to party $P_j \in \mathcal{P}$.
   For $k = 1, \ldots, n$, let x_{ki} denote the share, received from the party $P_k \in \mathcal{P}$ at the end of the input stage.
 – *Computation Stage*: Let $G_1, \ldots, G_m$ be a publicly-known topological ordering of the gates of cir. For $k = 1, \ldots, m$, do the following for gate G_k:
   • If G_k *is an addition gate*: Let $\alpha_i^{(k)}$ and $\beta_i^{(k)}$ be the shares held by P_i, corresponding to the gate-inputs. Set $\alpha_i^{(k)} + \beta_i^{(k)}$ to be the share, corresponding to the gate-output.
   • If G_k *is a multiplication-with-a-constant gate with constant* c: Let $\alpha_i^{(k)}$ be the share held by P_i, corresponding to the gate-input. Set $c \cdot \alpha_i^{(k)}$ to be the share, corresponding to the gate-output.
   • If G_k *is an addition-with-a-constant gate with constant* c: Let $\alpha_i^{(k)}$ be the share held by P_i, corresponding to the gate-input. Set $c + \alpha_i^{(k)}$ to be the share, corresponding to the gate-output.
   • If G_k *is a multiplication gate*: Let G_k be the ℓth multiplication gate in cir where $\ell \in \{1, \ldots, c_M\}$ and let $(a_i^{(\ell)}, b_i^{(\ell)}, c_i^{(\ell)})$ be the shares of the ℓth multiplication-triple, received from $\mathcal{F}_{\text{Triple}}$. Moreover, let $\alpha_i^{(k)}$ and $\beta_i^{(k)}$ be the shares held by P_i, corresponding to the gate-inputs of G_k. Then do the following:
     1. Compute $d_i^{(\ell)} = \alpha_i^{(k)} - a_i^{(\ell)}$.   % Parties collectively compute $[d^{(\ell)}]_t = [\alpha^{(k)}]_t - [a^{(\ell)}]_t$.
     2. Compute $e_i^{(\ell)} = \beta_i^{(k)} - b_i^{(\ell)}$.   % Parties collectively compute $[e^{(\ell)}]_t = [\beta^{(k)}]_t - [b^{(\ell)}]_t$.
     3. Do the following to publicly reconstruct $d^{(\ell)}$ and $e^{(\ell)}$:
       – Send the shares $d_i^{(\ell)}$ and $e_i^{(\ell)}$ *only* to party P_1.
       – (If $P_i = P_1$): Upon receiving the shares $d_j^{(\ell)}, e_j^{(\ell)}$ from $P_j \in \mathcal{P}$, compute $d^{(\ell)} = \mathsf{R}_{\text{Sha}}(\mathcal{P}, \{d_1^{(\ell)}, \ldots, d_n^{(\ell)}\})$ and $e^{(\ell)} = \mathsf{R}_{\text{Sha}}(\mathcal{P}, \{e_1^{(\ell)}, \ldots, e_n^{(\ell)}\})$. Then send $d^{(\ell)}$ and $e^{(\ell)}$ to every $P_j \in \mathcal{P}$.
     4. Set $\gamma_i^{(k)} \stackrel{def}{=} d^{(\ell)} e^{(\ell)} + d^{(\ell)} b_i^{(\ell)} + e^{(\ell)} a_i^{(\ell)} + c_i^{(\ell)}$ to be the share, corresponding to the gate-output.   % Parties collectively compute $[\gamma^{(k)}]_t = d^{(\ell)} e^{(\ell)} + d^{(\ell)} [b^{(\ell)}]_t + e^{(\ell)} [a^{(\ell)}]_t + [c^{(\ell)}]_t$.

 – *Output Stage*:
   • Send the share y_i to every party in $\mathcal{P}$.
   • Upon receiving the shares $y_1, \ldots, y_n$, output $y = \mathsf{R}_{\text{Sha}}(\mathcal{P}, \{y_1, \ldots, y_n\})$.

Fig. 7.2 A perfectly-secure protocol in pre-processing model for any deterministic function in the $\mathcal{F}_{\text{Triple}}$-hybrid model. The above steps are executed by each $P_i \in \mathcal{P}$

Lemma 7.1 *Let $y = f(x_1, \ldots, x_n)$ be an n-ary deterministic function over $\mathbb{F}$ with P_i holding the private input x_i. Moreover, let $t < n$. Then protocol Π_{Beaver} is t-perfectly-secure for f in the $\mathcal{F}_{\text{Triple}}$-hybrid model.*

The protocol requires one call to $\mathcal{F}_{\text{Triple}}$ during the pre-processing phase. Let c_M and D_M denote the number of multiplication gates and multiplicative depth of the circuit cir representing f respectively. Then in the circuit-evaluation phase, the protocol requires $\mathcal{O}(D_M)$ communication rounds and communication of $\mathcal{O}(c_M n)$ field elements.

Proof The round and communication complexity follow easily from the protocol discussion and formal steps. The *correctness* follows from the fact that $\mathcal{F}_{\mathsf{Triple}}$ generates t-Shamir-sharing of multiplication-triples, which ensures that the parties hold a correct t-Shamir-sharing of the output of multiplication gates.

During the pre-processing phase, the adversary receives from $\mathcal{F}_{\mathsf{Triple}}$ at most t shares, corresponding to t-Shamir-sharing of random multiplication-triples. From the properties of Shamir-sharing, these shares are randomly distributed and hence can be easily simulated, by setting the simulated multiplication-triples to arbitrary multiplication-triples, say $(0, 0, 0)$. During the evaluation of multiplication gates, the adversary learns the complete vector of shares corresponding to the masked gate-inputs. However, since these masked gate-inputs are randomly distributed over $\mathbb{F}$ (as the corresponding masks are randomly distributed), the vector of shares learnt by the adversary in the protocol Π_{Beaver} can be also easily simulated, by setting them to uniformly random values (subject to the condition that they are consistent with the shares of the corrupt parties). The formal steps of the simulator are shown in Fig. 7.3. For simplicity, we assume that the adversary Adv corrupts exactly t parties in the protocol Π_{Beaver}.

To complete the proof, we need to show that the view of Adv during the execution of the protocol Π_{Beaver} is distributed identically to the simulated view generated by $\mathcal{S}$. This can be done similarly as done in the proofs of Theorems 5.9 and 6.3. We leave the details as an exercise for the interested readers.   □

7.2.1 Securely Computing the Functionality $\mathcal{F}_{\mathsf{Triple}}$

Protocol Π_{Beaver} is in the $\mathcal{F}_{\mathsf{Triple}}$-hybrid model. To execute the protocol Π_{Beaver} in the *plain* model, we need a protocol to securely compute the function $\mathcal{F}_{\mathsf{Triple}}$. In this section, we present a protocol Π_{Triple} for the same purpose, assuming $t < n/2$ holds.[2] Recall that the functionality $\mathcal{F}_{\mathsf{Triple}}$ is defined as follows:

$$\mathcal{F}_{\mathsf{Triple}}(\lambda, \ldots, \lambda) = (O_1, \ldots, O_n),$$

where for $i = 1, \ldots, n$,

$$O_i = \left(\{(a_i^{(\ell)}, b_i^{(\ell)}, c_i^{(\ell)})\}_{\ell=1,\ldots,c_M} \right).$$

Here for $\ell = 1, \ldots, c_M$ and $i = 1, \ldots, n$, the conditions $a_i^{(\ell)} = f_{a^{(\ell)}}(\alpha_i)$, $b_i^{(\ell)} = f_{b^{(\ell)}}(\alpha_i)$ and $c_i^{(\ell)} = f_{c^{(\ell)}}(\alpha_i)$ hold, where $f_{a^{(\ell)}}(Z)$, $f_{b^{(\ell)}}(Z)$ and $f_{c^{(\ell)}}(Z)$ are random polynomials from the set $\mathcal{P}^{a^{(\ell)},t}$, $\mathcal{P}^{b^{(\ell)},t}$ and $\mathcal{P}^{c^{(\ell)},t}$ respectively, such that $c^{(\ell)} = a^{(\ell)}b^{(\ell)}$ holds.

---

[2] Recall that $t < n/2$ is the *optimal* threshold for any t-perfectly-secure protocol for arbitrary functions.

Simulator $\mathcal{S}$

The input of the simulator is the index set $I \subset \{1, \ldots, n\}$ of the corrupt parties where $|I| = t$, the inputs $\{x_i\}_{i \in I}$ of the corrupt parties and the function output y.

- *Simulating the Pre-processing Phase*:
  - For $\ell = 1, \ldots, c_M$, the simulator sets $(\widetilde{a}^{(\ell)}, \widetilde{b}^{(\ell)}, \widetilde{c}^{(\ell)}) = (0, 0, 0)$ and generates the shares $(\widetilde{a}_1^{(\ell)}, \ldots, \widetilde{a}_n^{(\ell)}) \leftarrow \mathsf{G}_{\mathsf{Sha}}(\widetilde{a}^{(\ell)})$, $(\widetilde{b}_1^{(\ell)}, \ldots, \widetilde{b}_n^{(\ell)}) \leftarrow \mathsf{G}_{\mathsf{Sha}}(\widetilde{b}^{(\ell)})$ and $(\widetilde{c}_1^{(\ell)}, \ldots, \widetilde{c}_n^{(\ell)}) \leftarrow \mathsf{G}_{\mathsf{Sha}}(\widetilde{c}^{(\ell)})$.
  - The simulator then sets $\{(\widetilde{a}_i^{(\ell)}, \widetilde{b}_i^{(\ell)}, \widetilde{c}_i^{(\ell)})\}_{\ell \in 1, \ldots, c_M, i \in I}$ to be the view of the adversary for the pre-processing phase.
- *Simulating the Input Stage*: The steps remain the same as in Fig 5.3.
- *Simulating the Computation Stage*: For every gate $G_k \in \{G_1, \ldots, G_m\}$, the simulator does the following:
  - If G_k *is an addition gate*: Let $\{\widetilde{\alpha}_i^{(k)}\}_{i \in I}$ and $\{\widetilde{\beta}_i^{(k)}\}_{i \in I}$ be the shares of the corrupt parties, corresponding to the gate-inputs. For every $i \in I$, set $\widetilde{\alpha}_i^{(k)} + \widetilde{\beta}_i^{(k)}$ to be the share of P_i, corresponding to the gate-output and add it to the view of Adv.
  - If G_k *is a multiplication-with-a-constant gate with constant* c: Let $\{\widetilde{\alpha}_i^{(k)}\}_{i \in I}$ be the shares of the corrupt parties, corresponding to the gate-input. For every $i \in I$, set $c \cdot \widetilde{\alpha}_i^{(k)}$ to be the share of P_i, corresponding to the gate-output and add it to the view of Adv.
  - If G_k *is an addition-with-a-constant gate with constant* c: Let $\{\widetilde{\alpha}_i^{(k)}\}_{i \in I}$ be the shares of the corrupt parties, corresponding to the gate-input. For every $i \in I$, set $c + \widetilde{\alpha}_i^{(k)}$ to be the share of P_i, corresponding to the gate-output and add it to the view of Adv.
  - If G_k *is a multiplication gate*: Let G_k be the ℓth multiplication gate in cir where $\ell \in \{1, \ldots, c_M\}$. Let $\{\widetilde{\alpha}_i^{(k)}\}_{i \in I}$ and $\{\widetilde{\beta}_i^{(k)}\}_{i \in I}$ be the shares of the corrupt parties, corresponding to the gate-inputs. Moreover, let $\{(\widetilde{a}_i^{(\ell)}, \widetilde{b}_i^{(\ell)}, \widetilde{c}_i^{(\ell)})\}_{i \in \{1, \ldots, n\}}$ be the shares of the ℓth multiplication-triple, generated by the simulator.
    - For every $i \in I$, compute $\widetilde{\alpha}_i^{(k)} - \widetilde{a}_i^{(\ell)}$ and $\widetilde{\beta}_i^{(k)} - \widetilde{b}_i^{(\ell)}$.
    - Randomly pick $\widetilde{d}^{(\ell)}$ and $\widetilde{e}^{(\ell)}$ from $\mathbb{F}$. Then randomly select t-degree polynomials $f_{\widetilde{d}^{(\ell)}}(Z) \in \mathcal{P}^{\widetilde{d}^{(\ell)}, t}$ and $f_{\widetilde{e}^{(\ell)}}(Z) \in \mathcal{P}^{\widetilde{e}^{(\ell)}, t}$, subject to the constraints that $f_{\widetilde{d}^{(\ell)}}(\alpha_i) = (\widetilde{\alpha}_i^{(k)} - \widetilde{a}_i^{(\ell)})$ and $f_{\widetilde{e}^{(\ell)}}(\alpha_i) = (\widetilde{\beta}_i^{(k)} - \widetilde{b}_i^{(\ell)})$ hold for every $i \in I$.
    - Corresponding to every $i \in I$, compute $\widetilde{\gamma}_i^{(k)} \overset{def}{=} \widetilde{d}^{(\ell)} \widetilde{e}^{(\ell)} + \widetilde{d}^{(\ell)} \widetilde{b}_i^{(\ell)} + \widetilde{e}^{(\ell)} \widetilde{a}_i^{(\ell)} + \widetilde{c}_i^{(\ell)}$
    - If $1 \in I$ (i.e., if P_1 is under the control of Adv), then add $\{(f_{\widetilde{d}^{(\ell)}}(\alpha_1), \ldots, f_{\widetilde{d}^{(\ell)}}(\alpha_n)), (f_{\widetilde{e}^{(\ell)}}(\alpha_1), \ldots, f_{\widetilde{e}^{(\ell)}}(\alpha_n)), \widetilde{\gamma}_1^{(k)}\}$ to the view of P_1.
    - For every $i \in I$, add $(f_{\widetilde{d}^{(\ell)}}(\alpha_i), f_{\widetilde{e}^{(\ell)}}(\alpha_i), \widetilde{d}^{(\ell)}, \widetilde{e}^{(\ell)}, \widetilde{\gamma}_i^{(k)})$ to the view of P_i.
- *Simulating the Output Stage*: The steps remain the same as in Fig 5.3.

Fig. 7.3 Simulator for simulating the view of the corrupt parties in the protocol Π_{Beaver}

Protocol Π_{Triple} follows a *two-stage* approach for securely generating the t-Shamir-shared random multiplication-triples. In the *first* stage, the parties jointly and securely generate random t-Shamir-sharing of the first two components of the required multiplication-triples, namely $\{a^{(\ell)}\}_{\ell=1, \ldots, c_M}$ and $\{b^{(\ell)}\}_{\ell=1, \ldots, c_M}$. In the *second* stage, the parties securely generate a random t-Shamir-sharing of the third component of the multiplication-triples, namely $\{c^{(\ell)}\}_{\ell=1, \ldots, c_M}$.

For the first stage, to generate a random t-Shamir-sharing of a pair of random values (a, b), each party "contributes" by generating a random t-Shamir-sharing of a pair of uniformly random values. The sum of all these t-Shamir-shared pairs is then taken as the resultant t-Shamir-shared (a, b). This resultant pair is both random and unknown to the adversary, due to the contributions from the honest parties in the summation. Since the goal is to

---

Protocol Π_{Triple}

- *Stage I*: Generating random t-Shamir-shared pairs:
  - For $\ell = 1, \ldots, c_M$, randomly pick $(a^{(i,\ell)}, b^{(i,\ell)}) \in \mathbb{F}^2$. Compute $(a_1^{(i,\ell)}, \ldots, a_n^{(i,\ell)}) \leftarrow \mathsf{G}_{\mathsf{Sha}}(a^{(i,\ell)})$ and $(b_1^{(i,\ell)}, \ldots, b_n^{(i,\ell)}) \leftarrow \mathsf{G}_{\mathsf{Sha}}(b^{(i,\ell)})$.
  - For $j = 1, \ldots, n$, send the shares $\{(a_j^{(i,\ell)}, b_j^{(i,\ell)})\}_{\ell=1,\ldots,c_M}$ to party P_j.
  - For $\ell = 1, \ldots, c_M$, compute $a_i^{(\ell)} = \sum\limits_{j=1}^{j=n} a_i^{(j,\ell)}$ and $b_i^{(\ell)} = \sum\limits_{j=1}^{j=n} b_i^{(j,\ell)}$. Here $a_i^{(j,\ell)}, b_i^{(j,\ell)}$ denote the shares received from P_j.   % Parties compute $[a^{(\ell)}]_t = \sum\limits_{j=1}^{j=n} [a^{(j,\ell)}]_t$ and $[b^{(\ell)}]_t = \sum\limits_{j=1}^{j=n} [b^{(j,\ell)}]_t$.
- *Stage II*: Computing random t-Shamir-sharing of the product of the pairs:
  - For $\ell = 1, \ldots, c_M$, invoke $\mathcal{F}_{\mathsf{Mult}}$ with input $(a_i^{(\ell)}, b_i^{(\ell)})$. % Parties compute $[a^{(\ell)} b^{(\ell)}]_t$.
  - For $\ell = 1, \ldots, c_M$, let $c_i^{(\ell)}$ be the output received from $\mathcal{F}_{\mathsf{Mult}}$ in response to the ℓth call to $\mathcal{F}_{\mathsf{Mult}}$. Output the shares $\{(a_i^{(\ell)}, b_i^{(\ell)}, c_i^{(\ell)})\}_{\ell=1,\ldots,c_M}$.

Fig. 7.4 A t-perfectly-secure protocol for $\mathcal{F}_{\mathsf{Triple}}$ in the $\mathcal{F}_{\mathsf{Mult}}$-hybrid model. The above steps are executed by each $P_i \in \mathcal{P}$

generate c_M such secret-shared (a, b) pairs, the above process is executed in parallel and independently c_M number of times.

Once the secret-shared $(a^{(\ell)}, b^{(\ell)})$ pairs are generated during the first stage, to securely generate a random t-Shamir-sharing of the corresponding value $c^{(\ell)}$ during the second stage, the parties use either the protocol Π_{BGWMult} (see Fig. 6.4) or Π_{GRRMult} (see Fig. 6.7).[3]

The formal details of the protocol Π_{Triple} are presented in Fig. 7.4. For the sake of modular analysis, the protocol is presented in the $\mathcal{F}_{\mathsf{Mult}}$-hybrid model (see Sect. 6.4 for the details of the $\mathcal{F}_{\mathsf{Mult}}$ function). To implement the protocol Π_{Triple} in the plain model, the calls to $\mathcal{F}_{\mathsf{Mult}}$ have to be substituted, either through the sub-protocol Π_{BGWMult} or Π_{GRRMult}.

The properties of the protocol Π_{Triple} are stated in Lemma 7.2. The round and communication complexity trivially follows from the protocol description. We have intuitively argued about the security of the protocol and have left completing the formal details as an exercise for the interested readers.

Lemma 7.2 *Protocol Π_{Triple} is a t-perfectly-secure protocol for $\mathcal{F}_{\mathsf{Triple}}$ in the $\mathcal{F}_{\mathsf{Mult}}$-hybrid model, for any $t < n$. The protocol requires one round of communication, c_M calls to $\mathcal{F}_{\mathsf{Mult}}$ and has communication complexity of $\mathcal{O}(c_M n^2)$ field elements.*

By replacing the calls to $\mathcal{F}_{\mathsf{Mult}}$ in Π_{Triple} with either the protocol Π_{BGWMult} or Π_{GRRMult}, we get the following corollary of Lemma 7.2 on protocol Π_{Triple} in the plain model.

Corollary 7.3 *Let $t < n/2$. Then there exists a t-perfectly-secure protocol for $\mathcal{F}_{\mathsf{Triple}}$, which requires $\mathcal{O}(1)$ rounds of communication and communication of $\mathcal{O}(c_M n^2)$ field elements.*

---

[3] Note that the use of a multiplication protocol requires the condition $t < n/2$ to hold.

Now combining Corollary 7.3 with Lemma 7.1, we get the following theorem on the protocol Π_{Beaver} in the plain model.

Theorem 7.4 (BGW Protocol with Pre-computed Beaver's Multiplication-Triples) *Let* $y = f(x_1, \ldots, x_n)$ *be an n-ary deterministic function over* $\mathbb{F}$ *with* P_i *holding the private input* x_i. *Moreover, let* $t < n/2$. *Then protocol* Π_{Beaver} *is a t-perfectly-secure protocol for* f.

During the pre-processing phase, the protocol requires $\mathcal{O}(1)$ *rounds of communication and has communication complexity of* $\mathcal{O}(c_M n^2)$ *field elements. Let* c_M *and* D_M *denote the number of multiplication gates and multiplicative depth of the circuit* cir *representing* f *respectively. Then in the circuit-evaluation phase, the protocol requires* $\mathcal{O}(D_M)$ *communication rounds and communication of* $\mathcal{O}(c_M n)$ *field elements.*

Remark 7.5 (*On the usage of functionality* $\mathcal{F}_{\text{Mult}}$ *in protocols* Π_{BGW} *and* Π_{Beaver}) A closer look into the protocols Π_{BGW} and Π_{Beaver} reveals that both these protocols invoke the TTP $\mathcal{F}_{\text{Mult}}$ in a different way. In the protocol Π_{BGW}, these invocations are during the circuit-evaluation phase. Hence, these invocations are *dependent* on the function f (namely the cir) and the inputs of the parties for f. All invocations *cannot* be clubbed together and parallelized due to the dependency amongst the multiplication gates (i.e. output of one multiplication may act as the input for another). So, the circuit-evaluation phase of the protocol Π_{BGW} in the plain model requires a communication of $\mathcal{O}(n^2)$ field elements per multiplication gate and a resilience of $t < n/2$.

On the other hand, in the protocol Π_{Beaver}, *all* the invocations of $\mathcal{F}_{\text{Mult}}$ are done in the pre-processing phase *independent* of cir and the inputs of the parties for f. Consequently, all of them can be clubbed together and parallelized. The evaluation of a multiplication gate in the circuit-evaluation phase becomes simpler, where the parties only need to publicly reconstruct two secret-shared values. As a result, as shown in Theorem 7.4, the pre-processing and circuit-evaluation phases have different complexities and resilience. While the pre-processing phase has an amortized communication complexity of $\mathcal{O}(n^2)$ per multiplication gate and can tolerate only up to $t < n/2$ faults, the circuit-evaluation phase has a better amortized communication complexity of $\mathcal{O}(n)$ per multiplication gate and a better resilience of $t < n$.

These positive points inspire the study of MPC protocols in the pre-processing model. Indeed, we can envision a scenario where a TTP (say a trusted cloud service-provider) is available only for generating the pre-processing data as required in the protocol Π_{Beaver}. Later the actual circuit-evaluation can be carried out in the *absence* of any TTP at a faster pace while tolerating all but one corruptions.

7.3   Perfectly-Secure MPC Using Double-Shared Randomness

In this section, we show a different form of correlated randomness (than Beaver's multiplication-triples), which allows the parties for a faster shared circuit-evaluation in the BGW protocol. The method is attributed to Damgård-Nielsen [63] (we refer to this protocol as the DN protocol for the rest of the discussion). The pre-processing data required in this method are $(t, 2t)$-*Shamir-sharing* of random values. Informally, a value is said to be $(t, 2t)$-Shamir-shared, if it is shared among the parties both through a t-degree polynomial, as well as through a $2t$-degree polynomial. More formally:

Definition 7.6 $((t, 2t)$-*double-sharing* [63]) A value $s \in \mathbb{F}$ is said to be $(t, 2t)$-double-shared where $2t < n$, if there exist t-degree and $2t$-degree polynomials over $\mathbb{F}$, say $f(Z)$ and $g(Z)$ respectively, where $f(Z) \in \mathcal{P}^{s,t}$ and $g(Z) \in \mathcal{P}^{s,2t}$, such that each party $P_i \in \mathcal{P}$ holds the *double-share* $s_i \overset{def}{=} f(\alpha_i)$ and $\mathsf{s}_i \overset{def}{=} g(\alpha_i)$.[4]

We use the notation $[s]_{t,2t}$ to denote the vector of shares corresponding to a $(t, 2t)$-double-sharing of s. That is, $[s]_{t,2t} \overset{def}{=} ((s_1, \mathsf{s}_1), \dots, (s_n, \mathsf{s}_n))$. A $(t, 2t)$-double-sharing of a value s is said to be *random*, if the underlying sharing-polynomials $f(Z)$ and $g(Z)$ are random polynomials from the set $\mathcal{P}^{s,t}$ and $\mathcal{P}^{s,2t}$ respectively. That is, all the coefficients of $f(Z)$ and $g(Z)$ are random elements from $\mathbb{F}$, except for the constant term, which is s.

It is easy to see that similar to d-sharing (see Definition 5.1), $(t, 2t)$-double-sharing also satisfies the *linearity* property. That is, if a and b are two $(t, 2t)$-double-shared values and if c_1, c_2 are *publicly-known* constants from $\mathbb{F}$, then the following holds:

$$c_1 \cdot [a]_{t,2t} + c_2 \cdot [b]_{t,2t} = [c_1 \cdot a + c_2 \cdot b]_{t,2t}$$

In general, the parties can locally compute any *publicly-known* linear function of $(t, 2t)$-double-shared values.

The high level idea behind the shared evaluation of multiplication gates using a double-sharing is the following. Consider a multiplication gate in cir with inputs x, y and output z, where $z = xy$. Moreover, let x and y be randomly t-Shamir-shared and the goal is to securely generate a random t-Shamir-sharing of z. Furthermore, let the parties have access to a random $(t, 2t)$-double-sharing of a uniformly random value, say r. That is, as part of the double-sharing, the parties hold independent shares, corresponding to $[r]_{2t}$, as well as $[r]_t$. The parties first locally generate a $2t$-Shamir-sharing of the value $xy + r$, which utilizes the shares corresponding to $[r]_{2t}$. This is followed by *publicly* reconstructing $xy + r$.

Note that $xy + r$ being a masked version of xy, masked with a uniformly random r, Adv does not learn anything additional on x, y. Treating $xy + r$ as a *public* constant, the parties

---

[4] The term *double-share* here signifies that each party holds two shares, one corresponding to t-Shamir-sharing of s and another corresponding to $2t$-Shamir-sharing of s. We use different fonts, to differentiate between the two types of shares.

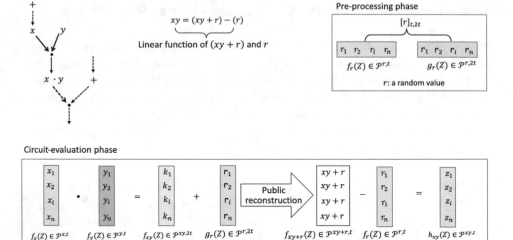

Fig. 7.5 Pictorial depiction of evaluating a multiplication gate in the circuit, using a pre-processed $(t, 2t)$-double-shared random value

can now locally generate a t-Shamir-sharing of z as $xy + r - [r]_t = [xy]_t$, thanks to the linearity property of t-Shamir-sharing. For this, the shares corresponding to $[r]_t$ are utilized which were not "touched" till this step. Note that the resultant t-Shamir-sharing of z will be random, since the sharing $[r]_t$ is a random t-Shamir-sharing of r. For a pictorial depiction of the protocol, see Fig. 7.5.

One can view the entire process as reconstructing a masked version of z in public and then a joint removal of the mask in a t-shared fashion. Similar to the case of Beaver's multiplication-triples, if there are c_M multiplication gates in cir, then the parties require c_M number of $(t, 2t)$-double-shared random values from the pre-processing phase. To abstract out the requirements of the pre-processing phase, we envision a TTP $\mathcal{F}_{\text{Double}}$ as follows:

$$\mathcal{F}_{\text{Double}}(\lambda, \ldots, \lambda) = \left(\{r_1^{(\ell)}, \mathsf{r}_1^{(\ell)}\}_{\ell=1,\ldots,c_M}, \ldots, \{r_n^{(\ell)}, \mathsf{r}_n^{(\ell)}\}_{\ell=1,\ldots,c_M} \right),$$

where for $\ell = 1, \ldots, c_M$, the vector of shares $((r_1^{(\ell)}, \mathsf{r}_1^{(\ell)}), \ldots, (r_n^{(\ell)}, \mathsf{r}_n^{(\ell)}))$ corresponds to a random $(t, 2t)$-double-sharing of a uniformly random value $r^{(\ell)} \in \mathbb{F}$. That is, there exist random t and $2t$-degree polynomials, say $f_{r^{(\ell)}}(Z)$ and $g_{r^{(\ell)}}(Z)$, belonging to the sets $\mathcal{P}^{r^{(\ell)}, t}$ and $\mathcal{P}^{r^{(\ell)}, 2t}$ respectively, such that each P_i holds the double-share $(r_i^{(\ell)}, \mathsf{r}_i^{(\ell)})$ where $r_i^{(\ell)} = f_{r^{(\ell)}}(\alpha_i)$ and $\mathsf{r}_i^{(\ell)} = g_{r^{(\ell)}}(\alpha_i)$.

The formal details of the DN protocol called Π_{DN} are presented in Fig. 7.6. The protocol is designed in the $\mathcal{F}_{\text{Double}}$-hybrid model. To reconstruct the values $xy + r$ during the evaluation of the multiplication gates in the circuit-evaluation phase, we use the communication-efficient method, where the value is first reconstructed only towards a protocol-designated party, say P_1, who then relays the value to every other party.

Protocol Π_{DN}

The Pre-processing Phase

- Invoke $\mathcal{F}_{\text{Double}}$ with input λ. In response, let $\{(r_i^{(\ell)}, \mathsf{r}_i^{(\ell)})\}_{\ell \in 1, \ldots, c_M}$ be the shares received from $\mathcal{F}_{\text{Double}}$.
  % For $\ell = 1, \ldots, c_M$, parties generate $[r^{(\ell)}]_t = (r_1^{(\ell)}, \ldots, r_n^{(\ell)})$ and $[r^{(\ell)}]_{2t} = (\mathsf{r}_1^{(\ell)}, \ldots, \mathsf{r}_n^{(\ell)})$.

The Circuit-evaluation Phase

- *Input Stage*: same steps as in the protocol Π_{BGW}.
- *Computation Stage*: Let $G_1, \ldots, G_m$ be a publicly-known topological ordering of the gates of cir. For $k = 1, \ldots, m$, do the following for gate G_k:
  - If G_k *is an addition gate*: Same steps as in the protocol Π_{BGW}.
  - If G_k *is a multiplication-with-a-constant gate with constant* c: Same steps as in the protocol Π_{BGW}.
  - If G_k *is an addition-with-a-constant gate with constant* c: Same steps as in the protocol Π_{BGW}.
  - If G_k *is a multiplication gate*: Let G_k be the ℓth multiplication gate in cir where $\ell \in \{1, \ldots, c_M\}$ and let $(r_i^{(\ell)}, \mathsf{r}_i^{(\ell)})$ be the shares of the ℓth $(t, 2t)$-double-shared value, received from $\mathcal{F}_{\text{Double}}$. Moreover, let $\alpha_i^{(k)}$ and $\beta_i^{(k)}$ be the shares held by P_i, corresponding to the gate-inputs of G_k. Then do the following:
    1. Compute $d_i^{(k)} = \alpha_i^{(k)} \cdot \beta_i^{(k)}$.   % Parties compute $[d^{(k)} = \alpha^{(k)} \cdot \beta^{(k)}]_{2t} = [\alpha^{(k)}]_t \cdot [\beta^{(k)}]_t$.
    2. Compute $e_i^{(\ell)} = d_i^{(k)} + \mathsf{r}_i^{(\ell)}$.   % Parties compute $[e^{(\ell)}]_{2t} = [d^{(k)}]_{2t} + [r^{(\ell)}]_{2t}$.
    3. Do the following to publicly reconstruct $e^{(\ell)}$:
       - Send the share $e_i^{(\ell)}$ *only* to party P_1.
       - (If $P_i = P_1$): Upon receiving the shares $e_j^{(\ell)}$ from $P_j \in \mathcal{P}$, compute $e^{(\ell)} = \mathsf{R}_{\text{Sha}}(\mathcal{P}, \{e_1^{(\ell)}, \ldots, e_n^{(\ell)}\})$. Then send $e^{(\ell)}$ to every $P_j \in \mathcal{P}$.
    4. Set $\gamma_i^{(k)} \stackrel{def}{=} e^{(\ell)} - r_i^{(\ell)}$ to be the share, corresponding to the gate-output.   % Parties computing $[\gamma^{(k)}]_t = e^{(\ell)} - [r^{(\ell)}]_t$.
- *Output Stage*: Same as in the protocol Π_{BGW}.

Fig. 7.6 The DN perfectly-secure protocol for any deterministic function in the $\mathcal{F}_{\text{Double}}$-hybrid model. The above steps are executed by each $P_i \in \mathcal{P}$

The properties of the protocol Π_{DN} are formally stated in Lemma 7.7. The round and communication complexity follow easily from the protocol inspection. The formal security proof will be similar to that of Lemma 7.1. We leave working out the formal proof as an exercise for the interested readers.

A closer look into the protocols Π_{Beaver} (Fig. 7.2) and Π_{DN} (Fig. 7.6) reveals that the resilience bounds are different for the two protocols; while the former protocol can tolerate up to $t < n$ corruptions, the latter can withstand only up to $t < n/2$ corruptions in the circuit-evaluation phase. The condition $t < n/2$ is required in the protocol Π_{DN} to reconstruct the $2t$-Shamir-shared masked gate-outputs during the evaluation of multiplication gates. On the other hand, in the protocol Π_{Beaver}, the parties need to reconstruct only t-Shamir-shared values during the evaluation of multiplication gates, for which the condition $t < n$ is sufficient.

Lemma 7.7 *Let $y = f(x_1, \ldots, x_n)$ be an n-ary deterministic function over $\mathbb{F}$ with P_i holding the private input x_i. Moreover, let $t < n/2$. Then protocol Π_{DN} is t-perfectly-secure for f in the $\mathcal{F}_{\mathsf{Double}}$-hybrid model.*

The protocol requires one call to $\mathcal{F}_{\mathsf{Double}}$ during the pre-processing phase. Let c_M and D_M denote the number of multiplication gates and multiplicative depth of the circuit cir *representing f respectively. Then in the circuit-evaluation phase, the protocol requires $\mathcal{O}(D_M)$ communication rounds and communication of $\mathcal{O}(c_M n)$ field elements.*

7.3.1 Securely Computing Function $\mathcal{F}_{\mathsf{Double}}$

In this section, we discuss how to securely compute the function $\mathcal{F}_{\mathsf{Double}}$. We first discuss a naive approach, followed by a more efficient approach.

Recall that the function $\mathcal{F}_{\mathsf{Double}}$ outputs a random $(t, 2t)$-double-sharing of c_M number of uniformly random values, where the view of the adversary is independent of these random values. The naive approach for generating one such double-shared random value is as follows: each party P_i "contributes" by picking a uniformly random element, say $R^{(i)}$, and generating a random $(t, 2t)$-double-sharing of $R^{(i)}$. The parties then set $r \stackrel{def}{=} R^{(1)} + \ldots + R^{(n)}$ and can locally compute a $(t, 2t)$-double-sharing of r as $[r]_{t,2t} = [R^{(1)}]_{t,2t} + \ldots + [R^{(n)}]_{t,2t}$, thanks to the linearity property of $(t, 2t)$-double-sharing. The resultant value r will be a uniformly random element from $\mathbb{F}$, since each element $R^{(i)}$ is a random element. Moreover, the resultant $(t, 2t)$-double-sharing of r will be random, as each of the double-sharings $[R^{(i)}]_{t,2t}$ is a random double-sharing. Finally, the view of the adversary will be independent of r, owing to the "contribution" of the honest parties which are unknown to the adversary.

To generate c_M number of random $(t, 2t)$-double-shared values, the above idea can be executed c_M number of times in parallel. We call the resultant protocol as Π_{Double}, which is formally presented in Fig. 7.7. In the protocol, we use the notation $R^{(i,\ell)}$ to denote the random value contributed by the party P_i, for the generation of the ℓth random double-sharing.

The properties of the protocol Π_{Double} are stated in Lemma 7.8 and are easy to prove.

Lemma 7.8 *Protocol Π_{Double} is a t-perfectly-secure protocol for $\mathcal{F}_{\mathsf{Double}}$ for any $t < n/2$. The protocol requires one round and has communication complexity of $\mathcal{O}(c_M n^2)$ field elements.*

A more efficient protocol for $\mathcal{F}_{\mathsf{Double}}$: In the protocol Π_{Double} one random $(t, 2t)$-double-shared value r is generated from n number of $(t, 2t)$-double-shared values $R^{(1)}, \ldots, R^{(n)}$. We argued that r is uniformly random from the point of view of Adv, since the $R^{(i)}$ values shared by the *honest* parties P_i are uniformly random and unknown from the point of view of Adv. In a more detail, there exists a *one-to-one correspondence* (injective mapping) between the $R^{(i)}$ values shared by the *honest* parties P_i and the resultant r. That is, for every

---

Protocol Π_{Double}

- For $\ell = 1, \ldots, c_M$, do the following:
  - Randomly pick $R^{(i,\ell)} \in \mathbb{F}$.
  - Compute the vector of shares $[R^{(i,\ell)}]_t = (R_1^{(i,\ell)}, \ldots, R_n^{(i,\ell)})$ by randomly picking a t-degree polynomial $f_{R^{(i,\ell)}}(Z)$ from the set $\mathcal{P}^{R^{(i,\ell)},t}$ and setting $R_j^{(i,\ell)} = f_{R^{(i,\ell)}}(\alpha_j)$, for $j = 1, \ldots, n$.
  - Compute the vector of shares $[R^{(i,\ell)}]_{2t} = (\mathsf{R}_1^{(i,\ell)}, \ldots, \mathsf{R}_n^{(i,\ell)})$ by randomly picking a $2t$-degree polynomial $g_{R^{(i,\ell)}}(Z)$ from the set $\mathcal{P}^{R^{(i,\ell)},2t}$ and setting $\mathsf{R}_j^{(i,\ell)} = g_{R^{(i,\ell)}}(\alpha_j)$, for $j = 1, \ldots, n$.
  - For $j = 1, \ldots, n$, send the double-share $(R_j^{(i,\ell)}, \mathsf{R}_j^{(i,\ell)})$ to party P_j.
  - Compute $r_i^{(\ell)} = \sum_{j=1}^{j=n} R_i^{(j,\ell)}$ and $\mathsf{r}_i^{(\ell)} = \sum_{j=1}^{j=n} \mathsf{R}_i^{(j,\ell)}$. Here $(R_i^{(j,\ell)}, \mathsf{R}_i^{(j,\ell)})$ denotes the double-share received from P_j. % Parties jointly compute $[r^{(\ell)}]_{t,2t} = \sum_{j=1}^{j=n} [R^{(j,\ell)}]_{t,2t}$.
- Output the double-shares $\{(r_i^{(\ell)}, \mathsf{r}_i^{(\ell)})\}_{\ell=1,\ldots,c_M}$.

Fig. 7.7 A t-perfectly-secure protocol for $\mathcal{F}_{\text{Double}}$ with $t < n/2$. The above steps are executed by each $P_i \in \mathcal{P}$

candidate $R^{(i)}$ value shared by the honest parties P_i from the point of view of Adv, there exists a corresponding r, consistent with the view of Adv (namely, the shares received by Adv). Since the $R^{(i)}$ values shared by the honest parties are distributed uniformly over $\mathbb{F}$ (and not known to Adv), due to the injective mapping, the resultant value r will also be uniformly distributed over $\mathbb{F}$ (and not known to Adv).

The idea behind the more efficient protocol $\Pi_{\text{EfficientDouble}}$ for $\mathcal{F}_{\text{Double}}$ is that there are at least $n - t$ *honest* parties P_i, whose double-shared $R^{(i)}$ values are uniformly random for Adv. Hence, one can "extract out" $n - t$ double-shared random values out of the values $R^{(1)}, \ldots, R^{(n)}$ via a "better" injective mapping.

In a more detail, let $F(Z)$ be the $(n - 1)$-degree polynomial, passing through the n distinct points $(\alpha_1, R^{(1)}), \ldots, (\alpha_n, R^{(n)})$. Notice that the polynomial $F(Z)$ is well defined, as there exists a unique $(n - 1)$-degree polynomial, passing through the points $(\alpha_1, R^{(1)}), \ldots, (\alpha_n, R^{(n)})$. Then consider the $n - t$ values $F(\beta_1), \ldots, F(\beta_{n-t})$, where $\beta_1, \ldots, \beta_{n-t}$ are *distinct* elements from $\mathbb{F}$, *different* from $\alpha_1, \ldots, \alpha_n$. The values $F(\beta_1), \ldots, F(\beta_{n-t})$ are distinct points on the polynomial $F(Z)$, different from the points $F(\alpha_1), \ldots, F(\alpha_n)$. Moreover, from the properties of Lagrange's interpolation, the new points $F(\beta_1), \ldots, F(\beta_{n-t})$ can be expressed as a *publicly-known linear* function of the n points $F(\alpha_1), \ldots, F(\alpha_n)$ on the polynomial $F(Z)$ (see Sect. 2.2 and Example 5.2). Most importantly, there exists an *injective* mapping between the points $F(\alpha_i)$ shared by the *honest* parties P_i (which are the same as the $R^{(i)}$ values shared by P_i) and the points $F(\beta_1), \ldots, F(\beta_{n-t})$. Hence from the point of view of Adv, the values $F(\beta_1), \ldots, F(\beta_{n-t})$ are uniformly distributed over $\mathbb{F}$ and unknown. That is, for every candidate $R^{(i)}$ value shared by the honest parties P_i from the point of view of Adv, there exist corresponding values $F(\beta_1), \ldots, F(\beta_{n-t})$, consistent with the view of Adv (namely the shares received by Adv).

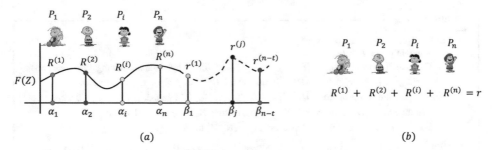

(a)   (b)

Fig. 7.8 Pictorial depiction of the randomness-extraction methods used in the protocols Π_{Double} and $\Pi_{\mathsf{EfficientDouble}}$. Figure **a** shows the method used in the protocol $\Pi_{\mathsf{EfficientDouble}}$, where $n - t$ uniformly random values are extracted out of the n values contributed by the parties, where P_i contributes $R^{(i)}$. This is done by fitting a $(n - 1)$-degree polynomial through the contributed values and extending the polynomial at $n - t$ new points. Figure **b** shows the method used in the protocol Π_{Double}, where all the contributed values are simply added to extract out a single random value

Since the values $F(\beta_1), \ldots, F(\beta_{n-t})$ are publicly-known linear combination of $F(\alpha_1),$ $\ldots, F(\alpha_n)$, it follows that once the values $F(\alpha_1), \ldots, F(\alpha_n)$ are available in $(t, 2t)$-double-shared fashion, the parties can locally compute a $(t, 2t)$-double-sharing of $F(\beta_1), \ldots,$ $F(\beta_{n-t})$ by applying the linear combination to the $(t, 2t)$-double-sharings of $F(\alpha_1), \ldots,$ $F(\alpha_n)$. For a pictorial comparison of protocols Π_{Double} and $\Pi_{\mathsf{EfficientDouble}}$, see Fig. 7.8.

For simplicity, let us assume that c_M is a multiple of $n - t$; i.e., $c_M = k(n - t)$ holds, for some integer $k \geq 1$. Then the above idea can be executed k number of times in parallel, to generate c_M number of double-shared random values. The overall communication complexity of the protocol will be $\mathcal{O}(kn^2)$, as each party needs to contribute k number of double-shared random values. Since $k = \frac{c_M}{n-t}$, if $n - t = \Theta(n)$ holds, then the overall communication complexity of the protocol will be $\mathcal{O}(c_M n)$. Protocol $\Pi_{\mathsf{EfficientDouble}}$ is due to [21, 63] and presented in Fig. 7.9.

While all the previous protocols require $|\mathbb{F}| > n$ to hold, protocol $\Pi_{\mathsf{EfficientDouble}}$ require $|\mathbb{F}| > 2n - t$ to hold. This is because we need a total of $2n - t$ distinct elements $\alpha_1, \ldots, \alpha_n,$ $\beta_1, \ldots, \beta_{n-t}$ from $\mathbb{F}$. While $\alpha_1, \ldots, \alpha_n$ are needed to define the $F(Z)$ polynomials, the elements $\beta_1, \ldots, \beta_{n-t}$ are needed for extracting out the random values. In the protocol, $c_{j1}, \ldots, c_{jn}$ denote the publicly-known *Lagrange's interpolation coefficients*, such that $F(\beta_j)$ is expressed as a linear combination of $F(\alpha_1), \ldots, F(\alpha_n)$, with respect to the linear combiners $c_{j1}, \ldots, c_{jn}$. That is, the following relation holds for $j = 1, \ldots, n - t$:

$$F(\beta_j) = c_{j1} \cdot F(\alpha_1) + \ldots + c_{jn} \cdot F(\alpha_n).$$

The properties of the protocol $\Pi_{\mathsf{EfficientDouble}}$ are stated in Lemma 7.9, which can be proved easily. We leave the proof as an exercise.

Protocol $\Pi_{\mathsf{EfficientDouble}}$

- For $\ell = 1, \ldots, \frac{c_M}{n-t}$, do the following:
  - Randomly pick $R^{(i,\ell)} \in \mathbb{F}$.
  - Compute the vector of shares $[R^{(i,\ell)}]_t = (R_1^{(i,\ell)}, \ldots, R_n^{(i,\ell)})$ by randomly picking a t-degree polynomial $f_{R^{(i,\ell)}}(Z)$ from the set $\mathcal{P}^{R^{(i,\ell)},t}$ and setting $R_j^{(i,\ell)} = f_{R^{(i,\ell)}}(\alpha_j)$, for $j = 1, \ldots, n$.
  - Compute the vector of shares $[R^{(i,\ell)}]_{2t} = (\mathsf{R}_1^{(i,\ell)}, \ldots, \mathsf{R}_n^{(i,\ell)})$ by randomly picking a $2t$-degree polynomial $g_{R^{(i,\ell)}}(Z)$ from the set $\mathcal{P}^{R^{(i,\ell)},2t}$ and setting $\mathsf{R}_j^{(i,\ell)} = g_{R^{(i,\ell)}}(\alpha_j)$, for $j = 1, \ldots, n$.
  - For $j = 1, \ldots, n$, send the double-share $(R_j^{(i,\ell)}, \mathsf{R}_j^{(i,\ell)})$ to party P_j.
  - Let $F^{(\ell)}(Z)$ be the $(n-1)$-degree polynomial, passing through the points $\{(\alpha_j, R^{(j,\ell)})\}_{j=1,\ldots,n}$. Moreover, for $j = 1, \ldots, n-t$, let $c_{j1}^{(\ell)}, \ldots, c_{jn}^{(\ell)}$ be the *publicly-known* linear combiners (Lagrange's interpolation coefficients), such that the following holds:

$$r^{(j,\ell)} \overset{def}{=} F^{(\ell)}(\beta_j) = c_{j1}^{(\ell)} \cdot R^{(1,\ell)} + \ldots + c_{jn}^{(\ell)} \cdot R^{(n,\ell)}.$$

- Compute $r_i^{(j,\ell)} = c_{j1}^{(\ell)} \cdot R_i^{(1,\ell)} + \ldots + c_{jn}^{(\ell)} \cdot R_i^{(n,\ell)}$ and $\mathsf{r}_i^{(j,\ell)} = c_{j1}^{(\ell)} \cdot \mathsf{R}_i^{(1,\ell)} + \ldots + c_{jn}^{(\ell)} \cdot \mathsf{R}_i^{(n,\ell)}$, where $(R_i^{(k,\ell)}, \mathsf{R}_i^{(k,\ell)})$ denotes the double-share received from P_k. % Parties jointly compute $[r^{(j,\ell)}]_{t,2t} = c_{j1}^{(\ell)} \cdot [R^{(1,\ell)}]_{t,2t} + \ldots + c_{jn}^{(\ell)} \cdot [R^{(n,\ell)}]_{t,2t}$.

- Output the double-shares $\{(r_i^{(j,\ell)}, \mathsf{r}_i^{(j,\ell)})\}_{\ell=1,\ldots,\frac{c_M}{n-t}, j=1,\ldots,n-t}$.

Fig. 7.9 A more efficient t-perfectly-secure protocol for $\mathcal{F}_{\mathsf{Double}}$. The above steps are executed by each $P_i \in \mathcal{P}$

Lemma 7.9 *Protocol* $\Pi_{\mathsf{EfficientDouble}}$ *is a* t-*perfectly-secure protocol for* $\mathcal{F}_{\mathsf{Double}}$ *for any* $t < n/2$. *The protocol requires one round of communication and has communication complexity of* $\mathcal{O}(\frac{c_M}{n-t} \cdot n^2)$ *field elements. If* $n - t = \Theta(n)$, *then the communication complexity is* $\mathcal{O}(c_M n)$ *field elements.*

Now by using the protocol $\Pi_{\mathsf{EfficientDouble}}$ in Π_{DN} (Fig. 7.6) for securely computing $\mathcal{F}_{\mathsf{Double}}$ and using the fact that for any $t < n/2$, the condition $n - t = \Theta(n)$ holds, we get the following result for the protocol Π_{DN} in the plain model.

Theorem 7.10 (BGW Protocol with Pre-computed Double-Shared Random Values) *Let* $y = f(x_1, \ldots, x_n)$ *be an* n-*ary deterministic function over* $\mathbb{F}$ *with* P_i *holding the private input* x_i. *Moreover, let* $t < n/2$. *Then protocol* Π_{DN} *is a* t-*perfectly-secure protocol for* f.

During the pre-processing phase, the protocol requires 1 *round of communication and has communication complexity of* $\mathcal{O}(c_M n)$ *field elements. Let* c_M *and* D_M *denote the number of multiplication gates and multiplicative depth of the circuit* cir *representing* f *respectively. Then in the circuit-evaluation phase, the protocol requires* $\mathcal{O}(D_M)$ *communication rounds and communication of* $\mathcal{O}(c_M n)$ *field elements.*

From Theorem 7.10, one can consider the protocol Π_{DN} in the plain model as *scalable* in the sense that *per-party* communication cost for evaluating *each* multiplication gate is $\mathcal{O}(1)$ field elements, which is *independent* of the number of parties n. Hence *asymptotically,* the per-party communication cost *does not* increase if the number of parties n increases. Comparing this with the complexity of protocol Π_{Beaver} in the plain model (see Theorem 7.4), we note that the per-party communication cost for evaluating each multiplication gate is $\mathcal{O}(n)$ field elements, which depends upon the number of parties. So, the protocol Π_{Beaver} (in the plain model) is *not* scalable.

A natural question is whether one can further improve the communication complexity of the protocol Π_{DN} for evaluating the multiplication gates in cir. An obvious related question is: what is the lower bound on the communication complexity of *any* t-perfectly-secure MPC protocol, with the *optimal resilience* of $t < n/2$? Another complexity measure of MPC protocols, as discussed earlier is the round complexity. We note that with or without preprocessing, all the protocols we have discussed require $\mathcal{O}(D_M)$ rounds. Therefore, another interesting question is: what is the round complexity lower bound of *any* t-perfectly-secure MPC protocol, with the *optimal resilience* of $t < n/2$? We cite the related works below.

7.4 On Lower Bounds for Optimally-Resilient Perfectly-Secure MPC

The work of [61] shows a lower bound on the communication complexity of MPC both in the standard model with $n = 2t + 1$ parties and in the pre-processing model with $n = t + 1$ parties. Their result holds for passively-secure protocols which is our current focus. They show that for any natural number g, there exists a Boolean circuit C with g gates, such that any MPC protocol securely evaluating C must communicate $\Omega(ng)$ bits. The result easily extends to constructing similar circuits over any fixed finite field. This implies that the protocol Π_{DN} is *optimal* for arithmetic circuits over $\mathbb{F}$.

We note that there are two possible ways to circumvent the necessary $\mathcal{O}(n)$ overhead in the communication complexity. The first option is to consider a *non-optimal* resilience of $t < (\frac{1}{2} - \epsilon)n$ instead of $t < n/2$, for some non-zero $\epsilon > 0$. The readers are referred to [60, 70] for this line of work. The second option is to consider a *weaker* level of security, namely *cryptographic security* (also known as computational security), where the adversary is assumed to be *computationally bounded*. In this setting, one may consider deploying *fully homomorphic encryption* (FHE) [76], which are based on computational-hardness assumptions and are less efficient than traditional public-key encryption schemes. The interested readers are referred to [10] for this line of work.

We now move on to the discussion on round complexity lower bounds. Firstly, it is known that two rounds of interaction are essential for *any* MPC protocol, irrespective of the setting. This is because in any 1-round protocol, a corrupt party could repeatedly compute the "residual function" on many different inputs of its own (referred as "residual function" attack) [87]. The residual function refers to the function f to be computed with the input of the honest parties being fixed. In more detail, let Π be a 1-round MPC protocol for securely computing $f(x_1, \ldots, x_n)$ and without loss of generality, has the following structure: every party computes n messages based on its input and randomness and communicates the relevant message to every other party in the single round. Following this, every party outputs $f(x_1, \ldots, x_n)$, based on its internal state and the messages received from the other parties. Now consider a scenario where the adversary controls the last t parties. Let us fix the inputs of the honest parties to $x_1, \ldots, x_{n-t}$. In protocol Π, the adversary has the "capability" to compute $f(x_1, \ldots, x_{n-t}, x_{n-t+1}, \ldots, x_n)$, for *every possible* vector of the inputs $x_{n-t+1}, \ldots, x_n$, based on the messages received from the honest parties $P_1, \ldots, P_{n-t}$ in Π. After an execution of Π, the adversary can simply re-run the protocol Π "in its head", with different possible values of $x_{n-t+1}, \ldots, x_n$, while fixing the received messages from $P_1, \ldots, P_{n-t}$ in the execution of Π. This clearly allows the adversary to learn the output of f on more than one combination of inputs $(x_1, \ldots, x_n)$ from a single execution of Π, breaching the security of Π. Notice that the residual function attack *cannot* be launched on an MPC protocol having more than one rounds. The adversary can *no* longer re-run such a protocol multiple times in its head, while changing the inputs of the corrupted parties in each rerun. Specifically, the messages of the honest parties for the second round onwards will depend on the messages from the adversary. Without the internal state (consisting of the input and the randomness) of an honest party, the adversary cannot generate an honest party's messages on its behalf for any possible vector of the inputs $x_{n-t+1}, \ldots, x_n$, except the one used in the instance of Π.

Constant-round unconditionally-secure protocols were first constructed by Bar-Ilan and Beaver [14] and were later extended in several works (for instance [69]). Ishai and Kushilevitz [96, 97] approached the 2-round lower bound and presented a 3-round protocol. In fact, they showed that a 2-round protocol is possible if instead of honest majority, one requires that more than two-third of the parties are honest. Recently, [5, 6] presented a 2-round honest-majority protocol for all functions, settling the long standing open question. All the constant round protocols mentioned above have computation and communication complexity which are polynomial in the number of parties and in the size of the *formula* that computes the function f.[5] This means that their complexity is polynomial *only* for NC^1 circuits (which can be represented by polynomial-sized formulas). This is unlike the $\mathcal{O}(D_M)$-round protocols discussed so far, whose complexity is polynomial for *any* polynomial-sized circuit and not just for NC^1 circuits.

7.5 Dealing with Malicious Adversaries

We conclude this chapter by briefly discussing the issues that may occur if the protocols Π_{Beaver} and Π_{DN} (and the associated sub-protocols) are executed in the presence of a *malicious* adversary. The issues of corrupt parties *not* sharing their inputs using a t-degree sharing-polynomial and corrupt parties producing incorrect shares during the output stage,

---

[5] A formula is a special type of circuit where each gate has fan-out at most 1. They represent computation where the results of subcomputations cannot be used more than once.

hold for Π_{Beaver} and Π_{DN} as well and can be taken care of by using maliciously-secure VSS [44]. Additionally, during the evaluation of multiplication gates, the corrupt parties may lead to the reconstruction of incorrect masked values, either by producing incorrect shares (of the masked values) or by relaying incorrect masked values. Dealing with these require additional techniques, apart from VSS (see, for instance [21, 63]).

Unfortunately, VSS alone is *not* sufficient to deal with malicious behaviour during the pre-processing phase of Π_{Beaver} and Π_{DN}. For instance, the protocol Π_{Triple} (for securely computing $\mathcal{F}_{\text{Triple}}$) needs to be replaced with a *maliciously-secure* protocol for securely computing the $\mathcal{F}_{\text{Mult}}$ function. In the protocols Π_{Double} and $\Pi_{\text{EfficientDouble}}$ (for securely computing $\mathcal{F}_{\text{Double}}$), a potentially *corrupt* dealer may share *different* values through t and $2t$-degree polynomials, during its designated instances of secret-sharing.[6] Hence the parties need to check if the *same* value is secret-shared, during the various instances of $(t, 2t)$-double-sharing, such that the shared values remain private for an *honest* dealer. Dealing with these challenges require additional technicalities and discussing them is out of scope of the current lecture series. We refer the interested readers to [2, 8, 21, 54, 63, 83] for more details.

---

[6] Recall that to generate a $(t, 2t)$-double-sharing of a value, the corresponding dealer has to share the *same* value *twice*, using t and $2t$-degree polynomials.

Perfectly-Secure MPC Tolerating General Adversaries

8

Till now, our focus was on perfectly-secure MPC tolerating *threshold* adversaries. In this chapter, we shift our attention to perfectly-secure MPC tolerating general (*non-threshold*) adversaries.

8.1 Motivation for General Adversaries

Recall that in any MPC protocol, the distrust among the parties is modelled by a centralized entity called *adversary*, who can corrupt a subset of parties during the protocol execution. Till now, we have considered a *threshold* adversary, who can corrupt any t out of the n parties. The threshold model fits well in a scenario where all the n parties are equally "hard" to corrupt and adversary has the "resources" to corrupt *any* t of them. However, in reality this need not be true as some of the parties may be better guarded than others. Hence, a more realistic model might be to consider an adversary who can corrupt a *small* number of well-protected parties or a *large* number of poorly-protected parties. Unfortunately, the threshold model does not allow for such expressibility. Another limitation with the threshold model is that it seems quite restrictive to assume that *any* subset of t parties might collaborate to cheat others. Instead, which subsets we should actually worry about may depend on the composition of the set of parties and their relation to each other, rather than on the size of the subsets.

Motivated by the above problems, Hirt and Maurer [91] initiated the study of MPC in the *non-threshold* adversarial model under a more general constraint on the adversary's corruption capability. In this model, the adversary is allowed to corrupt any set of parties from a *pre-defined* collection of subsets of $\mathcal{P}$ called a *general adversary-structure*. Moreover, they presented necessary and sufficiency conditions for the existence of MPC protocols tolerating such an adversary. The flexibility of non-threshold model makes it applicable in many

© The Author(s), under exclusive license to Springer Nature Switzerland AG 2022   111
A. Choudhury and A. Patra, *Secure Multi-Party Computation Against Passive Adversaries*,
Synthesis Lectures on Distributed Computing Theory,
https://doi.org/10.1007/978-3-031-12164-7_8

real-world scenarios, especially when the number of parties n is not too large. We note that the size of the adversary structure can be exponential in n due to the number of possible subsets of $\mathcal{P}$. So, as remarked in [92], non-threshold model comes with a downside that the resultant MPC protocol for a given exponential-sized adversary structure can have exponential communication and computation complexities.

It was shown in [91] that there are several scenarios where modelling the distrust through a non-threshold adversary may lead to better fault-tolerance, compared to the threshold model. For instance, let $\mathcal{P} = \{P_1, \ldots, P_6\}$ and consider an adversary-structure, consisting of the subsets $\{P_1, P_2, P_3, P_4\}$, $\{P_2, P_3, P_4, P_5\}$ and $\{P_4, P_6\}$; i.e. the adversary can control any of these three subsets of parties during the protocol execution (notice the difference in the size of the individual subsets). Looking ahead, we will show that there exists a perfectly-secure MPC tolerating the above adversary. On the other hand, if we model the distrust through a threshold adversary, then from the results discussed for threshold adversaries, any perfectly-secure protocol can tolerate at most 2 corruptions. Hence through a non-threshold adversary, we can tolerate more number of corruptions (namely 4, corresponding to the potentially corrupt subset $\{P_1, P_2, P_3, P_4\}$ or $\{P_2, P_3, P_4, P_5\}$).

Another advantage of MPC protocols against non-threshold adversaries is that we can design protocols over algebraic structures, whose size *need not* depend upon the number of parties n. This is unlike the protocols discussed till now based on Shamir's secret-sharing, where all computations have to performed over a field $\mathbb{F}$ where $|\mathbb{F}| > n$.

8.2   Preliminaries and Definitions

We assume a set of n mutually distrusting parties $\mathcal{P} = \{P_1, \ldots, P_n\}$, connected by pair-wise secure channels. The distrust in the system is modelled by a *computationally-unbounded passive* (semi-honest) adversary Adv, specified by an *adversary structure* $\mathcal{Z} \subseteq 2^{\mathcal{P}}$. The adversary Adv can corrupt a set of parties $Z^\star \subset \mathcal{P}$ during the execution of any protocol, where $Z^\star$ is subset of some set in the adversary structure (i.e., $Z^\star \subseteq Z_c$ for some $Z_c \in \mathcal{Z}$). The adversary structure $\mathcal{Z}$ is *monotone* in the sense that if $Z \in \mathcal{Z}$, then any $Z' \subseteq Z$ also belongs to $\mathcal{Z}$. The basis of $\mathcal{Z}$ denoted by $\mathcal{Z}_0$ consists of the *maximal* subsets from $\mathcal{Z}$. That is, if $Z \in \mathcal{Z}_0$, then there exists no $Z' \in \mathcal{Z}$, such that $Z \subset Z'$ and $Z' \in \mathcal{Z}$. We next give the definition of the $\mathcal{Q}^{(k)}$ condition.

Definition 8.1 ($\mathcal{Q}^{(k)}(S, \mathcal{Z})$ *Condition*) Given a set of parties $S \subseteq \mathcal{P}$, we say that an adversary-structure $\mathcal{Z}$ satisfies the $\mathcal{Q}^{(k)}(S, \mathcal{Z})$ condition, where $k \geq 1$, if the union of no k subsets from $\mathcal{Z}$ spans the entire set S. That is, for every $Z_{i_1}, \ldots, Z_{i_k} \in \mathcal{Z}$:

$$S \not\subseteq Z_{i_1} \cup \ldots \cup Z_{i_k}.$$

An obvious implication which follows from the above definition is the following: if $\mathcal{Z}$ satisfies the $Q^{(k)}(S, \mathcal{Z})$ condition, then it also satisfies the $Q^{(k')}(S, \mathcal{Z})$ condition for any $1 \leq k' < k$. Moreover, for any $Z \in \mathcal{Z}$, the adversary structure $\mathcal{Z}$ satisfies the $Q^{(k-1)}(S', \mathcal{Z})$ condition, where $S' \stackrel{def}{=} (S \setminus Z)$, provided $k \geq 2$. Finally, if $\mathcal{Z}$ satisfies the $Q^{(k)}(S, \mathcal{Z})$ condition, then the basis $\mathcal{Z}_0$ of $\mathcal{Z}$ satisfies the $Q^{(k)}(S, \mathcal{Z}_0)$ condition.

We assume that the parties want to securely compute a function f over some finite algebraic structure $(\mathcal{K}, +, \cdot)$, which could be a finite ring or a field.[1] Function f is represented by a *publicly* known arithmetic circuit cir over $\mathcal{K}$. For simplicity and without loss of generality, we assume that each $P_i \in \mathcal{P}$ has a single input x_i for the function f, and there is a single output $y = f(x_1, \ldots, x_n)$, which is supposed to be learnt by all the parties. Moreover, the function f is a *deterministic* function and cir consists of c_M number of multiplication gates and has multiplicative depth D_M.

8.2.1 Definitions

We next present the definition of perfectly-secure MPC against non-threshold adversaries, for which we generalize the Definition 5.5. We refer the readers to Sect. 5.4.4 for the definition of $\mathsf{view}_i^{\Pi}(\vec{x})$, which denotes the *view* of the party P_i during the execution of a protocol Π with inputs $\vec{x} = (x_1, \ldots, x_n)$. For every $I = \{i_1, \ldots, i_\ell\}$, the notation $\mathsf{view}_I^{\Pi}(\vec{x})$ denotes the view of the parties $P_{i_1}, \ldots, P_{i_\ell}$. That is, $\mathsf{view}_I^{\Pi}(\vec{x}) = (\mathsf{view}_{i_1}^{\Pi}(\vec{x}), \ldots, \mathsf{view}_{i_\ell}^{\Pi}(\vec{x}))$. Finally, the output of all the parties from an execution of Π on inputs $\vec{x}$ is denoted by $\mathsf{output}^{\Pi}(\vec{x})$. The formal definition of securely computing any function f against a non-threshold adversary is given as follows.

Definition 8.2 (*Perfect Security of n-party Deterministic Protocols Against Non-Threshold Adversaries*) Let $f : (\{0, 1\}^\star)^n \rightarrow (\{0, 1\}^\star)^n$ be a *deterministic n*-ary function and let Π be an *n*-party protocol. Moreover, let $\mathcal{Z} = \{Z_1, \ldots, Z_q\} \subseteq 2^{\mathcal{P}}$ be an adversary-structure, where each $Z_m \subset \mathcal{P}$. We say that Π is a $\mathcal{Z}$-*perfectly-secure* protocol for f, if for every $\vec{x} = (x_1, \ldots, x_n) \in (\{0, 1\}^\star)^n$ where $|x_1| = |x_2| = \ldots = |x_n|$ and for every adversary Adv controlling any subset of parties $Z^\star$ with indices in $I \subset \{1, \ldots, n\}$ where $Z^\star \subseteq Z_c$ for some $Z_c \in \mathcal{Z}$, the following two conditions hold:

– *Correctness*:

$$\mathsf{output}^{\Pi}(\vec{x}) = f(x_1, \ldots, x_n).$$

---

[1] This is unlike the protocols discussed for threshold adversaries, where f is over a finite field $\mathbb{F}$ with $|\mathbb{F}| > n$.

- *Privacy*: there exists a probabilistic polynomial-time algorithm S called *simulator*, such that the probability distribution of the output generated by S is identical to the view of the adversary. That is:

$$\left\{ S(I, \vec{x}_I, f_I(x_1, \ldots, x_n)) \right\} \equiv \left\{ \mathsf{view}_I^\Pi(\vec{x}) \right\}.$$

Here $\vec{x}_I$ denotes the inputs corresponding to the parties with index in I and $f_I(x_1, \ldots, x_n)$ denotes the function output, restricted to the parties with index in I.

Similarly, one can give a corresponding definition of perfect-security for randomized functionalities against non-threshold adversaries, by generalizing the Definition 5.7. We leave the formal details as an exercise. Looking ahead, the design principle of an MPC protocol against a non-threshold adversary will again follow the shared circuit-evaluation, where the parties jointly and securely evaluate each gate in cir, with each party holding a share of each value during the evaluation as per some secret-sharing scheme. But now instead of a t-out-of-n secret-sharing scheme, the underlying secret-sharing scheme needs to be "secure" against a non-threshold adversary. Moreover, we prefer to use a *linear* secret-sharing to ensure that the linear gates in cir are evaluated *non-interactively*. We next present the definition of the secret-sharing used for circuit-evaluation.

Definition 8.3 ([·]-*sharing*) Let $\mathcal{Z}$ be an adversary-structure with basis $\mathcal{Z}_0 = \{Z_1, \ldots, Z_q\}$, where each $Z_m \subset \mathcal{P}$. Moreover, for $m = 1, \ldots, q$, let $\mathcal{G}_m \overset{def}{=} \mathcal{P} \setminus Z_m$. A value $s \in \mathcal{K}$ is said to be [·]-shared, if there exist values $s_1, \ldots, s_q \in \mathcal{K}$ where $s = s_1 + \ldots + s_q$, such that for each $m = 1, \ldots, q$, all parties in the group $\mathcal{G}_m$ hold the *share* s_m. The notation $[s]_{\mathcal{Z}}$ denotes the vector of shares $(s_1, \ldots, s_q)$.[2]

A vector of shares $(s_1, \ldots, s_q)$ is called a *random* [·]$_{\mathcal{Z}}$-sharing of s, if $s_1, \ldots, s_q$ are random elements from $\mathcal{K}$, subject to the condition that $s = s_1 + \ldots + s_q$ holds.

Note that a party P_i may possess more than one share in the vector $[s]_{\mathcal{Z}}$, depending upon the number of groups $\mathcal{G}_m$ in which P_i is present, which further depends upon the adversary structure $\mathcal{Z}$. Namely, P_i holds the shares $\{s_m\}_{\mathcal{G}_m: P_i \in \mathcal{G}_m}$. A closer look into the definition of [·]-sharing immediately reveals that the sharing semantics is *identical* to that of Ito's general secret-sharing scheme (see the algorithm $\mathsf{G}_{\mathsf{Ito}}$ in Fig. 3.1). Hence the security properties of the Ito's scheme (which are proved in Theorem 3.4) also hold in the context of [·]-sharing.

It is easy to see that [·]-sharing satisfies the following linearity property: given secret-shared values a and b, namely $[a]$ and $[b]$ and *publicly-known* constants $c_1, c_2 \in \mathcal{K}$, then the parties can *locally* compute their shares corresponding to $[c_1 \cdot a + c_2 \cdot b]$. In general, the parties can locally compute any *publicly* known linear function of [·]-shared values.

---

[2] We will drop $\mathcal{Z}$ from the notation $[s]_{\mathcal{Z}}$, if it is clear from the context.

8.3   Necessary Condition for Perfectly-Secure MPC Against Non-threshold Adversaries

Recall that $t < n/2$ is the necessary condition for the existence of any t-perfectly-secure MPC protocol for arbitrary functions (see Theorem 6.9). One can interpret this condition as the union of any two subsets of parties of size at most t *should not* cover the entire set of parties. In this section, we generalize this result and show that for the existence of any $\mathcal{Z}$-*perfectly-secure* MPC protocol for an arbitrary function with respect to a given adversary-structure $\mathcal{Z}$, the adversary-structure should satisfy the $\mathcal{Q}^{(2)}(\mathcal{P}, \mathcal{Z})$ condition. To prove this result, we show that the existence of a $\mathcal{Z}$-*perfectly-secure* MPC protocol where $\mathcal{Z}$ *does not* satisfy the $\mathcal{Q}^{(2)}(\mathcal{P}, \mathcal{Z})$ condition implies the existence of 1-perfectly-secure protocol for securely computing the 2-party AND function, which according to Theorem 6.8 is not possible. To prove the implication, we use the *player-partitioning* technique (see Sect. 6.5.1).

Theorem 8.4 *Let* $f : \{0, 1\}^n \to \{0, 1\}$ *be the n-party Boolean AND function where* $f(B_1, \dots, B_n) \overset{def}{=} B_1 \wedge \dots \wedge B_n$, *with each party P_i having the private input-bit B_i. Moreover, let $\mathcal{Z}$ be an adversary-structure such that $\mathcal{Z}$ does not satisfy the $\mathcal{Q}^{(2)}(\mathcal{P}, \mathcal{Z})$ condition. Then there exists no $\mathcal{Z}$-perfectly-secure protocol for f.*

Proof Let $\mathcal{Z}$ be an adversary-structure such that $\mathcal{Z}$ does not satisfy the $\mathcal{Q}^{(2)}(\mathcal{P}, \mathcal{Z})$ condition. Without loss of generality, let $Z_1, Z_2 \in \mathcal{Z}$, such that $Z_1 \cup Z_2 = \mathcal{P}$. Moreover, for simplicity, assume that $Z_1 \cap Z_2 = \emptyset$. We prove the theorem using a contradiction. So let us assume the existence of a $\mathcal{Z}$-perfectly-secure protocol for f, say Π_{nAND}. Using Π_{nAND}, we design a 1-perfectly-secure protocol Π_{2AND}, which allows two mutually-distrusting parties P_A and P_B with input-bits a and b respectively, to securely compute the function $\mathcal{F}_{\text{2AND}}$, where

$$\mathcal{F}_{\text{2AND}}(a, b) = (a \wedge b, a \wedge b).$$

However, since protocol Π_{2AND} is impossible due to Theorem 6.8, it implies that there exists no such protocol Π_{nAND}. The steps of the protocol Π_{2AND} are as follows (see Fig. 8.1 for a pictorial depiction):

- Party P_A plays the role of the parties in Z_1 as per the protocol Π_{nAND} with inputs of all the parties in Z_1 being set to a. While P_B plays the role of the parties in Z_2 as per the protocol Π_{nAND} with inputs of all the parties in Z_2 being set to b.
- If in the protocol Π_{nAND}, any party $P_i \in Z_1$ needs to send some message m to any party $P_j \in Z_2$, then in the protocol Π_{2AND}, party P_A sends m to P_B.
- If in the protocol Π_{nAND}, any party $P_k \in Z_2$ needs to send some message m' to any party $P_\ell \in Z_1$, then in the protocol Π_{2AND}, party P_B sends m' to P_A.
- If in the protocol Π_{nAND}, any party $P_i \in Z_1$ needs to send some message to any party $P_j \in Z_1$, then in the protocol Π_{2AND}, party P_A keeps the message with itself. In the same

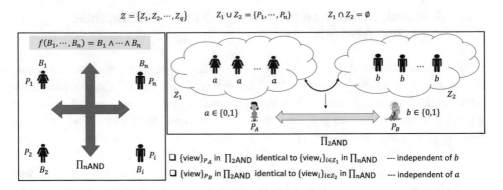

Fig. 8.1 Pictorial depiction of the transformation of $\Pi_{n\mathsf{AND}}$ into $\Pi_{2\mathsf{AND}}$

way, if in the protocol $\Pi_{n\mathsf{AND}}$, any party $P_i \in Z_2$ needs to send some message to any party $P_j \in Z_2$, then in the protocol $\Pi_{2\mathsf{AND}}$, party P_B keeps the message with itself.

- Party P_A outputs whatever the first party in Z_1 outputs, while P_B outputs whatever the first party in Z_2 outputs.

The *correctness* property of $\Pi_{n\mathsf{AND}}$ ensures that in the protocol $\Pi_{2\mathsf{AND}}$, parties P_A and P_B obtain the output $a \wedge b$. In the protocol $\Pi_{2\mathsf{AND}}$, if P_A is under adversary's control, then its view will be the same as the view of the parties in Z_1 in the protocol $\Pi_{n\mathsf{AND}}$. From the *privacy* property of the protocol $\Pi_{n\mathsf{AND}}$, the view of the parties in Z_1 will be independent of the inputs of the parties in $\mathcal{P} \setminus Z_1$, which is b. Using a similar argument, if P_B is under adversary's control in the protocol $\Pi_{2\mathsf{AND}}$, then its view will be the same as the view of the parties in Z_2 in the protocol $\Pi_{n\mathsf{AND}}$. From the *privacy* property of the protocol $\Pi_{n\mathsf{AND}}$, it follows that the view of P_B will be independent of a. Thus the privacy property of $\Pi_{n\mathsf{AND}}$ translates to the privacy property of $\Pi_{2\mathsf{AND}}$. $\qquad\square$

8.4 Various Building Blocks

In this section, we present the various building blocks for a perfectly-secure MPC protocol against a non-threshold adversary. Throughout, we assume that $\mathcal{Z}$ is a given adversary-structure, with basis $\mathcal{Z}_0 = \{Z_1, \ldots, Z_q\}$. While for few of the building blocks, it is sufficient to have $\mathcal{Z}$ satisfying the $\mathcal{Q}^{(1)}(\mathcal{P}, \mathcal{Z})$ condition, for the multiplication sub-protocol, we require $\mathcal{Z}$ to satisfy the $\mathcal{Q}^{(2)}(\mathcal{P}, \mathcal{Z})$ condition.

Protocol Sh$_{\text{ISN}}$

- Randomly pick $s_1, \ldots, s_q \in \mathcal{K}$, such that $s = s_1 + \ldots + s_q$ holds
- For $m = 1, \ldots, q$, send s_m to all the parties in $\mathcal{G}_m$.

Fig. 8.2 Secret-sharing protocol for generating a random $[\cdot]_{\mathcal{Z}}$ sharing of a secret. The above code is executed only by the dealer D

8.4.1   The Secret-Sharing Protocol

Protocol Sh$_{\text{ISN}}$ (Fig. 8.2) allows a designated dealer D $\in \mathcal{P}$ to generate a random $[\cdot]_{\mathcal{Z}}$-sharing of its private input s, such that the view of the adversary is independent of s. To do this, D generates a random vector of shares of s as per the algorithm G$_{\text{Ito}}$ (see Fig. 3.1) and distributes the respective shares to the corresponding parties in each group $\mathcal{G}_m$.

The properties of the protocol Sh$_{\text{ISN}}$ are stated in Lemma 8.5. While the round and communication complexity follows from the protocol inspection, the privacy property follows from the *privacy* property of G$_{\text{Ito}}$, as proved in Theorem 3.4.

Lemma 8.5 *Let $\mathcal{Z}$ be an adversary-structure satisfying the $\mathcal{Q}^{(1)}(\mathcal{P}, \mathcal{Z})$ condition. Then protocol* Sh$_{\text{ISN}}$ *allows a dealer* D $\in \mathcal{P}$ *with private input s to generate a random $[\cdot]_{\mathcal{Z}}$-sharing of s, such that the view of the adversary is independent of s for an honest* D. *The protocol requires one round of communication and incurs a communication of $\mathcal{O}(|\mathcal{Z}| \cdot \mathsf{poly}(n))$ elements from $\mathcal{K}$.*

8.4.2   The Reconstruction Protocol

Let s be a value which is $[\cdot]_{\mathcal{Z}}$-shared. Protocol Rec$_{\text{ISN}}$ (see Fig. 8.3) then allows all the parties to reconstruct the value s. For this, a *designated* party from each group $\mathcal{G}_m$ (say for instance, the party with the *least* index) is asked to make public the share of s, corresponding to the group $\mathcal{G}_m$. This ensures that all the shares of s are publicly available, enabling the parties to reconstruct s.

Protocol Rec$_{\text{ISN}}$

Let $[s] = (s_1, \ldots, s_q)$, where for $m = 1, \ldots, q$, each party in the group $\mathcal{G}_m$ holds the share s_m.
- For $m = 1, \ldots, q$, do the following: If $P_i \in \mathcal{G}_m$ and P_i is the least indexed party in $\mathcal{G}_m$, then send the share s_m to all the parties in $\mathcal{P}$.
- Upon receiving $s_1, \ldots, s_q$ from the least indexed party in $\mathcal{G}_1, \ldots, \mathcal{G}_q$ respectively, output $s_1 + \ldots + s_q$.

Fig. 8.3 Protocol for publicly reconstructing a $[\cdot]_{\mathcal{Z}}$-shared value. The above code is executed by every $P_i \in \mathcal{P}$

The properties of the protocol $\mathsf{Rec_{ISN}}$ are stated in Lemma 8.6, which follow in a straightforward way from the protocol inspection.

Lemma 8.6 *Let $\mathcal{Z}$ be an adversary-structure and let s be $[\cdot]_{\mathcal{Z}}$-shared. Then protocol $\mathsf{Rec_{ISN}}$ allows the parties to publicly reconstruct s. The protocol requires one round of communication and incurs a communication of $\mathcal{O}(|\mathcal{Z}| \cdot \mathsf{poly}(n))$ elements from $\mathcal{K}$.*

8.4.3 Multiplication Protocol

Consider the generalized n-party multiplication functionality $\mathcal{F}_{\mathsf{GenMult}}$, which takes input a $[\cdot]$-sharing of $a, b \in \mathcal{K}$ and outputs a *random* $[\cdot]$-sharing of $c \stackrel{def}{=} ab$. More formally, let $[a] = (a_1, \ldots, a_q)$ and $[b] = (b_1, \ldots, b_q)$ be a $[\cdot]$-sharing of a and b respectively, with each party P_i in the group $\mathcal{G}_m$ holding the shares a_m, b_m. And let $[c] = (c_1, \ldots, c_q)$ denote a *random* $[\cdot]$-sharing of ab. Then the functionality $\mathcal{F}_{\mathsf{GenMult}}$ is defined as follows:

$$\mathcal{F}_{\mathsf{GenMult}}\Big((\{a_m, b_m\}_{\mathcal{G}_m : P_1 \in \mathcal{G}_m}), \ldots, (\{a_m, b_m\}_{\mathcal{G}_m : P_n \in \mathcal{G}_m})\Big) = \Big((\{c_m\}_{\mathcal{G}_m : P_1 \in \mathcal{G}_m}), \ldots$$
$$(\{c_m\}_{\mathcal{G}_m : P_n \in \mathcal{G}_m})\Big).$$

We present a $\mathcal{Z}$-*perfectly-secure* protocol Π_{GenMult} for $\mathcal{F}_{\mathsf{GenMult}}$ due to [120], provided $\mathcal{Z}$ satisfies the $\mathcal{Q}^{(2)}(\mathcal{P}, \mathcal{Z})$ condition. The high level idea of the protocol is as follows. From the definition of $[\cdot]$-sharing, it follows that the following relation holds:

$$ab = a_1 b_1 + \ldots + a_i b_j + \ldots + a_q b_q = \sum_{j=1, k=1}^{j=q, k=q} a_j b_k.$$

Hence from the linearity property of $[\cdot]$-sharing, a $[\cdot]$-sharing of ab can be computed *non-interactively*, if each of the summands $a_j b_k$ is available in a $[\cdot]$-shared fashion. Based on this observation, in protocol Π_{GenMult}, a *publicly-known designated* party is assigned the task of acting as a dealer and generating a *random* $[\cdot]$-sharing of $a_j b_k$. A random $[\cdot]$-sharing of ab is then generated by summing all the individual random $[\cdot]$-shared summands. The crux of the protocol is to carefully identify the designated party, who can do a random $[\cdot]$-sharing of the summand $a_j b_k$.

Let $\mathcal{S}_{jk} \stackrel{def}{=} \mathcal{G}_j \cap \mathcal{G}_k = \mathcal{P} \setminus (Z_j \cup Z_k)$, where $\mathcal{G}_j = \mathcal{P} \setminus Z_j$ and $\mathcal{G}_k = \mathcal{P} \setminus Z_k$. Since $\mathcal{Z}$ is assumed to satisfy the $\mathcal{Q}^{(2)}(\mathcal{P}, \mathcal{Z})$ condition, it follows that the set $\mathcal{S}_{jk}$ is *non-empty*, else $\mathcal{P} \subseteq Z_j \cup Z_k$, which is a contradiction. Hence the parties in $\mathcal{S}_{jk}$ possess both the shares a_j as well as b_k and hence can compute the summand $a_j b_k$. Then the *least-indexed* party in $\mathcal{S}_{jk}$ is designated to carry out the task of randomly $[\cdot]$-sharing the summand $a_j b_k$. Note that there will be at least one set $\mathcal{S}_{jk}$ which will consist of only *honest* parties. Specifically, $\mathcal{S}_{jk}$ where either Z_j or Z_k is the corrupt set, contains only honest parties. Consequently, the

> **Protocol Π_{GenMult}**
>
> Let $[a] = (a_1, \ldots, a_q)$ and $[b] = (b_1, \ldots, b_q)$, where for $m = 1, \ldots, q$, each party in the group $\mathcal{G}_m$ holds the shares a_m and b_m. Moreover, for $1 \leq j, k, \leq q$, let $\mathcal{S}_{jk} \overset{def}{=} \mathcal{G}_j \cap \mathcal{G}_k$.
>
> - Corresponding to each set $\mathcal{S}_{jk}$, do the following:
>   - If P_i is the least indexed party in $\mathcal{S}_{jk}$, then act as a dealer D and invoke an instance of the protocol $\mathsf{Sh}_{\mathsf{Ito}}$ with input $a_j b_k$ to generate a random $[\cdot]$-sharing of $a_j b_k$.
>   - Participate in the instance of $\mathsf{Sh}_{\mathsf{ISN}}$ invoked by the least-indexed party in the set $\mathcal{S}_{jk}$. Let $\{(a_j b_k)_m\}_{\mathcal{G}_m : P_i \in \mathcal{G}_m}$ be the shares received by the party P_i in this instance of $\mathsf{Sh}_{\mathsf{Ito}}$.
> - Output the shares $\left\{ \sum_{j=1,k=1}^{j=q,k=q} (a_j b_k)_m \right\}_{\mathcal{G}_m : P_i \in \mathcal{G}_m}$. % Parties jointly compute $[ab] = \sum_{j=1,k=1}^{j=q,k=q} [a_j b_k]$.

Fig. 8.4 A $\mathcal{Z}$-*perfectly-secure* protocol for computing $\mathcal{F}_{\mathsf{GenMult}}$. The above code is executed by every $P_i \in \mathcal{P}$

corresponding summand $a_j b_k$ which is randomly $[\cdot]$-shared by the designated party in $\mathcal{S}_{jk}$ will be random from the point of view of adversary, ensuring that adversary does not learn any additional information. Protocol Π_{GenMult} is formally presented in Fig. 8.4.

The properties of the protocol Π_{GenMult} are stated in Lemma 8.7. The communication complexity follows from the fact that there are $q^2 = \mathcal{O}(|\mathcal{Z}|^2)$ instances of $\mathsf{Sh}_{\mathsf{ISN}}$ involved. Intuitively the protocol is secure as the adversary only learns shares of the summands shared by the honest parties as per the protocol $\mathsf{Sh}_{\mathsf{ISN}}$. From the *privacy* property of $\mathsf{Sh}_{\mathsf{ISN}}$, these shares are distributed randomly, independent of the actual summand and hence these shares can be easily simulated. We leave the formal details as an exercise.

Lemma 8.7 *Let $\mathcal{Z}$ be an adversary-structure satisfying the $\mathcal{Q}^{(2)}(\mathcal{P}, \mathcal{Z})$ condition. Then protocol Π_{GenMult} is a $\mathcal{Z}$-perfectly-secure protocol for $\mathcal{F}_{\mathsf{GenMult}}$ with one round of communication and communication complexity of $\mathcal{O}(|\mathcal{Z}|^3 \cdot \mathsf{poly}(n))$ elements from $\mathcal{K}$.*

A more efficient protocol for $\mathcal{F}_{\mathsf{GenMult}}$: Protocol Π_{GenMult} requires a communication of $\mathcal{O}(|\mathcal{Z}|^3 \cdot \mathsf{poly}(n))$ elements from $\mathcal{K}$, owing to the fact that an instance of $\mathsf{Sh}_{\mathsf{ISN}}$ is executed for generating a random $[\cdot]$-sharing of each of the q^2 summands $a_j b_k$, where each instance requires a communication of $\mathcal{O}(|\mathcal{Z}| \cdot \mathsf{poly}(n))$ elements. In [120], it was observed that one can reduce the number of instances of $\mathsf{Sh}_{\mathsf{ISN}}$ in Π_{GenMult} to $\mathcal{O}(n)$, thus bringing down the communication complexity to $\mathcal{O}(|\mathcal{Z}| \cdot \mathsf{poly}(n))$ elements from $\mathcal{K}$.

The idea behind the reduction is as follows: let party P_i is designated to generate a random $[\cdot]$-sharing of ℓ number of summands in the protocol Π_{GenMult}. Now instead of invoking ℓ independent instances of $\mathsf{Sh}_{\mathsf{ISN}}$ to share those ℓ summands, party P_i can instead invoke a *single* instance of Π_{GenMult} to generate a $[\cdot]$-sharing of sum of those summands. This ensures that there will be at most n instances of $\mathsf{Sh}_{\mathsf{ISN}}$ executed in the protocol Π_{GenMult} (one instance executed on the behalf of each party P_i to let P_i share the sum of all the designated summands). It is easy to see that the end result will be still a random $[\cdot]$-sharing of ab. To avoid repetition, we do not present the formal details of the modified protocol, denoted as Π_{GenMult}.

Protocol Π_{GenMPC}

- *Input Stage*: On having the input x_i, invoke an instance $\text{Sh}_{\text{ISN}}^{(i)}$ as D to generate a random $[\cdot]_{\mathcal{Z}}$-sharing of x_i. For $k = 1, \ldots, n$, let $\{s_{km}\}_{\mathcal{G}_m : P_i \in \mathcal{G}_m}$ be the shares, received from the dealer P_k, during $\text{Sh}_{\text{ISN}}^{(k)}$.
- *Computation Stage*: Let $G_1, \ldots, G_\ell$ be a publicly-known topological ordering of the gates of cir. For $k = 1, \ldots, \ell$, do the following for gate G_k:
    - If G_k *is an addition gate*: Let $\{a_m^{(k)}\}_{\mathcal{G}_m : P_i \in \mathcal{G}_m}$ and $\{b_m^{(k)}\}_{\mathcal{G}_m : P_i \in \mathcal{G}_m}$ be the shares held by P_i, corresponding to the gate-inputs. Set $\{a_m^{(k)} + b_m^{(k)}\}_{\mathcal{G}_m : P_i \in \mathcal{G}_m}$ to be the share, corresponding to the gate-output.
    - If G_k *is a multiplication-with-a-constant gate with constant* c: Let $\{a_m^{(k)}\}_{\mathcal{G}_m : P_i \in \mathcal{G}_m}$ be the share held by P_i, corresponding to the gate-input. Set $\{c \cdot a_m^{(k)}\}_{\mathcal{G}_m : P_i \in \mathcal{G}_m}$ to be the share, corresponding to the gate-output.
    - If G_k *is a multiplication gate*: Let $\{a_m^{(k)}\}_{\mathcal{G}_m : P_i \in \mathcal{G}_m}$ and $\{b_m^{(k)}\}_{\mathcal{G}_m : P_i \in \mathcal{G}_m}$ be the shares held by P_i, corresponding to the gate-inputs. Call $\mathcal{F}_{\text{GenMult}}$ by sending $\{(a_m^{(k)}, b_m^{(k)})\}_{\mathcal{G}_m : P_i \in \mathcal{G}_m}$ to $\mathcal{F}_{\text{GenMult}}$. Set $\{c_m^{(k)}\}_{\mathcal{G}_m : P_i \in \mathcal{G}_m}$ to be the shares, corresponding to the gate-output, where $\{c_m^{(k)}\}_{\mathcal{G}_m : P_i \in \mathcal{G}_m}$ are the shares returned back by $\mathcal{F}_{\text{GenMult}}$.
- *Output Stage*: Let $\{y_m\}_{\mathcal{G}_m : P_i \in \mathcal{G}_m}$ denote the shares held by P_i, corresponding to the function-output. Participate in an instance of Rec_{ISN} with these shares to reconstruct the output y.

Fig. 8.5 A $\mathcal{Z}$-*perfectly-secure* protocol for f in the $\mathcal{F}_{\text{GenMult}}$-hybrid model. The above code is executed by every $P_i \in \mathcal{P}$

8.5   A Perfectly-Secure MPC Protocol for Non-threshold Adversaries

In this section, we present a perfectly-secure MPC protocol Π_{GenMPC} tolerating a non-threshold adversary. The protocol is based on the idea of shared circuit-evaluation, where each value during the evaluation is randomly $[\cdot]_{\mathcal{Z}}$-shared, with the parties finally reconstructing the $[\cdot]_{\mathcal{Z}}$-shared output. The protocol is presented in the $\mathcal{F}_{\text{GenMult}}$-hybrid model and its formal details are available in Fig. 8.5.

The properties of the protocol Π_{GenMPC} are stated in Lemma 8.8. The security proof will be similar to the proof of Theorem 6.3 and we leave the formal details as an exercise.

Lemma 8.8 *Let* $y = f(x_1, \ldots, x_n)$ *be an n-ary deterministic function over* $\mathcal{K}$ *with* P_i *holding the private input* x_i. *Moreover, let* Adv *be a computationally-unbounded adversary, characterized by a non-threshold adversary* $\mathcal{Z}$ *satisfying the* $\mathcal{Q}^{(2)}(\mathcal{P}, \mathcal{Z})$ *condition. Then protocol* Π_{GenMPC} *is* $\mathcal{Z}$-*perfectly-secure for* f *in the* $\mathcal{F}_{\text{GenMult}}$-*hybrid model.*

The protocol requires 2 rounds and communication of $\mathcal{O}(|\mathcal{Z}| \cdot \text{poly}(n))$ *elements from* $\mathcal{K}$ *for the input and output stage. In addition,* c_M *calls to* $\mathcal{F}_{\text{GenMult}}$ *are made to evaluate the multiplication gates, where* c_M *denotes the number of multiplication gates in the circuit* cir *representing* f.

From Lemma 8.7 and the follow-up discussion, we know that protocol Π_{GenMult} is a $\mathcal{Z}$-perfectly-secure for $\mathcal{F}_{\text{GenMult}}$, provided $\mathcal{Z}$ satisfies the $\mathcal{Q}^{(2)}(\mathcal{P}, \mathcal{Z})$ condition. Hence, overall we get the following result regarding Π_{GenMPC}. The round complexity of $\mathcal{O}(D_M)$ is achieved, since all the multiplication-gates at the same multiplication layer can be evaluated in parallel, by invoking the corresponding instances of Π_{GenMult} in parallel.

Theorem 8.9 *Let* $y = f(x_1, \dots, x_n)$ *be an n-ary deterministic function over* $\mathcal{K}$ *with* P_i *holding the private input* x_i. *Moreover, let* Adv *be a computationally-unbounded adversary, characterized by a non-threshold adversary* $\mathcal{Z}$, *such that* $\mathcal{Z}$ *satisfies the* $\mathcal{Q}^{(2)}(\mathcal{P}, \mathcal{Z})$ *condition. Then protocol* Π_{GenMult} *is* $\mathcal{Z}$-*perfectly-secure for* f *in the plain model.*

The protocol requires 2 *rounds and communication of* $\mathcal{O}(|\mathcal{Z}| \cdot \mathsf{poly}(n))$ *elements from* $\mathcal{K}$ *for the input and output stage. During the computation stage, the protocol requires* $\mathcal{O}(D_M)$ *rounds of communication and incurs a communication of* $\mathcal{O}(c_M \cdot |\mathcal{Z}| \cdot \mathsf{poly}(n))$ *elements from* $\mathcal{K}$, *where* c_M *and* D_M *denote the number of multiplication gates and the multiplicative depth of the circuit* cir *respectively, representing the function* f.

Protocol Π_{GenMPC} **in the pre-processing model:** One can recast the protocol Π_{GenMPC} in the pre-processing model, where the protocol is divided into a *circuit-independent pre-processing phase*, followed by a *circuit-dependent circuit-evaluation* phase. In the pre-processing phase, the parties can generate random $[\cdot]_{\mathcal{Z}}$-sharing of c_M number of random multiplication-triples $(a, b, c) \in \mathcal{K}^3$, where $c = ab$. These triples can be then later used to evaluate the multiplication-gates in the circuit cir using the Beaver's method, since $[\cdot]$-sharing satisfies the linearity property.

In more detail, consider an arbitrary multiplication gate, with gate-inputs x and y being randomly $[\cdot]$-shared. Moreover, let parties have access to random $[\cdot]$-sharings of a random multiplication-triple (a, b, c) from the pre-processing phase. Then to generate a random $[\cdot]$-sharing of xy, the parties first *non-interactively* compute a $[\cdot]$-sharing of d and e, since the following hold:

$$[d] = [x] - [a], \quad [e] = [y] - [b].$$

The parties then *publicly* reconstruct the secret-shared values d and e. Once d and e are public, the parties can then *non-interactively* generate a $[\cdot]$-sharing of xy, since the following hold:

$$[xy] = de + d[b] + e[a] + [c].$$

To generate the $[\cdot]$-secret-shared random multiplication-triples in the pre-processing phase, the parties can first generate $[\cdot]$-secret-shared random pairs of values and then can use instances of the protocol Π_{GenMult} to generate a $[\cdot]$-sharing of product of each pair. To generate the secret-shared pairs, each party can "contribute" by $[\cdot]$-sharing a random pair of values and then all these $[\cdot]$-shared pairs can be summed up to generate a resultant $[\cdot]$-shared random pair of values. The idea used here is exactly the same as in protocol Π_{Triple}

(see Fig. 7.4), except that all computations are now done over $[\cdot]$-shared values and in the presence of a non-threshold adversary. We leave the complete formal details as an exercise for the interested readers.

8.6   Dealing with Malicious Adversaries

We conclude this chapter by briefly discussing the issues that may occur if the protocol Π_{GenMPC} (and the associated sub-protocols) are executed in the presence of a *malicious* adversary. Similar to the case of the protocol Π_{BGW}, corrupt parties *may not* generate $[\cdot]$-sharing of their inputs during the input stage and may produce incorrect shares during the output stage, leading the parties to reconstruct incorrect output. These problems can be sorted out by using a VSS scheme against non-threshold adversaries. A more serious problem occurs during the evaluation of multiplication gates (in the protocol Π_{GenMult} for computing $\mathcal{F}_{\mathsf{GenMult}}$), where the *designated* party to share the summands $a_j b_k$ may be maliciously corrupt and share incorrect summands, leading to incorrect evaluation of multiplication gates. Dealing with these challenges require additional technicalities and discussing them is out of scope of the current lecture series. We refer the interested readers to [93, 120] for more details.

Perfectly-Secure MPC for Small Number of Parties 9

So far our focus was on general n-party secure MPC, where the emphasis was on *asymptotic* efficiency. In this chapter, we discuss a special case of perfectly-secure MPC, namely MPC for small number of parties. Instead of asymptotic efficiency, our focus will be on *concrete* efficiency. The use case considered in this chapter is that of secure 3-*party computation* (secure 3PC), with one passive corruption. We discuss two different protocols in this setting, the first one due to [9] and the second one due to [47]. In a later chapter, we will show further improvements in the concrete efficiency of these protocols, settling for a *cryptographically-secure* variant of these protocols.

9.1   MPC for Small Number of Parties: Motivation

While secure MPC, in general, has been a subject of extensive research, the area of MPC with a small number of parties has drawn popularity of late mainly due to its efficiency and simplicity (see for instance [9, 39, 40, 45, 48, 71, 121, 122, 130] and their references). Furthermore, most real-time applications of secure MPC involve a small number of parties. Applications such as statistical and financial data analysis [35], email-filtering [112], distributed credential encryption [122], Danish sugar beet auction [36] involve only 3 parties. Well-known MPC frameworks such as VIFF [74], Sharemind [34] have been deployed with 3 parties. Recent advances in secure machine learning (ML) based on MPC have shown applications with a small number of parties [121, 123, 130]. MPC with a small number of parties helps solve MPC over large population as well via server-aided computation, where a small number of servers jointly hold the input data of the large population and run an MPC protocol evaluating the desired function.

As we will see in this chapter, there are tailor-made techniques for the secure 3PC setting, which can lead to more efficient circuit-evaluation by several order of magnitude, instead of adapting the protocols for the n-party setting to the the case of $n = 3$. Another advantage

A. Choudhury and A. Patra, *Secure Multi-Party Computation Against Passive Adversaries*,
Synthesis Lectures on Distributed Computing Theory,
https://doi.org/10.1007/978-3-031-12164-7_9

of designing customized secure 3PC protocols is that the resultant protocols *do not* impose any stringent requirements on the underlying algebraic structure. For instance, unlike the BGW protocol (and its variants) which require a finite *field* for operation, the 3PC protocols discussed in this chapter can work even over a finite *ring*. If the ring of ℓ-bit integers modulo 2^ℓ is used, the protocols directly utilize the integer arithmetic used inside the computer for deploying these protocols, resulting in faster implementations. The network model and the adversary setting considered in this chapter are the same as in Chap. 6 where $n = 3$ and $t = 1$.

9.2   Secure 3PC Protocol of [9]

In this section, we present the 1-perfectly-secure 3PC protocol of [9]. Throughout this section, we assume a finite ring $(\mathbb{R}, +, \cdot)$. The set of parties $\mathcal{P} = \{P_1, P_2, P_3\}$. The function f to be securely computed is expressed as a publicly-known arithmetic circuit cir over $\mathbb{R}$. Without loss of generality, we assume that f is a *deterministic* function, where each P_i has a private input $x_i \in \mathbb{R}$ and there is a single output $y \overset{def}{=} f(x_1, x_2, x_3)$ which is supposed to be learnt by all the parties.

The idea behind the secure 3PC protocol of [9] is based on the shared circuit-evaluation. However, instead of Shamir's secret-sharing, the underlying values during the circuit-evaluation are secret-shared as per *replicated secret-sharing* (RSS). We next present the definition of RSS.

Definition 9.1 (*Replicated Secret-Sharing (RSS)*) A value $s \in \mathbb{R}$ is said to be *RSS-shared*, if there exist values $s_1, s_2, s_3 \in \mathbb{R}$ where $s = s_1 + s_2 + s_3$, such that P_1 holds the *shares* (s_1, s_2), party P_2 holds the shares (s_2, s_3) and P_3 holds the shares (s_3, s_1). The notation $[s]_1$ denotes the vector of shares (s_1, s_2, s_3).

A vector of shares $(s_1, s_2, s_3) \in \mathbb{R}^3$ is called a *random* RSS-sharing of s, if s_1, s_2, s_3 are random elements from $\mathbb{R}$, subject to the condition that $s = s_1 + s_2 + s_3$ holds.

The term *replicated* here signifies that each piece s_i is possessed by two parties. Namely, party P_i holds the pieces s_i and s_{i+1}, where $s_{i+1} = s_{(i+1) \mod 3}$ if $i = 3$. A closer look into the semantics of RSS reveals that it is a special case of the $[\cdot]_{\mathcal{Z}}$-sharing (Definition 8.3) with respect to the adversary-structure $\mathcal{Z} = \{\{P_2\}, \{P_3\}, \{P_1\}\}$. Hence, RSS satisfies the *linearity* property, thus allowing the parties to *non-interactively* compute any linear function over RSS-shared inputs.

We next discuss the various building blocks, which will be used in the RSS-based secure 3PC protocol.

9.2.1 The Secret-Sharing and Reconstruction Protocols

Protocol $\mathsf{Sh}_{\mathsf{RSS}}$ (Fig. 9.1) allows a designated *dealer* $\mathsf{D} \in \mathcal{P}$ to generate a *random* RSS-sharing of a private input s held by D. The protocol steps are explained assuming $\mathsf{D} = P_1$ and similar steps are executed if $\mathsf{D} \in \{P_2, P_3\}$.

Protocol $\mathsf{Sh}_{\mathsf{RSS}}$ in the pre-processing model: It is easy to see that in protocol $\mathsf{Sh}_{\mathsf{RSS}}$, if D is *honest*, then the view of the adversary will be independent of s, since there will be one piece among s_1, s_2 and s_3 which will not be available with the adversary (we leave the formal security proof as an exercise). Protocol $\mathsf{Sh}_{\mathsf{RSS}}$ needs a communication of 4 ring elements (D does not communicate the shares of s to itself). We next show that if we design the protocol $\mathsf{Sh}_{\mathsf{RSS}}$ in the *pre-processing* model, then one can reduce the communication complexity of the protocol to 3 ring elements. This is a significant improvement, since in the context of secure 3PC, the focus is on the *concrete* efficiency, rather than *asymptotic* efficiency. In real-world applications (for example, secure ML) where a party may need to share thousands of values during the run-time, the above saving is significant.

The pre-processing based secret-sharing protocol is in the $\mathcal{F}_{\mathsf{Zero}}$-hybrid model (we will later present a 1-perfectly-secure protocol for $\mathcal{F}_{\mathsf{Zero}}$ in the *plain* model), where the functionality generates a *random* 3-party *additive* secret-sharing of the element 0. Formally, the function $\mathcal{F}_{\mathsf{Zero}}$ is as follows:

$$\mathcal{F}_{\mathsf{Zero}}(\lambda, \lambda, \lambda) = (\alpha_1, \alpha_2, \alpha_3),$$

where α_1, α_2 and α_3 are random elements from $\mathbb{R}$, such that $\alpha_1 + \alpha_2 + \alpha_3 = 0$ and party P_i holds the value α_i.

Now consider P_1 to be the dealer, who wants to generate a random RSS-sharing of its input s. And let P_1, P_2 and P_3 have access to random α_1, α_2 and α_3 respectively, such that $\alpha_1 + \alpha_2 + \alpha_3 = 0$ holds. Then we note that $s + (\alpha_1 + \alpha_2 + \alpha_3) = s$ holds. Hence, if we define $s_1 \overset{def}{=} s + \alpha_1$, $s_2 \overset{def}{=} \alpha_2$ and $s_3 \overset{def}{=} s_3$, then each P_i already holds s_i and the vector (s_1, s_2, s_3) already constitutes a *random* vector of shares as per RSS-sharing of s. Now to ensure that s is secret-shared as per the semantics of RSS-sharing, we need to ensure that each P_i holds s_{i+1} as well, which can be given to P_i by the party holding s_{i+1}. Hence, the resultant protocol requires each of the 3 parties to send a *single* ring element to exactly one other party, resulting in a total communication of 3 ring elements during the actual sharing

---

Protocol $\mathsf{Sh}_{\mathsf{RSS}}$

- On having the input s, randomly pick $s_1, s_2, s_2 \in \mathbb{R}$, such that $s = s_1 + s_2 + s_3$ holds.
- Send the *shares* (s_2, s_3) and (s_3, s_1) to P_2 and P_3 respectively.

Fig. 9.1 Secret-sharing protocol for generating a random RSS-sharing of a secret held by the dealer $\mathsf{D} = P_1$. The above code is executed only by P_1. Similar steps are executed if P_2 or P_3 is the dealer

---

Protocol Sh$_{RSS}$

 – *Pre-processing Phase*: Invoke $\mathcal{F}_{Zero}$ with input λ and receive α_i from $\mathcal{F}_{Zero}$.
 – *Sharing Phase*:
   • *If $P_i = P_1$*: On having the input s, compute $s_1 \overset{def}{=} s + \alpha_1$. Send s_1 to P_3.
   • *If $P_i = P_2$*: Set $s_2 \overset{def}{=} \alpha_2$. Send s_2 to P_1.
   • *If $P_i = P_3$*: Set $s_3 \overset{def}{=} \alpha_3$. Send s_3 to P_2.

Fig. 9.2 Modified secret-sharing protocol for generating a random RSS-sharing of a secret held by the dealer $D = P_1$ in the $\mathcal{F}_{Zero}$-hybrid model. The above code is executed by every $P_i \in \mathcal{P}$. Similar steps are executed if P_2 or P_3 is the dealer

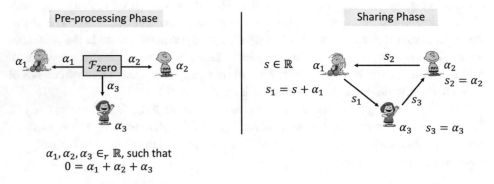

$\alpha_1, \alpha_2, \alpha_3 \in_r \mathbb{R}$, such that
$0 = \alpha_1 + \alpha_2 + \alpha_3$

Fig. 9.3 Pictorial depiction of the protocol Sh$_{RSS}$ in the $\mathcal{F}_{Zero}$-hybrid model where P_1 is the dealer

protocol.[1] The modified Sh$_{RSS}$ protocol is presented in Fig. 9.2 and for a pictorial illustration, see Fig. 9.3. We note that as it was the case with all the protocols discussed so far in the pre-processing model, the parties *cannot* re-use the same $(\alpha_1, \alpha_2, \alpha_3)$ for multiple instance of Sh$_{RSS}$, as it will *breach* privacy. Hence, for every instance of Sh$_{RSS}$, the parties need to have an independent and random additive sharing $(\alpha_1, \alpha_2, \alpha_3)$ of 0 from the pre-processing phase.

Reconstruction Protocol: Let s be a value which is RSS-shared. Then protocol Rec$_{RSS}$ (Fig. 9.4) allows the parties to *publicly* reconstruct s. In the protocol, each party P_i needs to send a single ring element to another party, which ensures that all the parties hold all the shares of s.

---

[1] This property of every party sending only one ring element to one another party will be a common feature, achieved by all the building blocks related to RSS.

Protocol Rec$_{RSS}$

Let $[s]_1 = (s_1, s_2, s_3)$, with P_1, P_2 and P_3 holding the shares $(s_1, s_2), (s_2, s_3)$ and (s_3, s_1) respectively.
  – *Steps for P_1:*
     • Send s_2 to P_3.
     • Upon receiving s_3 from P_2, output $s = s_1 + s_2 + s_3$.
  – *Steps for P_2:*
     • Send s_3 to P_1.
     • Upon receiving s_1 from P_3, output $s = s_1 + s_2 + s_3$.
  – *Steps for P_3:*
     • Send s_1 to P_2.
     • Upon receiving s_2 from P_1, output $s = s_1 + s_2 + s_3$.

Fig. 9.4 Reconstruction protocol to publicly reconstruct a RSS-shared value s

9.2.2 The Multiplication Protocol

Let a and b be two RSS-shared values and the goal is to securely compute the functionality $\mathcal{F}_{RSSMult}$, which generates a *random* RSS-sharing of ab. Formally, the functionality $\mathcal{F}_{RSSMult}$ is as follows:

$$\mathcal{F}_{RSSMult}\Big((a_1, a_2, b_1, b_2), (a_2, a_3, b_2, b_3), (a_3, a_1, b_3, b_1)\Big) = \Big((c_1, c_2), (c_2, c_3), (c_3, c_1)\Big),$$

where $[a]_1 = (a_1, a_2, a_3)$, $[b]_1 = (b_1, b_2, b_3)$ and $[c]_1 \stackrel{def}{=} (c_1, c_2, c_3)$ is a *random* RSS-sharing of $c \stackrel{def}{=} ab$. We now present a 1-*perfectly-secure* protocol $\Pi_{RSSMult}$ for $\mathcal{F}_{RSSMult}$. The high-level idea behind the protocol is as follows: since $a = a_1 + a_2 + a_3$ and $b = b_1 + b_2 + b_3$ holds, it follows that the following relation holds:

$$\begin{aligned} ab &= (a_1 + a_2 + a_3)(b_1 + b_2 + b_3) \\ &= (a_1 b_1 + a_1 b_2 + a_2 b_1) + (a_2 b_2 + a_2 b_3 + a_3 b_2) + (a_3 b_3 + a_3 b_1 + a_1 b_3) \\ &= z_1 + z_2 + z_3, \end{aligned}$$

where $z_1 \stackrel{def}{=} (a_1 b_1 + a_1 b_2 + a_2 b_1)$, $z_2 \stackrel{def}{=} (a_2 b_2 + a_2 b_3 + a_3 b_2)$ and $z_3 \stackrel{def}{=} (a_3 b_3 + a_3 b_1 + a_1 b_3)$. The vector of values (z_1, z_2, z_3) constitutes an *additive* secret-sharing of ab, with P_1, P_2 and P_3 having the ability to *locally* compute z_1, z_2 and z_3 respectively. One may think that the vector (z_1, z_2, z_3) can be treated as an RSS-sharing of ab as well, if P_1 sends z_1 to P_3, party P_2 sends z_2 to P_1 and P_3 sends z_3 to P_2. This will ensure that P_1, P_2 and P_3 holds $(z_1, z_2), (z_2, z_3)$ and (z_3, z_1) respectively. However, this is not sufficient for security, since the vector (z_1, z_2, z_3) *does not* constitute a *random* RSS-sharing of ab, which is the desired output of $\mathcal{F}_{RSSMult}$. Hence exchanging information as above may lead to security breach. For instance, if P_2 is under adversary's control, then it learns $a_3 b_1 + a_1 b_3$ after receiving z_3 from P_3, since a_3 and b_3 are also available with P_2. Hence clearly the view of adversary is no longer independent of a and b, as it learns some information about the values a_1 and b_1.

To make it more concrete, if $a_3 = b_3 = 1$ (the probability of this event is non-zero), then adversary actually learns $a_1 + b_1$ and hence it can rule out certain values of a and b from its point of view.[2]

To tackle the above problem, the parties need to jointly randomize the vector of shares (z_1, z_2, z_3) computed above, before exchanging the respective components of the resultant vector. To do the randomization, we assume that the parties have access to a *random* additive sharing $(\alpha_1, \alpha_2, \alpha_3)$ of 0 from the pre-processing phase. Hence the protocol Π_{RSSMult} is designed in the $\mathcal{F}_{\mathsf{Zero}}$-hybrid model, where P_1, P_2 and P_3 holds α_1, α_2 and α_3 respectively from the pre-processing phase, with α_1, α_2 and α_3 being random elements from $\mathbb{R}$, subject to the condition that $\alpha_1 + \alpha_2 + \alpha_3 = 0$ holds. Assuming that such a pre-processed correlated randomness is available to the parties, the parties randomize the vector (z_1, z_2, z_3), owing to the following relation:

$$
\begin{aligned}
ab &= (z_1 + z_2 + z_3) + (\alpha_1 + \alpha_2 + \alpha_3) \\
&= (z_1 + \alpha_1) + (z_2 + \alpha_2) + (z_3 + \alpha_3) \\
&= c_1 + c_2 + c_3,
\end{aligned}
$$

where $c_1 \overset{def}{=} z_1 + \alpha_1$, $c_2 \overset{def}{=} z_2 + \alpha_2$ and $c_3 \overset{def}{=} z_3 + \alpha_3$ and where P_1, P_2 and P_3 can *locally* compute c_1, c_2 and c_3 respectively. Notice that the vector (c_1, c_2, c_3) constitutes a *random* additive sharing of ab, since the vector of values $(\alpha_1, \alpha_2, \alpha_3)$ constitutes a *random* additive sharing of 0. Once the vector (c_1, c_2, c_3) is ready, to ensure that it constitutes an RSS-sharing of ab, party P_1, P_2 and P_3 sends c_1, c_2 and c_3 to P_3, P_1 and P_2 respectively. One can verify that now the view of the adversary will be independent of a and b.[3] It can be proved formally that protocol Π_{RSSMult} is a 1-perfectly-secure protocol for $\mathcal{F}_{\mathsf{RSSMult}}$ in the $\mathcal{F}_{\mathsf{Zero}}$-hybrid model; we leave the formal proof as an exercise. The formal steps of the protocol Π_{RSSMult} are presented in Fig. 9.6 and for a pictorial illustration, see Fig. 9.5. We note that the parties *cannot* reuse the same $(\alpha_1, \alpha_2, \alpha_3)$ across all the instances of Π_{RSSMult}, as it will violate the perfect-privacy (due to the same reason for which a Beaver's multiplication-triple cannot be reused for multiple multiplication gates). Hence for each instance of Π_{RSSMult}, the parties need to get an independent additive sharing $(\alpha_1, \alpha_2, \alpha_3)$ of 0 from $\mathcal{F}_{\mathsf{Zero}}$.

9.2.3 Protocol for Securely Computing $\mathcal{F}_{\mathsf{Zero}}$

We present a protocol Π_{Zero} (see Fig. 9.7), which is a 1-perfectly-secure protocol for $\mathcal{F}_{\mathsf{Zero}}$. The high-level idea of the protocol is very simple. Each party P_i picks a uniformly random element β_i from $\mathbb{R}$. We then note that the following relation holds:

---

[2] One can relate this problem with the degree-reduction problem in the context of the multiplication-gate evaluation in the BGW approach.

[3] One can imagine the above randomization process as equivalent of the randomization done in the GRR degree-reduction method.

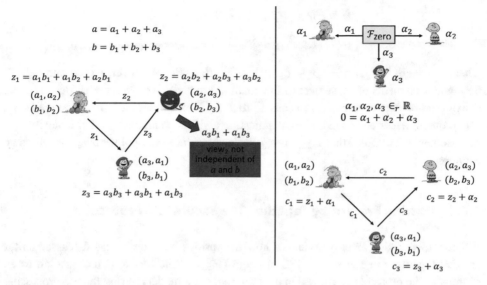

Fig. 9.5 Pictorial depiction of the protocol Π_{RSSMult}. The picture in the left shows the insecure method, where parties exchange the values z_1, z_2 and z_3 without randomizing the values. The picture in the right shows the actual protocol in the $\mathcal{F}_{\text{Zero}}$-hybrid model

---

Protocol Π_{RSSMult}

Let $[a]_1 = (a_1, a_2, a_3)$ and $[b]_1 = (b_1, b_2, b_3)$, with P_1, P_2 and P_3 holding the shares $(a_1, a_2, b_1, b_2), (a_2, a_3, b_2, b_3)$ and (a_3, a_1, b_3, b_1) respectively.
- *Pre-processing phase*: Invoke $\mathcal{F}_{\text{Zero}}$ with input λ and receive the output α_i from $\mathcal{F}_{\text{Zero}}$.
- *Circuit-evaluation phase*:
  - Compute $c_i \stackrel{def}{=} a_i b_i + a_i b_{i+1} + a_{i+1} b_i + \alpha_i$, where $i + 1 \stackrel{def}{=} 1$, if $i = 3$.
  - Send c_i to party P_{i-1}, where $i - 1 \stackrel{def}{=} 3$, if $i = 1$.

Fig. 9.6 A 1-perfectly-secure protocol for $\mathcal{F}_{\text{RSSMult}}$ in the $\mathcal{F}_{\text{Zero}}$-hybrid model. The above code is executed by every party P_i

---

Protocol Π_{Zero}

- Randomly pick β_i from $\mathbb{R}$ and send β_i to P_{i-1}, where $i - 1 \stackrel{def}{=} 3$, if $i = 1$.
- Upon receiving β_{i+1} from P_{i+1}, where $i + 1 \stackrel{def}{=} 1$ for $i = 3$, compute $\alpha_i = \beta_i - \beta_{i+1}$.

Fig. 9.7 A 1-perfectly-secure protocol for $\mathcal{F}_{\text{Zero}}$. The above code is executed by every party P_i

$$0 = (\beta_1 - \beta_2) + (\beta_2 - \beta_3) + (\beta_3 - \beta_1)$$
$$= \alpha_1 + \alpha_2 + \alpha_3,$$

where $\alpha_1 \stackrel{def}{=} \beta_1 - \beta_2$, $\alpha_2 \stackrel{def}{=} \beta_2 - \beta_3$ and $\alpha_3 \stackrel{def}{=} \beta_3 - \beta_1$. Moreover, α_1, α_2 and α_3 will be random elements of $\mathbb{R}$, subject to the condition that $\alpha_1 + \alpha_2 + \alpha_3 = 0$. Based on the above relationship, each party P_i sends β_i to P_{i-1}. This allows each P_j to compute α_j. The protocol needs one round of communication and has communication complexity of 3 ring elements. The proof that Π_{Zero} is a 1-perfectly-secure protocol for $\mathcal{F}_{\mathsf{Zero}}$ is left as an exercise.

9.2.4 Putting Everything Together: The Secure 3PC Protocol

We now give a high level overview of how the various building blocks discussed so far are tied together to get a secure 3PC protocol Π_{RSS3PC} (the formal details are left as an exercise). The protocol is designed in the pre-processing model. During the pre-processing phase, the parties generate random additive sharings of 0. Since we assumed that each P_i has a single input x_i for f, assuming that the circuit cir representing f has c_M number of multiplication gates, the parties generate $c_M + 3$ random additive sharings of 0, by executing $c_M + 3$ instances of protocol Π_{Zero} in parallel. While 3 of these additive sharings are used for generating RSS-sharing of the inputs of the parties for f, the remaining c_M sharings are used for evaluating the multiplication gates.

During the circuit-evaluation phase, the parties start jointly evaluating cir, where each value is randomly RSS-shared. To begin with, each P_i generates a random RSS-sharing of its input x_i using a pre-processed additive sharing of 0 as per protocol $\mathsf{Sh}_{\mathsf{RSS}}$. The linear gates in cir are evaluated non-interactively, owing to the linearity property of RSS-sharing. For evaluating a multiplication gate, the parties use an instance of Π_{RSSMult} by deploying a pre-processed additive sharing of 0. Finally, once the function output is ready in RSS-shared fashion, the parties execute an instance of $\mathsf{Rec}_{\mathsf{RSS}}$ to publicly reconstruct it. The properties of the protocol Π_{RSS3PC} are stated in Theorem 9.2; while the complexity figures are easy to verify, we leave the security proof as an exercise.

Theorem 9.2 *Let $y = f(x_1, x_2, x_3)$ be a ternary deterministic function over $\mathbb{R}$ with P_i holding the private input x_i. Moreover, let Adv be a computationally-unbounded adversary, which can control any one out of the 3 parties P_1, P_2 or P_3 in a passive fashion. Then protocol Π_{RSS3PC} is a 1-perfectly-secure for f in the plain model.*

For evaluating a single multiplication gate, the protocol requires a communication of 3 ring elements in the pre-processing phase and a communication of 3 ring elements in the circuit-evaluation phase. The protocol requires one round of communication during the pre-processing phase and $2 + D_M$ rounds of communication during the circuit-evaluation phase, where D_M is the multiplicative depth of the circuit cir representing f.

Comparing Π_{RSS3PC} **with Protocol** Π_{BGW}: We conclude this section by showing that the *concrete* efficiency of the protocol Π_{RSS3PC} (as stated in Theorem 9.2) is indeed better than the secure 3PC protocol, derived from the generic n-party MPC protocol Π_{BGW} by substituting $n = 3$ and $t = 1$. For comparison, we focus on the concrete cost of evaluating a multiplication gate (recall that the cost of any generic MPC protocol is pre-dominated by the complexity of evaluating *multiplication* gates). For this, we consider three distinct variants of Π_{BGW}: one *without* pre-processing where protocol Π_{GRRMult} is used for evaluating multiplication gates during the circuit-evaluation phase and two variants in the pre-processing model. Moreover, we focus only on the cost during the *circuit-evaluation* phase, which is function and circuit-dependent.

- If protocol Π_{GRRMult} (Fig. 6.7) is used to evaluate a multiplication gate, then each $P_i \in \{P_1, P_2, P_3\}$ needs to generate a random 1-Shamir-sharing of its *product-share*. This will require P_i to send 2 *field* elements (Shamir-shares) to every other party and hence a total communication of 6 field elements.
- Let us next consider the variants of Π_{BGW} in the pre-processing model. If we consider the variant based on Beaver's multiplication-triple (protocol Π_{Beaver} in Fig. 7.2), then the protocol requires public reconstruction of two 1-Shamir-shared values for evaluating each multiplication gate. This will require a communication of 6 elements, 2 elements for first letting only P_1 to reconstruct those values and 4 elements for P_1 to relay those reconstructed values to remaining two parties.
  If we consider the variant based on double-shared random values (protocol Π_{DN} in Fig. 7.6), then it requires the parties to publicly reconstruct a 2-Shamir-shared value. This needs a communication of 4 elements: 2 elements for first letting only P_1 to reconstruct the value and further 2 elements to let P_1 relay the reconstructed value to the remaining two parties.

Hence in all the cases, the *concrete* efficiency of Π_{RSSMult} for evaluating the *multiplication* gates during the *circuit-evaluation* phase is clearly better than the generic protocols. With the goal of further improving this concrete efficiency, we next discuss a more efficient 3PC protocol.

9.3   ASTRA: Secure 3PC of [47]

All the MPC protocols discussed till now assign "symmetric" role to all the parties. The idea behind the secure 3PC protocol ASTRA of [47] (which is inherited from [101]) is to break this symmetry and instead assign "asymmetric" roles to the parties. In more detail, one of the designated parties in $\mathcal{P}$ is assigned the role of a *distributor*, denoted by D, while the remaining two parties are designated as *evaluators*, denoted by E_1 and E_2; hence $\mathcal{P} = \{D, E_1, E_2\}$. The protocol is designed in the pre-processing model. During the pre-processing phase, the distributor D distributes correlated randomness among the evaluators. This entire phase is executed *only* by D. The presence of E_1 and E_2 *is not* required and they can receive the values sent by D as soon as they "wake up" at a later point of time. During the circuit-evaluation phase, the evaluators jointly evaluate the circuit in a secret-shared fashion using the correlated randomness generated in the pre-processing phase. The distributor is *not* allowed to participate during the circuit-evaluation phase (otherwise it will violate the privacy). One can observe the "asymmetry" involved here in terms of the roles played by the different parties.

The protocol does not put any restriction regarding who is assigned the role of the distributor and evaluators. The deployer can do the role assignment, based on the parameters of the network among the various parties. For instance, since a fast circuit-evaluation phase is preferred, one can assign the role of evaluators to the parties who have fast computing resources and connected through high speed network. We note that such a design flexibility is *absent* in the secure 3PC protocol Π_{RSSMult}, where all the three parties play a symmetric role, both during the pre-processing phase, as well as during the circuit-evaluation phase.

In terms of *concrete* efficiency, the ASTRA 3PC protocol requires a communication of 4 ring elements and 2 ring elements per multiplication gate, during the pre-processing and circuit-evaluation phase respectively. While the *total* communication cost per multiplication gate is *same* as Π_{RSSMult} (namely 6 ring elements), the cost-distribution across the two phases are different: protocol Π_{RSSMult} requires 3 ring elements during both the phases, while ASTRA needs 4 elements during the pre-processing phase and 2 elements during the circuit-evaluation phase, offering a better circuit-evaluation phase. The downside is that unlike protocol Π_{RSSMult} where the pre-processing phase is *circuit-independent*, the pre-processing phase of ASTRA is *circuit-dependent*. However this is not an issue in real-world applications like MLaaS, where the same circuit needs to be evaluated several times by the same set of parties, but over different inputs.

To exploit the above idea of incorporating asymmetry in the role parties, a new secret-sharing is introduced in [47], which we call as *masked secret-sharing* (MSS) and where parties are assigned "asymmetric" shares. Informally, here the evaluators hold a *one-time pad* (OTP) encryption of the underlying secret and each evaluator holds an additive-share of the corresponding OTP. The OTP and its additive shares are selected randomly by the distributor. More formally:

Definition 9.3 (*Masked Secret-Sharing (MSS)*) A value $s \in \mathbb{R}$ is said to be *MSS-shared*, if there exist values $\lambda_{s,1}, \lambda_{s,2}, m_s \in \mathbb{R}$ where $m_s = s + \lambda_{s,1} + \lambda_{s,2}$, such that D holds the share $(\lambda_{s,1}, \lambda_{s,2})$, while each E_i holds the share $(\lambda_{s,i}, m_s)$. The notation $\langle s \rangle$ denotes the vector of shares $\left((\lambda_{s,1}, \lambda_{s,2}), (\lambda_{s,1}, m_s), (\lambda_{s,2}, m_s) \right)$, where the first, second and third component belongs to D, E_1 and E_2 respectively.

A vector of shares $\left((\lambda_{s,1}, \lambda_{s,2}), (\lambda_{s,1}, m_s), (\lambda_{s,2}, m_s) \right)$ is called a *random* MSS-sharing of s, if $\lambda_{s,1}$ and $\lambda_{s,2}$ are random elements from $\mathbb{R}$ (implying that m_s is also a random element of $\mathbb{R}$).

It is easy to see that MSS satisfies the linearity property and hence allows the parties to *non-interactively* compute any *linear* function of MSS-shared inputs. We next present the various building blocks, which are used in the ASTRA 3PC protocol.

9.3.1   The Secret-Sharing and Reconstruction Protocols

Protocol $\mathsf{Sh_{MSS}}$ allows a designated *dealer* to generate a random MSS-sharing of its private input, such that the view of the adversary is independent of the input for an *honest* dealer. Since MSS-sharing has asymmetric sharing-semantics, the steps of $\mathsf{Sh_{MSS}}$ will be different, depending upon whether the dealer is the distributor or one of the evaluators. The protocol is in the pre-processing model. During the pre-processing phase, D generates shares of a random OTP and distributes it to the respective parties, with the dealer holding both the OTP-shares. During the circuit-evaluation phase, the dealer computes the OTP encryption of the secret and distributes it to the respective parties. The protocol is presented in Fig. 9.9 and is pictorially depicted in Fig. 9.8.

It is easy to see that if the dealer is *honest*, then the underlying secret remains perfectly-secure. For instance, if D is the dealer, then either E_1 or E_2 could be corrupt. If E_1 is corrupt, then it does not learn $\lambda_{s,2}$ which is randomly chosen from $\mathbb{R}$ and hence m_s will be a random element for E_1. Similar argument holds for the case when E_2 is corrupt. On the other hand,

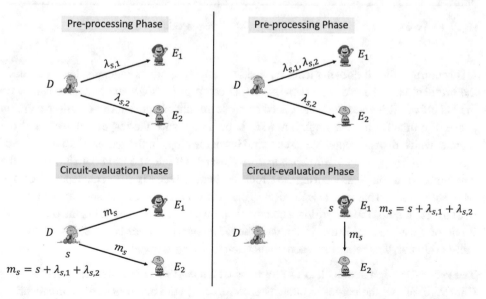

Fig. 9.8 Pictorial depiction of the protocol $\mathsf{Sh_{MSS}}$. The picture in the left shows the protocol when D is the dealer, while the picture in the right shows the protocol when E_1 is the dealer (similar steps are executed when E_2 is the dealer)

Protocol Sh$_{\text{MSS}}$

- *Pre-processing Phase*: Only D executes the following steps:
  - Randomly select $\lambda_{s,1}$ and $\lambda_{s,2}$ from $\mathbb{R}$.
  - If D is the dealer, then send λ_{s_i} to E_i, for $i = 1, 2$.
  - If E_1 is the dealer, then send $(\lambda_{s,1}, \lambda_{s,2})$ and $\lambda_{s,2}$ to E_1 and E_2 respectively.
  - If E_2 is the dealer, then send $(\lambda_{s,1}, \lambda_{s,2})$ and $\lambda_{s,1}$ to E_2 and E_1 respectively.
- *Circuit-evaluation Phase*: On having the input $s \in \mathbb{R}$, the dealer computes $m_s \stackrel{def}{=} s + \lambda_{s,1} + \lambda_{s,2}$ and does the following, depending upon the case.
  - If D is the dealer, then send m_s to E_1 and E_2.
  - If E_1 is the dealer, then send m_s to E_2.
  - If E_2 is the dealer, then send m_s to E_1.

Fig. 9.9 Protocol for generating a random MSS-sharing of a secret held by a dealer

---

Protocol Rec$_{\text{MSS}}$

Let the MSS-sharing of s be denoted by the vector of shares $\big((\lambda_{s,1}, \lambda_{s,2}), (\lambda_{s,1}, m_s), (\lambda_{s,2}, m_s)\big)$.
- *Steps for* D:
  - Send $\lambda_{s,1}$ to E_2.
  - Upon receiving m_s from E_1, compute $s = m_s - (\lambda_{s,1} + \lambda_{s,2})$.
- *Steps for* E_1:
  - Send m_s to D.
  - Upon receiving $\lambda_{s,2}$ from E_2, compute $s = m_s - (\lambda_{s,1} + \lambda_{s,2})$.
- *Steps for* E_2:
  - Send $\lambda_{s,2}$ to E_1.
  - Upon receiving $\lambda_{s,1}$ from D, compute $s = m_s - (\lambda_{s,1} + \lambda_{s,2})$.

Fig. 9.10 Protocol for publicly reconstructing a MSS-shared value

if D is corrupt, then it does not learn m_s and the pads $\lambda_{s,1}, \lambda_{s,2}$ are independent of s. Since the protocol is in the pre-processing model, D can *pre-distribute* the pads in advance on the behalf of all the secrets which need to be secret-shared during the circuit-evaluation phase. For this, D (and the parties) need to know in advance the respective dealers of the secrets, which depends upon the circuit cir. Hence the steps in the pre-processing phase of the protocol Sh$_{\text{MSS}}$ are *circuit-dependent*. A closer look into the protocol shows that the communication complexity during the circuit-evaluation phase is different, depending upon who is the dealer. That is, if D is the dealer, then the OTP encryption m_s needs to be sent to both the evaluators, thus requiring a communication of 2 ring elements. On the other hand, if one of the evaluators is the dealer, then the OTP encryption needs to be sent to *only* the other evaluator, thus requiring a communication of 1 ring element.

The reconstruction protocol: Let s be a value which is MSS-shared. Then protocol Rec$_{\text{MSS}}$ (Fig. 9.10) allows the parties to publicly reconstruct s, with one round of communication, involving a communication of 3 ring elements. The high level idea of the protocol is as follows: from the semantics of MSS, it follows that each party lacks a single "piece" to completely learn s. That is, D is missing the OTP encryption m_s, while E_1 and E_2 are missing

$\lambda_{s,2}$ and $\lambda_{s,1}$ respectively. Hence to publicly reconstruct s, it is enough if the corresponding missing piece is made available to each party. This is done carefully in the protocol to ensure that each party is burdened with the load of providing a desired missing piece to exactly one other party.

9.3.2   The Multiplication Protocol

While MSS-sharing satisfies the linearity property allowing for local evaluation of any linear gate, it does not allow local evaluation of a multiplication gate. In this section, we present a protocol Π_{MSSMult}, which allows the parties to solve this problem. More specifically, the protocol securely computes the functionality $\mathcal{F}_{\text{MSSMult}}$, which takes input two MSS-shared values and generates a *random* MSS-sharing of the product of those values. More formally:

$$\mathcal{F}_{\text{MSSMult}}\Big(((\lambda_{a,1}, \lambda_{a,2}), (\lambda_{b,1}, \lambda_{b,2})), ((\lambda_{a,1}, m_a), (\lambda_{b,1}, m_b)), ((\lambda_{a,2}, m_a), (\lambda_{b,2}, m_b)) \Big) =$$

$$\Big((\lambda_{c,1}, \lambda_{c,2}), (\lambda_{c,1}, m_c), (\lambda_{c,2}, m_c) \Big),$$

where $\Big((\lambda_{c,1}, \lambda_{c,2}), (\lambda_{c,1}, m_c), (\lambda_{c,2}, m_c) \Big)$ denotes a *random* MSS-sharing of ab, such that $a = m_a - (\lambda_{a,1} + \lambda_{a,2})$ and $b = m_b - (\lambda_{b,1} + \lambda_{b,2})$. The high level idea of the protocol is as follows: during the *pre-processing* phase, D picks random OTP-shares $\lambda_{c,1}$ and $\lambda_{c,2}$ and distributes it to E_1 and E_2 respectively. Now to generate a MSS-sharing of ab, the evaluators E_1 and E_2 need to compute the OTP encryption $m_c \stackrel{def}{=} ab + \lambda_{c,1} + \lambda_{c,2}$ during the *circuit-evaluation* phase. For this, we note that the following relationship holds:

$$m_c = ab + (\lambda_{c,1} + \lambda_{c,2})$$
$$= [m_a - (\lambda_{a,1} + \lambda_{a,2})][m_b - (\lambda_{b,1} + \lambda_{b,2})] + (\lambda_{c,1} + \lambda_{c,2})$$
$$= m_a m_b - m_a(\lambda_{b,1} + \lambda_{b,2}) - m_b(\lambda_{a,1} + \lambda_{a,2}) + (\lambda_{c,1} + \lambda_{c,2}) + (\lambda_{a,1} + \lambda_{a,2})(\lambda_{b,1} + \lambda_{b,2})$$

Let $\gamma_c \stackrel{def}{=} (\lambda_{a,1} + \lambda_{a,2})(\lambda_{b,1} + \lambda_{b,2})$. It follows that the value γ_c will be available with D in the pre-processing phase, as all the OTP-shares are selected by D. Hence D can generate a random 2-party additive-sharing of γ_c during the *pre-processing* phase by picking random shares $\gamma_{c,1}$ and $\gamma_{c,2}$, subject to the condition that $\gamma_{c,1} + \gamma_{c,2} = \gamma_c$ and distributes $\gamma_{c,1}$ and $\gamma_{c,2}$ to E_1 and E_2 respectively. Notice that this makes the pre-processing phase steps *circuit-dependent*, as γ_c depends upon the OTP-shares used in the MSS-sharing of the inputs a and b. Now once γ_c is additively-shared among E_1 and E_2, it then follows that m_c can be computed, based on the following relationship:

$$m_c = (m_a m_b - m_a \lambda_{b,1} - m_b \lambda_{a,1} + \lambda_{c,1} + \gamma_{c,1}) + (0 - m_a \lambda_{b,2} - m_b \lambda_{a,2} + \lambda_{c,2} + \gamma_{c,2})$$
$$= m_{c,1} + m_{c_2},$$

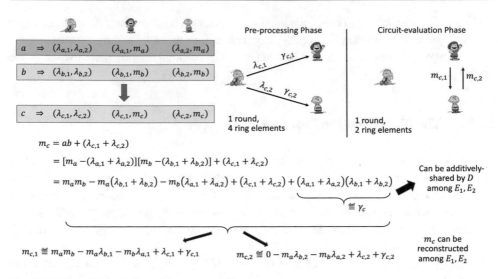

$$m_c = ab + (\lambda_{c,1} + \lambda_{c,2})$$

$$= [m_a - (\lambda_{a,1} + \lambda_{a,2})][m_b - (\lambda_{b,1} + \lambda_{b,2})] + (\lambda_{c,1} + \lambda_{c,2})$$

$$= m_a m_b - m_a(\lambda_{b,1} + \lambda_{b,2}) - m_b(\lambda_{a,1} + \lambda_{a,2}) + (\lambda_{c,1} + \lambda_{c,2}) + \underbrace{(\lambda_{a,1} + \lambda_{a,2})(\lambda_{b,1} + \lambda_{b,2})}_{\stackrel{\text{def}}{=} \gamma_c}$$

$$\underbrace{m_{c,1} \stackrel{\text{def}}{=} m_a m_b - m_a \lambda_{b,1} - m_b \lambda_{a,1} + \lambda_{c,1} + \gamma_{c,1}}_{} \qquad m_{c,2} \stackrel{\text{def}}{=} 0 - m_a \lambda_{b,2} - m_b \lambda_{a,2} + \lambda_{c,2} + \gamma_{c,2}$$

Fig. 9.11 Pictorial depiction of the protocol Π_{MSSMult}

where $m_{c,1} \stackrel{def}{=} (m_a m_b - m_a \lambda_{b,1} - m_b \lambda_{a,1} + \lambda_{c,1} + \gamma_{c,1})$ and $m_{c,2} \stackrel{def}{=} (0 - m_a \lambda_{b,2} - m_b \lambda_{a,2} + \lambda_{c,2} + \gamma_{c,2})$. Hence during the circuit-evaluation phase, E_1 and E_2 can compute $m_{c,1}$ and $m_{c,2}$ respectively and reconstruct m_c by exchanging these values, *only* among themselves. The protocol is formally presented in Fig. 9.12 and is pictorially illustrated in Fig. 9.11.

Protocol Π_{MSSMult}

- *Pre-processing Phase*: In this phase, D has the inputs $(\lambda_{a,1}, \lambda_{a,2})$ and $(\lambda_{b,1}, \lambda_{b,2})$, corresponding to the gate-inputs and it executes the following steps:
  - Compute $\gamma_c \stackrel{def}{=} (\lambda_{a,1} + \lambda_{a,2})(\lambda_{b,1} + \lambda_{b,2})$.
  - Randomly pick $\gamma_{c,1}$ and $\gamma_{c,2}$ from $\mathbb{R}$, such that $\gamma_c = \gamma_{c,1} + \gamma_{c,2}$ holds.
  - Randomly pick $\lambda_{c,1}$ and $\lambda_{c,2}$.
  - Send $\lambda_{c,i}$ and $\gamma_{c,i}$ to E_i, for $i = 1, 2$.
- *Circuit-evaluation Phase*: In this phase, each evaluator E_i has inputs $(\lambda_{a,i}, m_a)$ and $(\lambda_{b,i}, m_b)$ corresponding to gate-inputs and $(\lambda_{c,i}, \gamma_{c,i})$ corresponding to gate-output.
  - *Steps for E_1*:
    - Send $m_{c,1} \stackrel{def}{=} (m_a m_b - m_a \lambda_{b,1} - m_b \lambda_{a,1} + \lambda_{c,1} + \gamma_{c,1})$ to E_2.
    - Upon receiving $m_{c,2}$ from E_2, compute $m_c = m_{c,1} + m_{c,2}$.
  - *Steps for E_2*:
    - Send $m_{c,2} \stackrel{def}{=} (0 - m_a \lambda_{b,2} - m_b \lambda_{a,2} + \lambda_{c,2} + \gamma_{c,2})$ to E_1.
    - Upon receiving $m_{c,1}$ from E_1, compute $m_c = m_{c,1} + m_{c,2}$.

Fig. 9.12 A 1-perfectly-secure protocol for $\mathcal{F}_{\text{MSSMult}}$

From the protocol inspection, it follows that protocol Π_{MSSMult} needs a communication of 4 ring elements during the pre-processing phase (to distribute the additive-shares of λ_c and γ_c) and a communication of 2 ring elements during the circuit-evaluation phase (to let the evaluators reconstruct m_c). One can easily prove that the protocol is a 1-perfectly-secure protocol for $\mathcal{F}_{\text{MSSMult}}$ and we leave the formal details as an exercise.

9.3.3 The ASTRA 3PC Protocol

The various building blocks in the context of MSS-sharing discussed so far can be easily tied together to get the secure 3PC protocol Π_{MSS3PC} (the protocol is referred by the name ASTRA in the literature). The protocol has a *circuit-dependent* pre-processing phase, executed only by D, where D distributes random OTP-shares for each value in the circuit. To ensure that linear gates can be later evaluated locally (by using the linearity property of MSS-sharing), the OTP-shares of the output of the linear gates are set as the corresponding linear function of OTP-shares of the gate-input(s). Moreover, for the multiplication gates in the circuit, D also distributes random additive-shares of the product of the OTP-shares of the gate-inputs. Namely, it executes the steps corresponding to the pre-processing phase as per the protocol Π_{MSSMult}.

The circuit-evaluation phase is executed only by the evaluators, where the output of each gate is made available in a random MSS-shared fashion. While the linearity property of MSS allows the evaluators to maintain this invariant *non-interactively*, for evaluating multiplication gates, the evaluators execute the steps corresponding to the circuit-evaluation phase as per the protocol Π_{MSSMult}. The participation of D is not required in this phase, as D would have already got its shares (namely the OTP-shares) corresponding to the MSS-sharing of each value during the pre-processing phase itself. Once the function output is ready in a MSS-shared fashion, it is publicly reconstructed by executing an instance of Rec_{MSS}. As the same principle of shared circuit-evaluation has been used throughout in all the protocols so far (albeit with different secret-sharing semantics), we leave the formal details of Π_{MSS3PC} and its formal security proof as an exercise.

9.4 Dealing with Malicious Adversaries

We conclude this chapter by briefly discussing the issues that may occur if the protocols Π_{RSS3PC} and Π_{MSS3PC} (and the associated sub-protocols) are executed in the presence of a *malicious* adversary. Let us first consider the protocol Π_{RSS3PC}, where the following problems may occur if one of the parties among P_1, P_2 and P_3 gets maliciously corrupt: (a) The corrupt party *may not* secret-share its input as per the semantics of RSS; (b) The corrupt party may produce incorrect share during the reconstruction of a RSS-shared value, leading to incorrect values being reconstructed and (c) The corrupt party may send incorrect values during the evaluation of multiplication gates. These issues can be handled by incorporating additional verification mechanisms in the sub-protocols Sh_{RSS}, Rec_{RSS}, $\Pi_{RSSMult}$ and Π_{Zero} to verify if all the parties (including the corrupt party) are following the protocol steps, without revealing anything additional about the values of the honest parties (see [50, 121]). However, we stress that the verification mechanisms can *only* enable the parties to *detect* whether any of the parties have deviated from the protocol instructions, *without* disclosing the exact identity of the maliciously-corrupt party. Consequently, the notion of security achieved by the resultant maliciously-secure 3PC protocol is that of *security with abort*, where the honest parties have to pre-maturely halt the protocol execution in the face of any malicious corruption, without getting the function output. For instance, consider the reconstruction protocol Rec_{RSS} for publicly-reconstructing an RSS-shared value s, where the shares of P_1, P_2 and P_3 are (s_1, s_2), (s_2, s_3) and (s_3, s_1) respectively. In the protocol, every party receives the "missing" share from another party. In the *maliciously*-secure Rec_{RSS} protocol, to verify if a party has received the correct missing share, the missing share needs to be supplied by two parties and then compared. For instance, P_1 should ask for the missing s_3 from *both* P_2 and P_3 and compare whether it has received the *same* s_3 from both the parties, which will guarantee that the received s_3 is correct, as there will be at least one honest party among P_2 and P_3. However, if P_1 receives different copies of s_3, then it can only conclude that one among the P_2 and P_3 is corrupt, without knowing the exact identity of the corrupt party and hence the only option available to P_1 is to abort. We also stress that *any* perfectly-secure 3PC protocol (and *not just* the protocol Π_{RSS3PC}) can only provide security with abort in the face of one malicious corruption [78].

Next consider the protocol Π_{MSS3PC} in the presence of one *malicious* corruption. As usual, the corrupt party may not secret-share its input as per the semantics of the MSS and can send incorrect values during the reconstruction protocol. Additionally, if the distributor is the corrupt party, then it may distribute inconsistent information during the pre-processing phase, while a corrupt evaluator can lead to an incorrect evaluation of multiplication gates. To deal with these issues, one need to augment the various building blocks with verification mechanisms to ensure that everyone is following the protocol instructions, without disclosing anything additional about the inputs of the honest parties (see [47, 108, 130]). However, similar to the case of Π_{RSS3PC}, the resultant maliciously-secure 3PC can only provide security with abort. The work of [38] shows how to deal with malicious corruption in the protocol Π_{MSS3PC} and achieve full security. However, the resultant protocol is only cryptographically-secure.

The GMW MPC Protocol

10

All the MPC protocols discussed so far offer *perfect-security* against *computationally-unbounded* adversaries. For the next few chapters, we shift our attention to *cryptographic-security* (also known as *computational* or *conditional* security), where the security is provided only against *computationally-bounded* adversaries.[1] We first discuss the motivation for studying cryptographically-secure MPC protocols, followed by certain definitions. We then present the seminal protocol in this regime, namely the protocol due to Goldreich-Micali-Wigderson [80], which is popularly called as the GMW MPC protocol. We conclude the chapter by discussing the challenges faced by the GMW protocol in the face of *malicious* corruptions.

10.1 Cryptographically-Secure MPC: The Motivation

Even though *perfectly-secure* MPC protocols provide ever-lasting security, as they are secure against computationally-unbounded adversaries, they come with their own restrictions. First of all, the *resilience* offered by these protocols is low. For instance, in the threshold setting, a generic MPC protocol can tolerate only up to $t < n/2$ corruptions (this setting is often called as the *honest-majority* setting). Second, for security, these protocols rely on the existence of pair-wise perfectly-secure channels. Third, these protocols impose strict restrictions on the underlying algebraic structures. For instance, the generic BGW protocol (and its variants) require a finite field for operation.

---

[1] The term *cryptographic-security* stems from the fact that certain cryptographic techniques are used in these protocols, whose security hold only against *computationally-bounded* adversaries, as they are based on certain number-theoretic hardness *assumptions*. Due to this, the level of security is also called as *computational* or *conditional* security.

A. Choudhury and A. Patra, *Secure Multi-Party Computation Against Passive Adversaries*,
Synthesis Lectures on Distributed Computing Theory,
https://doi.org/10.1007/978-3-031-12164-7_10

As it turns out, all these restrictions disappear, if one settles for *cryptographic security*. We can design (efficient) cryptographically-secure MPC protocols tolerating all but one corrupt parties. That is, we can achieve a resilience of up to $t < n$ (this setting is often called as the *dishonest-majority* setting). We also do not require pair-wise secure channels, as we can easily emulate them using cryptographic mechanisms, such as (public-key) encryption.[2] Finally, we can directly design generic protocols, operating over bits. A very special case of cryptographically-secure MPC is that of secure *two-party* computation (secure 2PC), which captures varieties of real-world problems, such as privacy-preserving pattern-matching, private set-intersection, private comparison, to name a few.

Various Paradigms of cryptographically-secure MPC protocols: Unlike the generic perfectly-secure MPC protocols, all of which are based on secret-sharing, there are *three different* design principles used in the context of cryptographically-secure MPC protocols.

– *Secret-Sharing Approach*: This approach which was pioneered in [80] is similar to the BGW approach, where the circuit representing the function is jointly evaluated in a secret-shared fashion. These protocols are computationally-efficient and are *bandwidth friendly*, as they involve very less communication. However, the down side is that the amount of interaction among the parties is proportional to the multiplicative-depth of the circuit. Hence these protocols are *not* suitable for *high-latency* network, where the round-trip message delay is high.
– *Garbled-Circuit Approach*: This approach which was first pioneered in [138] in the context of secure 2PC and later in [18] for the n-party setting, requires only a *constant* round of interactions among the parties and hence they are apt for high-latency networks. The down side is that compared to the secret-sharing based protocols, they require heavier computation and communication.
– *Threshold Public-key Encryption Based Approach*: This approach was first pioneered in [58] where all the values during the circuit-evaluation are available in an encrypted fashion under a *threshold public-key encryption* scheme. On a very high level, it is a special form of public-key encryption scheme, where the encryption-key is available *publicly*, while the decryption-key is secret-shared among the parties, with each party holding a share of the decryption-key. The system allows any party to encrypt any message using the encryption-key. However the decryption of a ciphertext is possible only when $t + 1$ parties jointly decrypt the ciphertext.
   Under this approach, the MPC protocols can be further classified, depending upon the type of threshold encryption scheme used. The first category of protocols use *linearly-homomorphic* scheme, which allows the parties to *non-interactively* evaluate the linear gates in the circuit and requires interaction for evaluating the multiplication gates. Hence

---

[2] We note that one can use one-time pad encryption in the perfect-security setting to get a secure channel from an insecure one, but that requires prior setup of the pads between the sender and the receiver.

their round-complexity is proportional to the multiplicative-depth of the underlying circuit. The second category of protocols are based on *fully homomorphic encryption* (FHE) [76], which allows the parties to non-interactively evaluate the *entire* circuit, once the inputs of the respective parties are available in an encrypted fashion. Similar to the protocols based on the garbled-circuit approach, these protocols require only a constant round of interactions. However, the protocols involve heavy computations and are several order of magnitude slower than the garbled-circuit based protocols, intuitively due to the use of *symmetric-key* primitives in the latter protocols, which are several order of magnitude faster compared to *public-key* primitives.

In summary, all the approaches are interesting and they richly contribute to the theoretical expanse of cryptographically-secure MPC protocols. Based on the application scenario, one may rightly choose the paradigm for the required MPC solution. Moreover, mixing the approaches for evaluating different parts of the circuits have been proven to offer huge efficiency benefits. These line of works are denoted as mixed protocols [66, 121, 129]. In this lecture series, we will focus only on the first two approaches.

10.2   Preliminaries and Definitions

We follow almost the same network and adversarial setting that we have considered till now, with certain modifications. The distrust in the system is modelled by a centralized adversary Adv, who can control any t out of the n parties in the passive fashion, where $t < n$. The adversary is *computationally-bounded*, whose running time is some polynomial function of a *security parameter* λ, which is typically the size of keys used in the underlying cryptographic primitives. Moreover, the running time of the parties in the protocol are now expressed as a function of λ and an algorithm is called *efficient*, if its running time is some polynomial function of λ. This automatically implies that the size of the underlying circuit cir representing the function f, is also some polynomial function of λ.[3] We assume that there is a mechanism for every party P_i to send any message securely to any other party P_j, such that if P_i and P_j are both honest, then adversary does not learn the underlying message. Such a mechanism can be easily instantiated using any real-world cryptographically-secure communication protocol, such as SSL or TSL. We do not go into the exact instantiation and instead abstract out the underlying secure communication mechanism by assuming a pair-wise secure channel among every pair of parties. Since we are going to deploy

---

[3] In any MPC protocol, the parties at least need to process each gate in cir and in order for the MPC protocol to be efficient, the overall running time for the parties to process each gate should be upper bounded by some polynomial function of λ.

cryptographic primitives in our protocols, there might be a small (negligible) error in the protocol outcome(s).[4] We next formally define negligible functions.

Definition 10.1 (*Negligible Function* [102]) A function f from the natural numbers to the non-negative real numbers is *negligible*, if for every positive polynomial p, there is an X, such that for all integers $x > X$, it holds that $f(x) < \frac{1}{p(x)}$.

Equivalently, it must be the case that for all constants c, there exists an X, such that for all $x > X$ it holds that $f(x) < x^{-c}$. We will denote an arbitrary negligible function by negl.

The function f to be securely computed by the parties is over a ring $(\mathbb{R}, +, \cdot)$. For simplicity and without loss of generality, we assume that f is a *deterministic* function of the form $f : \mathbb{R}^n \to \mathbb{R}$, where $y \stackrel{def}{=} f(x_1, \ldots, x_n)$ and where each party P_i has a private input $x_i \in \mathbb{R}$, such that the output y is supposed to be learnt by all the parties. We next focus on the security definitions of *cryptographically-secure* MPC. The definitions will be similar to the definitions presented in Sect. 5.4.4, except that now instead of the requirement that certain probability distributions should be identical, it is only needed that they are computationally-indistinguishable. Before we proceed, we first present the definition of computational indistinguishability.

Definition 10.2 (*Computational Indistinguishability*) Two probability ensembles (infinite sequences of random variable) $\{X_\lambda\}_{\lambda \in \mathbb{N}}$ and $\{Y_\lambda\}_{\lambda \in \mathbb{N}}$, indexed by the security parameter λ are called computationally indistinguishable, denoted by $X_\lambda \stackrel{c}{=} Y_\lambda$, if for every probabilistic polynomial-time (PPT) algorithm A, the following condition holds:

$$\left| \Pr_{x \leftarrow X_\lambda} [A(x) = 1] - \Pr_{x \leftarrow Y_\lambda} [A(x) = 1] \right| \leq \mathsf{negl}(\lambda).$$

That is, as λ tends to ∞ then every efficient algorithm A's behaviour (output) does not change significantly, when given uniformly random samples according to X_λ or Y_λ.

Intuitively, the above definition captures the idea that PPT algorithms cannot "significantly" distinguish between the ensemble X_λ and Y_λ and it can perform only negligibly better than just guessing whether a given random sample is sampled according to X_λ or Y_λ. We next adapt the definitions in Sect. 5.4.4 in the context of cryptographic-security.

Definition 10.3 (*Cryptographic/Computational Security of n-party Protocols for Deterministic Functions* [78]) Let $f : (\{0, 1\}^\star)^n \to (\{0, 1\}^\star)^n$ be a *deterministic n-ary function* and let Π be an n-party protocol. We say that Π is a *t-cryptographically-secure* protocol for

---

[4] On a very high level, this small error stems from the fact that the keys for the underlying cryptographic mechanisms are generated using randomized algorithms and there is always a negligible (but non-zero) error probability that these algorithms end up picking candidate keys which do not have the "desired" properties.

f, if for every $\vec{x} = (x_1, \ldots, x_n) \in (\{0, 1\}^\star)^n$ where $|x_1| = |x_2| = \cdots = |x_n|$ and for every PPT adversary Adv controlling a subset of at most t parties with indices in $I \subset \{1, \ldots, n\}$ where $|I| \leq t$, the following two conditions hold:

- *Correctness*: $\text{output}^\Pi(\vec{x})$ should be the same as $f(x_1, \ldots, x_n)$, except with probability $\text{negl}(\lambda)$.
- *Privacy*: there exists a probabilistic polynomial-time algorithm $\mathcal{S}$ called *simulator*, such that the probability distribution of the output generated by $\mathcal{S}$ is computationally indistinguishable from view of the adversary. That is:

$$\left\{ \mathcal{S}(I, \vec{x}_I, f_I(x_1, \ldots, x_n)) \right\} \overset{c}{\equiv} \left\{ \text{view}_I^\Pi(\vec{x}) \right\}.$$

Here $\vec{x}_I$ denotes the inputs corresponding to the parties with index in I and $f_I(x_1, \ldots, x_n)$ denotes the function output, restricted to the parties with indices in I.

Definition 10.4 (*Cryptographic/Computational Security of General n-party Protocols* [78]) Let $f : (\{0, 1\}^\star)^n \to (\{0, 1\}^\star)^n$ be a *randomized n-ary* function and let Π be an n-party protocol. We say that Π is a *t-cryptographically-secure* protocol for f, if for every $\vec{x} = (x_1, \ldots, x_n) \in (\{0, 1\}^\star)^n$ where $|x_1| = |x_2| = \cdots = |x_n|$ and for every PPT adversary Adv controlling a subset of at most t parties with indices in $I \subset \{1, \ldots, n\}$ where $|I| \leq t$, there exists a probabilistic polynomial-time algorithm $\mathcal{S}$ called *simulator*, such that the following holds:

$$\left\{ (\mathcal{S}(I, \vec{x}_I, f_I(x_1, \ldots, x_n)), f(x_1, \ldots, x_n)) \right\} \overset{c}{\equiv} \left\{ (\text{view}_I^\Pi(\vec{x}), \text{output}^\Pi(\vec{x})) \right\}.$$

10.3   The GMW Protocol in the Pre-processing Model

In this section, we present the GMW protocol in the pre-processing model, assuming that the parties have access to secret-shared random multiplication-triples. Assuming that the parties have access to such pre-processed triples, the circuit-evaluation phase of the protocol is *perfectly-secure*. Later we will see how to instantiate the pre-processing phase using a cryptographic mechanism. This makes the overall protocol *cryptographically-secure*. We first recap the additive secret-sharing and related properties, which are used in the protocol.

10.3.1 Additive Secret-Sharing and Related Protocols

Informally, a value is said to be additively-shared if it is divided into n shares which sum up to the secret, with each party holding one of these shares. Formally:

Protocol Sh_{ASS}

- On having the input $s \in \mathbb{R}$, randomly select $s_1, \ldots, s_n$ from $\mathbb{R}$, such that $s_1 + \ldots + s_n = s$ holds.
- For $i = 1, \ldots, n$, send the *share* s_i to party P_i.

Fig. 10.1 A perfectly-secure protocol for generating a random ASS of a value. The above code is executed only by the dealer D

Definition 10.5 (*Additive Secret-Sharing (ASS)*) A value $s \in \mathbb{R}$ is said to be ASS-shared, if there exist $s_1, \ldots, s_n \in \mathbb{R}$ where $s_1 + \cdots + s_n = s$, such that each $P_i \in \mathcal{P}$ holds the share s_i.

Let $(s_1, \ldots, s_n)$ be a vector of shares, corresponding to an ASS of s. Then we write $\langle s \rangle = (s_1, \ldots, s_n)$. An ASS $(s_1, \ldots, s_n)$ of a value s is said to be *random*, if the shares $s_1, \ldots, s_n$ are random elements from $\mathbb{R}$.

It is easy to see that ASS satisfies the *linearity* property. That is, given ASS-shared values a and b and *publicly-known* constants $c_1, c_2 \in \mathbb{R}$, then the following holds:

$$c_1 \cdot \langle a \rangle + c_2 \cdot \langle b \rangle = \langle c_1 \cdot a + c_2 \cdot b \rangle.$$

In general, parties can *locally* compute any *publicly-known* linear function of ASS-shared values.

Secret-sharing protocol: Protocol Sh_{ASS} (Fig. 10.1) allows a designated *dealer* $D \in \mathcal{P}$ to generate a *random* ASS of its input, such that the view of the adversary remains independent of this input if D is *honest*. Moreover, the protocol is *perfectly-secure* and achieve this property, even if the adversary is *computationally-unbounded*.

The properties of the protocol Sh_{ASS} are stated in Lemma 10.6. The security trivially follows from the fact that the protocol is same as D generating the shares as per the algorithm G_{Add} (Fig 3.2), where the operations are now performed over the ring $\mathbb{R}$, instead of the group $\mathbb{G}$.

Lemma 10.6 *Let* Adv *be a computationally-unbounded adversary, who can control any t out of the n parties, where $t < n$. Then protocol* Sh_{ASS} *allows* D *to generate a random ASS of* D*'s input s, such that the view of* Adv *is independent of s if* D *is honest. The protocol needs one round of interaction and communication of $\mathcal{O}(n)$ ring elements.*

Reconstruction protocols: Let s be a value which is ASS-shared. Then protocol Rec_{ASS} allows the parties to publicly reconstruct s. In the *round-efficient* version of the protocol, every party P_i can send its share, say s_i, to every other party. This allows *all* the parties to have the shares $s_1, \ldots, s_n$, using which they can compute $s = s_1 + \cdots + s_n$. This requires a single round of interaction and communication of $\mathcal{O}(n^2)$ ring elements.

In the *communication-efficient* version of $\mathsf{Rec}_{\mathsf{ASS}}$, the parties first send their shares *only* to a designated party, say P_1, thus allowing P_1 to reconstruct s. Party P_1 can then send the reconstructed s to every other party. This will require two rounds of interaction, but a communication of only $\mathcal{O}(n)$ ring elements. As both these variants are straight forward, we avoid giving the formal details.

10.3.2 The GMW Protocol in the $\mathcal{F}_{\mathsf{Triple}}$-hybrid Model

The GMW protocol Π_{GMW} in the pre-processing model is presented in Fig. 10.2. The protocol is in the $\mathcal{F}_{\mathsf{Triple}}$-hybrid model, assuming the presence of a TTP computing the functionality $\mathcal{F}_{\mathsf{Triple}}$, which generates random ASS of c_M number of random multiplication-triples for the parties. Formally the functionality $\mathcal{F}_{\mathsf{Triple}}$ is as follows:

$$\mathcal{F}_{\mathsf{Triple}}(\lambda, \ldots, \lambda) = \Big(\{(a_1^{(\ell)}, b_1^{(\ell)}, c_1^{(\ell)})\}_{\ell=1,\ldots,c_M}, \ldots, \{(a_n^{(\ell)}, b_n^{(\ell)}, c_n^{(\ell)})\}_{\ell=1,\ldots,c_M} \Big),$$

where for $\ell = 1, \ldots, c_M$, the vector of shares $(a_1^{(\ell)}, \ldots, a_n^{(\ell)})$, $(b_1^{(\ell)}, \ldots, b_n^{(\ell)})$ and $(c_1^{(\ell)}, \ldots, c_n^{(\ell)})$ correspond to a *random* ASS-sharing of $a^{(\ell)}, b^{(\ell)}$ and $c^{(\ell)}$ respectively, such that $a^{(\ell)}$ and $b^{(\ell)}$ are random elements of $\mathbb{R}$ and $c^{(\ell)} = a^{(\ell)} b^{(\ell)}$. A closer look into $\mathcal{F}_{\mathsf{Triple}}$ above reveals that it is very similar to the functionality $\mathcal{F}_{\mathsf{Triple}}$ considered in Sect. 7.2, except that now the functionality outputs random ASS of the underlying multiplication-triples, instead of random t-Shamir-secret-sharing of the triples.

Protocol Π_{GMW} is exactly the same as the protocol Π_{Beaver} (see Fig 7.2) with the difference that now all the computations are performed over ASS-shared values, rather than t-Shamir-shared values. Namely, the inputs for the function are randomly ASS-shared by the respective parties through instances of $\mathsf{Sh}_{\mathsf{ASS}}$. And then the parties evaluate each gate in the circuit by maintaining the variant that given a random ASS-sharing of the gate-input(s), the parties generate a random ASS-sharing of the gate-output. Maintaining the invariant for *linear* gates is "free" and does not require any interaction among the parties due to the linearity of ASS. For the multiplication gates, the parties use Beaver's trick [16] and deploy a multiplication-triple generated in the pre-processing phase. We note that Beaver's trick will work even with ASS-shared values (in fact, it works with *any* linear secret-sharing scheme). More specifically, consider a multiplication gate in the circuit cir, with inputs x, y and output z, where $z = xy$. Let the inputs x and y be ASS-shared among the parties and the goal is to securely compute a random ASS of z. Moreover, let (a, b, c) be a random multiplication-triple from the pre-processing phase, which is randomly ASS-shared among the parties. The parties then first locally compute ASS of $d \stackrel{def}{=} x - a$ and $e \stackrel{def}{=} y - b$, since the following hold:

$$\langle x - a \rangle = \langle x \rangle - \langle a \rangle \quad \text{and} \quad \langle y - b \rangle = \langle y \rangle - \langle b \rangle.$$

Protocol Π_{GMW}

The Pre-processing Phase
- Invoke the functionality $\mathcal{F}_{\mathsf{Triple}}$ with input λ. In response, let $\{(a_i^{(\ell)}, b_i^{(\ell)}, c_i^{(\ell)})\}_{\ell \in 1,\ldots,c_M}$ be the shares received.

The Circuit-evaluation Phase
- *Input Stage*:
  - On having the input x_i, execute an instance $\mathsf{Sh}_{\mathsf{ASS}}^{(i)}$ of $\mathsf{Sh}_{\mathsf{ASS}}$ to generate a random ASS of x_i.
  - For $j = 1, \ldots, n$, participate in the instance $\mathsf{Sh}_{\mathsf{ASS}}^{(j)}$ executed by the dealer P_j.
  For $k = 1, \ldots, n$, let x_{ki} denote the share, received from the party $P_k \in \mathcal{P}$ at the end of the input stage.
- *Computation Stage*: Let $G_1, \ldots, G_m$ be a publicly-known topological ordering of the gates of cir. For $k = 1, \ldots, m$, do the following for gate G_k:
  - If G_k *is an addition gate*: Let $\alpha_i^{(k)}$ and $\beta_i^{(k)}$ be the shares held by P_i, corresponding to the gate-inputs. Set $\alpha_i^{(k)} + \beta_i^{(k)}$ to be the share, corresponding to the gate-output.
  - If G_k *is a multiplication-with-a-constant gate with constant* c: Let $\alpha_i^{(k)}$ be the share held by P_i, corresponding to the gate-input. Set $c \cdot \alpha_i^{(k)}$ to be the share, corresponding to the gate-output.
  - If G_k *is an addition-with-a-constant gate with constant* c: Let $\alpha_i^{(k)}$ be the share held by P_i, corresponding to the gate-input.
    - If $P_i = P_1$, then set $c + \alpha_i^{(k)}$ to be the share, corresponding to the gate-output.
    - Else set $\alpha_i^{(k)}$ to be the share, corresponding to the gate-output.
  - If G_k *is a multiplication gate*: Let G_k be the ℓth multiplication gate in cir where $\ell \in \{1, \ldots, c_M\}$ and let $(a_i^{(\ell)}, b_i^{(\ell)}, c_i^{(\ell)})$ be the shares of the ℓth multiplication-triple, received from $\mathcal{F}_{\mathsf{Triple}}$. Moreover, let $\alpha_i^{(k)}$ and $\beta_i^{(k)}$ be the shares held by P_i, corresponding to the gate-inputs of G_k. Then do the following:
    1. Compute $d_i^{(\ell)} = \alpha_i^{(k)} - a_i^{(\ell)}$.   % Parties collectively compute $\langle d^{(\ell)} \rangle = \langle \alpha^{(k)} \rangle - \langle a^{(\ell)} \rangle$.
    2. Compute $e_i^{(\ell)} = \beta_i^{(k)} - b_i^{(\ell)}$.   % Parties collectively compute $\langle e^{(\ell)} \rangle = \langle \beta^{(k)} \rangle - \langle b^{(\ell)} \rangle$.
    3. Do the following to publicly reconstruct $d^{(\ell)}$ and $e^{(\ell)}$:
       - Send the shares $d_i^{(\ell)}$ and $e_i^{(\ell)}$ *only* to party P_1.
       - (If $P_i = P_1$): Upon receiving the shares $d_j^{(\ell)}, e_j^{(\ell)}$ from each party $P_j \in \mathcal{P}$, compute $d^{(\ell)} = d_1^{(\ell)} + \ldots + d_n^{(\ell)}$ and $e^{(\ell)} = e_1^{(\ell)} + \ldots + e_n^{(\ell)}$. Then send $d^{(\ell)}$ and $e^{(\ell)}$ to every $P_j \in \mathcal{P}$.
    4. Computing output share: % $\mathcal{P}$ compute $\langle \gamma^{(k)} \rangle = d^{(\ell)} e^{(\ell)} + d^{(\ell)} \langle b^{(\ell)} \rangle + e^{(\ell)} \langle a^{(\ell)} \rangle + \langle c^{(\ell)} \rangle$.
       - If $P_i = P_1$, then set $\gamma_i^{(k)} \stackrel{def}{=} d^{(\ell)} e^{(\ell)} + d^{(\ell)} b_i^{(\ell)} + e^{(\ell)} a_i^{(\ell)} + c_i^{(\ell)}$ to be the share, corresponding to the gate-output.
       - Else set $\gamma_i^{(k)} \stackrel{def}{=} 0 + d^{(\ell)} b_i^{(\ell)} + e^{(\ell)} a_i^{(\ell)} + c_i^{(\ell)}$ to be the share, corresponding to the gate-output.

- *Output Stage*:
  - Send the share y_i to every party in $\mathcal{P}$.
  - Upon receiving the shares $y_1, \ldots, y_n$, output $y = y_1 + \ldots + y_n$.

Fig. 10.2 The GMW MPC protocol in the $\mathcal{F}_{\mathsf{Triple}}$-hybrid model. The above steps are executed by each $P_i \in \mathcal{P}$

The parties then publicly reconstruct $x - a$ and $y - b$. Then a random ASS of z is computed locally as a linear function of ASS of the multiplication-triple (a, b, c), since the following relation holds:

$$\langle z \rangle = de + d\langle b \rangle + e\langle a \rangle + \langle c \rangle.$$

Once all the gates are evaluated and the function output is ready in ASS-shared fashion, the parties publicly reconstruct it. Intuitively, the privacy is maintained as throughout adversary learns at most t shares corresponding to a random ASS of each value during the circuit-evaluation.

The properties of the protocol Π_{GMW} are stated in Lemma 10.7, which is analogous to Lemma 7.1 and can be proved similarly, with random t-Shamir-sharings being replaced by random ASS. We leave the proof as an exercise.

Lemma 10.7 *Let $y = f(x_1, \ldots, x_n)$ be an n-ary deterministic function over $\mathbb{R}$ with P_i holding the private input x_i. Moreover, let $t < n$. Then protocol Π_{GMW} is t-perfectly-secure for f in the $\mathcal{F}_{\mathsf{Triple}}$-hybrid model.*

The protocol requires one call to $\mathcal{F}_{\mathsf{Triple}}$ during the pre-processing phase. Let c_M and D_M denote the number of multiplication gates and multiplicative depth respectively of the circuit cir representing f. Then in the circuit-evaluation phase, the protocol requires $\mathcal{O}(D_M)$ communication rounds and communication of $\mathcal{O}(c_M n)$ ring elements.

10.3.3 Protocol for $\mathcal{F}_{\mathsf{Triple}}$ in the $\mathcal{F}_{\mathsf{Mult}}$-hybrid Model

From Lemma 10.7, for a plain-model realization of the protocol Π_{GMW}, we need a protocol to securely compute the functionality $\mathcal{F}_{\mathsf{Triple}}$. In this section, we discuss a *perfectly-secure* protocol for computing $\mathcal{F}_{\mathsf{Triple}}$ in the $\mathcal{F}_{\mathsf{Mult}}$-hybrid model. The *multiplication* functionality $\mathcal{F}_{\mathsf{Mult}}$ here is exactly the same as discussed in Sect. 6.4, except that the inputs and output are now ASS-shared, rather than t-Shamir-shared. Formally, the functionality $\mathcal{F}_{\mathsf{Mult}}$ is defined as follows:

$$\mathcal{F}_{\mathsf{Mult}}\Big((a_1, b_1), \ldots, (a_n, b_n)\Big) = (c_1, \ldots, c_n),$$

where the input and output of P_i are (a_i, b_i) and c_i respectively. Here $\langle a \rangle = (a_1, \ldots, a_n)$ and $\langle b \rangle = (b_1, \ldots, b_n)$ and the vector $(c_1, \ldots, c_n)$ constitutes a *random* ASS-sharing of ab; i.e., $\langle ab \rangle = (c_1, \ldots, c_n)$. Assuming the existence of a TTP who can securely compute the functionality $\mathcal{F}_{\mathsf{Mult}}$, we present a protocol $\Pi_{\mathsf{ASSTriple}}$ for securely computing $\mathcal{F}_{\mathsf{Triple}}$. The protocol is exactly the same as the protocol Π_{Triple} (see Fig 7.4), except that all the computations are now over ASS-shared values rather than t-Shamir-shared values.

Protocol $\Pi_{\mathsf{ASSTriple}}$ (see Fig. 10.3) follows a two-stage approach. In the first stage, the parties together generate random ASS of random pairs of values, unknown to the adversary. In the second stage, the parties call $\mathcal{F}_{\mathsf{Mult}}$ to generate random ASS of the product of the ASS-shared pairs. For the first stage, each party "contributes" random pairs of values in ASS-shared fashion and the sum of all these ASS-shared pairs is set to be the resultant outputs for the first stage. The resultant shared pairs are random and unknown to the adversary owing to the contributions made by the honest parties that are bound to exist due to the condition $t < n$.

Protocol $\Pi_{\mathsf{ASSTriple}}$

- *Stage I*: Generating random ASS-shared pairs:
  - For $\ell = 1, \ldots, c_M$, randomly pick $(a^{(i,\ell)}, b^{(i,\ell)}) \in \mathbb{R}^2$. Act as a dealer and invoke instances of $\mathsf{Sh}_{\mathsf{ASS}}$ to generate random ASS of $(a^{(i,\ell)}, b^{(i,\ell)})$.
  - For $j = 1, \ldots, n$, participate in the instances of $\mathsf{Sh}_{\mathsf{ASS}}$ executed by P_j as the dealer. For $\ell = 1, \ldots, c_M$, let $a_i^{(j,\ell)}, b_i^{(j,\ell)}$ denote the shares received from P_j.
  - For $\ell = 1, \ldots, c_M$, compute $a_i^{(\ell)} = \sum\limits_{j=1}^{j=n} a_i^{(j,\ell)}$ and $b_i^{(\ell)} = \sum\limits_{j=1}^{j=n} b_i^{(j,\ell)}$. $\%$ Parties compute $\langle a^{(\ell)} \rangle = \sum\limits_{j=1}^{j=n} \langle a^{(j,\ell)} \rangle$ and $\langle b^{(\ell)} \rangle = \sum\limits_{j=1}^{j=n} \langle b^{(j,\ell)} \rangle$.
- *Stage II*: Computing random ASS of the product of the pairs:
  - For $\ell = 1, \ldots, c_M$, invoke $\mathcal{F}_{\mathsf{Mult}}$ with input $(a_i^{(\ell)}, b_i^{(\ell)})$. $\%$ Parties compute $\langle a^{(\ell)} b^{(\ell)} \rangle$.
  - For $\ell = 1, \ldots, c_M$, let $c_i^{(\ell)}$ be the output received from $\mathcal{F}_{\mathsf{Mult}}$ in response to the ℓth call to $\mathcal{F}_{\mathsf{Mult}}$. Output the shares $\{(a_i^{(\ell)}, b_i^{(\ell)}, c_i^{(\ell)})\}_{\ell=1,\ldots,c_M}$.

Fig. 10.3 A t-perfectly-secure protocol for $\mathcal{F}_{\mathsf{Triple}}$ in the $\mathcal{F}_{\mathsf{Mult}}$-hybrid model. The above steps are executed by each $P_i \in \mathcal{P}$

The properties of the protocol $\Pi_{\mathsf{ASSTriple}}$ are stated in Lemma 10.8, which can be proved easily.

Lemma 10.8 *Protocol $\Pi_{\mathsf{ASSTriple}}$ is a t-perfectly-secure protocol for $\mathcal{F}_{\mathsf{Triple}}$ in the $\mathcal{F}_{\mathsf{Mult}}$-hybrid model for any $t < n$. The protocol requires one round of interaction among the parties and a communication of $\mathcal{O}(c_M n^2)$ elements from $\mathbb{R}$, along with c_M calls to the functionality $\mathcal{F}_{\mathsf{Mult}}$.*

From the discussion so far, we conclude that the GMW protocol is a t-perfectly-secure protocol in the $\mathcal{F}_{\mathsf{Mult}}$-hybrid model. We next shift our attention to design protocols for computing $\mathcal{F}_{\mathsf{Mult}}$ in the plain model. For this, we will introduce another important cryptographic primitive called *oblivious transfer* (OT) [132] which is known to be "complete" for securely realizing any function [104]. By completeness, we mean that given OT, no further cryptographic assumptions are required to securely realize any function. We will show that $\mathcal{F}_{\mathsf{Mult}}$ can be securely computed in the $\mathcal{F}_{\mathsf{OT}}$-hybrid model, even with *dishonest* majority (where $t < n$ holds). This is in contrast to the $\mathcal{F}_{\mathsf{Mult}}$ functionality considered in the Sect. 6.2, which can be computed with *perfect security* only in the *honest* majority setting (where $t < n/2$ holds).

10.4   Protocols for Computing $\mathcal{F}_{\mathsf{Mult}}$ in $\mathcal{F}_{\mathsf{OT}}$-hybrid Model

In this section, we present different protocols for computing $\mathcal{F}_{\mathsf{Mult}}$. We first consider the case of a Boolean ring, followed by the case of a general ring. All these protocols are in the $\mathcal{F}_{\mathsf{OT}}$-hybrid model, where $\mathcal{F}_{\mathsf{OT}}$ denotes the 2-party OT function as shown below.

$$\mathcal{F}_{\mathsf{OT}}\Big((m_0, m_1), (b)\Big) = (\bot, m_b).$$

An OT primitive is a 2-party primitive, involving a *sender* S and a *receiver* R. S's input is a pair of *private* messages (m_0, m_1) (from some domain) and R's input is a *private choice-bit* b. The primitive outputs the message m_b for R. The primitive should guarantee *sender's security*, implying that a corrupt R should not learn about the message m_{1-b} and *receiver's security*, implying that a corrupt sender should not learn about the choice bit b. These requirements are captured by the above function $\mathcal{F}_{\mathsf{OT}}$.

In the rest of this section, we assume the presence of a TTP which computes $\mathcal{F}_{\mathsf{OT}}$ for the parties. In the next chapter, we will discuss various protocols for securely computing $\mathcal{F}_{\mathsf{OT}}$. Looking ahead, all these instantiations *necessarily* require some cryptographic primitive to be deployed, thus making the overall GMW protocol *cryptographically-secure*.

10.4.1 Computing $\mathcal{F}_{\mathsf{Mult}}$ for 2-party Case over Boolean Ring

For simplicity, we begin with a protocol for securely computing $\mathcal{F}_{\mathsf{Mult}}$ for the 2-party case with one corruption; i.e., $n = 2$ and $t = 1$. Moreover, for an easy understanding, we consider the ring $\mathbb{R}$ to be the *Boolean* ring $(\{0, 1\}, \oplus, \wedge)$, where the $+$ and $\cdot$ operations are Boolean XOR ($\oplus$) and AND ($\wedge$) operations respectively. We present a protocol $\Pi_{\mathsf{2BoolMult}}$ in the $\mathcal{F}_{\mathsf{OT}}$-hybrid for securely computing the functionality $\mathcal{F}_{\mathsf{Mult}}$. In the protocol, P_1 and P_2 have inputs (a_1, b_1) and (a_2, b_2) respectively, where $a_1, a_2, b_1, b_2 \in \{0, 1\}$ and where $a_1 \oplus a_2 = a$ and $b_1 \oplus b_2 = b$. The output of P_1 and P_2 in the protocol are *random* bits c_1 and c_2 respectively, such that $c_1 \oplus c_2 = a \wedge b$.[5]

Our first attempt in designing $\Pi_{\mathsf{2BoolMult}}$ is based on the following relation:

$$ab = (a_1 \oplus a_2)(b_1 \oplus b_2)$$
$$= (a_1 b_1 \oplus a_2 b_1) \oplus (a_1 b_2 + a_2 b_2)$$

One may be tempted to set c_1 and c_2 as $(a_1 b_1 \oplus a_2 b_1)$ and $(a_1 b_2 + a_2 b_2)$ respectively. For this, we have to enable P_1 to learn $a_2 b_1$, since P_1 can compute $a_1 b_1$ itself. Similarly, we have to enable P_2 to learn $a_1 b_2$, since P_2 can compute $a_2 b_2$. For the former, parties P_1 and P_2 can invoke $\mathcal{F}_{\mathsf{OT}}$, where P_2 plays the role S with input messages $(0, a_2)$ and P_1 plays the role of R with choice-bit b_1. As a result, P_1 will receive the output $a_2 b_1$ from $\mathcal{F}_{\mathsf{OT}}$. Similarly, for the latter, party P_1 and P_2 can invoke $\mathcal{F}_{\mathsf{OT}}$ as S and R, with inputs $(0, a_1)$ and b_2 respectively (see the first figure in Fig. 10.4).

Unfortunately, the above idea is insecure, as revealing $a_1 b_2$ and $a_2 b_1$ in the clear to the respective parties may lead to revealing a or b, which is forbidden as per the function $\mathcal{F}_{\mathsf{Mult}}$. For instance, if $b_2 = 1$ (the probability of this is *non-zero*), then $a_1 b_2$ is the same as a_1. This completely leaks a to P_2 that holds the other share a_2 of a. The above idea needs a slight

---

[5] In the rest of the discussion, we interchangeably use $a \wedge b$ and ab.

twist to tackle these security issues. We will now allow P_1 and P_2 to learn a_2b_1 and a_1b_2 only in a masked fashion.

In more detail, P_1 and P_2 invoke $\mathcal{F}_{OT}$ as S and R, with inputs $(r_1, r_1 \oplus a_1)$ and b_2 respectively, where r_1 is a *random* mask, selected by P_1. This allows P_2 to receive the output $r_1 \oplus a_1b_2$ from $\mathcal{F}_{OT}$. Now a potentially corrupt P_2 does not learn anything about a_1, since r_1 is random from its point of view. On the other hand, a corrupt P_1 does not learn anything about b_2, which follows from *receiver's security* of OT.

In the same way, to take care of the other "cross-term" a_2b_1, parties P_2 and P_1 invoke $\mathcal{F}_{OT}$ by enacting the role of S and R respectively, with inputs $(r_2, r_2 \oplus a_2)$ and b_1 respectively, where r_2 is a random mask chosen by P_2. This allows P_1 to receive the output $r_2 \oplus a_2b_1$. Protocol $\Pi_{2BoolMult}$ is now formally presented in Fig. 10.5 and is pictorially depicted in the second figure in Fig. 10.4.

Intuitively, the protocol is secure and the view of the corrupt party can be easily simulated. For instance, consider the case when P_1 is *corrupt*. Then it learns $r_2 \oplus a_2b_1$ as the output from $\mathcal{F}_{OT}$. However, since r_2 is a uniformly random bit, unknown to P_1, the bit $r_2 \oplus a_2b_1$ will be a random bit for P_1. Hence it can be easily simulated, with the simulator outputting a uniformly random bit as the output from $\mathcal{F}_{OT}$ for P_1. Similarly, the view of a potentially corrupt P_2 can be easily simulated. We leave the complete formal proof as an exercise and directly state the property of the protocol $\Pi_{2BoolMult}$ in Lemma 10.9.

Lemma 10.9 *Protocol* $\Pi_{2BoolMult}$ *is a 1-perfectly-secure protocol for* $\mathcal{F}_{Mult}$ *for the 2-party case over Boolean ring in the* $\mathcal{F}_{OT}$*-hybrid model. The protocol requires two calls to* $\mathcal{F}_{OT}$.

An Alternative and More Efficient Approach for Computing $\mathcal{F}_{Mult}$: Protocol $\Pi_{2BoolMult}$ requires 2 calls to $\mathcal{F}_{OT}$. A natural question is whether one can reduce the number of OT calls.

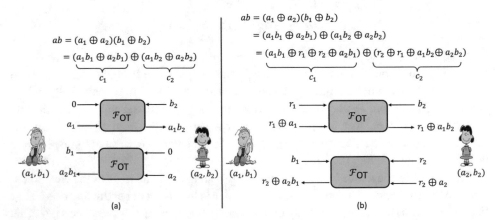

Fig. 10.4 Pictorial depiction of the protocol $\Pi_{2BoolMult}$. The first figure shows the insecure method, while the second figure denotes the actual protocol

---

Protocol $\Pi_{\text{2BoolMult}}$

The inputs for P_1 and P_2 are (a_1, b_1) and (a_2, b_2) respectively, where $a_1 \oplus a_2 = a$ and $b_1 \oplus b_2 = b$.
- *Taking care of the cross-term $a_1 b_2$:*
    - P_1 randomly selects $r_1 \in \{0, 1\}$.
    - P_1 invokes $\mathcal{F}_{\text{OT}}$ as S with input messages $(r_1, r_1 \oplus a_1)$ and P_2 invokes $\mathcal{F}_{\text{OT}}$ as R with choice-bit b_2.
    - P_2 receives the output $r_1 \oplus a_1 b_2$ from $\mathcal{F}_{\text{OT}}$.
- *Taking care of the cross-term $a_2 b_1$:*
    - P_2 randomly selects $r_2 \in \{0, 1\}$.
    - P_2 invokes $\mathcal{F}_{\text{OT}}$ as S with input messages $(r_2, r_2 \oplus a_2)$ and P_1 invokes $\mathcal{F}_{\text{OT}}$ as R with choice-bit b_1.
    - P_1 receives the output $r_2 \oplus a_2 b_1$ from $\mathcal{F}_{\text{OT}}$.
- *Computing the output:*
    - P_1 outputs $c_1 = a_1 b_1 \oplus r_1 \oplus r_2 \oplus a_2 b_1$.
    - P_2 outputs $c_2 = a_2 b_2 \oplus r_2 \oplus r_1 \oplus a_1 b_2$.

Fig. 10.5 A 1-perfectly-secure protocol for $\mathcal{F}_{\text{Mult}}$ in the $\mathcal{F}_{\text{OT}}$-hybrid model for the 2-party case over Boolean ring

The OT function $\mathcal{F}_{\text{OT}}$ considered in the protocol $\Pi_{\text{2BoolMult}}$ is called as the 1-*out-of-2-OT*, since receiver obliviously receives one out of the two messages. We next consider a different OT functionality $\mathcal{F}_{\text{4OT}}$, called 1-*out-of-4-OT*, where S's input consists of 4 messages and R obliviously receives one of these messages, depending upon a pair of choice-bits held by R. Formally, the function $\mathcal{F}_{\text{4OT}}$ is as follows:

$$\mathcal{F}_{\text{4OT}}\Big((m_{00}, m_{01}, m_{10}, m_{11}), (b_1 b_2)\Big) = (\perp, m_{b_1 b_2}).$$

We next give a high level overview of how the parties can securely compute $\mathcal{F}_{\text{Mult}}$ in the $\mathcal{F}_{\text{4OT}}$-hybrid model, where *only one* call to $\mathcal{F}_{\text{4OT}}$ is made in the protocol. The resultant protocol is more efficient compared to $\Pi_{\text{2BoolMult}}$, as in the next chapter we will show that $\mathcal{F}_{\text{4OT}}$ can be more efficiently computed, compared to efficiently computing $\mathcal{F}_{\text{OT}}$ *twice*.

The idea behind the modified protocol is that P_1 randomly selects its share $c_1 \in \{0, 1\}$ and then the goal is to ensure that P_2 learns the share $c_2 \overset{\text{def}}{=} (a \wedge b) \oplus c_1$, without revealing any additional information. For this, we observe that c_2 can be expressed in terms of a_1, b_1 and c_1, once a_2 and b_2 are fixed. This is because the following relation holds:

$$c_2 = (a \wedge b) \oplus c_1 = [(a_1 \oplus a_2) \wedge (b_1 \oplus b_2)] \oplus c_1$$

For instance, if $a_2 = b_2 = 0$, then $c_2 = (a_1 \wedge b_1) \oplus c_1$, while for $a_2 = b_2 = 1$, the condition $c_2 = (\neg a_1 \wedge \neg b_1) \oplus c_1$ holds. Based on this observation, P_1 acts as S and calls $\mathcal{F}_{\text{4OT}}$ with inputs $m_{00} = (a_1 \wedge b_1) \oplus c_1$, $m_{01} = (a_1 \wedge \neg b_1) \oplus c_1$, $m_{10} = (\neg a_1 \wedge b_1) \oplus c_1$ and $m_{11} = (\neg a_1 \wedge \neg b_1) \oplus c_1$. Notice that P_1 can compute these messages, as it has a_1, b_1 and c_1. Now P_2 obliviously receives one of these 4 messages by invoking $\mathcal{F}_{\text{4OT}}$ as R with $a_2 b_2$ as choice-bits. From the properties of $\mathcal{F}_{\text{4OT}}$, it follows that P_2 receives the desired value c_2. If P_1 is *corrupt*, then the *receiver's security* ensures that P_1 does not learn anything about a_2 and b_2. On the other hand, if P_2 is *corrupt*, then the *sender's security* ensures that P_2

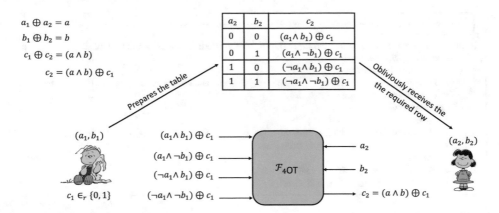

Fig. 10.6 Pictorial depiction of a more efficient way of computing $\mathcal{F}_{\mathsf{Mult}}$ over Boolean ring in the 2-party setting in the $\mathcal{F}_{\mathsf{4OT}}$-hybrid model

does not learn anything beyond c_2. Since c_2 is a masked version of $a \wedge b$, with the mask c_1 being unknown to P_2, the value c_2 will be a uniformly random value for P_2. The modified protocol is pictorially depicted in Fig. 10.6 and the formal details and security proof are left as an exercise.

10.4.2 Computing $\mathcal{F}_{\mathsf{Mult}}$ for *n*-party Case over Boolean Ring

Protocol $\Pi_{\mathsf{2BoolMult}}$ can be easily extended to the n-party setting for securely computing $\mathcal{F}_{\mathsf{Mult}}$ in the $\mathcal{F}_{\mathsf{OT}}$-hybrid model. The idea is that the following relation holds:

$$ab = (a_1 \oplus \ldots \oplus a_n)(b_1 \oplus \ldots \oplus b_n).$$

Hence, every pair of *distinct* parties (P_i, P_j) needs to securely compute a 2-party ASS of the cross-terms $a_i b_j$ and $a_j b_i$. Similar to the protocol $\Pi_{\mathsf{2BoolMult}}$, for each such cross-term, one of the parties randomly select a mask and the other party receives a masked version of the cross-term. Thus for every pair of distinct parties, two calls to $\mathcal{F}_{\mathsf{OT}}$ are made, corresponding to the two cross-terms involving these parties. Hence there will be overall $\mathcal{O}(n^2)$ calls to $\mathcal{F}_{\mathsf{OT}}$. For a pictorial depiction of the protocol steps for the case of $n = 3$ parties, see Fig. 10.7.

10.4.3 Computing $\mathcal{F}_{\mathsf{Mult}}$ over a General Ring

In this section, we discuss how to securely compute $\mathcal{F}_{\mathsf{Mult}}$ over a general ring $(\mathbb{R}, +, \cdot)$, where each element of $\mathbb{R}$ is represented by ℓ bits. For simplicity, we consider the case of $n = 2$ parties, with $t = 1$ corruption. The protocol is due to [77] and can be easily extended

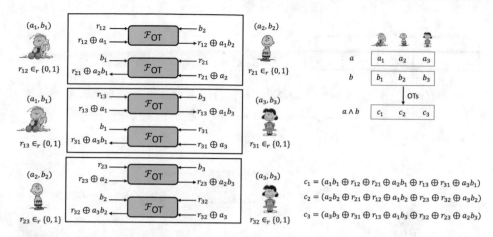

Fig. 10.7 Pictorial depiction of the protocol for computing $\mathcal{F}_{\mathsf{Mult}}$ over Boolean ring in the $\mathcal{F}_{\mathsf{OT}}$-hybrid for the case of $n = 3$ parties

to the n-party case. The idea behind the protocol is as follows. Since $a = a_1 + a_2$ and $b = b_1 + b_2$, then the following holds:

$$ab = a_1b_1 + a_1b_2 + a_2b_1 + a_2b_2.$$

While P_1 and P_2 can locally compute a_1b_1 and a_2b_2 respectively, we need a mechanism which can allow P_1 and P_2 to securely compute a 2-party random ASS of the cross-terms a_1b_2 and a_2b_1 respectively by making calls to $\mathcal{F}_{\mathsf{OT}}$. Let us focus on how a random ASS of a_1b_2 can be computed and a similar method can be used to generate a random 2-party ASS of a_2b_1.

Let us denote the inputs of P_1 and P_2 as x and y respectively, where $x, y \in \mathbb{R}$. The goal is to securely generate a random 2-party ASS of xy, with P_1 and P_2 holding random z_1 and z_2 respectively from $\mathbb{R}$, such that $z_1 + z_2 = xy$ holds. Since x can be represented by ℓ bits, let $(x_{\ell-1}, \ldots, x_0)$ be the bit-representation of x, with x_0 being the LSB. Then the following holds:

$$
\begin{aligned}
xy &= (x_0 2^0 + \cdots + x_{\ell-1} 2^{\ell-1})y \\
&= (x_0 2^0 y) + \cdots + (x_{\ell-1} 2^{\ell-1} y)
\end{aligned}
$$

In the protocol, the parties securely generate a random 2-party ASS of each of the ℓ summands in the above expression. Then from the linearity of ASS, the sum of all these ASSs will result in a random ASS of xy. Consider the ith summand $x_i 2^i y$ in the above expression, where x_i and y are held by P_1 and P_2 respectively. To generate a random ASS of this summand, P_2 and P_1 call $\mathcal{F}_{\mathsf{OT}}$ as S and R respectively. The input for P_2 are the messages $m_0 = r_i$ and $m_1 = 2^i y + r_i$ respectively, where r_i is a random mask from $\mathbb{R}$, picked by P_2. On the other

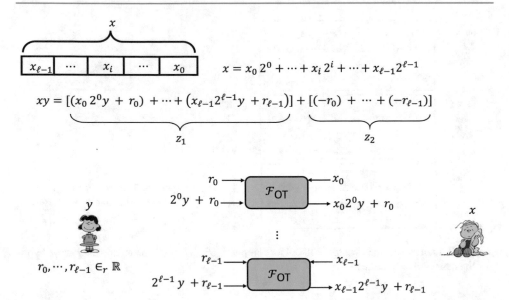

Fig. 10.8 Pictorial depiction of the Gilboa's method [77] to generate a random ASS of xy, where the inputs of P_1 and P_2 are x and y respectively. To securely compute $\mathcal{F}_{\mathsf{Mult}}$ for the 2-party case, the above protocol needs to be executed twice, once for the cross-term a_1b_2 (where $x = a_1$ and $y = b_2$) and once for a_2b_1 (where $x = a_2$ and $y = b_1$)

hand, the choice-bit of P_1 is x_i. It then follows from the property of $\mathcal{F}_{\mathsf{OT}}$, that P_1 receives the output $x_i 2^i y + r_i$ from $\mathcal{F}_{\mathsf{OT}}$ as R. The received value is a random element from $\mathbb{R}$ for P_1, due to the random mask r_i. This ensures that P_1 does not learn anything about y. On the other hand, P_2 does not learn any information about x_i, which follows from the *receiver's security of OT*. It then follows that the vector of values $(x_i 2^i y + r_i, -r_i)$, with P_1 and P_2 holding $x_i 2^i y + r_i$ and $-r_i$ respectively, can be considered as a random ASS of the summand $x_i 2^i y$. By following the above process for each of the ℓ summands (which requires ℓ calls to $\mathcal{F}_{\mathsf{OT}}$), parties P_1 and P_2 can generate a random ASS of each of the summands. For a pictorial depiction of the protocol, see Fig. 10.8.

To securely compute $\mathcal{F}_{\mathsf{Mult}}$, parties P_1 and P_2 have to invoke the above process *twice*, once for the cross-term a_1b_2 (where the inputs x and y of P_1 and P_2 are a_1 and b_2 respectively) and once for the cross-term a_2b_1 (where the inputs x and y of P_1 and P_2 are a_2 and b_1 respectively). Hence there will be total 2ℓ calls to $\mathcal{F}_{\mathsf{OT}}$. The overall output of P_1 will be then the sum of a_1b_1 and P_1's shares corresponding to ASS of a_1b_2 and ASS of a_2b_1, while the output of P_2 will be the sum of a_2b_2 and P_2's shares corresponding to ASS of a_1b_2 and ASS of a_2b_1. Since the protocol steps follow easily from the above description, we do not provide the complete formal details.

10.5   Dealing with Malicious Adversaries

We conclude this chapter by briefly discussing the challenges faced while executing the GMW protocol in the face of a *malicious* adversary. The simplest possible attack that a malicious adversary can launch on the protocol is by *not* providing any share on the behalf of the corrupt parties during the reconstruction of the function output (or during the reconstruction of the desired values while evaluating multiplication gates in the circuit), thus causing the honest parties to abort the protocol execution *without* obtaining any output. In fact, it can be shown that *any* maliciously-secure MPC protocol in the *dishonest-majority* setting (where $t < n$) has to settle with security with abort [78]. Additionally, the corrupt parties can participate with incorrect values during the evaluation of multiplication gates and so the parties need to incorporate verification mechanisms to verify if all the parties are following the protocol instructions, without disclosing anything additional about the values of the honest parties. Several such verification mechanisms have been proposed in the literature and discussing them is out of scope of the current lecture series. We refer the interested readers to [15, 28, 64, 103, 111] and their references for some of the recent advancements in this area.

Oblivious Transfer

11

In the previous chapter, we have shown that one can implement the GMW protocol in the *plain model*, if we know how to securely compute the OT function $\mathcal{F}_{OT}$. In this chapter, our focus will be to securely compute $\mathcal{F}_{OT}$. As mentioned earlier, OT in itself is a very important cryptographic primitive and has been studied in depth. There are many instantiations available based on a spectrum of assumptions. Our goal is not to cover all of them. We refer the interested readers to [88] for a more detailed and rigorous coverage of OT.

We begin by first showing that one *cannot* securely compute $\mathcal{F}_{OT}$ tolerating *computationally-unbounded* adversaries. Next, we discuss various variants of OT. Their equivalences are well-studied in the literature. Here we present a few hand-picked implications between them. We then discuss the realization of $\mathcal{F}_{OT}$ based on enhanced trapdoor permutations. This is followed by an efficiency study of OT which includes domain extension and the foundational concept of OT extension. We conclude by briefly discussing the challenges faced while designing OT protocols in the face of a malicious adversary.

11.1 $\mathcal{F}_{OT}$ Cannot Be Computed Against Unbounded Adversaries

In this section, we show that there is *no* protocol for securely computing $\mathcal{F}_{OT}$ against computationally-unbounded adversaries. The impossibility works via a reduction from any unconditionally-secure protocol for computing $\mathcal{F}_{OT}$ to a 2-party unconditionally-secure protocol for computing the AND of two bits. The latter is known to be impossible due to Theorem 6.8.

In more detail, let Π_{OT} be a protocol for securely computing $\mathcal{F}_{OT}$ in the presence of a computationally-unbounded adversary, corrupting either S or R. Thus Π_{OT} provides *sender's security* against a computationally-unbounded R and *receiver's security* against a computationally-unbounded S. Now using Π_{OT}, we design the protocol Π_{2AND}, which

© The Author(s), under exclusive license to Springer Nature Switzerland AG 2022
A. Choudhury and A. Patra, *Secure Multi-Party Computation Against Passive Adversaries*,
Synthesis Lectures on Distributed Computing Theory,
https://doi.org/10.1007/978-3-031-12164-7_11

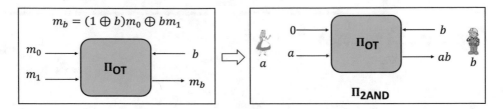

Fig. 11.1 Pictorial depiction of the transformation of Π_{OT} into Π_{2AND}

allows Alice and Bob to securely compute $a \wedge b$, where a and b are private bits, held by Alice and Bob respectively.

In protocol Π_{2AND}, Alice and Bob execute an instance of Π_{OT}, by playing the role of S and R respectively, where Alice's inputs are $(m_0 = 0, m_1 = a)$ and Bob's input is b. It then follows from the properties of Π_{OT}, that Bob as R, receives the output $a \wedge b$, which it can then send to Alice, so that both the parties learn $a \wedge b$. For security, if Alice is corrupt, then it does not learn anything about b in the protocol, which follows from *receiver's security* of Π_{OT}. On the other hand, if Bob is corrupt, then it does not learn anything beyond $a \wedge b$ due to *sender's security* of Π_{OT}. Specifically, if Bob's input $b = 0$, then the privacy of a is preserved. For a pictorial depiction of the transformation of Π_{OT} to Π_{2AND}, see Fig. 11.1.

From Theorem 6.8, we know that there exists no 2-party protocol Π_{2AND} with the above properties, implying that our assumption about the existence of Π_{OT} is incorrect.

11.2   Variants of OT

The definition of OT as captured through the functionality $\mathcal{F}_{OT}$ is due to [68] and is different from the original definition of OT, as proposed by Rabin in [132]. In the Rabin's variant of OT (which we call as Rabin-OT), S has *only one* private input m and with probability $\frac{1}{2}$, R receives m and with probability $\frac{1}{2}$, R receives $\perp$, with S being oblivious of R's output. This models a noisy communication, where S's message may get lost, with S being unaware of the exact situation. Interestingly, in [59] it is shown that both these variants are *equivalent*. That is, given a secure protocol for computing $\mathcal{F}_{OT}$, one can use it to design a secure protocol for Rabin-OT and vice-versa.

Recall that $\mathcal{F}_{OT}$ is also called as 1-*out-of*-2-OT, since one of the two messages of S gets obliviously transferred to R. In the literature, the following variants of OT have also been considered:

- 1-*out-of-N*-OT: Here S has N private inputs $m_0, \ldots, m_{N-1}$ and R has a private *index* $b \in \{0, \ldots, N - 1\}$. The output for R is the message m_b. We need the following security properties: a corrupt S should not learn b (*receiver's security*) and a corrupt R should learn only the message m_b (*Sender's* security).

- k-*out-of-N*-OT: This is a generalized form of the 1-*out-of-N*-OT, where S has N private inputs $m_0, \ldots, m_{N-1}$ and R has k private *indices* $i_1, \ldots, i_k \in \{0, \ldots, N-1\}$. The output for R are the message $m_{i_1}, \ldots, m_{i_k}$. A corrupt S should not learn about R's indices (*receiver's security*) and a corrupt R should learn only the messages it is interested in (*Sender's* security).

One can show that given a protocol for securely computing $\mathcal{F}_{\text{OT}}$, one can design secure protocols for 1-*out-of-N*-OT and k-*out-of-N*-OT (see [125]). Hence it is sufficient to focus on designing protocols for securely computing $\mathcal{F}_{\text{OT}}$. For completeness, we show how to construct a 1-out-of-4-OT using a secure protocol for computing $\mathcal{F}_{\text{OT}}$ (recall that a secure 1-out-of-4-OT protocol was used in the previous chapter to securely compute $\mathcal{F}_{\text{Mult}}$ for the 2-party setting over a Boolean ring).

11.2.1 1-out-of-2-OT $\Rightarrow$ 1-out-of-N-OT

We demonstrate the design of a 1-out-of-N-OT protocol for $N = 4$; the idea can be easily generalized for any N of the form 2^k. Let S has private inputs $m_{00}, m_{01}, m_{10}, m_{11} \in \{0, 1\}^\lambda$ and let R has the private choice indices $b_1, b_2 \in \{0, 1\}$. The goal is to let R obtain $m_{b_1 b_2}$, without S learning b_1 and b_2. Since S should not learn the exact message R is interested in, it has to send all the four messages in some "encrypted" fashion, such that R should be able to "decrypt" and learn exactly the message $m_{b_1 b_2}$. Towards this, S picks two random pairs of keys (k_0', k_1') and (k_0, k_1). While the key-pair (k_0', k_1') corresponds to the MSB bit-position with index 0 and 1 respectively, the key-pair (k_0, k_1) corresponds to the LSB bit-position with index 0 and 1 respectively. The idea is to then encrypt m_{ij} to ciphertext c_{ij} using the keys k_i' and k_j and send the ciphertexts $c_{00}, c_{01}, c_{10}, c_{11}$ to R, along with a provision for R to receive *only* the keys k_{b_1}' and k_{b_2}, with S being *oblivious* of the keys received by R. This will allow R to decrypt the ciphertext $c_{b_1} c_{b_2}$ and recover $m_{b_1 b_2}$.

The mechanism for R to obliviously receive the desired keys is taken care through OTs. Namely S and R call $\mathcal{F}_{\text{OT}}$ *twice*, once for letting R receive the key k_{b_1}' and once for receiving the key k_{b_2}. In more detail, during the first call to $\mathcal{F}_{\text{OT}}$, S and R participate with inputs (k_0', k_1') and b_1 respectively, while during the second call, their respective inputs are (k_0, k_1) and b_2. The challenging part is the encryption process. One may be tempted to use the keys k_i' and k_j as *one-time pads* (OTP) for encrypting m_{ij} to c_{ij} by setting $c_{ij} = m_{ij} \oplus k_i' \oplus k_j$. Since R will have the keys k_{b_1}' and k_{b_2} from $\mathcal{F}_{\text{OT}}$s, it will be able to recover $m_{b_1 b_2}$ by computing $m_{b_1 b_2} = c_{b_1 b_2} \oplus k_{b_1}' \oplus k_{b_2}$. However, the above method of encryption violates *sender's security*, as a *corrupt* R will be able to learn additional information about the remaining messages, other than $m_{b_1 b_2}$. For instance, by computing $c_{00} \oplus c_{01} \oplus c_{10} \oplus c_{11}$, R will be able to learn $m_{00} \oplus m_{01} \oplus m_{10} \oplus m_{11}$.

To get around the above problem, instead of directly encrypting the messages with the key-pairs, we use them for generating *pseudo-random* pads through a *pseudo-random function*

(PRF) [102]. In the sequel, we recall the definition of PRF, followed by the encryption process used in the above construction. Intuitively, a PRF is a *deterministic* keyed-function, whose "behaviour" is almost similar to that of a *true random function* (TRF) in the sense that any polynomial time *distinguisher* algorithm cannot distinguish outputs generated by the PRF from the output generated by a TRF.

In more detail, let $F : \{0, 1\}^{\ell_{key}} \times \{0, 1\}^{\ell_{in}} \rightarrow \{0, 1\}^{\ell_{out}}$ be an efficient, keyed function. A keyed function is a two-input function, where the first input is called the *key* and denoted by k. We say F is efficient if $F(k, x)$ can be computed in polynomial time, given k and x. While using a keyed function, typically a key k is chosen randomly and fixed, and we are then interested in the single-input function $F_k : \{0, 1\}^{\ell_{in}} \rightarrow \{0, 1\}^{\ell_{out}}$, defined as $F_k(x) \stackrel{def}{=} F(k, x)$. Let $\mathsf{Func}_{\ell_{in}, \ell_{out}}$ denote the set of all functions with domain $\{0, 1\}^{\ell_{in}}$ and codomain $\{0, 1\}^{\ell_{out}}$ and let f be a *random* function from the set $\mathsf{Func}_{\ell_{in}, \ell_{out}}$, implying that f is a TRF. Then F is called a PRF, if no PPT distinguisher A can distinguish the outputs generated by F_k from the outputs generated by f.

To formally capture the above essence, A is given an *oracle-access* to an oracle, which is either F_k or f, with A being *unaware* of which one it is. The algorithm A may query its oracle at any input x, in response to which the oracle returns either $F_k(x)$ or $f(x)$, depending upon whether the oracle is F_k or f respectively. The algorithm A may ask its queries adaptively during its interaction with the oracle, based on the outputs of previous queries; however it can ask only polynomially many queries, since A is a PPT algorithm. We use the notation $A^{F_k(\cdot)}$ and $A^{f(\cdot)}$ respectively, to denote A's interaction with the oracle when the oracle is F_k and f respectively. Then F is called a PRF, if A outputs 1 when A's oracle is F_k with almost the same probability with which A outputs 1, when its oracle is f. This would imply that A cannot significantly distinguish apart whether the oracle is F_k or f. Formally, we have the following definition:

Definition 11.1 (*Pseudorandom Function (PRF)* [102]) Let $F : \{0, 1\}^{\ell_{key}} \times \{0, 1\}^{\ell_{in}} \rightarrow \{0, 1\}^{\ell_{out}}$ be an efficient, keyed function. Then F is a pseudorandom function if for every PPT algorithm A, there is a negligible function negl such that:

$$\left| \Pr[A^{F_k(\cdot)}(1^\lambda) = 1] - \Pr[A^{f(\cdot)}(1^\lambda) = 1] \right| \leq \mathsf{negl}(\lambda),$$

where the first probability is taken over uniform choice of $k \in \{0, 1\}^{\ell_{key}}$ and randomness of A, and the second probability is taken over uniform choice of $f \in \mathsf{Func}_{\ell_{in}, \ell_{out}}$ and randomness of A.

One can construct PRFs based on the assumption that one-way function (OWF) exists. The popular block-ciphers such as AES and 3DES can be used as practical instantiations of PRFs (see [102] for more details). Assuming the existence of a PRF, the encryption process used in the 1-out-of-4-OT construction is as follows: to encrypt the message m_{ij} using the keys k_i' and k_j, the sender computes $c_{ij} \stackrel{def}{=} F_{k_i'}(ij) \oplus F_{k_j}(ij) \oplus m_{ij}$. Thus the outputs of

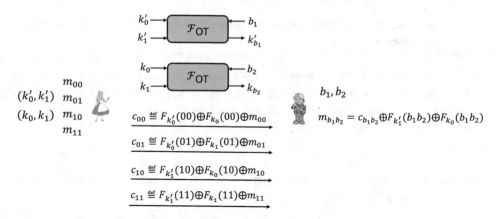

Fig. 11.2 Pictorial depiction of the 1-out-of-4-OT protocol in the $\mathcal{F}_{\mathsf{OT}}$-hybrid model

$F_{k_i'}$ and F_{k_j} are used as pseudo-random pads for encrypting the message. To recover the message $m_{b_1 b_2}$, the receiver can compute $m_{b_1 b_2} = c_{b_1 b_2} \oplus F_{k'_{b_1}}(b_1 b_2) \oplus F_{b_2}(b_1 b_2)$. For a pictorial illustration, see Fig. 11.2.

Intuitively, *sender's security* is achieved because R will be able to decrypt *only* $c_{b_1 b_2}$. For every other ciphertext, there will be at least one key which will be unknown to R and hence the corresponding pseudorandom pad will be unknown. The encryption process used here is also called as *double-encryption*, since two keys are used for encrypting each message. Looking ahead, such encryptions are also used in the context of Yao's secure 2PC protocol, which we will discuss in the next chapter. One can formally prove that if there exists a PPT adversary who by corrupting R can break *sender's security* with a non-negligible probability, then the adversary's algorithm can be used to design an efficient distinguisher to break the security of PRF F (see for instance [86] for more details).

11.3 Securely Computing $\mathcal{F}_{\mathsf{OT}}$

As mentioned earlier, there are a range of protocols for computing $\mathcal{F}_{\mathsf{OT}}$ with different trade-offs, based on various assumptions, such as difficulty of factoring large random composite numbers, the difficulty of the Diffie-Hellman problem, existence of trapdoor one-way permutations (such as RSA) and homomorphic encryption, to name a few. In this chapter, we will discuss the construction of bit-OT protocol (where S's messages are bits) based on *any one-way trapdoor permutation* (OWTP) and refer the interested readers to [88] for various other ways of designing protocols for securely computing $\mathcal{F}_{\mathsf{OT}}$. In the sequel, we first give the formal definition of OWTP, enhanced OWTP, and hard-core predicates, followed by the construction of the bit-OT protocol.

11.3.1 Enhanced One-Way Trapdoor Permutation (OWTP) and Hard-core Predicates

One-way permutation (OWP) and *one-way trapdoor permutation* (OWTP) are fundamental concepts in modern cryptography. Informally, a OWP is a permutation (bijection), where the output of the permutation can be efficiently computed, while the inverse of any random element cannot be computed in polynomial time, except with a negligible probability. Formally:

Definition 11.2 (*One-way Permutation (OWP)* [37, 102]) A permutation (bijection) $f : \mathcal{X} \to \mathcal{X}$ is called a OWP, if the following two conditions hold:

- *Easy to compute*: The value $f(x)$ can be computed in polynomial (in λ) time for every $x \in \mathcal{X}$.
- *Hard to invert*: For every PPT algorithm A, there is a negligible function negl, such that

$$\Pr_{x \leftarrow \mathcal{X}}\Big[A(1^\lambda, f(x)) = x\Big] \leq \mathsf{negl}(\lambda),$$

where the probability is taken over the random choice of x (the notation $x \leftarrow \mathcal{X}$ denotes that x is chosen uniformly at random from $\mathcal{X}$) and the randomness of A.

A OWTP is a *special* type of OWP, which has an associated trapdoor, using which the inverse of any element can be efficiently computed. Formally:

Definition 11.3 (*One-way Trapdoor Permutation (OWTP)* [37, 102]) A OWTP scheme $\mathcal{T}$ over a finite set $\mathcal{X}$ is a triplet of polynomial time algorithms (Gen, f, Inv), such that:

- $\mathsf{Gen}(1^\lambda) \to (\mathsf{pk}, \mathsf{sk})$: the key-generation algorithm Gen is a *randomized* algorithm, which outputs a *public-key* pk and a *secret-key* sk.[1]
- $f_{\mathsf{pk}} : \mathcal{X} \to \mathcal{X}$: the keyed function f_{pk} is a bijection from $\mathcal{X}$ to $\mathcal{X}$, which takes input $x \in \mathcal{X}$ (apart from pk) and gives the output $y = f_{\mathsf{pk}}(x)$.
- $\mathsf{Inv}_{\mathsf{sk}} : \mathcal{X} \to \mathcal{X}$: the keyed function f_{sk} is a bijection from $\mathcal{X}$ to $\mathcal{X}$, which takes input $y \in \mathcal{X}$ (apart from sk) and gives the output $x = f_{\mathsf{sk}}(y)$.

The scheme satisfies the following two properties:

- *Correctness*: For every (pk, sk) generated by Gen and for every $x \in \mathcal{X}$, the following should hold except with a negligible probability.

$$\mathsf{Inv}_{\mathsf{sk}}(f_{\mathsf{pk}}(x)) = x$$

---

[1] The secret-key is also called as the *trapdoor information*.

– *One-wayness*: function f_{pk} should be a one-way permutation (as per the previous definition), even if an adversary knows the public-key pk.

There are several well-known instantiations of OWTP based on varieties of assumptions, such as the RSA OWTP based on the assumption that factoring large composite numbers is difficult (see for instance [37, 102]).

We next define a related concept called *hard-core predicate*, which will be used in the construction of the OT protocol. One may think that if f is a OWP, then it is difficult to invert it *completely* in the sense that given $y = f(x)$ for a random x, the value of x *cannot* be computed in its *entirety* in polynomial time, just based on the description of f and y. However, this *need not* be always true. Indeed it is possible for a OWP f to "leak" something about the input x through $f(x)$ (see [37, 102]). The idea behind the hard-core predicate is to formally identify a specific piece of information about x, that is *always* guaranteed to be "hidden" by $f(x)$. Formally, we have the following definition:

Definition 11.4 (*Hard-Core Predicate* [37, 102]) A function hc : $\{0, 1\}^\star \to \{0, 1\}$ is called a hard-core predicate for a function f, if the following conditions hold:

– For *any* given $x \in \{0, 1\}^\lambda$, the value $\mathsf{hc}(x)$ can be computed in polynomial (in λ) time.
– For *every* PPT algorithm A, there is a negligible function negl, such that[2]

$$\Pr_{x \leftarrow \{0,1\}^\lambda}\left[A(1^\lambda, f(x)) = \mathsf{hc}(x)\right] \le \frac{1}{2} + \mathsf{negl}(\lambda),$$

where the probability is taken over the uniform choice of x (the notation $x \leftarrow \{0, 1\}^\lambda$ denotes that x is chosen uniformly at random from $\{0, 1\}^\lambda$) and the randomness of A.
An *equivalent* formulation of the above condition is in terms of the inability of A to significantly distinguish $\mathsf{hc}(x)$ from a uniform random bit. That is, the following should hold:

$$\left| \Pr_{x \leftarrow \{0,1\}^\lambda} [A(1^\lambda, f(x), \mathsf{hc}(x)) = 1] - \Pr_{b \leftarrow \{0,1\}} [A(1^\lambda, b) = 1] \right| \le \mathsf{negl}(\lambda),$$

where first probability is taken over the uniform choice of x from $\{0, 1\}^\lambda$ and the randomness of A and the second probability is over the uniform choice of b and randomness of A.

---

[2] Since hc is a Boolean function, it is *always* possible to compute $\mathsf{hc}(x)$ with probability $\frac{1}{2}$ by a random guessing. The following expression captures the essence that A *should not* be able to do anything significantly better than randomly guessing $\mathsf{hc}(x)$.

A fundamental result due to Goldreich and Levin [79] shows that given *any* OWP, one can construct a *different* OWP and its corresponding hard-core predicate. Formally, they proved the following (we refer the readers to [102] for the proof).

Theorem 11.5 (Goldreich-Levin Theorem [79]) *Let f be a OWP. Then the following holds:*

- *The function* $g(x, r) \stackrel{def}{=} (f(x), r)$ *where* $|x| = |r|$ *is a OWP*[3].
- *The function* $\mathsf{hc}(x, r) \stackrel{def}{=} \bigoplus_{i=1}^{n} x_i \cdot r_i$ *is a hard-core predicate for g, where x_i and r_i denotes the ith bit of x and r respectively.*

Although OWTP suffices for many applications, OT will need an enhanced hardness condition from OWTP (and its corresponding hard-core predicates). For this, we need to introduce another standard algorithm associated with OWTP. We denote this by Sam which, on input pk, samples the (co)domain of f_{pk}, returning an almost uniformly distributed element from it. A OWTP is now defined as a set of four polynomial time algorithms (Gen, Sam, f, Inv), where the *one-wayness* property is equivalently rewritten utilizing Sam as follows: for every PPT algorithm A, there is a negligible function negl, such that

$$\Pr_{(\mathsf{pk},\mathsf{sk}) \leftarrow \mathsf{Gen}(1^\lambda), r \leftarrow R_\lambda} \left[A(1^\lambda, \mathsf{pk}, \mathsf{Sam}(\mathsf{pk}; r)) = \mathsf{Inv}_{\mathsf{sk}}(\mathsf{Sam}(\mathsf{pk}; r)) \right] \leq \mathsf{negl}(\lambda),$$

where R_λ denotes the distribution of the coins of Sam on λ-bit long inputs. That is, given a random element sampled by Sam, it should be computationally difficult for A to compute the inverse function of that element, except with a negligible probability.

Now for an *enhanced* OWTP, we will require that it is computationally hard for any PPT A to compute the inverse function of a random element sampled by Sam, even if the coins used by Sam to sample that element is given to A. Note that, given the coins used by Sam and pk, the resultant element x is fully determined. But the opposite direction need not be true always; i.e., given *only* x and pk, it may not be possible to determine the randomness used by Sam to sample that x. Therefore, conceptually A is given more power in an enhanced OWTP compared to OWTP, since it has access to both the random element (for which the inverse needs to be computed), along with the randomness used to pick that element.

Definition 11.6 (*Enhanced trapdoor permutations* [81]) Let $\mathcal{T} = (\mathsf{Gen}, \mathsf{Sam}, f, \mathsf{Inv})$ be a OWTP scheme. We say that $\mathcal{T}$ is enhanced if for every PPT algorithm A, there is a negligible function negl, such that

---

[3] The notation $|x|$ and $|r|$ denotes the length of the bit-strings x and r respectively.

$$\Pr_{(\text{pk},\text{sk})\leftarrow\text{Gen}(1^\lambda),r\leftarrow R_\lambda}\left[A(1^\lambda,\text{pk},r)=\text{Inv}_{\text{sk}}(\text{Sam}(\text{pk};r))\right]\leq\text{negl}(\lambda),$$

where R_λ denotes the distribution of the coins of Sam on λ-bit long inputs.

Any enhanced OWTP can be augmented with an enhanced hard-core predicate. Loosely speaking, such a predicate should be easy to compute. But given only pk and $r\leftarrow R_\lambda$, it should *not* be possible for any PPT algorithm to compute $\text{hc}(\text{Inv}_{\text{sk}}(\text{Sam}(\text{pk};r)))$ in the absence of sk, non-negligibly better than a random guess. In other words, $\text{hc}(\text{Inv}_{\text{sk}}(\text{Sam}$ $(\text{pk};r)))$ should be computationally indistinguishable from a uniformly random bit, in the *absence* of sk, even if r is given to the adversary. Formally:

Definition 11.7 (*Enhanced Hard-Core Predicate* [81]) A function $\text{hc}:\{0,1\}^\star\to\{0,1\}$ is called an enhanced hard-core predicate for f of an enhanced OWTP scheme $\mathcal{T}=$ (Gen, Sam, f, Inv) if the following conditions hold:

- For *any* given $x\in\mathcal{X}$, the value $\text{hc}(x)$ can be computed in polynomial (in λ) time.
- For *every* PPT algorithm A, there is a negligible function negl, such that

$$\Pr_{(\text{pk},\text{sk})\leftarrow\text{Gen}(1^\lambda),r\leftarrow R_\lambda}\left[A(1^\lambda,\text{pk},r)=\text{hc}(\text{Inv}_{\text{sk}}(\text{Sam}(\text{pk};r)))\right]\leq\frac{1}{2}+\text{negl}(\lambda),$$

where R_λ denotes the distribution of the coins of Sam on λ-bit long inputs. Equivalently, the following should hold:

$$\left|\Pr_{(\text{pk},\text{sk})\leftarrow\text{Gen}(1^\lambda),r\leftarrow R_\lambda}[A(1^\lambda,\text{pk},r,\text{hc}(\text{Inv}_{\text{sk}}(\text{Sam}(\text{pk};r))))=1]\right.$$

$$\left.-\Pr_{b\leftarrow\{0,1\}}[A(1^\lambda,b)=1]\right|\leq\text{negl}(\lambda).$$

There are well-known instantiations for enhanced OWTP (and corresponding enhanced hard-core predicate), such as the one based on RSA assumption (see [81])

11.3.2 Protocol for Computing $\mathcal{F}_{OT}$ from OWTP

In this section, we present a protocol Π_{OT} due to [80], for securely computing $\mathcal{F}_{OT}$, where $m_0,m_1\in\{0,1\}$. The protocol assumes the existence of an enhanced OWTP scheme $\mathcal{T}=$ (Gen, Sam, f, Inv) and an associated hard-core predicate hc for f. The high level idea of the protocol is to let S compute OTP-encryptions of m_0 and m_1 and send to R in such a way that R will be able to decrypt and recover only m_b. To implement the above idea, S runs the algorithm Gen and generates the key-pair (pk, sk) and provides pk to R. The receiver

R then randomly picks two elements s and T from $\mathcal{X}$, the domain (and co-domain) of f and it computes the output $S = f_{\mathsf{pk}}(s)$. The idea is then to let S use the elements S and T to generate the OTP-pads for encrypting m_0 and m_1 in such a way that the message m_b is always encrypted using a pad, which is also available with R and the pad which is used to encrypt m_{1-b} remains unknown to R. Moreover, this is done in such a way that S remains *oblivious* of the choice-bit b of R.

Based on the above intuition, S encrypts m_b using $\mathsf{hc}(s)$ as the pad. This will allow R to recover m_b, as R can compute the pad itself using the knowledge of s. Let $t \stackrel{def}{=} \mathsf{Inv}_{\mathsf{sk}}(T)$. Notice that R *cannot* compute $\mathsf{hc}(t)$ in polynomial time, which follows from the definition of hc and the fact that sk is unavailable to R. To ensure that R does not have the pad to recover m_{1-b}, the encryption mechanism ensures that S uses $\mathsf{hc}(t)$ as the pad to encrypt m_{1-b}.

To allow S to compute the pads as above, R sends S and T to S, from which S computes s and t, using the trapdoor sk and finds $\mathsf{hc}(s)$ and $\mathsf{hc}(t)$. However, S and T need to be sent in such a way that S being oblivious of b, ends up using $\mathsf{hc}(s)$ as the pad for encrypting m_b. For this, R sends S followed by T if $b = 0$, else it sends T followed by S. From the point of view of S, it receives two uniformly random elements from $\mathcal{X}$ and hence it cannot figure out whether $b = 0$ or $b = 1$, thus guaranteeing *receiver's security* (note that this holds, even if S is *computationally-unbounded*). Now irrespective of the order in which S receives the two elements from R, it uses the pad generated from the first element to encrypt m_0 and the pad generated from the second element to encrypt m_1. It is easy to see that due to the order in which R sends S and T, the message m_b ends up being encrypted using the pad $\mathsf{hc}(s)$. Protocol Π_{OT} is formally presented in Fig. 11.4 and is pictorially illustrated in Fig. 11.3.

We next give a high level overview of why protocol Π_{OT} is a 1-cryptographically-secure protocol for computing $\mathcal{F}_{\mathsf{OT}}$. The *correctness* of the protocol is obvious, so we focus on *privacy*. For simplicity, we assume that the protocol is executed in the $\mathcal{F}_{\mathsf{SetUp}}$-hybrid, with the setup for $\mathcal{T}$ being done by $\mathcal{F}_{\mathsf{SetUp}}$. We have to argue that the view of a corrupt S can be simulated (for receiver's security) and the view of a corrupt receiver can be simulated (for sender's security).

First consider a *corrupt* S. Then in the protocol, S receives c_0 and c_1 from R, both of which are random elements of $\mathcal{X}$ (while T is a random element from $\mathcal{X}$, the element S is also random, since s is selected randomly and f_{pk} is a bijection). These two messages can be

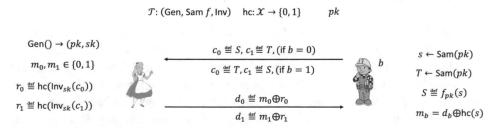

Fig. 11.3 Pictorial depiction of the protocol Π_{OT} based on enhanced OWTP

Protocol Π_{OT}

The public input is an enhanced OWTP scheme $\mathcal{T} = (\mathsf{Gen}, \mathsf{Sam}, f, \mathsf{Inv})$ and an associated hard-core predicate hc for f, where the domain and co-domain of f is $\mathcal{X}$.

- *Set-up phase*: The following set-up is done *once* by S at the beginning and the same set-up can be used for polynomially many instances of Π_{OT}:[a]
  - Compute $\mathsf{Gen}(1^\lambda) \to (\mathsf{pk}, \mathsf{sk})$.
  - Send pk to R.
- *Round I*: On having the input $b \in \{0, 1\}$, R executes the following steps:
  - Pick $s \leftarrow \mathsf{Sam}(\mathsf{pk})$ and $T \leftarrow \mathsf{Sam}(\mathsf{pk})$, where $s, T \in \mathcal{X}$.[b]
  - Compute $S \stackrel{def}{=} f_{\mathsf{pk}}(s)$.
  - If $b = 0$, then set $c_0 = S$ and $c_1 = T$. Else set $c_0 = T$ and $c_1 = S$.
  - Send (c_0, c_1) to S.
- *Round II*: On having the input $m_0, m_1 \in \{0, 1\}$, S executes the following steps:
  - Upon receiving (c_0, c_1) from R, compute $r_0 \stackrel{def}{=} \mathsf{hc}(\mathsf{Inv}_{\mathsf{sk}}(c_0))$ and $r_1 \stackrel{def}{=} \mathsf{hc}(\mathsf{Inv}_{\mathsf{sk}}(c_1))$.
  - Send $d_0 \stackrel{def}{=} m_0 \oplus r_0$ and $d_1 \stackrel{def}{=} m_1 \oplus r_1$ to R.
- *Local computation at the end of Round II*: Upon receiving (r_0, r_1) from S, compute $m_b = r_b \oplus \mathsf{hc}(s)$.

---
[a]Instead of S generating the set-up, one can also assume the existence of a TTP $\mathcal{F}_{\mathsf{SetUp}}$ which does the setup once for all for S and R and the resultant protocol will be then in the $\mathcal{F}_{\mathsf{SetUp}}$-hybrid model.
[b]To avoid additional notations, we avoid the randomness used by Sam to sample the elements s and T.

Fig. 11.4 A generic 1-cryptographically-secure protocol for computing $\mathcal{F}_{\mathsf{OT}}$ over a Boolean ring from enhanced OWTP

easily simulated by a simulator, who (without knowing the choice-bit b) simply outputs two random elements from $\mathcal{X}$. It is easy to see that any (computationally-unbounded) adversary will not be able to distinguish between the real-view of S and the view generated by the simulator, implying that *receiver's security* is achieved, even against a computationally-unbounded S.

Next consider the case when R is *corrupt*. Apart from its input b and output m_b, the view of R in the protocol consists of the random pair of elements (s, T) picked by R, the element S and the messages (d_0, d_1) received from S, where $d_b = m_b \oplus \mathsf{hc}(s)$ holds. Intuitively, d_{1-b} does not reveal any information about m_{1-b}, since the pad $\mathsf{hc}(\mathsf{Inv}_{\mathsf{sk}}(T))$ used in d_{1-b} cannot be computed by R, in the absence of sk, even when the randomness used for sampling T is given (as T is an enhanced OWTP). Thus for a PPT R, the bit $\mathsf{hc}(\mathsf{Inv}_{\mathsf{sk}}(T))$ is computationally indistinguishable from a uniformly random bit (follows from the definition of (enhanced) hc) and hence d_{1-b} is al most like a random bit for R.

Based on the above intuition, a simulator with inputs b and m_b can simulate the view of R as follows: the simulator first picks random $\widetilde{s}$ and $\widetilde{T}$ from $\mathcal{X}$, to simulate the elements s and T picked by R in the protocol. It is easy to see that the probability distribution of (s, T) and $(\widetilde{s}, \widetilde{T})$ are identical. Next, the simulator sets $\widetilde{d_b} = m_b \oplus \mathsf{hc}(\widetilde{s})$ to be one of the messages received by R from S. Again, it is easy to see that the probability distribution of the message d_b received by R in the protocol is identical to the distribution of $\widetilde{d_b}$. Specifically, both d_b as well as $\widetilde{d_b}$ upon getting decrypted, produces m_b. To simulate the other message received by R from S, the simulator sets $\widetilde{d_{1-b}}$ to be a random bit.

The only difference between the view of R in the protocol and the view generated by the simulator is between d_{1-b} and $\widetilde{d}_{1-b}$. A careful observation reveals that if in the protocol d_{1-b} is set as $m_{1-b} \oplus p$, where p is a uniformly random bit, then the probability distribution of the modified d_{1-b} will be exactly the *same* as $\widetilde{d}_{1-b}$, as both of them will be then a random bit. However, in the protocol, d_{1-b} is actually $m_{1-b} \oplus \mathsf{hc}(\mathsf{Inv}_{\mathsf{sk}}(T))$. To show that a PPT adversary cannot distinguish between d_{1-b} and $\widetilde{d}_{1-b}$, it is sufficient to show that $\mathsf{hc}(\mathsf{Inv}_{\mathsf{sk}}(T))$ is computationally indistinguishable from a uniformly random bit p. However, this follows from the definition of (enhanced) hard-core predicated. Specifically, it can be shown that if a PPT adversary can non-negligibly distinguish apart the view of R in the protocol and the view generated by the simulator, then the adversary can be used to non-negligibly distinguish apart $\mathsf{hc}(\mathsf{Inv}_{\mathsf{sk}}(T))$ from a uniformly random bit, given just the random T and the randomness used to sample T. However, this will violate the assumption that hc is an (enhanced) hard-core predicate; we refer the interested readers to [81] for the complete formal details of the above reduction.

11.4   Efficiency of OT

The protocol for OT presented in the previous section relies on OWTP, which can be instantiated based on public-key operations. It is important at this stage to demarcate the performance difference between public-key and symmetric-key primitives. With the modern computing speed, to get 128-bit security,[4] one can deploy *symmetric-key* cryptographic primitives like AES with key-size of 128 bits, thus setting the security parameter λ to 128. However, to get the same 128-bit security using *asymmetric-key* (namely *public-key*) cryptographic primitives, one has to operate with prime numbers of order 3072 bits, allowing for a security parameter $\lambda = 3072$. Due to working over a much larger algebraic structure, public-key-based protocols are several order of magnitude slower than symmetric-key-based protocols. Therefore, within the regime of cryptographically-secure MPC protocols, protocols based on symmetric-key primitives are preferred over those based on asymmetric-key primitives.

Given the known efficiency benefits of symmetric-key primitives, a natural question is whether OT can be realized based on symmetric-key primitives. However, [94] shows that OT is unlikely to be built from symmetric-key primitives.

Based on the above impossibility result, protocols based on OT would seem to necessarily suffer from low efficiency. For instance, consider the GMW MPC protocol discussed in the previous chapter. The protocol requires $\mathcal{O}(n^2)$ calls to $\mathcal{F}_{\mathsf{OT}}$ for each multiplication gate and hence overall $\mathcal{O}(c_M n^2)$ calls to $\mathcal{F}_{\mathsf{OT}}$. This implies that the parties need to perform $\mathcal{O}(c_M n^2)$ *public-key* operations. When public-key primitives are unavoidable, the next natural question is whether it is possible to reduce the number of public-key operations. This will be a

---

[4] A λ-bit security refers to that fact that in order to break security, an adversary needs to perform computations of order 2^{128}.

commendable progress even when achieved at the expense of performing certain number of symmetric-key operations. Specifically, an interesting efficiency question is:

Can the $\mathcal{O}(c_M n^2)$ instances of computing Π_{OT} in the GMW protocol be implemented with only $\mathcal{O}(\lambda)$ instances of an OT protocol plus $\mathcal{O}(c_M n^2)$ symmetric-key operations?

Generalizing the above question, we ask the following:

Let $L = \mathsf{poly}(\lambda)$ and let Π_{OT} be a protocol for securely computing $\mathcal{F}_{OT}$. Then can we implement L instances of securely computing $\mathcal{F}_{OT}$ by executing $\mathcal{O}(\lambda)$ instances of Π_{OT} and performing $\mathcal{O}(L)$ symmetric-key operations?

The above question is clearly of practical importance, since OT is used extensively not only in the GMW protocol, but also in the Yao's secure 2PC protocol, which we discuss in the next chapter. A positive answer to the above question will imply that the number of OT operations that the parties need to perform will be *independent* of the circuit-size. This will further imply that the number of public-key operations will be independent of the circuit-size.

In this section, we show how to answer the question posed above positively through *OT extension* [17]. The idea is to let parties execute some *base OTs* (also called as *seed OTs*) and then use them to generate a "large" number of OTs. One can conceptually compare OT extension with *pseudo-random generators* (PRG), where a "small" seed is "expanded" to a "large" pseudorandom string. Looking ahead, while implementing the GMW (and Yao's) protocol in practice, the parties can first execute the base OTs in a *function-independent* pre-processing phase. Once the parties start evaluating the circuit, the precomputed base OTs are expanded to generate the "actual" OTs via OT extension. One can see the similarity of this approach with the MPC in the pre-processing model, where raw data generated in the pre-processing phase is used later for efficiently evaluating the circuit. We note that symmetric-key primitives are necessary for OT extension. Indeed, the work of [17] proves that an OT extension cannot be done information-theoretically. That is, it is impossible to produce large number of OTs starting from a small number of base OTs information-theoretically. In fact, the results of [119] show that an OT extension protocol implies OWFs.

The OT extension protocol that we describe here is due to [95]. The whole process of OT extension consists of two different sub-protocols for different purposes. In the next two sections, we discuss these two sub-protocols and then discuss the OT extension protocol. For more efficient state-of-the-art OT extension protocols, we refer to [55].

11.4.1 Domain Extension for OT

Let Π_{ShOT} be a protocol for securely computing $\mathcal{F}_{OT}$ where S's messages are of size λ bits. Then the goal of the *domain-extension* for OT is to use Π_{ShOT} and design a protocol Π_{LongOT}

for securely computing $\mathcal{F}_{\mathsf{OT}}$, where S's messages are of size k bits, where $k = \mathsf{poly}(\lambda)$.[5] Since the domain-extension is based on PRG, we first present the formal definition of PRG.

Informally, a PRG is a deterministic algorithm, which expands an input seed to generate a longer output. The output is pseudorandom in the sense that no PPT "distinguisher" algorithm can significantly distinguish apart a random output generated by a PRG from a uniformly random string.

Definition 11.8 (Pseudorandom Generator (PRG) [102]) Let ℓ be a polynomial and let G be a deterministic, polynomial-time algorithm, such that for any λ and any input $s \in \{0, 1\}^{\lambda}$, the output $G(s)$ is a string of length $\ell(\lambda)$. We say that G is a pseudorandom generator (PRG), if the following conditions hold:

- *Expansion*: For every λ, it holds that $\ell(\lambda) > \lambda$.
- *Pseudorandomness*: For any PPT algorithm D, there is a negligible function negl such that:
$$\left| \Pr[D(G(s)) = 1] - \Pr[D(r) = 1] \right| \leq \mathsf{negl}(\lambda),$$

where the first probability is over the uniform choice of $s \in \{0, 1\}^{\lambda}$ and randomness of D, and the second probability is over the uniform choice of $r \in \{0, 1\}^{\ell(\lambda)}$ and randomness of D.

The idea behind the protocol Π_{LongOT} is to let S use a pair of random PRG seeds and expand these seeds to generate pseudorandom pads for encrypting its inputs of Π_{LongOT}. The encrypted inputs are then communicated to R. In order for R to receive the desired message, we need to enable R obtain the appropriate seed, while keeping S oblivious of it. For this, S and R invoke an instance of Π_{ShOT}, where the inputs of S are the PRG seeds. The domain extension is pictorially illustrated in Fig. 11.5.

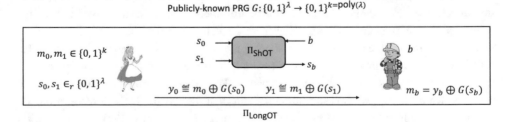

Fig. 11.5 Pictorial depiction of the domain-extension protocol

---

[5] The term Sh and Long in Π_{ShOT} and Π_{LongOT} signifies that the inputs of S are short and long respectively.

As the protocol is straightforward and easily understood through the pictorial illustration, we do not give the formal details of the protocol. The *receiver's security* for Π_{LongOT} directly follows from the *receiver's security* of Π_{ShOT}, as a *corrupt* S remains oblivious of the choice-bit b during the protocol Π_{ShOT}. The *sender's security* in Π_{LongOT} follows from the *sender's security* in Π_{ShOT} and the pseudorandomness property of the PRG. Namely, if R is *corrupt*, then the *sender's security* during Π_{ShOT} ensures that R does not learn anything about the seed s_{1-b}. This further implies that the pad $G(s_{1-b})$ remains unknown to R and hence y_{1-b} does not reveal anything about m_{1-b}. We refer the readers to [95] for a formal security proof.

11.4.2 Oblivious Transfer of a Matrix

We next present a protocol $\Pi_{\text{MatTransfer}}$, which is a secure 2-party protocol, executed between two parties, say Alice and Bob. In the protocol, Bob has private inputs T and B, where T is a *random* Boolean matrix of size $k \times \lambda$, where the ith row and jth column of T is denoted by T_i and $T^{(j)}$ respectively. Moreover, $B = (b_1, \ldots, b_k)$ is a Boolean vector of size k bits. The private input for Alice is a Boolean vector $S = (s_1, \ldots, s_\lambda)$ of size λ. The goal is to let Alice receive the Boolean matrix Q of size $k \times \lambda$, where the ith row Q_i of the matrix Q satisfies the following property:

$$
Q_i = \begin{cases} T_i & \text{if } b_i = 0 \\ T_i \oplus S & \text{if } b_i = 1 \end{cases}
$$

The protocol ensures that Alice does not learn any information about B and Bob does not learn any information about S. To achieve the above goal, Alice and Bob execute λ instances of the OT protocol Π_{LongOT} from the previous section (where S's messages are of size k bits).[6] While Bob plays the role of S, the role of R is assigned to Alice. In the ith invocation of the OT, the input messages of Bob (as S) will be $(T^{(i)}, T^{(i)} \oplus B)$, while the choice-bit of Alice (as R) will be s_i.

Let $Q^{(i)} \in \{0, 1\}^k$ denote the output received by Alice from the ith instance of Π_{LongOT}. It then follows that $Q^{(i)} = T^{(i)} \oplus s_i B$ holds. Now let Q be the matrix of size $k \times \lambda$, where the ith column of Q is $Q^{(i)}$. One can now easily verify that the ith row Q_i of Q satisfies the above required property. For a pictorial illustration of the protocol $\Pi_{\text{MatTransfer}}$, see Fig. 11.6.

If Bob is *corrupt*, then the *receiver's security* of Π_{LongOT} guarantees that Bob does not learn the choice-bits $s_1, \ldots, s_\lambda$ and hence S. On the other hand, if Alice is *corrupt*, then the *sender's security* of Π_{LongOT} guarantees that from the ith instance, Alice learns either $T^{(i)}$ (which is independent of B) or $B \oplus T^{(i)}$, with $T^{(i)}$ being unknown to Alice. Moreover, since $T^{(1)}, \ldots, T^{(\lambda)}$ are random and independent of each other, the privacy of B is maintained.

---

[6] Note that internally, this requires executing λ instances of the OT protocol Π_{ShOT}, where S's messages are of size only λ bits, where $k = \text{poly}(\lambda)$.

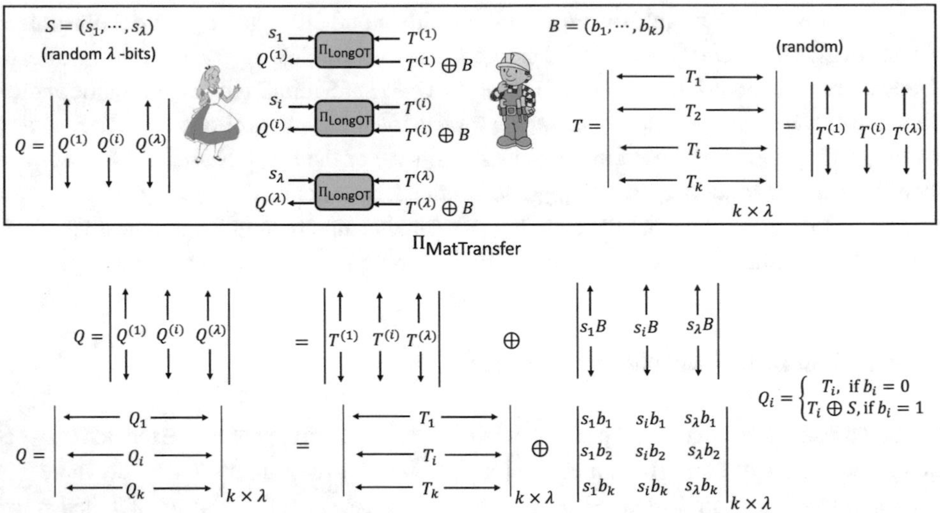

Fig. 11.6 Pictorial depiction of the protocol $\Pi_{\mathsf{MatTransfer}}$

The protocol requires *only* λ instances of Π_{LongOT}, which is *independent* of the number of the rows k of the matrix T and Q.

11.4.3 The OT-Extension Protocol

In this section, we present the highly efficient OT-extension protocol of [95]. Let Alice and Bob be two parties, where the private input of Alice consists of k pairs of messages $\{(m_{i0}, m_{i1})\}_{i \in \{1,\ldots,k\}}$, where each message is of size ℓ bits and where $k = \mathsf{poly}(\lambda)$. The private input for Bob is a Boolean choice vector $B = (b_1, \ldots, b_k)$. The goal is to let Bob receive the messages $m_{1b_1}, \ldots, m_{kb_k}$, with Alice being oblivious of the choice vector B. Thus the protocol securely computes $\mathcal{F}_{\mathsf{OT}}$ k number of times, where S's messages are of size ℓ bits. The interesting property of the protocol is that it involves Alice and Bob executing *only* λ instances of an OT protocol, where S's messages are of size *only* λ bits. The protocol uses the protocol $\Pi_{\mathsf{MatTransfer}}$ discussed in the previous section.

The high level idea of the protocol is to let Alice send each pair of messages in a masked fashion to Bob in such a way that for each pair, Bob can unmask exactly one message, depending upon the choice-bit for that pair. To materialize this idea, Alice picks a *random* Boolean vector $S = (s_1, \ldots, s_\lambda)$ of size λ bits, while Bob picks a *random* Boolean array T of size $k \times \lambda$ bits. Alice and Bob then execute an instance of the protocol $\Pi_{\mathsf{MatTransfer}}$, where Alice's input is S and Bob's inputs are B and T. This ensures that Alice obtains a matrix Q of size $k \times \lambda$ bits, where the ith row Q_i of the matrix Q satisfies the following property:

$$Q_i = \begin{cases} T_i & \text{if } b_i = 0 \\ T_i \oplus S & \text{if } b_i = 1 \end{cases}$$

As discussed in the previous section, executing $\Pi_{\mathsf{MatTransfer}}$ will require Alice and Bob to execute *only* λ instances of an OT protocol, where S's messages are of size *only* λ bits. Once Alice obtains the matrix Q, one may consider the following naive approach of sending Alice's messages in a masked message: for the ith pair of messages (m_{i0}, m_{i1}), let Alice use Q_i and $Q_i \oplus S$ to mask m_{i0} and m_{i1} respectively. This will ensure that the message m_{ib_i} gets masked with T_i and $m_{i(1-b_i)}$ gets masked with $T_i \oplus S$. Since Bob will know T_i, it can unmask T_i and recover m_{ib_i} and since S will be unknown to Bob, it cannot obtain the message $m_{i(1-b_i)}$. Unfortunately, there are two problems with this naive approach:

- *Incompatibility in the size of mask and messages*: While Alice's messages m_{i0} and m_{i1} are of size ℓ bits, the proposed masks Q_i and $Q_i \oplus S$ are of size k bits.
- *Correlation in the masks*: The masks Q_i and $Q_i \oplus S$ are not independent of each other. Hence masking m_{i0} and m_{i1} with these pads and sending to Bob will breach the security for Alice. For instance, let us assume $k = \ell$ (so that length-incompatibility becomes a non-issue). If we consider the ith and jth pair of messages, then apart from m_{ib_i} and m_{jb_j}, Bob also learns $m_{i(1-b_i)} \oplus T_i \oplus S$ and $m_{j(1-b_j)} \oplus T_j \oplus S$. Since T_i and T_j are known to Bob, it ends up learning $m_{i(1-b_i)} \oplus m_{j(1-b_j)}$. This is clearly a violation of *sender's security*.

To get around the above problems, Alice needs to do some processing on Q_i and $Q_i \oplus S$, so that the resultant outputs are of size ℓ bits and the correlation between Q_i and $Q_i \oplus S$ is broken. This is done by using the notion of correlation robust hash function [95]. Informally, it is a special type of (cryptographic) hash function, where the output of the hash function is pseudorandom, even if its inputs are correlated. Formally, we have the following definition:

Definition 11.9   (Correlation Robust Hash Function [95]) Let $H : \{0, 1\}^{\ell_{in}} \rightarrow \{0, 1\}^{\ell_{out}}$ be a cryptographic hash function and let $k = \mathsf{poly}(\lambda)$. Then H is said to be correlation robust, if for any PPT algorithm D, there is a negligible function negl such that the following is at most $\mathsf{negl}(\lambda)$.

$$\Big| \Pr[D(T_1, \ldots, T_k, H(T_1 \oplus S), \ldots, H(T_k \oplus S)) = 1] - \Pr[D(T_1, \ldots, T_k, R_1, \ldots, R_k) = 1] \Big|$$

where the first probability is taken over random choice of $T_1, \ldots, T_k, S$ over $\{0, 1\}^{\ell_{in}}$ and the random choices of D. The second probability is taken over random choice of $T_1, \ldots, T_k, S$ over $\{0, 1\}^{\ell_{in}}$, random choice of $R_1, \ldots, R_k$ over $\{0, 1\}^{\ell_{out}}$ and the random choices of D.

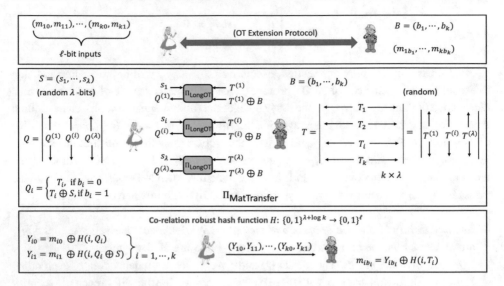

Fig. 11.7 Pictorial depiction of the OT extension protocol of [95]. The first box shows the inputs of the parties and required output. The second box denotes the instance of $\Pi_{\text{MatTransfer}}$ executed between the parties. The third box denotes the masked messages sent by Alice to Bob

The above definition captures the essence that the outputs $H(T_1 \oplus S), \ldots, H(T_k \oplus S)$ are pseudorandom from the point of view of any PPT adversary. Correlation robust hash functions can be constructed based on various cryptographic assumptions, see for instance [84, 95].

Now assuming the existence of a correlation robust hash function $H : \{0, 1\}^{\lambda + \log k} \to \{0, 1\}^{\ell}$, Alice can mask the message-pair (m_{i0}, m_{i1}) using $(Q_i, Q_i \oplus S)$ by computing $Y_{i0} \overset{def}{=} m_{i0} \oplus H(i, Q_i)$ and $Y_{i1} \overset{def}{=} m_{i1} \oplus H(i, Q_i \oplus S)$ and send (Y_{i0}, Y_{i1}) to Bob. Upon receiving the pair, Bob can recover m_{ib_i} by computing $m_{ib_i} = y_{ib_i} \oplus H(i, T_i)$. Thus by using H, Alice gets rid of both the issues stated earlier. Namely, the pads $H(Q_i)$ and $H(Q_i \oplus S)$ will be pseudorandom and will be of length ℓ bits, with Bob knowing exactly one of these two pads. For a pictorial depiction of the full OT extension protocol, see Fig. 11.7. We refer the readers to [95] for the formal security proof of the OT extension protocol.

11.5   Dealing with Malicious Adversaries

There are several challenges while designing OT protocols in the presence of a *malicious* adversary. For instance, consider the protocol Π_{OT} based on enhanced OWTP. In the protocol, if R behaves maliciously, then it can completely break the *sender's security* and end up learning both the messages. For this, instead of picking the element T randomly, a *malicious* R can compute the element T in the *same* way, as it has computed S. That is, it can first pick an element t randomly and then set T to be $f_{pk}(t)$. Consequently, R will now know *both* $hc(s)$, as well as $hc(t)$ and hence can decrypt both d_0 as well as d_1 and in the process ends up learning both m_0 as well as m_1. The breach of *sender's security* in Π_{OT} automatically implies a security breach when used in higher level protocols such as the domain extension and OT extension protocols. To deal with a malicious adversary, one needs to incorporate additional verification mechanisms to enforce even a potentially corrupt party to follow the protocol instructions correctly and that too without revealing anything additional about the data of the honest party. We refer the interested readers to [88] (and its references) for maliciously-secure OT protocols.

Yao's Protocol for Secure 2-party Computation **12**

In this chapter, we present the seminal secure two-party computation (secure 2PC) proto-col due to Yao [138]. The striking feature of the protocol is that unlike all the protocols discussed till now where the number of interactions among the parties is proportional to the multiplicative depth of the underlying circuit, Yao's protocol requires only a *constant* number of interactions among the parties, irrespective of the circuit size. Thus the protocol can be deployed in *high-latency* networks, where the round-trip delay between the parties is high. The protocol is cryptographically-secure. Unlike the GMW protocol, where OT oper-ations are performed for evaluating the multiplication gates, the Yao's protocol involves OT operations *only* for the input gates of only one of the two parties and relies on *symmetric-key* operations for the rest of the computation.

The down sides of the Yao's protocol are as follows. First, the techniques of garbling used here, which we elaborate shortly, are primarily restricted to the Boolean circuits. There have been very few attempts to extend them to the arithmetic-circuit regime, but the results have not led to as efficient solutions as Yao's construction [7, 12]. Second, in the OT-hybrid model, GMW protocol is perfectly-secure, whereas Yao's protocol is not. This is due to the use of a symmetric-key encryption scheme inside a primitive called *garbling* scheme which is the corner-stone of Yao's protocol. While unconditionally-secure garbling schemes secure against computationally-unbounded adversaries (and hence unconditionally-secure Yao's protocol in OT-hybrid model) are known, the shortcoming is that such protocols are efficient (polynomial-time) only for NC^1 circuits or circuits with logarithmic depth [105]. Third, it involves huge communication complexity and hence is *not* suitable for *low bandwidth* networks. Lastly, while GMW protocol can be almost immediately generalized to the n-party setting, the generalization of Yao's protocol to the n-party setting is non-trivial (see for instance [18, 23]). In this chapter, we focus our attention only on the classic 2-party setting.

© The Author(s), under exclusive license to Springer Nature Switzerland AG 2022   177
A. Choudhury and A. Patra, *Secure Multi-Party Computation Against Passive Adversaries*,
Synthesis Lectures on Distributed Computing Theory,
https://doi.org/10.1007/978-3-031-12164-7_12

As mentioned, the Yao's protocol is based on the concept of *garbling* scheme, which in itself is a fundamental cryptographic primitive. While the notion of garbling was used informally in several earlier works related to Yao's protocol and its variants, the notion of garbling was first formalized in [22]. Unlike the previous presentations of Yao's protocol, we follow the formalism of [22] and present the Yao's protocol in the framework of [22]. While a rigorous (and the first) formal security proof of Yao's protocol appeared in [116], we show how to adapt the proof and recast it in the framework of abstract garbling. We then proceed to elaborate on the rich literature on the optimization techniques for Yao's garbling scheme which, in effect, impact the computation and communication complexity of Yao's protocol. We further extend our efficiency discussion on Yao's protocol in preprocessing model and it's round complexity. We conclude this chapter with the attacks that may be possible on Yao's protocol in the face of an active adversary.

12.1   Preliminaries and Definitions

We start with the formal definition of Boolean circuits, presented in [22].

Definition 12.1 (*Boolean Circuits [22]*) A circuit is a tuple $\mathsf{cir} = (n, m, q, A, B, G)$. The parameters n, m and q are positive integers which define the number of input, output, and non-input wires respectively. Wires are indexed from 1 to $n + q$, with 1 to n being input wires, and $n + q - m + 1$ to $n + q$ being output wires. A gate is identified by its outgoing wire index and $\mathsf{Gates} = \{n + 1, \ldots, n + q\}$ denotes the set of gates.

For a gate $g \in \mathsf{Gates}$, the notation $A(g)$ and $B(g)$ denotes the left and right incoming wire indices respectively. For every gate g, we have $B(g) \in \{1, n + q - m\}$ and $A(g) \in \{0, n + q - m\}$. The value $A(g) = 0$ if g has fan-in of 1 (i.e. if g is a NOT gate). In order to avoid cycles, we require that $A(g) < g$ and $B(g) < g$ holds.

The function $G : \mathsf{Gates} \times \{0, 1\}^2 \rightarrow \{0, 1\}$ is a function that determines the functionality of each gate. For $g \in \mathsf{Gates}$, the notation $G_g(\cdot, \cdot)$ denotes the function $G(g, \cdot, \cdot)$, which is a mapping $G_g : \{0, 1\}^2 \rightarrow \{0, 1\}$.

For a pictorial illustration of a Boolean circuit as per Definition 12.1, see Fig. 12.1. From the above definition, it is clear that evaluating a circuit $\mathsf{cir} = (n, m, q, A, B, G)$ comprises of executing the gate functionality of each gate $g \in \{n + 1, \ldots, n + q\}$ in increasing order, starting with a given input $x \in \{0, 1\}^n$ populating the values on the input wires $w \in \{1, \ldots, n\}$. We use $\mathsf{cir}(x)$ to denote the evaluation of input $x \in \{0, 1\}^n$ on circuit cir. The size of cir is denoted by $|\mathsf{cir}|$, and we have $|\mathsf{cir}| = n + q$.

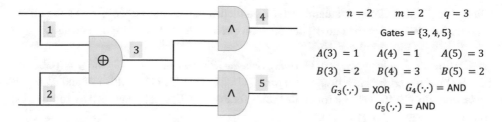

Fig. 12.1 An example of a Boolean circuit and associated parameters as per Definition 12.1

12.1.1 Garbling Scheme as a Primitive

We recall the definition of an abstract garbling-scheme from [22].

Definition 12.2 (*Garbling Scheme [22]*) A garbling scheme $\mathcal{G}$ is characterised by a tuple of algorithms $\mathcal{G} = (\mathsf{Gb}, \mathsf{En}, \mathsf{Ev}, \mathsf{De})$. All of these algorithms are polynomial time, and with the exception of Gb, they are deterministic. The sequence of invoking these algorithms is as follows (see Fig. 12.2 for a pictorial depiction):

- $(\mathsf{GC}, e, d) \leftarrow \mathsf{Gb}\left(1^\lambda, \mathsf{cir}\right)$: the *garbling algorithm* Gb is invoked on a circuit cir to produce a *garbled-circuit* GC, *input-encoding information e*, and *output-decoding information d*.
- $\mathsf{En}\,(x, e) = X$: the *encoding algorithm* En encodes a clear input x with encoding-information e in order to produce a *garbled/encoded input X*.
- $\mathsf{Ev}\,(\mathsf{GC}, X) = Y$: the *evaluation algorithm* Ev evaluates X upon GC to produce a *garbled-output Y*.
- $\mathsf{De}\,(Y, d) = y$: the *decoding algorithm* De translates Y into a clear output y as per the decoding-information d.

The *correctness* requirement of the garbling scheme follows naturally from the above definition of its components. Informally, it requires that decoding a garbled-output obtained

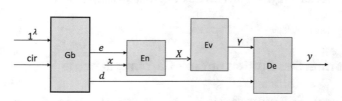

Fig. 12.2 Block diagram of garbling a circuit cir, encoding an input x, and decoding the garbled output to retrieve $y = \mathsf{cir}(x)$

through a garbled circuit-evaluation over a garbled-input should be the *same* as the output obtained by evaluating the underlying Boolean circuit over the clear input. Formally:

Definition 12.3 (*Correctness of Garbling Scheme [22]*) A garbling scheme $\mathcal{G} = $ (Gb, En, Ev, De) has the *correctness* property, if *for all* circuits cir : $\{0, 1\}^n \rightarrow \{0, 1\}^m$ and *all* inputs in its domain $x \in \{0, 1\}^n$, the following holds for *every* (GC, e, d) generated by running Gb on cir:

$$\text{De}\left(\text{Ev}\left(\text{GC}, \text{En}(x, e)\right), d\right) = \text{cir}(x).$$

We next proceed to define the privacy property of a garbling scheme, which captures the privacy of the inputs. Informally, a *private* garbling scheme requires the garbled-circuit, encoded-input, and decoding-information to be simulatable, given only the clear output and the description of the circuit. This requirement captures the intuition that the garbled evaluation itself leaks no information about the clear inputs and intermediate values in the circuit. Formally:

Definition 12.4 (*Privacy of a Garbling Scheme [22]*) A garbling scheme $\mathcal{G} = $ (Gb, En, Ev, De) achieves the *privacy* property, if there exists a PPT simulator $\mathcal{S}$ such that for *every* circuit cir : $\{0, 1\}^n \rightarrow \{0, 1\}^m$ where $|\text{cir}| = \text{poly}(\lambda)$, every input $x \in \{0, 1\}^n$ and every PPT algorithm D, there exists a negligible function negl, such that following holds:

$$\left| \Pr_{(GC,e,d) \leftarrow \text{Gb}(1^\lambda, \text{cir})} [D(\text{GC}, \text{En}(x, e), d) = 1] - \Pr_{(\widetilde{GC}, \widetilde{X}, \widetilde{d}) \leftarrow \mathcal{S}(1^\lambda, \text{cir}, \text{cir}(x))} [D(\widetilde{GC}, \widetilde{X}, \widetilde{d}) = 1] \right| \leq \text{negl}(\lambda),$$

where the first probability is over the random choice used by the algorithm Gb and the randomness used by D, while the second probability is over the randomness used by $\mathcal{S}$ and D.

12.2   Yao's Garbling Scheme

In this section, we present the Yao's garbling scheme in the abstract framework of garbling, as per Definition 12.2. As the approach used in the scheme is highly subtle and non-trivial, for a better understanding, we first give an informal description of the scheme, following [116].

12.2.1 Informal Description of Yao's Garbling Scheme

We informally explain the idea used in Yao's garbling scheme using the concept of "locked boxes", as used in [116]. To garble the circuit cir, the garbler associates two padlock keys with each wire in the circuit. One of these keys corresponds to the bit 0, while the other corresponds to 1. The keys are *indistinguishable* in the sense that later if the evaluator is given one of these two keys, it is not possible to distinguish whether the given key corresponds to the bit value 0 or 1 (the association of the keys and the corresponding bit values will be known only to the garbler).

To garble a gate, four doubly locked boxes are constructed, where each box corresponds to one row in the truth table of the underlying gate. That is, one box corresponds to the input combination $(0, 0)$, another box corresponds to the input combination $(1, 0)$ and so on. Each box is locked using one of the two keys associated with each input wire of the gate. The choice of the input keys for locking a box depends upon which row in the truth table the box corresponds to. For example, the box corresponding to the input combination $(1, 0)$ will be locked using the key corresponding to bit 1 along the left input wire and the key corresponding to bit 0 along the right input wire. This way of double locking ensures that later given one key corresponding to each input wire of the gate, *only one* of the four doubly locked boxes gets opened using the available keys.

Inside each of the four doubly locked boxes, one of the two keys associated with the gate-output wire is stored. The key to be stored is such that it correctly associates the input bits with the output bit of the gate. For instance, if the gate is an XOR gate and if the doubly locked box corresponds to the input combination $(0, 1)$, then it will be locked with the left input wire key corresponding to 0 and right input wire key corresponding to 1. Moreover, since the XOR of 0 and 1 is 1, the gate-output wire key corresponding to bit 1 will be stored inside this doubly locked box. After constructing the four doubly locked boxes, they are *randomly* shuffled by the garbler. This ensures that later during the evaluation, the "relative position" of the opened box does not reveal its correspondence with the corresponding row in the truth table. The collection of randomly permuted doubly locked boxes for each gate constitutes the *garbled-circuit*. The *encoding-information* is the pairs of keys along with their semantic (i.e. whether they correspond to 0 or 1), associated with the input wires of the circuit. The *decoding-information* is constituted by the pairs of keys along with their semantic, associated with the output wires of the circuit.

To garble an input x, one key from each key pair associated with the input wires of the circuit is given, depending upon the individual bits of x. Notice that no information about the individual bits of x is revealed *just* from the garbled-input. This is because the garbled-input is a collection of indistinguishable padlock keys, whose semantics are available only through the encoding-information. Given the garbled-input and the garbled-circuit, the garbled circuit-evaluation proceeds by opening the doubly locked boxes associated with each gate one at a time (for each gate, only one doubly locked box will open). The process gets over, once the doubly locked boxes associated with the circuit-output wires are opened; the keys obtained by the opening of these doubly locked boxes constitute the garbled circuit-output. Notice that during the garbled circuit-evaluation, no information about the actual values of the intermediate gates is revealed. This is because for each such gate, the evaluation makes available one of the keys associated with the output of these gates, whose semantic is not available to the evaluation algorithm. Given the garbled circuit-output, the actual output is obtained by using the decoding-information and learning the semantics of the corresponding keys.

In [116] it is shown how to instantiate the concept of doubly locked boxes in the Yao's garbling scheme via a symmetric-key encryption scheme. With each wire, a randomly chosen pair of encryption keys is associated, where one key corresponds to bit 0, while the other corresponds to bit 1. Each doubly locked box is then substituted by a double-encryption, encrypting an appropriate gate-output wire key. Recall that in the locked-box description of the Yao's garbling scheme, it is important to ensure that given one of the keys associated with each input wire of the gate, exactly one of the four doubly locked boxes gets opened; this is required to ensure the correctness property. To ensure that the same holds even when we replace the doubly locked boxes by double-encryptions, we require the underlying symmetric-key encryption scheme to have some "special" properties. Informally we require the encryption scheme to satisfy the following requirements:

- It should have *indistinguishable* encryptions for *multiple messages*. That is, no PPT algorithm should be able to distinguish between an encryption of a vector $\vec{x}$ and an encryption of a vector $\vec{y}$, for any pair of vectors $(\vec{x}, \vec{y})$. We stress that we require security for multiple messages. This is because a wire can serve as input to multiple gates and in such a case, the keys associated with the wire will be used for encrypting multiple gate-output keys.
- An encryption under one key will fall in the range of an encryption under another key with a negligible probability. Moreover, given a key k and a ciphertext c, it should be possible to efficiently verify if c is in the range of k. In [116], these two properties are called *elusive range* and *efficiently verifiable range* respectively. Looking ahead, these two requirements ensure that given a pair of keys associated with the input wires of a gate and the garbled-gate (which will be a set of randomly permuted double-encryptions), the evaluator is able to identify the intended decryption.

We next formalize the requirements from the underlying symmetric-key encryption scheme.

12.2.2 Special Symmetric-Key Encryption Used in Yao's Garbling

We first start by recalling the syntax of symmetric-key encryption scheme from [102].

Definition 12.5 (*Symmetric-key Encryption [102]*) A symmetric-key encryption scheme Π is a triplet of algorithms (Gen, Enc, Dec) with $\mathcal{K}, \mathcal{M}, \mathcal{C}$ being the key space, plaintext space and ciphertext space respectively, where

- $k \leftarrow \mathsf{Gen}(1^\lambda)$: the key-generation algorithm Gen is a randomized algorithm, which outputs a key k, uniformly at random from $\mathcal{K}$.

- $c \leftarrow$ Enc(k, m): the encryption algorithm Enc is a randomized algorithm, which takes input a plaintext m and a key k and outputs a ciphertext c from $\mathcal{C}$. The notation Enc$_k(m)$ denotes an encryption of m, under the key k.
- Dec$(k, c) = m$: the decryption algorithm Dec is a deterministic algorithm, which takes input a ciphertext c and a key k and outputs m. The notation Dec$_k(c)$ denotes the output of Dec for input m, under the key k.

The scheme Π is said to have the *correctness* property, if for *every* k obtained from Gen and *every* $m \in \mathcal{M}$, the following holds:

$$\mathsf{Dec}_k(\mathsf{Enc}_k(m)) = m$$

We next formalize the security properties needed from the underlying symmetric-key encryption scheme used in the Yao's garbling scheme. The first requirement of indistinguishable encryptions for multiple messages is captured through the notion of *chosen plaintext attack* (CPA)-security [102]. Informally, an encryption scheme is CPA-secure for multiple messages, if no PPT adversary A can distinguish between encryptions of two vectors of messages, chosen by A itself, under a random key k *unknown* to A. Moreover, this holds even if A is given an oracle access to the encryption algorithm under the key k, where A can query the oracle for encryption of any message of A's choice (under the key k) and the oracle responds with an encryption of the corresponding message. Following [102], in [116] it is shown that it is sufficient to consider CPA-security for a *single* pair of messages for proving the security of Yao's garbling scheme. This is formalized through the security experiment described in Fig. 12.3.

Let $\mathsf{Exp}_A^{\mathsf{cpa}}(\lambda, \sigma)$ denote the instance of the experiment $\mathsf{Exp}_A^{\mathsf{cpa}}$, when the message pair (x_σ, y_σ) is selected for encryption in the challenge ciphertexts. Informally, an encryption scheme is CPA-secure for a single pair of messages, if no PPT adversary A can significantly distinguish apart between a random instance of the experiment $\mathsf{Exp}_A^{\mathsf{cpa}}(\lambda, 0)$ from a random

---

Experiment $\mathsf{Exp}_A^{\mathsf{cpa}}(\lambda)$

- A key $k \leftarrow$ Gen(1^λ) is generated and the adversary A is invoked with input 1^λ and oracle access to Enc$_k(\cdot)$.[a]
  The adversary A outputs two pairs of messages (x_0, y_0) and (x_1, y_1), where $x_0, x_1, y_0, y_1 \in \mathcal{M}$, such that $|x_0| = |x_1|$ and $|y_0| = |y_1|$.
- A uniformly random bit σ is selected and the challenge ciphertexts $c_1 \leftarrow$ Enc$_k(x_\sigma)$ and $c_2 \leftarrow$ Enc$_k(y_\sigma)$ are computed.
- A is given the pair (c_1, c_2), as well as continued oracle access to Enc$_k(\cdot)$.
- A outputs a bit b and this is taken as the output of the experiment.

[a]The adversary A can query the oracle with *any* input $m \in \mathcal{M}$ of A's choice and the oracle responds back with output Enc$_k(m)$.

Fig. 12.3 The CPA-security experiment for a single pair of messages with respect to a symmetric-key encryption scheme $\Pi = $ (Gen, Enc, Dec) and a PPT adversary A

instance of the experiment $\mathsf{Exp}_A^{\mathsf{cpa}}(\lambda, 1)$. That is, the adversary's output in both the instances of the experiment remains almost the same. Formally:

Definition 12.6 (*Indistinguishable Encryptions Under CPA [102]*) Let $\Pi = (\mathsf{Gen}, \mathsf{Enc}, \mathsf{Dec})$ be a symmetric-key encryption scheme with $\mathcal{K}, \mathcal{M}, \mathcal{C}$ being the key space, plaintext space and ciphertext space respectively. Then Π has indistinguishable encryptions under CPA attacks (shortly written as Π *is CPA-secure*), if for every PPT adversary A participating in the experiment in Fig. 12.3, there is a negligible function negl, such that the following holds:

$$\left| \Pr[\mathsf{Exp}_A^{\mathsf{cpa}}(\lambda, 0) = 1] - \Pr[\mathsf{Exp}_A^{\mathsf{cpa}}(\lambda, 1) = 1] \right| \leq \mathsf{negl}(\lambda),$$

where both the probabilities are taken over the random choice of the key k generated in the experiment, the randomness used in the corresponding instances of $\mathsf{Enc}_k(\cdot)$ and the randomness of A.

We next shift our attention to the other properties required from the underlying symmetric-key encryption scheme used in the Yao's garbling scheme, namely the elusive range and the efficiently verifiable range. However, instead of using these properties, we use a simplified variant of it, which is called the *special correctness* [99] and which is sufficient for the correctness of the Yao's garbling scheme. Before giving the definition of special correctness, we first define the *range* of a key, which is the set of all ciphertexts which can be generated by using that key. Formally:

Definition 12.7 (*Range of a Key [116]*) Let $(\mathsf{Gen}, \mathsf{Enc}, \mathsf{Dec})$ be a symmetric-key encryption scheme, with $\mathcal{K}, \mathcal{M}, \mathcal{C}$ being the key space, plaintext space and ciphertext space respectively. Then the range of a key $k \in \mathcal{K}$ is defined as $\mathsf{Range}(k) \stackrel{def}{=} \{\mathsf{Enc}_k(x) : x \in \mathcal{M}\}$.

The formal definition of the special correctness property is as follows.

Definition 12.8 (*Special Correctness [99]*) A symmetric-key encryption scheme $(\mathsf{Gen}, \mathsf{Enc}, \mathsf{Dec})$ has *special correctness*, if there is a negligible function negl, such that the following holds for *every* message $m \in \mathcal{M}$:

$$\Pr[\mathsf{Dec}_{k_2}(\mathsf{Enc}_{k_1}(m)) \neq \perp : k_1 \leftarrow \mathsf{Gen}(1^\lambda), k_2 \leftarrow \mathsf{Gen}(1^\lambda)] \leq \mathsf{negl}(\lambda),$$

where the probability is taken over random choices of the keys k_1 and k_2 generated by the algorithm Gen.

In [99], the following construction for a symmetric-key encryption scheme with special correctness is proposed (this is exactly the same construction as in [116] with elusive and efficiently verifiable range).

Example 12.9 (*[99]*) Let $F : \{0, 1\}^\lambda \times \{0, 1\}^\lambda \to \{0, 1\}^{2\lambda}$ be a PRF. Then consider the symmetric-key encryption scheme (Gen, Enc, Dec) for the message space $\mathcal{M} = \{0, 1\}^\lambda$, where:

- $k \leftarrow \mathsf{Gen}(1^\lambda)$: the key generation algorithm outputs a uniformly random PRF key k.
- $(c_1, c_2) \leftarrow \mathsf{Enc}_k(m)$: where $c_1 \in_r \{0, 1\}^\lambda$ and $c_2 \stackrel{def}{=} F_k(c_1) \oplus m0^\lambda$, where $m0^\lambda$ denotes the concatenation of m and 0^λ.
- $\mathsf{Dec}_k(c) \in \{m, \bot\}$: parse $c = (c_1, c_2)$ and compute $w = F_k(c_1) \oplus c_2$. Output the first λ bits of w as m if the last λ bits of w are 0, else output $\bot$.

It is well known that the above encryption scheme is CPA-secure (see for instance [102]). It can be shown easily that the scheme also has the special correctness property if F is a secure PRF. Intuitively this is because if the special correctness does not hold, then it implies that with a non-negligible probability, there exists a ciphertext c, where c is in $\mathsf{Range}(k_1)$ as well as in $\mathsf{Range}(k_2)$. Let $c = (c_1, c_2)$. Now as per the construction, in order that c belongs to $\mathsf{Range}(k_1)$ as well as $\mathsf{Range}(k_2)$, it must hold that the last λ bits of $F_{k_1}(c_1)$ as well as $F_{k_2}(c_1)$ should be identical. However this can happen only with a negligible probability. This is because if instead of the PRF F_{k_1}, a truly random function (TRF) f is used, then the last λ bits of $f(c_1)$ and $F_{k_2}(c_1)$ will be same with probability at most $2^{-\lambda}$; the same should hold even if F_{k_1} is used instead of f, as otherwise one can distinguish f from F_{k_1}, which is a contradiction. We refer the interested readers to [116] for the formal security proof.

Double-encryption security: In the Yao's garbling scheme, for each gate the evaluator will see four randomly permuted double-encryptions and it will have a pair of keys, one for each input wire of the gate, corresponding to the actual bit values for the gate-input wires. Using these keys, the evaluator can decrypt only one ciphertext. For security, it is required that the evaluator learns nothing "additional" from the remaining three ciphertexts. For instance, it should not even learn whether the unopened ciphertexts encrypt the same (unknown) gate-output key; if the gate is an AND gate, then a violation of this property will let the evaluator learn that the gate-output key it has obtained corresponds to 1, while the remaining three unopened ciphertexts encrypt the gate-output key corresponding to 0. Formally the security requirement of the underlying double-encryption scheme is captured by the double-encryption security experiment [116], which is given in Fig. 12.4. In the experiment, the expression $\overline{\mathsf{Enc}}(k_1, k_2, m)$ denotes a double-encryption $\mathsf{Enc}_{k_1}(\mathsf{Enc}_{k_2}(m))$.

Let $\mathsf{Exp}_A^{\mathsf{double}}(\lambda, \sigma)$ denote the instance of the experiment $\mathsf{Exp}_A^{\mathsf{double}}$, when the message triplet $(x_\sigma, y_\sigma, z_\sigma)$ is selected for encryption in the challenge ciphertexts. Informally an encryption scheme has security under double encryption if any PPT adversary A cannot distinguish apart between a random instance of the experiment $\mathsf{Exp}_A^{\mathsf{double}}$ with $\sigma = 0$ from a random instance of $\mathsf{Exp}_A^{\mathsf{double}}$ with $\sigma = 1$. That is, the adversary has the same output, say 1, in both the instances of the experiment, except with a negligible probability. Formally:

Experiment $\mathsf{Exp}_A^{\mathsf{double}}(\lambda)$

- The adversary A is invoked with input 1^λ and outputs two keys k_0, k_1 of length λ and two triplets of messages (x_0, y_0, z_0) and (x_1, y_1, z_1), where all messages are of the same length.
- Two uniformly random keys $k_0' \leftarrow \mathsf{Gen}(1^\lambda), k_1' \leftarrow \mathsf{Gen}(1^\lambda)$ are chosen for the encryption scheme.
- A uniformly random bit σ is selected and A is given the challenge ciphertexts

$$\left\langle \overline{\mathsf{Enc}}(k_0, k_1', x_\sigma), \overline{\mathsf{Enc}}(k_0', k_1, y_\sigma), \overline{\mathsf{Enc}}(k_0', k_1', z_\sigma) \right\rangle,$$

as well as oracle access to $\overline{\mathsf{Enc}}(\cdot, k_1', \cdot)$ and $\overline{\mathsf{Enc}}(k_0', \cdot, \cdot)$.[a]
- A outputs a bit b and this is taken as the output of the experiment.

---
[a]Here oracle access means that A can provide any k and m to $\overline{\mathsf{Enc}}(\cdot, k_1', \cdot)$, who responds back with an output $\overline{\mathsf{Enc}}(k, k_1', m)$. Similar interpretation holds for the oracle access to $\overline{\mathsf{Enc}}(k_0', \cdot, \cdot)$.

Fig. 12.4 The double-encryption security experiment with respect to a symmetric-key encryption scheme $\Pi = (\mathsf{Gen}, \mathsf{Enc}, \mathsf{Dec})$ and a PPT adversary A

Definition 12.10 (*Chosen Double-encryption (CDE Security) [116]*) A symmetric-key encryption scheme $\Pi = (\mathsf{Gen}, \mathsf{Enc}, \mathsf{Dec})$ is said to be secure under *chosen double-encryption* (shortly written as Π *is CDE-secure*), if for every PPT algorithm A participating in the experiment $\mathsf{Exp}_A^{\mathsf{double}}$, there is a negligible function negl, such that the following holds:

$$\left| \Pr[\mathsf{Exp}_A^{\mathsf{double}}(\lambda, 1) = 1] - \Pr[\mathsf{Exp}_A^{\mathsf{double}}(\lambda, 0) = 1] \right| \leq \mathsf{negl}(\lambda),$$

where both the probabilities are taken over the randomness used by A and the randomness used in the corresponding experiments.

Before proceeding further, let us take a closer look into the experiment $\mathsf{Exp}_A^{\mathsf{double}}$ and analyse what exactly it tries to capture in the context of Yao's garbling. Let g be an arbitrary Boolean gate in a circuit, with left-input wire w_x, right-input wire w_y and gate-output wire w_g. Let (k_x^0, k_x^1), (k_y^0, k_y^1) and (k_g^0, k_g^1) be the pair of keys, associated with w_x, w_y and w_g respectively. Here k_x^0 corresponds to bit value $b_x = 0$ over wire w_x, while k_x^1 corresponds to the bit value $b_x = 1$ over w_x; the same interpretation holds for (k_y^0, k_y^1) and (k_g^0, k_g^1). The garbled gate g will consists of four double-encryptions $c_{00} \overset{def}{=} \overline{\mathsf{Enc}}(k_x^0, k_y^0, k_g^{g(0,0)})$, $c_{01} \overset{def}{=} \overline{\mathsf{Enc}}(k_x^0, k_y^1, k_g^{g(0,1)})$, $c_{10} \overset{def}{=} \overline{\mathsf{Enc}}(k_x^1, k_y^0, k_g^{g(1,0)})$ and $c_{11} \overset{def}{=} \overline{\mathsf{Enc}}(k_x^1, k_y^1, k_g^{g(1,1)})$, in a randomly permuted order. During the garbled evaluation of g, the evaluator will have these four double-encryptions. In addition, it will have the left-wire key $k_x^{b_x}$ and the right-wire key $k_y^{b_y}$, depending upon the value of b_x and b_y respectively. Using these keys, the evaluator can decrypt the double-encryption c_{b_x, b_y}. The remaining keys $k_x^{1-b_x}$ and $k_y^{1-b_y}$ will be not revealed to the evaluator. The remaining three unopened ciphertexts will be under the key combinations $(k_x^{b_x}, \mathbf{k_y^{1-b_y}})$, $(\mathbf{k_x^{1-b_x}}, k_y^{1-b_y})$ and $(\mathbf{k_x^{1-b_x}}, \mathbf{k_y^{1-b_y}})$, where the keys unknown to the evaluator are highlighted in bold face. Notice that in each of these three combinations, there is at least one key not available to the evaluator.

Now comparing the above scenario with the experiment $\mathsf{Exp}_A^{\mathsf{double}}$, the keys k_0 and k_1 available with A correspond to the gate-input keys $k_x^{b_x}$ and $k_y^{b_y}$ respectively, available with the evaluator. The keys k_0' and k_1' correspond to the remaining gate-input keys $k_x^{1-b_x}$ and $k_y^{1-b_y}$ respectively, which are *not* available with the evaluator. The three challenge ciphertexts in the experiment correspond to the three unopened double-encryptions available with the evaluator. Notice that for each of the three challenge ciphertexts in the experiment, there is at least one key from the key-pair (k_0', k_1'), unknown to A. This captures the scenario that for each of the three unopened double-encryptions available with the evaluator, there is at least one key not available with the evaluator.

Next, the oracle access $\overline{\mathsf{Enc}}(k_0', \cdot, \cdot)$ and $\overline{\mathsf{Enc}}(\cdot, k_1', \cdot)$ in the experiment captures the following: in the circuit, apart from the gate g, the left gate-input wire w_x may serve as the gate-input wire for several other gates as well.[1] As part of the garbling of such gates, the evaluator will see double-encryptions, under the unknown key $\mathbf{k_x^{1-x}}$, which is captured in the experiment by providing A the oracle access to $\overline{\mathsf{Enc}}(k_0', \cdot, \cdot)$. In the same way, the right gate-input wire w_y may serve as the gate-input wire for several other gates as well.[2] As part of the garbling of such gates, the evaluator will see double-encryptions, under the unknown key $\mathbf{k_y^{1-y}}$, which is captured in the experiment by providing A the oracle access to $\overline{\mathsf{Enc}}(\cdot, k_1', \cdot)$. Now the requirement that the evaluator should not learn anything additional from the three unopened double-encryptions corresponding to gate g is captured in the experiment by requiring that A should not be able to distinguish if the three challenge ciphertexts encrypt (x_0, y_0, z_0) or (x_1, y_1, z_1), for any (x_0, y_0, z_0) and (x_1, y_1, z_1) of A's choice. For a pictorial depiction of the above explanation, see Fig. 12.5.

In [116], the equivalence of CPA-security and CDE-security was proved, which is stated in the following lemma.

Lemma 12.11 ([116]) *Let $\Pi = (\mathsf{Gen}, \mathsf{Enc}, \mathsf{Dec})$ be a symmetric-key encryption scheme which is CPA-secure. Then Π is also CDE-secure.*

Since the encryption scheme in Example 12.9 is CPA-secure [102], from Lemma 12.11 it follows that the encryption scheme is CDE-secure as well and hence can be used as a candidate symmetric-key encryption scheme in the Yao's garbling scheme.

---

[1] Without loss of generality, we can assume that if w_x serves as the gate-input wire for any other gate, then it serves as the *left* gate-input wire for those gates. If this is not the case, then it is always possible to re-assign the wire labels to ensure that the above holds.

[2] Without loss of generality, we can assume that if w_y serves as the gate-input wire for any other gate, then it serves as the *right* gate-input wire for those gates. If this is not the case, then it is always possible to re-assign the wire labels to ensure that the above holds.

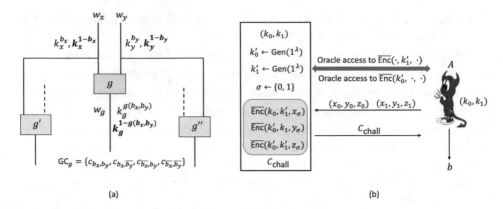

Fig. 12.5 Figure **a** denotes the information available with the garbler and the evaluator for a gate g in the Yao's garbling scheme, where the bold values will be unknown for the evaluator. Figure **b** depicts $\mathsf{Exp}_A^{\mathsf{double}}$ pictorially. In the garbling scheme, the evaluator will not know the keys $k_x^{1-b_x}$ and $k_y^{1-b_y}$, which correspond to the random keys k_0' and k_1' being picked in the experiment. There might be other gates in the circuit where the wires w_x and w_y may serve as one of the input wires and through those gates, the evaluator gets oracle service to $\overline{\mathsf{Enc}}(k_0', \cdot, \cdot)$ and $\overline{\mathsf{Enc}}(\cdot, k_1', \cdot)$. The CDE-security demands that the evaluator should not learn anything about the underlying messages, encrypted in the remaining three unopened double-encryptions $c_{b_x,\overline{b_y}}, c_{\overline{b_x},b_y}$ and $c_{\overline{b_x},\overline{b_y}}$, which is captured by demanding that the adversary A should not identify the bit σ in the experiment

12.2.3 Yao's Garbling Scheme: The Formal Details

We now formally describe the Yao's garbling scheme. Let $f : \{0, 1\}^n \rightarrow \{0, 1\}^m$ be a Boolean function, represented by a Boolean circuit cir and let (Gen, Enc, Dec) be a CDE-secure symmetric-key encryption scheme with special correctness. To *garble* cir, two random and independent keys k_i^0, k_i^1 for Enc are associated with each wire w_i in the circuit, corresponding to two different bit values over the wire. The *encoding-information* consists of the pairs of keys associated with the circuit-input wires, while the *decoding-information* is the mapping of the keys associated with the circuit-output wires to the corresponding bit value.

To *garble* a gate g with gate-input wires w_a, w_b and gate function $G_g : \{0, 1\}^2 \rightarrow \{0, 1\}$, four double-encryptions are computed, using different combinations of the keys (k_a^0, k_a^1) and (k_b^0, k_b^1) associated with the gate-input wires. Each double-encryption encrypts the "appropriate" gate-output wire key k_g^0 or k_g^1. More specifically, the double-encryptions ensure that later during the garbled gate evaluation of g, given the keys k_a^α and k_b^β, where $\alpha, \beta \in \{0, 1\}$, the evaluator is able to compute the key $k_g^{G_g(\alpha,\beta)}$ by decrypting one of the double-encryptions, without learning anything additional. The four double-encryptions are randomly permuted. This is required from preventing the evaluator to learn the value of α and β based on the "relative position" of the double-encryption (among the available four double-encryptions) that is decrypted by the evaluator to obtain $k_g^{G_g(\alpha,\beta)}$. The *garbled-circuit* GC is the collection of four randomly permuted double-encryptions for each gate in cir. This completes the description of the *garbling algorithm* $\mathsf{Gb}_{\mathsf{Yao}}$.

To garble an input $x \in \{0, 1\}^n$, the *encoding algorithm* $\mathsf{En}_{\mathsf{Yao}}$ takes the encoding-information and outputs the appropriate circuit-input wire keys, corresponding to the bits of x. The *evaluation algorithm* $\mathsf{Ev}_{\mathsf{Yao}}$ takes the garbled-circuit GC and garbled-input X and produces the garbled-output Y. This is done by evaluating each garbled gate, without learning any information about the input and output values of the gate. In more detail, to evaluate a garbled gate g with gate-input wires w_a, w_b and gate function $G_g : \{0, 1\}^2 \to \{0, 1\}$, the evaluation algorithm will do the following: let k_a^α and k_b^β be the keys available for w_a and w_b respectively, where $\alpha, \beta \in \{0, 1\}$. Using these two keys, the evaluation algorithm tries to decrypt all the (randomly permuted) four double-encryptions, available as garbled g. The *special correctness* property of Enc ensures that given k_a^α and k_b^β, only one double-encryption out of the four double-encryptions, namely the one encrypting the message $k_g^{G_g(\alpha,\beta)}$ using the keys k_a^α and k_b^β, results in a non-$\bot$ output; the remaining three double-encryptions will result in $\bot$ as the output. The keys finally obtained for the output wires after evaluating the garbled-circuit constitute the garble-output Y.

The *decoding algorithm* $\mathsf{De}_{\mathsf{Yao}}$ takes input the garbled-output Y and the decoding-information. It simply returns the bits mapped to the circuit-output wire keys in Y, as per the decoding-information. The formal details of the Yao's garbling scheme are given in Fig. 12.6.

For a pictorial illustration of the Yao's garbling scheme, see Fig. 12.7.

We now proceed to prove the properties of $\mathcal{G}_{\mathsf{Yao}}$. We begin with the *correctness* property. In order to prove the correctness, we first prove the following claim, which states that every garbled gate will be evaluated "correctly" with a high probability. That is, given the keys associated with the input wires of a gate, the evaluation algorithm will correctly obtain the corresponding gate-output wire key by decrypting the double-encryptions. Intuitively, this comes from the special correctness property of the underlying encryption scheme.

Claim 5 Let g be an arbitrary gate in cir, with gate function $G_g : \{0, 1\}^2 \to \{0, 1\}$, left-input wire $A(g) = w_a$, right-input wire $B(g) = w_b$ and gate-output wire w_g. Moreover let c_1^g, c_2^g, c_3^g and c_4^g be the double-encryptions corresponding to g, computed as per $\mathsf{Gb}_{\mathsf{Yao}}$. Furthermore, let the encryption scheme (Gen, Enc, Dec) has special correctness. Then for every $\alpha, \beta \in \{0, 1\}$, given keys k_a^α, k_b^β, the evaluation algorithm $\mathsf{Ev}_{\mathsf{Yao}}$ will associate the key k_g^γ with w_g where $k_g^\gamma = k_g^{G_g(\alpha,\beta)}$, except with a negligible probability.

Proof In order to prove the claim, we show that out of the four double-encryptions associated with g, *only one* double-encryption will decrypt to an output, different from $\bot$. In other words, there exists a single c_i^g with $c_i^g \in \mathsf{Range}(k_a^\alpha)$ and $\mathsf{Dec}_{k_a^\alpha}(c_i^g) \in \mathsf{Range}(k_b^\beta)$. The proof is by contradiction. So assume that there exists two ciphertexts, say c_i^g and c_j^g, such that both $c_i^g, c_j^g \in \mathsf{Range}(k_a^\alpha)$ and both $\mathsf{Dec}_{k_a^\alpha}(c_i^g), \mathsf{Dec}_{k_a^\alpha}(c_j^g) \in \mathsf{Range}(k_b^\beta)$. Without loss of generality, let c_i^g be the double-encryption, which should decrypt to an output different

Scheme $\mathcal{G}_{\mathsf{Yao}}$

$$\mathcal{G}_{\mathsf{Yao}} = (\mathsf{Gb}_{\mathsf{Yao}}, \mathsf{En}_{\mathsf{Yao}}, \mathsf{Ev}_{\mathsf{Yao}}, \mathsf{De}_{\mathsf{Yao}})$$

Let $(\mathsf{Gen}, \mathsf{Enc}, \mathsf{Dec})$ be a CDE-secure symmetric-key encryption scheme with special correctness. Let $\mathsf{cir} = (n, m, q, A, B, G)$ be the given Boolean circuit, with wires $w_1, \ldots, w_{n+q}$, input wires $w_1, \ldots, w_n$, gate-output wires $w_{n+1}, \ldots, w_{n+q}$ and circuit-output wires $w_{n+q-m+1}, \ldots, w_{n+q}$. The set $\mathsf{Gates} = \{n + 1, \ldots, n + q\}$ denotes the gates in the circuit, with $G_g : \{0,1\}^2 \to \{0,1\}$ denoting the gate function for each gate $g \in \mathsf{Gates}$. The sets A and B identify the left-input wire and right-input wire respectively for each gate, with $A(g)$ and $B(g)$ denoting the left-input and right-input wires of a gate g respectively.

$$\underline{\mathsf{Gb}_{\mathsf{Yao}}\ (1^\lambda, \mathsf{cir})}$$

- For $i = 1, \ldots, n + q$, corresponding to wire w_i, select two independent and random keys $k_i^0 \leftarrow \mathsf{Gen}(1^\lambda)$ and $k_i^1 \leftarrow \mathsf{Gen}(1^\lambda)$. Here k_i^0 and k_i^1 denotes the key, corresponding to bit value $b_i = 0$ and $b_i = 1$ respectively over wire w_i.
- For every gate $g \in \mathsf{Gates}$ with gate function G_g and input-wires $A(g) = w_a, B(g) = w_b$, do the following:
  - Compute the double-encryptions:

$$c_{0,0} \leftarrow \mathsf{Enc}_{k_a^0}(\mathsf{Enc}_{k_b^0}(k_g^{G_g(0,0)})),$$

$$c_{0,1} \leftarrow \mathsf{Enc}_{k_a^0}(\mathsf{Enc}_{k_b^1}(k_g^{G_g(0,1)})),$$

$$c_{1,0} \leftarrow \mathsf{Enc}_{k_a^1}(\mathsf{Enc}_{k_b^0}(k_g^{G_g(1,0)})),$$

$$c_{1,1} \leftarrow \mathsf{Enc}_{k_a^1}(\mathsf{Enc}_{k_b^1}(k_g^{G_g(1,1)})).$$

  - Randomly permute $c_{0,0}, c_{0,1}, c_{1,0}$ and $c_{1,1}$ and let c_1^g, c_2^g, c_3^g and c_4^g denote the permuted ciphertexts.
- Set $\mathsf{GC} = \{(c_1^g, c_2^g, c_3^g, c_4^g) : g \in \mathsf{Gates}\}$, $e = \{(k_i^0, k_i^1) : i = 1, \ldots, n\}$ and $d = \{((k_i^0, 0), (k_i^1, 1)) : i = n + q - m + 1, \ldots, n + q\}$. Output GC, e and d.

$$\underline{\mathsf{En}_{\mathsf{Yao}}\ (e, x)}$$

Let $e = \{(k_i^0, k_i^1) : i = 1, \ldots, n\}$ and $x = (x_1, \ldots, x_n)$. Output $X = (k_1^{x_1}, \ldots, k_n^{x_n})$.

$$\underline{\mathsf{Ev}_{\mathsf{Yao}}\ (\mathsf{GC}, X)}$$

Let $\mathsf{GC} = \{(c_1^g, c_2^g, c_3^g, c_4^g) : g \in \mathsf{Gates}\}$ and $X = (k_1^{x_1}, \ldots, k_n^{x_n})$.
- For $i = 1, \ldots, n$, associate the key $k_i^{x_i}$ with input wire w_i.
- For every gate $g \in \mathsf{Gates}$, do the following:
  - Let G_g be the gate function and let $A(g) = w_a, B(g) = w_b$. Moreover, let k_a^α and k_b^β be the keys available, corresponding to the wires w_a and w_b respectively.
  - For $i = 1, \ldots, 4$, compute $\mathsf{Dec}_{k_a^\alpha}(\mathsf{Dec}_{k_b^\beta}(c_i^g))$.
  - If more than one decryption operation returns an output different from $\perp$, then output Abort. Else let k_g^γ be the unique value different from $\perp$ that is obtained. Associate k_g^γ with wire w_g.
- If Abort is not obtained for any of the gates then output $Y = (k_{n+q-m+1}^{y_1}, \ldots, k_{n+q}^{y_m})$, namely the keys obtained for the output wires.

$$\underline{\mathsf{De}_{\mathsf{Yao}}\ (Y, d)}$$

Let $Y = (k_{n+q-m+1}^{y_1}, \ldots, k_{n+q}^{y_m})$ and $d = \{((k_i^0, 0), (k_i^1, 1)) : i = n + q - m + 1, \ldots, n + q\}$.
- For $i = 1, \ldots, m$, do the following:
  - If $k_{n+q-(m-i)}^{y_i} = k_{n+1-(m-i)}^0$, then set $y_i = 0$.
  - Else if $k_{n+q-(m-i)}^{y_i} = k_{n+1-(m-i)}^1$, then set $y_i = 1$.
  - Else set $y_i = \perp$.
- If for any $i \in \{1, \ldots, m\}$, $y_i = \perp$, then output $\perp$. Else output $y = (y_1, \ldots, y_m)$.

Fig. 12.6 The Yao's garbling scheme

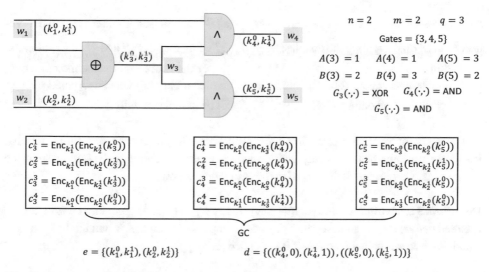

Fig. 12.7 A pictorial illustration of the Yao's garbling scheme

from $\perp$, given k_a^α and k_b^β. That is, $c_i^g = \mathsf{Enc}_{k_a^\alpha}(\mathsf{Enc}_{k_b^\beta}(k_g^{G_g(\alpha,\beta)}))$. Notice that in $\mathsf{Gb}_{\mathsf{Yao}}$, while garbling the gate g, independent and random pair of keys (k_a^0, k_a^1), (k_b^0, k_b^1) and (k_g^0, k_g^1) are associated with the wires w_a, w_b and w_g respectively. Now there are two possible cases regarding c_j^g:

- $c_j^g = \mathsf{Enc}_{k_a^\alpha}(\mathsf{Enc}_{k_b^{1-\beta}}(z))$ for $z \in \{k_g^0, k_g^1\}$: Since we have assumed that $\mathsf{Dec}_{k_a^\alpha}(c_j^g) \in$ $\mathsf{Range}(k_b^\beta)$, this further implies that $\mathsf{Enc}_{k_b^{1-\beta}}(z) \in \mathsf{Range}(k_b^\beta)$. However, since $(\mathsf{Gen}, \mathsf{Enc},$ $\mathsf{Dec})$ has special correctness, it follows that $\mathsf{Enc}_{k_b^{1-\beta}}(z) \in \mathsf{Range}(k_b^\beta)$, except with a negligible probability. This is because $\mathsf{Enc}_{k_b^{1-\beta}}(z) \in \mathsf{Range}(k_b^\beta)$ implies that the following holds,

$$\Pr[\mathsf{Dec}_{k_b^\beta}(\mathsf{Enc}_{k_b^{1-\beta}}(z)) \neq \perp : k_b^\beta \leftarrow \mathsf{Gen}(1^\lambda), k_b^{1-\beta} \leftarrow \mathsf{Gen}(1^\lambda)],$$

which as per the special correctness property of Enc can happen only with a negligible probability.

- $c_j^g = \mathsf{Enc}_{k_a^{1-\alpha}}(z)$ where $z = \mathsf{Enc}_{k'}(k'')$, where $k' \in \{k_b^0, k_b^1\}$ and $k'' \in \{k_g^0, k_g^1\}$: since $c_j^g \in$ $\mathsf{Range}(k_a^\alpha)$, it follows that $\mathsf{Enc}_{k_a^{1-\alpha}}(z) \in \mathsf{Range}(k_a^\alpha)$. Since $(\mathsf{Gen}, \mathsf{Enc}, \mathsf{Dec})$ has special correctness, it follows via similar arguments as above that $\mathsf{Enc}_{k_a^{1-\alpha}}(z) \in \mathsf{Range}(k_a^\alpha)$, with a negligible probability.

Now consider the ciphertext $c_i^g = \text{Enc}_{k_a^\alpha}(\text{Enc}_{k_b^\beta}(k_g^{G_g(\alpha,\beta)}))$. Assuming there are no decryption errors,[3] on decrypting the double-encryption c_i^g using the keys k_a^α and k_b^β, the evaluation algorithm Ev_{Yao} will obtain $k_g^{G_g(\alpha,\beta)}$. Moreover, as per the above arguments, the remaining three double-encryptions (corresponding to the garbled table of g) when decrypted with k_a^α and k_b^β will give the output $\perp$. Hence $k_g^{G_g(\alpha,\beta)}$ will be associated with w_g. $\square$

Using Claim 5, we prove the correctness property of $\mathcal{G}_{\text{Yao}}$ in Theorem 12.13. Informally, it follows from the fact that every garbled-gate is evaluated correctly. Before proving the correctness, we give the definition of *active* and *inactive* key.

Definition 12.12 (*Active and Inactive Key*) A key $k_a^\alpha \in \{k_a^0, k_a^1\}$ associated with wire w_a is called *active*, if on evaluating the circuit cir on input x, the bit that is obtained on wire w_a equals α. A key is called *inactive*, if it is not active.

Theorem 12.13 (Correctness of $\mathcal{G}_{\text{Yao}}$) *If* (Gen, Enc, Dec) *has special correctness, then except with a negligible probability, the garbling scheme* $\mathcal{G}_{\text{Yao}}$ *satisfies the correctness property. That is, for every circuit* cir $: \{0, 1\}^n \rightarrow \{0, 1\}^m$ *and input* $x \in \{0, 1\}^n$, *there is a negligible function* negl, *such that the following holds:*

$$Pr\left[\text{De}_{\text{Yao}}(\text{Ev}_{\text{Yao}}(\text{GC}_{\text{Yao}}, \text{En}_{\text{Yao}}(e, x)), d) \neq \text{cir}(x) : (\text{GC}, e, d) \leftarrow \text{Gb}_{\text{Yao}}(1^\lambda, \text{cir})\right] \leq \text{negl}(\lambda),$$

where the probability is taken over the randomness used in Gb_{Yao}.

Proof Let $x \in \{0, 1\}^n$ be an arbitrary input for the circuit cir. To prove the lemma, we first claim that given the garbled-input X and the gabled-circuit GC, the evaluation algorithm will associate the *active keys* with each wire. This is proved by induction on the circuit, starting with the input wires and working up to the circuit-output wires. Once we prove the claim then it follows easily that the decoding-information d will map the active circuit-output keys to the circuit-output $\text{cir}(x)$.

The claim is trivially true for the input wires, as the garbled-input X is nothing but the keys corresponding to each input wire, corresponding to the bits of x. This forms the base case of the induction. Next assume that the claim is true for an *arbitrary* gate g in cir, with $A(g) = w_a$ and $B(g) = w_b$. We show that the claim holds for the gate-output wire w_g as well. Let k_a^α and k_b^β be the active keys, corresponding to w_a and w_b respectively, where $\alpha, \beta \in \{0, 1\}$. From Claim 5, it follows that except with a negligible probability, say $\text{negl}_1(\lambda)$, the evaluation algorithm will associate the active key $k_g^{G_g(\alpha,\beta)}$ with w_g. This proves the inductive step.

Since there are $|\text{cir}| = \text{poly}(\lambda)$ number of gates in cir, it follows from the union bound that except with probability at most $\text{poly}(\lambda) \cdot \text{negl}_1(\lambda) = \text{negl}_2(\lambda)$, the evaluation algorithm

---

[3] This means that for every key k and message x, $\text{Dec}_k(\text{Enc}_k(x)) = x$ holds.

Simulator $\mathcal{S}_{\mathsf{Yao}}$

The inputs for the simulator are the circuit $\mathsf{cir} = (n, m, q, A, B, G)$ where Gates $= \{n+1, \ldots, n+q\}$ and $y = \mathsf{cir}(x)$. The simulator does the following:

- For $i = 1, \ldots, n+q$, corresponding to wire w_i, randomly select keys $\widetilde{k}_i^0 \leftarrow \mathsf{Gen}(1^\lambda)$, $\widetilde{k}_i^1 \leftarrow \mathsf{Gen}(1^\lambda)$.
- For every gate $g \in$ Gates with $A(g) = w_a$ and $B(g) = w_b$, do the following:
  - Compute the double-encryptions:

$$\widetilde{c_{0,0}} \leftarrow \mathsf{Enc}_{\widetilde{k}_a^0}(\mathsf{Enc}_{\widetilde{k}_b^0}(\widetilde{k}_g^0)),$$

$$\widetilde{c_{0,1}} \leftarrow \mathsf{Enc}_{\widetilde{k}_a^0}(\mathsf{Enc}_{\widetilde{k}_b^1}(\widetilde{k}_g^0)),$$

$$\widetilde{c_{1,0}} \leftarrow \mathsf{Enc}_{\widetilde{k}_a^1}(\mathsf{Enc}_{\widetilde{k}_b^0}(\widetilde{k}_g^0)),$$

$$\widetilde{c_{1,1}} \leftarrow \mathsf{Enc}_{\widetilde{k}_a^1}(\mathsf{Enc}_{\widetilde{k}_b^1}(\widetilde{k}_g^0)).$$

  - Randomly permute $\widetilde{c_{0,0}}, \widetilde{c_{0,1}}, \widetilde{c_{1,0}}$ and $\widetilde{c_{1,1}}$ and let $\widetilde{c}_1^g, \widetilde{c}_2^g, \widetilde{c}_3^g$ and $\widetilde{c}_4^g$ denote the permuted ciphertexts.[a]
- Set $\widetilde{\mathsf{GC}} = \{(\widetilde{c}_1^g, \widetilde{c}_2^g, \widetilde{c}_3^g, \widetilde{c}_4^g) : g \in$ Gates$\}$. Set $\widetilde{X} = \{\widetilde{k}_i^0 : i = 1, \ldots, n\}$.
- Let $y = (y_1, \ldots, y_m)$. Set $\widetilde{d} = \{((k_{n+q-m+i}^0, y_i), (k_{n+q-m+i}^1, 1 - y_i)) : i = 1, \ldots, m\}$.
- Output $\widetilde{\mathsf{GC}}, \widetilde{X}$ and $\widetilde{d}$.

---

[a]Note that the "other" key $\widetilde{k}_g^1$ is not encrypted in any of the double-encryptions.

Fig. 12.8 The input-independent simulator for Yao's garbling scheme

will associate the active keys with the circuit-output wires. That is, the keys obtained for the circuit-output wires all correspond to the output value $\mathsf{cir}(x)$, thus proving the theorem. $\square$

The privacy of Yao's garbling scheme: We next proceed to prove the privacy property of $\mathcal{G}_{\mathsf{Yao}}$. For this, we first design a simulator $\mathcal{S}_{\mathsf{Yao}}$ (Fig. 12.8), which when given cir and $\mathsf{cir}(x)$, produces a simulated garbled-circuit $\widetilde{\mathsf{GC}}$, simulated garbled-input $\widetilde{X}$ and simulated decoding-information $\widetilde{d}$. The simulator $\mathcal{S}_{\mathsf{Yao}}$ is "input independent", as it produces $\widetilde{\mathsf{GC}}, \widetilde{X}$ and $\widetilde{d}$, *without* the knowledge of input x. To prove the privacy, we need to show that the probability distribution of (GC, X, d) obtained from the "real" garbling is computationally indistinguishable from the probability distribution of $(\widetilde{\mathsf{GC}}, \widetilde{X}, \widetilde{d})$, generated by the simulator. We show the indistinguishability "indirectly" via the following two-step process:

- We first consider an *alternative* form of the simulator, called $\mathcal{S}_{\mathsf{Yao}}^{\mathsf{ID}}$ (Fig. 12.9), which is *input dependent* (here ID in $\mathcal{S}_{\mathsf{Yao}}^{\mathsf{ID}}$ denotes *input-dependent* simulation). The alternative simulator will possess the input x (apart from the output $\mathsf{cir}(x)$). We show that the probability distribution of the output generated by $\mathcal{S}_{\mathsf{Yao}}^{\mathsf{ID}}$ is exactly the *same* as the output generated by $\mathcal{S}_{\mathsf{Yao}}$ (Claim 6). Hence $\mathcal{S}_{\mathsf{Yao}}^{\mathsf{ID}}$ can be thought of as a mental experiment or a different description of $\mathcal{S}_{\mathsf{Yao}}$.
- In the second step, we show that the probability distribution of the output generated by $\mathcal{S}_{\mathsf{Yao}}^{\mathsf{ID}}$ is computationally indistinguishable from that of (GC, X, d), provided

---

Simulator $\mathcal{S}_{\text{Yao}}^{\text{ID}}$

The inputs for the simulator are the circuit $\text{cir} = (n, m, q, A, B, G)$ where $\text{Gates} = \{n+1, \dots, n+q\}$, x and $y = \text{cir}(x)$. The simulator does the following:

- For $i = 1, \dots, n+q$, corresponding to wire w_i, randomly select keys $\widetilde{k}_i^0 \leftarrow \text{Gen}(1^\lambda)$, $\widetilde{k}_i^1 \leftarrow \text{Gen}(1^\lambda)$.
- Evaluate cir on input x and identify the active keys over each wire in the circuit.
- For every gate $g \in \text{Gates}$, do the following:
  - Let $A(g) = w_a$ and $B(g) = w_b$. Moreover, let $\widetilde{k}_g^\gamma \in \{\widetilde{k}_g^0, \widetilde{k}_g^1\}$ be the the active key over w_g. Compute the double-encryptions:
  $$\widetilde{c_{0,0}} \leftarrow \text{Enc}_{\widetilde{k}_a^0}(\text{Enc}_{\widetilde{k}_b^0}(\widetilde{k_g^\gamma})),$$
  $$\widetilde{c_{0,1}} \leftarrow \text{Enc}_{\widetilde{k}_a^0}(\text{Enc}_{\widetilde{k}_b^1}(\widetilde{k_g^\gamma})),$$
  $$\widetilde{c_{1,0}} \leftarrow \text{Enc}_{\widetilde{k}_a^1}(\text{Enc}_{\widetilde{k}_b^0}(\widetilde{k_g^\gamma})),$$
  $$\widetilde{c_{1,1}} \leftarrow \text{Enc}_{\widetilde{k}_a^1}(\text{Enc}_{\widetilde{k}_b^1}(\widetilde{k_g^\gamma})).$$
  - Randomly permute $\widetilde{c_{0,0}}, \widetilde{c_{0,1}}, \widetilde{c_{1,0}}$ and $\widetilde{c_{1,1}}$ and let $\widetilde{c}_1^g, \widetilde{c}_2^g, \widetilde{c}_3^g$ and $\widetilde{c}_4^g$ denote the permuted ciphertexts.[a]
- Set $\widetilde{\text{GC}} = \{(\widetilde{c}_1^g, \widetilde{c}_2^g, \widetilde{c}_3^g, \widetilde{c}_4^g) : g \in \text{Gates}\}$. Set $\widetilde{X} = \{\widetilde{k}_i^{x_i} : i = 1, \dots, n\}$, where $x_1, \dots, x_n$ denotes the bits of x.
- Let $y = (y_1, \dots, y_m)$. Set $\widetilde{d} = \{((\widetilde{k_{n+q-m+i}^{y_i}}, y_i), (\widetilde{k_{n+q-m+i}^{1-y_i}}, 1-y_i)) : i = 1, \dots, m\}$.
- Output $\widetilde{\text{GC}}$, $\widetilde{X}$ and $\widetilde{d}$.

---
[a]Note that the inactive key $\widetilde{k_g^{1-\gamma}}$ is not encrypted in any of the double-encryptions.

Fig. 12.9 The alternate input-dependent simulator for Yao's garbling scheme

$(\text{Gen}, \text{Enc}, \text{Dec})$ is CDE-secure (Lemma 12.14). This will imply the indistinguishability of $(\widetilde{\text{GC}}, \widetilde{X}, \widetilde{d})$ and (GC, X, d), thus establishing the privacy of $\mathcal{G}_{\text{Yao}}$.

The reason to introduce the alternate simulator is to simplify the indistinguishability proof. More importantly, it is *not known* how to directly base the indistinguishability between the real garbling and input-independent simulated garbling on the CDE-security of the underlying encryption scheme; we will discuss more about this later after completing the privacy proof.

We begin with the description of *input-independent* simulator $\mathcal{S}_{\text{Yao}}$, which produces $(\widetilde{\text{GC}}, \widetilde{X}, \widetilde{d})$, just based on $\text{cir}(x)$ and cir. On a very high level, the simulator creates a garbled-circuit, which *always* evaluates to $\text{cir}(x)$, *irrespective* of which keys are used for the evaluation. This is achieved by creating garbled-gates, where all the four double-encryptions encrypt the *same* key, and so the values of the input wires do not affect the value of the output wire. In more detail, the simulator picks two random keys for each wire of the circuit. Next each gate is garbled by computing four double-encryptions using different combinations of the keys associated with the input wires of the gate. However, the simulator encrypts a *common* key in all the four double-encryptions. Namely, it picks one of the keys associated with the gate-output wire and encrypts this key in all the four double-encryptions. The simulated garbled-input $\widetilde{X}$ is computed by arbitrarily assigning one key from each key-pair, assigned for the circuit-input wires. The simulated decoding-information $\tilde{d}$ is computed by "programming" the keys encrypted in the garbled output-gates to the corresponding bits of $\text{cir}(x)$ (see Fig. 12.8 for the formal details).

We next describe the alternate *input-dependent* simulator $\mathcal{S}^{\text{ID}}_{\text{Yao}}$. Informally, the simulator $\mathcal{S}^{\text{ID}}_{\text{Yao}}$ generates its output in almost an identical fashion as Gb_{Yao}, except that while garbling any gate g, it encrypts only the *active key* over w_g in all the four double-encryptions. This is possible for $\mathcal{S}^{\text{ID}}_{\text{Yao}}$ because it will know the input x and cir and hence all the active and inactive keys. Similarly, the decoding-information is "cooked" to map the active keys over the circuit-output wires to the bits of $\text{cir}(x)$. The formal details of $\mathcal{S}^{\text{ID}}_{\text{Yao}}$ are given in Fig. 12.9.

Before we proceed further, we pictorially illustrate the outputs generated by Gb_{Yao}, $\mathcal{S}_{\text{Yao}}$ and $\mathcal{S}^{\text{ID}}_{\text{Yao}}$ in Fig. 12.10.

We next claim that the outputs generated by $\mathcal{S}^{\text{ID}}_{\text{Yao}}$ and $\mathcal{S}_{\text{Yao}}$ are identically distributed.

Claim 6 The probability distribution of the output of $\mathcal{S}^{\text{ID}}_{\text{Yao}}$ is identical to the probability distribution of the output of $\mathcal{S}_{\text{Yao}}$. That is, the following holds:

$$\left\{ (\widetilde{\text{GC}}, \tilde{X}, \tilde{d}) \leftarrow \mathcal{S}_{\text{Yao}}(1^\lambda, \text{cir}, \text{cir}(x)) \right\} \equiv \left\{ (\widetilde{\text{GC}}, \tilde{X}, \tilde{d}) \leftarrow \mathcal{S}^{\text{ID}}_{\text{Yao}}(1^\lambda, \text{cir}, x, \text{cir}(x)) \right\},$$

where $\equiv$ denotes that the two probability distributions are identical.

Proof It is easy to see that $\tilde{X}$ produced by both $\mathcal{S}^{\text{ID}}_{\text{Yao}}$ as well as $\mathcal{S}_{\text{Yao}}$ consists of n uniformly random keys and hence have the same distribution. So let us fix the garbled-input to some arbitrary common value (from the underlying domain) in both the distributions. Now conditioned on the garbled-input, the garbled gates generated by both $\mathcal{S}^{\text{ID}}_{\text{Yao}}$ as well as $\mathcal{S}_{\text{Yao}}$ consist of four randomly permuted double-encryptions, all of which encrypt a single random key. Hence $\widetilde{\text{GC}}$ is identically distributed in both the distributions and so let us fix the garbled-circuit to a common value in both the distributions.

Finally, conditioned on the garbled-input and garbled-circuit which are identically distributed in both the distributions, the decoding-information $\tilde{d}$ yields the same result, namely $\text{cir}(x)$, in both the distributions. This is because the $\tilde{d}$ produced by $\mathcal{S}^{\text{ID}}_{\text{Yao}}$ maps the active keys over the circuit-output wires to the bits in $y = \text{cir}(x)$. And these active keys are the only keys encrypted in the double-encryptions for gates from which the circuit-output wires exit. Similarly, for $\mathcal{S}_{\text{Yao}}$, the only keys encrypted in the gates from which circuit-output wires exit are the keys that are mapped to the bits in $y = \text{cir}(x)$ via $\tilde{d}$ generated by $\mathcal{S}_{\text{Yao}}$. $\qquad\square$

We next proceed to prove an important lemma, which forms the basis of proving the privacy property of $\mathcal{G}_{\text{Yao}}$. The lemma shows that the probability distribution of $(\widetilde{\text{GC}}, \tilde{X}, \tilde{d})$ produced by $\mathcal{S}^{\text{ID}}_{\text{Yao}}$ is computationally indistinguishable from the probability distribution of (GC, X, d) produced by $\mathcal{G}_{\text{Yao}}$, provided the underlying encryption scheme is CDE-secure. To simplify the proof of the lemma, we first describe a series of $q + 1$ hybrid experiments $H_0, \ldots, H_q$ (recall that q is the number of gates in cir) and claim that every two consec-

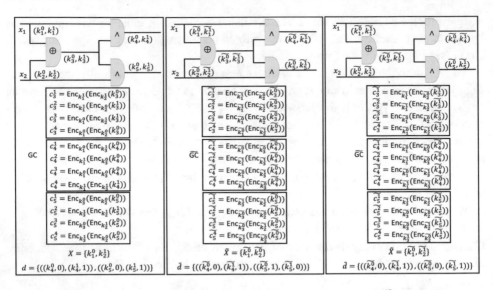

Fig. 12.10 Pictorial depiction of the outputs generated by $\mathsf{Gb}_{\mathsf{Yao}}$, $\mathcal{S}_{\mathsf{Yao}}$ and $\mathcal{S}_{\mathsf{Yao}}^{\mathsf{ID}}$ for the case when $x = (x_1, x_2) = (0, 1)$, resulting in the output $y = \mathsf{cir}(x) = (y_1, y_2) = (0, 1)$. The first box shows the garbled-circuit GC, garbled-input X and the decoding-information d generated by $\mathsf{Gb}_{\mathsf{Yao}}$. The second box shows the simulated garbled-circuit $\widetilde{\mathsf{GC}}$, simulated garbled-input $\widetilde{X}$ and the simulated decoding-information $\widetilde{d}$ generated by the input-independent simulator $\mathcal{S}_{\mathsf{Yao}}$. Notice that for the gates indexed 3, 4 and 5, all the corresponding double-encryptions encrypt only the key $\widetilde{k}_3^0$, $\widetilde{k}_4^0$ and $\widetilde{k}_5^0$ respectively (since simulator will *not know* the active and inactive keys, as x is unknown to the simulator). Accordingly, in $\widetilde{d}$, the keys $\widetilde{k}_4^0$ and $\widetilde{k}_5^0$ are mapped to 0 and 1 respectively, so as to be consistent with the function output $y = (0, 1)$. Since the input x is not known to the simulator, $\widetilde{X}$ is set to be the keys corresponding to $x_1 = x_2 = 0$. The third box shows the simulated garbled-circuit $\widetilde{\mathsf{GC}}$, simulated garbled-input $\widetilde{X}$ and the simulated decoding-information $\widetilde{d}$ generated by the input-dependent simulator $\mathcal{S}_{\mathsf{Yao}}^{\mathsf{ID}}$, which encrypts corresponding active keys in double-encryptions. Namely, for the gates indexed 3, 4 and 5, all the corresponding double-encryptions encrypt the active key $\widetilde{k}_3^1$, $\widetilde{k}_4^0$ and $\widetilde{k}_5^1$ respectively. The decoding-information is set so that the active output-wire keys are consistent with the bits of y_1 and y_2

utive hybrids in the series are computationally indistinguishable, provided the underlying encryption scheme is CDE-secure. Looking ahead, the hybrid H_0 will induce the probability distribution $\{(\mathsf{GC}, X, d)\}$, as produced by the real garbling. On the other hand, the hybrid H_q will induce the probability distribution $\{(\widetilde{\mathsf{GC}}, \widetilde{X}, \widetilde{d})\}$, as produced by $\mathcal{S}_{\mathsf{Yao}}^{\mathsf{ID}}$. As every two consecutive hybrids are computationally indistinguishable and there are $q + 1 = \mathsf{poly}(\lambda)$ number of such hybrids, using the standard hybrid argument [102] it follows that H_0 and H_q are computationally indistinguishable, thus proving the indistinguishability of real garbling and input-dependent simulated garbling. We next describe the hybrid experiments.

Hybrid Experiments $H_0(x, \text{cir}), H_1(x, \text{cir}), \ldots, H_q(x, \text{cir})$: The hybrid experiment $H_0(x, \text{cir})$ is the one which induces the probability distribution $\Big\{ (\text{GC}, X = \text{En}_{\text{Yao}}(x, e), d) :$ $(\text{GC}, e, d) \leftarrow \text{Gb}_{\text{Yao}}(1^\lambda, \text{cir}) \Big\}$, namely the one generated by the real garbling scheme $\mathcal{G}_{\text{Yao}}$. Hence GC, X and d are generated as per $\mathcal{G}_{\text{Yao}}$ in $H_0(x, \text{cir})$.

For $i = 1, \ldots, q$, we define the hybrid experiment $H_i(x, \text{cir})$ as follows: the garbled circuit $\widetilde{\text{GC}}$ in $H_i(x, \text{cir})$ consists of i garbled gates, generated as per $\mathcal{S}_{\text{Yao}}^{\text{ID}}$, while the remaining $q - i$ gates in the circuit are garbled as per the real garbling scheme $\mathcal{G}_{\text{Yao}}$. In more detail, in the experiment $H_i(x, \text{cir})$, random and independent pair of keys (k_i^0, k_i^1) is associated with each wire w_i of the circuit. Then a real garbling of cir is done as per Gb_{Yao}, input x is garbled to $\widetilde{X}$ as per the encoding-information and decoding-information $\widetilde{d}$ is generated as per Gb_{Yao}. Next using x, the circuit cir is evaluated and all active and inactive keys are identified. Next the garbling of the first i gates $g_{n+1}, \ldots, g_{n+i}$ in cir are modified as per $\mathcal{S}_{\text{Yao}}^{\text{ID}}$. More specifically, the following is done for each gate $g \in \{n + 1, \ldots, n + i\}$: let $A(g) = w_a$ and $B(g) = w_b$ and let $\widetilde{k}_g^\gamma$ be the active key over the wire w_g. Then the garbing of g is recomputed by encrypting $\widetilde{k}_g^\gamma$ with all the four combinations of $(\widetilde{k}_a^0, \widetilde{k}_a^1)$ and $(\widetilde{k}_b^0, \widetilde{k}_b^1)$. The remaining gates $g_{n+i+1}, \ldots, g_{n+q}$ are left unmodified and hence garbled as per the real garbling Gb_{Yao}.

For the sake of consistency, we let $(\widetilde{k}_i^0, \widetilde{k}_i^1)$ denote the pair of keys over wire w_i used in the experiment $H_0(x, \text{cir})$; moreover we let $\widetilde{\text{GC}}$, $\widetilde{X}$ and $\widetilde{d}$ denote the garbled-circuit, garbled-input and decoding-information respectively generated in $H_0(x, \text{cir})$.[4] For a pictorial depiction of the garbled-circuit generated in the various hybrid experiments, see Fig. 12.11.

We next claim that the probability distribution induced by any two consecutive hybrid experiments are indistinguishable, provided the underlying encryption scheme is CDE-secure.

Claim 7 If (Gen, Enc, Dec) is CDE-secure then the probability distributions induced by H_{i-1} and H_i are computationally indistinguishable for $i = 1, \ldots, q$.

Proof The proof is by contradiction. Assume there exists an $i \in \{1, \ldots, q\}$, such that the probability distributions induced by H_{i-1} and H_i are computationally distinguishable. Hence there exists a PPT distinguisher, say D, and several x, such that,

$$\Big| \Pr[D(H_{i-1}(x, \text{cir})) = 1] - \Pr[D(H_i(x, \text{cir})) = 1] \Big| \geq \mu(\lambda),$$

where $\mu(\lambda)$ is a non-negligible function in λ. We use D and x to construct a PPT adversary Adv, who can win the double-encryption security experiment $\text{Exp}_{\text{Adv}}^{\text{double}}$ with respect to (Gen, Enc, Dec) with probability at least $\mu(\lambda)$, which is a contradiction.

---

[4] While presenting $\mathcal{G}_{\text{Yao}}$ in Fig. 12.6, we used (k_i^0, k_i^1) to denote the key-pair associated with w_i. Moreover, GC, X and d represented the garbled circuit, garbled input and decoding information respectively. We change these notations here to ensure notational consistency across all the hybrids.

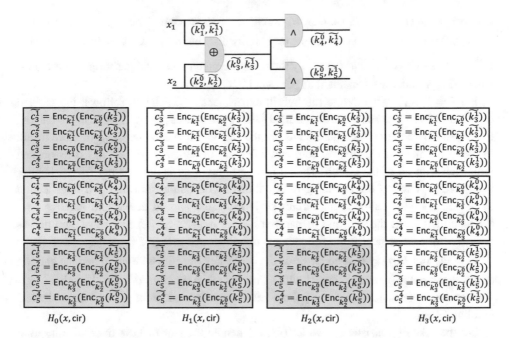

Fig. 12.11 Pictorial depiction of the garbled-circuits generated in the various hybrid experiments for the case when $x = (x_1, x_2) = (0, 1)$. In all the experiments, a pair of random keys is associated with each wire. In the hybrid $H_0(x, \text{cir})$, the double-encryptions for all the three gates are computed as per Gb_{Yao}. In the hybrid $H_1(x, \text{cir})$, the double-encryptions for the first gate (XOR gate) are computed as per $\mathcal{S}_{\text{Yao}}^{\text{ID}}$, where the active key $\widetilde{k}_3^1$ is encrypted in all the double-encryptions; the remaining garbled gates are computed as per Gb_{Yao}. In the hybrid $H_2(x, \text{cir})$, the double-encryptions for the first gate (XOR gate) and the second gate (AND gate) are computed as per $\mathcal{S}_{\text{Yao}}^{\text{ID}}$ and the remaining gate is garbled are computed as per Gb_{Yao}. Hence, the active key $\widetilde{k}_4^0$ is encrypted in all the double-encryptions corresponding to the second gate. In the hybrid $H_3(x, \text{cir})$, the double-encryptions for the all the gates are computed as per $\mathcal{S}_{\text{Yao}}^{\text{ID}}$

Let g be the ith gate in the circuit, with $A(g) = w_a$ and $B(g) = w_b$ and gate function $G_g : \{0, 1\}^2 \rightarrow \{0, 1\}$. Moreover, let $\alpha, \beta \in \{0, 1\}$ be the actual bit values over w_a and w_b respectively, while evaluating cir with input x. This means that the keys $\widetilde{k}_a^\alpha$ and $\widetilde{k}_b^\beta$ are the active keys, while $\mathbf{\widetilde{k}_a^{1-\alpha}}$ and $\mathbf{\widetilde{k}_b^{1-\beta}}$ are the inactive keys. The inactive keys are highlighted in bold face to distinguish them from active keys. Now the garbling of g in H_{i-1} will consist of the following double-encryptions, in a random order:

$$\text{Enc}_{\widetilde{k}_a^\alpha}(\text{Enc}_{\widetilde{k}_b^\beta}(\widetilde{k_g^{G_g(\alpha,\beta)}})), \quad \text{Enc}_{\widetilde{k}_a^\alpha}(\text{Enc}_{\mathbf{\widetilde{k}_b^{1-\beta}}}(\widetilde{k_g^{G_g(\alpha,1-\beta)}}))$$

$$\text{Enc}_{\mathbf{\widetilde{k}_a^{1-\alpha}}}(\text{Enc}_{\widetilde{k}_b^\beta}(\widetilde{k_g^{G_g(1-\alpha,\beta)}})), \quad \text{Enc}_{\mathbf{\widetilde{k}_a^{1-\alpha}}}(\text{Enc}_{\mathbf{\widetilde{k}_b^{1-\beta}}}(\widetilde{k_g^{G_g(1-\alpha,1-\beta)}})).$$

$$(12.1)$$

This is because, in H_{i-1}, gate g is garbled as per $\mathsf{Gb}_{\mathsf{Yao}}$, where *both* active as well as inactive keys are encrypted, according to various combinations of the keys over the gate-input wires. On the other hand, the garbling of g in H_i will consist of the following double-encryptions, in a random order:

$$\mathsf{Enc}_{\widetilde{k_a^\alpha}}(\mathsf{Enc}_{\widetilde{k_b^\beta}}(\widetilde{k_g^{G_g(\alpha,\beta)}})), \quad \mathsf{Enc}_{\widetilde{k_a^\alpha}}(\mathsf{Enc}_{\mathbf{k_b^{1-\beta}}}(\widetilde{k_g^{G_g(\alpha,\beta)}}))$$

$$\mathsf{Enc}_{\mathbf{k_a^{1-\alpha}}}(\mathsf{Enc}_{\widetilde{k_b^\beta}}(\widetilde{k_g^{G_g(\alpha,\beta)}})), \quad \mathsf{Enc}_{\mathbf{k_a^{1-\alpha}}}(\mathsf{Enc}_{\mathbf{k_b^{1-\beta}}}(\widetilde{k_g^{G_g(\alpha,\beta)}})). \tag{12.2}$$

This is because, in H_i, gate g is garbled as per the procedure followed by $\mathcal{S}_{\mathsf{Yao}}^{\mathsf{ID}}$, where *only* the active key in encrypted in all the four double-encryptions.

While the probability distribution of the *first* double-encryption in both Eqs. 12.1 and 12.2 are *identical*, a closer look into the remaining three double-encryptions in Eqs. 12.1 and 12.2 reveals that the indistinguishability between H_{i-1} and H_i depends upon the indistinguishability of these double-encryptions under the inactive keys $\mathbf{k_a^{1-\alpha}}$ and $\mathbf{k_b^{1-\beta}}$. Namely, the indistinguishability between H_{i-1} and H_i reduces to the indistinguishability between the distributions $\Big\{\mathsf{Enc}_{\widetilde{k_a^\alpha}}(\mathsf{Enc}_{\mathbf{k_b^{1-\beta}}}(k_g^{\widetilde{G_g(\alpha,1-\beta)}})), \mathsf{Enc}_{\mathbf{k_a^{1-\alpha}}}(\mathsf{Enc}_{\widetilde{k_b^\beta}}(k_g^{\widetilde{G_g(1-\alpha,\beta)}})),$

$\mathsf{Enc}_{\mathbf{k_a^{1-\alpha}}}(\mathsf{Enc}_{\mathbf{k_b^{1-\beta}}}(k_g^{\widetilde{G_g(1-\alpha,1-\beta)}}))\Big\}$ and $\Big\{\mathsf{Enc}_{\widetilde{k_a^\alpha}}(\mathsf{Enc}_{\mathbf{k_b^{1-\beta}}}(k_g^{\widetilde{G_g(\alpha,\beta)}})), \mathsf{Enc}_{\mathbf{k_a^{1-\alpha}}}$

$(\mathsf{Enc}_{\widetilde{k_b^\beta}}(k_g^{\widetilde{G_g(\alpha,\beta)}})), \mathsf{Enc}_{\mathbf{k_a^{1-\alpha}}}(\mathsf{Enc}_{\mathbf{k_b^{1-\beta}}}(k_g^{\widetilde{G_g(\alpha,\beta)}}))\Big\}$.

A closer look into the above two distributions reveals that the indistinguishability between these distributions reduces to the CDE-security of Enc. In more detail, in the experiment $\mathsf{Exp}^{\mathsf{double}}$ (see Fig. 12.4), if we let $k_0 = \widetilde{k_a^\alpha}, k_1 = \widetilde{k_b^\beta}, k_0' = \mathbf{k_a^{1-\alpha}}$ and $k_1' = \mathbf{k_b^{1-\beta}}$ and message triples (x_0, y_0, z_0) and (x_1, y_1, z_1) to $(k_g^{G_g(\alpha,1-\beta)}, k_g^{G_g(1-\alpha,\beta)}, k_g^{G_g(1-\alpha,1-\beta)})$ and $(k_g^{G_g(\alpha,\beta)}, k_g^{G_g(\alpha,\beta)}, k_g^{G_g(\alpha,\beta)})$ respectively, then it follows that no PPT distinguisher D can distinguish between the above two probability distributions. Otherwise, D can be used to break the CDE security. That is, using D we construct an adversary Adv for $\mathsf{Exp}^{\mathsf{double}}$, such that:

$$\left| \Pr[\mathsf{Exp}_{\mathsf{Adv}}^{\mathsf{double}}(\lambda, 1) = 1] - \Pr[\mathsf{Exp}_{\mathsf{Adv}}^{\mathsf{double}}(\lambda, 0) = 1] \right| \geq \mu(\lambda).$$

Informally, Adv participates in the experiment $\mathsf{Exp}^{\mathsf{double}}$ with k_0, k_1 and message triplets as above, while the experiment will randomly pick the keys k_0', k_1' and return the challenge ciphertexts (c', c'', c'''). To identify whether the challenge ciphertexts are encryptions of (x_0, y_0, z_0) or (x_1, y_1, z_1), the adversary Adv computes a garbling of cir. While the first $i-1$ gates are garbled as per $\mathcal{S}_{\mathsf{Yao}}^{\mathsf{ID}}$ (where cir is evaluated with input x to identify the active keys), the last $q-i$ gates are garbled as per $\mathsf{Gb}_{\mathsf{Yao}}$. The gate i is garbled using the challenge ciphertexts (c', c'', c''') in such a way that the overall garbled-circuit has either the same probability distribution as H_{i-1} or H_i, depending upon whether Adv received encryptions of (x_0, y_0, z_0) or (x_1, y_1, z_1) respectively. To identify what is the case, Adv invokes D and outputs whatever D outputs. Clearly, the distinguishing advantage of Adv will be exactly the same as that of D. Formally, the steps of the adversary Adv are as follows:

- Upon input 1^λ, pick two random keys $\widetilde{k}_i^0 \leftarrow \mathsf{Gen}(1^\lambda)$, $\widetilde{k}_i^1 \leftarrow \mathsf{Gen}(1^\lambda)$ for every wire w_i in cir, except for wires w_a and w_b. For w_a, select a random key $\widetilde{k}_a^\alpha \leftarrow \mathsf{Gen}(1^\lambda)$ and for w_b, select a random key $\widetilde{k}_b^\beta \leftarrow \mathsf{Gen}(1^\lambda)$, where $\alpha, \beta \in \{0, 1\}$ are the bit values over wires w_a and w_b respectively while evaluating cir on x.
- Evaluate cir on input x and label the active and inactive key over each wire, except for the wires w_a and w_b. For wire w_a and w_b, set $\widetilde{k}_a^\alpha$ and $\widetilde{k}_b^\beta$ as the *active* key. Note that Adv *does not* know the inactive keys over w_a and w_b.
- Set $\widetilde{X} = \{\widetilde{k}_i^{x_i} : 1 \le i \le n\}$, where $x = (x_1, \ldots, x_n)$.
- Set $\widetilde{d} = \{((k_{n+q-m+i}^{y_i}, y_i), (k_{n+q-m+i}^{1-y_i}, 1 - y_i)) : 1 \le i \le m\}$, where $y = (y_1, \ldots, y_m) = \mathsf{cir}(x)$.
- Construct the garbled circuit by garbling each gate in cir as follows:
  - To garble the gate g, do the following:
    1. participate in the experiment $\mathsf{Exp}_{\mathsf{Adv}}^{\mathsf{double}}$ by setting $k_0 = \widetilde{k}_a^\alpha$ and $k_1 = \widetilde{k}_b^\beta$. Send k_0, k_1 and the message triples $(x_0, y_0, z_0) = (k_g^{G_g(\alpha, 1-\beta)}, k_g^{G_g(1-\alpha, \beta)}, k_g^{G_g(1-\alpha, 1-\beta)})$ and $(x_1, y_1, z_1) = (k_g^{G_g(\alpha, \beta)}, k_g^{G_g(\alpha, \beta)}, k_g^{G_g(\alpha, \beta)})$ to the experiment.
    2. The experiment $\mathsf{Exp}_{\mathsf{Adv}}^{\mathsf{double}}$ chooses two random keys $\mathbf{k_a^{1-\alpha}}, \mathbf{k_b^{1-\beta}} \leftarrow \mathsf{Gen}(1^\lambda)$ and sends to Adv, either the double-encryptions[5]

$$\mathsf{Enc}_{\widetilde{k}_a^\alpha}(\mathsf{Enc}_{\mathbf{k_b^{1-\beta}}}(k_g^{G_g(\alpha, 1-\beta)})), \mathsf{Enc}_{\mathbf{k_a^{1-\alpha}}}(\mathsf{Enc}_{\widetilde{k}_b^\beta}(k_g^{G_g(1-\alpha, \beta)})),$$

$$\mathsf{Enc}_{\mathbf{k_a^{1-\alpha}}}(\mathsf{Enc}_{\mathbf{k_b^{1-\beta}}}(k_g^{G_g(1-\alpha, 1-\beta)})) \qquad (12.3)$$

or the double-encryptions

$$\mathsf{Enc}_{\widetilde{k}_a^\alpha}(\mathsf{Enc}_{\mathbf{k_b^{1-\beta}}}(k_g^{G_g(\alpha, \beta)})), \mathsf{Enc}_{\mathbf{k_a^{1-\alpha}}}(\mathsf{Enc}_{\widetilde{k}_b^\beta}(k_g^{G_g(\alpha, \beta)})),$$

$$\mathsf{Enc}_{\mathbf{k_a^{1-\alpha}}}(\mathsf{Enc}_{\mathbf{k_b^{1-\beta}}}(k_g^{G_g(\alpha, \beta)})) \qquad (12.4)$$

depending upon whether the choice bit $\sigma = 0$ or $\sigma = 1$ respectively, where the choice bit is selected uniformly at random by the experiment.

---

[5] Hence $k_0' = \mathbf{k_a^{1-\alpha}}$ and $k_1' = \mathbf{k_b^{1-\beta}}$ in the CDE experiment.

3. Let (c', c'', c''') be the received ciphertexts. Compute $c = \mathsf{Enc}_{\widetilde{k_a^\alpha}}(\mathsf{Enc}_{\widetilde{k_b^\beta}}(k_g^{\widetilde{G_g(\alpha,\beta)}}))$
    and set $\widetilde{c_1^g} = c$, $\widetilde{c_2^g} = c'$, $\widetilde{c_3^g} = c''$ and $\widetilde{c_4^g} = c'''$ as the garbling of g.
    Note that if Adv received ciphertexts as per $\sigma = 0$, then g is garbled as per H_{i-1}
    because the distribution of $(\widetilde{c_1^g}, \widetilde{c_2^g}, \widetilde{c_3^g}, \widetilde{c_4^g})$ will be identical to the distribution of
    the ciphertexts in (12.1). Otherwise g is garbled as per H_i because the distribution
    of $(\widetilde{c_1^g}, \widetilde{c_2^g}, \widetilde{c_3^g}, \widetilde{c_4^g})$ will be identical to the distribution of the ciphertexts in (12.2).
    The remaining gates are garbled as follows.

-   For every gate $g_j < g$, the gate g_j needs to be garbled as per $\mathcal{S}_{\mathsf{Yao}}^{\mathsf{ID}}$. This is because
    both in H_{i-1}, as well as H_i, gate g_j is garbled as per the input-dependent simulated
    garbling by encrypting *only* the active key over the gate-output wire w_j in all the
    double-encryptions, using the different combinations of active/inactive keys over the
    gate-input wires of g_j. If w_j is different from w_a or w_b, then Adv will know both the
    active as well as inactive key over w_j, as both are selected by Adv itself. On the other
    hand, if $w_j = w_a$ or $w_j = w_b$, then the active key over w_j is either $\widetilde{k_a^\alpha}$ or $\widetilde{k_b^\beta}$, both of
    which are known to Adv. So irrespective of the case, the active key over w_j is known
    to Adv, so it knows what to encrypt in all the four double-encryptions. However the
    inactive keys over the input wires of g_j need not be necessarily known to Adv.
    More specifically, if neither w_a nor w_b is an input-wire for g_j, then Adv knows the
    active as well inactive keys over the input wires of g_j (as they are picked by Adv
    itself) and so it can garble g_j, satisfying the above requirement. On the other hand,
    if either w_a or w_b is an input wire for g_j, then Adv needs the inactive key $\widetilde{k_a^{1-\alpha}}$ or
    $\widetilde{k_b^{1-\beta}}$ for computing the garbling of g. However, the inactive keys over w_a and w_b are
    known only to the experiment and cannot be revealed to Adv. To deal with this, Adv
    makes use of the oracle access to $\overline{\mathsf{Enc}}(k_0', \cdot, \cdot)$ and $\overline{\mathsf{Enc}}(\cdot, k_1', \cdot)$, available as part of
    the $\mathsf{Exp}_{\mathsf{Adv}}^{\mathsf{double}}$ experiment, where $k_0' = \widetilde{k_a^{1-\alpha}}$ and $k_1' = \widetilde{k_b^{1-\beta}}$. That is, depending upon
    the requirement (i.e. whether w_a or w_b is one of the input wires for g_j), Adv asks
    for encryptions under the required inactive key, to compute the garbling of g_j. Let
    $(\widetilde{c_1^{g_j}}, \widetilde{c_2^{g_j}}, \widetilde{c_3^{g_j}}, \widetilde{c_4^{g_j}})$ denote the garbling of g_j.
-   Every gate $g_j > g$ needs to be garbled as per the real garbling $\mathsf{Gb}_{\mathsf{Yao}}$. This is because
    both in H_{i-1}, as well as H_i, gate g_j is garbled as per the real garbling by encrypting
    active as well as inactive key over the gate-output wire w_j in the double-encryptions,
    using the different combinations of active/inactive keys over the gate-input wires of
    g_j. Since $g_j > g$, neither w_a nor w_b can be equal to w_j. So Adv will know both the
    active as well as inactive key over w_j, as both of them are picked by Adv itself. So
    it knows what to encrypt in the four double-encryptions, corresponding to g. Now
    similar to the previous case, depending upon whether w_a or w_b is one of the input
    wires for g_j, Adv makes use of the oracle access to $\overline{\mathsf{Enc}}(k_0', \cdot, \cdot)$ and $\overline{\mathsf{Enc}}(\cdot, k_1', \cdot)$ and

computes the required garbling of g_j. Let $(\widetilde{c_1^{g_j}}, \widetilde{c_2^{g_j}}, \widetilde{c_3^{g_j}}, \widetilde{c_4^{g_j}})$ denote the garbling of g_j.

- Set $\widetilde{\mathsf{GC}} = \{(\widetilde{c_1^g}, \widetilde{c_2^g}, \widetilde{c_3^g}, \widetilde{c_4^g}) : g \in \mathsf{Gates}\}$.
- Run the distinguisher D on input $(\widetilde{\mathsf{GC}}, \widetilde{X}, \widetilde{d})$ and output the bit obtained from D in the experiment $\mathsf{Exp}_{\mathsf{Adv}}^{\mathsf{double}}$.

It is easy to see that if Adv participates in the experiment $\mathsf{Exp}_{\mathsf{Adv}}^{\mathsf{double}}(\lambda, 0)$, then the distribution of $(\widetilde{\mathsf{GC}}, \widetilde{X}, \widetilde{d})$ generated by Adv is the same as generated by $H_{i-1}(x, \mathsf{cir})$. On the other hand, if it participates in $\mathsf{Exp}_{\mathsf{Adv}}^{\mathsf{double}}(\lambda, 1)$, then the distribution of $(\widetilde{\mathsf{GC}}, \widetilde{X}, \widetilde{d})$ generated by Adv is the same as generated by $H_i(x, \mathsf{cir})$. Hence it follows that,

$$\left| \Pr[\mathsf{Exp}_{\mathsf{Adv}}^{\mathsf{double}}(\lambda, 1) = 1] - \Pr[\mathsf{Exp}_{\mathsf{Adv}}^{\mathsf{double}}(\lambda, 0) = 1] \right| =$$

$$\left| \Pr[D(H_i(x, \mathsf{cir})) = 1] - \Pr[D(H_{i-1}(x, \mathsf{cir})) = 1] \right| \geq \mu(\lambda),$$

which is a contradiction to the CDE-security of $(\mathsf{Gen}, \mathsf{Enc}, \mathsf{Dec})$.

For a pictorial illustration of the interaction between Adv and D in the above reduction, see Fig. 12.12.   □

Using Claim 7, we next prove the crucial lemma, showing the indistinguishability of (GC, X, d) produced by the real garbling $\mathcal{G}_{\mathsf{Yao}}$ and $(\widetilde{\mathsf{GC}}, \widetilde{X}, \widetilde{d})$ produced by the input-dependent simulated garbling $\mathcal{S}_{\mathsf{Yao}}^{\mathsf{ID}}$. The proof is based on standard hybrid argument.

Lemma 12.14 *For every function $f : \{0, 1\}^n \to \{0, 1\}^m$ represented by a Boolean circuit* cir *and every input $x \in \{0, 1\}^n$, the probability distribution* $\Big\{ (\mathsf{GC}, X = \mathsf{En}_{\mathsf{Yao}}(x, e), d) :$ $(\mathsf{GC}, e, d) \leftarrow \mathsf{Gb}_{\mathsf{Yao}}(1^\lambda, \mathsf{cir}) \Big\}$ *is computationally indistinguishable from the probability distribution* $\Big\{ (\widetilde{\mathsf{GC}}, \widetilde{X}, \widetilde{d}) \leftarrow \mathcal{S}_{\mathsf{Yao}}^{\mathsf{ID}}(1^\lambda, \mathsf{cir}, x, \mathsf{cir}(x)) \Big\}$, *provided* $(\mathsf{Gen}, \mathsf{Enc}, \mathsf{Dec})$ *is CDE-secure.*

Proof We first note that the distribution of X and $\widetilde{X}$ are identical, as both consists of active keys for the circuit-input wires, corresponding to the bits in x. In the same way, both d and $\widetilde{d}$ maps the active keys over the circuit-output wires to the actual bits of $y = \mathsf{cir}(x)$. To show that the real garbled-circuit GC is computationally indistinguishable from $\widetilde{\mathsf{GC}}$, we use a hybrid argument. More specifically, we note that the probability distribution $\Big\{ (\mathsf{GC}, X = \mathsf{En}_{\mathsf{Yao}}(x, e), d) : (\mathsf{GC}, e, d) \leftarrow \mathsf{Gb}_{\mathsf{Yao}}(1^\lambda, \mathsf{cir}) \Big\}$ is the one induced by the hybrid experiment $H_0(x, \mathsf{cir})$.[6] On the other hand, the probability distribution $\Big\{ (\widetilde{\mathsf{GC}}, \widetilde{X}, \widetilde{d}) \leftarrow \mathcal{S}_{\mathsf{Yao}}^{\mathsf{ID}}(1^\lambda, \mathsf{cir}, x, \mathsf{cir}(x)) \Big\}$ is induced by the experiment $H_q(x, \mathsf{cir})$. There are $q = \mathsf{poly}(\lambda)$ intermediate hybrids between H_0 and H_q. Moreover, from Claim 7, for

---

[6] As mentioned in footnote 4, we used $\widetilde{\mathsf{GC}}$, $\widetilde{X}$ and $\widetilde{d}$ to denote the output of the experiment $H_0(x, \mathsf{cir})$ for the sake of notational consistency; the actual output is denoted as GC, X and d, namely the one used while presenting $\mathcal{G}_{\mathsf{Yao}}$.

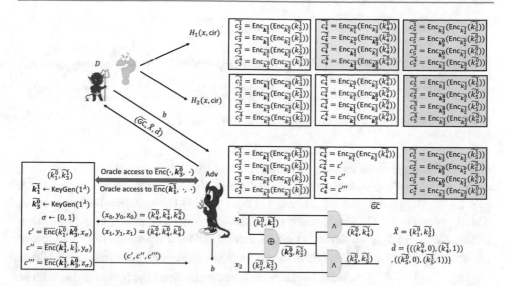

Fig. 12.12 Pictorial depiction of the interaction between the adversary Adv of the experiment $\text{Exp}_{\text{Adv}}^{\text{double}}$ and the distinguisher D in the proof by reduction of Claim 7, assuming that D can distinguish between the hybrids $H_1(x, \text{cir})$ and $H_2(x, \text{cir})$ (i.e., $i = 2$ in the proof of Claim 7) when $x = (x_1, x_2) = (0, 1)$. All the keys are randomly chosen from the underlying domain, with the keys in bold denoting the inactive keys over the gate-input wires of the second gate (AND) in cir. If $\sigma = 0$ in $\text{Exp}_{\text{Adv}}^{\text{double}}$, then the $\widetilde{\text{GC}}$ received by D will be distributed as per $H_1(x, \text{cir})$, otherwise $\widetilde{\text{GC}}$ will be distributed as per $H_2(x, \text{cir})$

$i = 1, \ldots, q$, the probability distributions induced by $H_{i-1}(x, \text{cir})$ and $H_i(x, \text{cir})$ are computationally indistinguishable, provided (Gen, Enc, Dec) is CDE-secure. Using hybrid argument [102], it then follows that H_0 and H_q are computationally indistinguishable as well, thus proving the lemma. $\qquad\square$

Finally the *privacy* property of $\mathcal{G}_{\text{Yao}}$ as stated in Theorem 12.15 follows from Claim 6 and Lemma 12.14.

Theorem 12.15 (Privacy of $\mathcal{G}_{\text{Yao}}$) *If* (Gen, Enc, Dec) *is CPA-secure then the garbling scheme* $\mathcal{G}_{\text{Yao}}$ *achieves the privacy property.*[7]

Before we conclude this section, we discuss the need for the input-dependent simulation while proving Theorem 12.15.

The need for input-dependent simulation: From the proof of Theorem 12.15, it follows that we are *not* able to "directly" prove the indistinguishability between the real garbling (output of Gb_{Yao}) and the *input-independent* simulated garbling (output of $\mathcal{S}_{\text{Yao}}$). The reason is

---

[7] Since (Gen, Enc, Dec) is CPA-secure, it implies that it is CDE-secure as well.

$\mathrm{Enc}_{k_a^\alpha}(\mathrm{Enc}_{k_b^\beta}(k_g^{G_g(\alpha,\beta)}))$	$\mathrm{Enc}_{k_a^\alpha}(\mathrm{Enc}_{k_b^\beta}(k_g^{G_g(\alpha,\beta)}))$	$\mathrm{Enc}_{k_a^\alpha}(\mathrm{Enc}_{k_b^\beta}(k_g^0))$
$\mathrm{Enc}_{k_a^\alpha}(\mathrm{Enc}_{\mathbf{k_b^{1-\beta}}}(k_g^{G_g(\alpha,1-\beta)}))$	$\mathrm{Enc}_{k_a^\alpha}(\mathrm{Enc}_{\mathbf{k_b^{1-\beta}}}(k_g^{G_g(\alpha,\beta)}))$	$\mathrm{Enc}_{k_a^\alpha}(\mathrm{Enc}_{\mathbf{k_b^{1-\beta}}}(k_g^0))$
$\mathrm{Enc}_{\mathbf{k_a^{1-\alpha}}}(\mathrm{Enc}_{k_b^\beta}(k_g^{G_g(1-\alpha,\beta)}))$	$\mathrm{Enc}_{\mathbf{k_a^{1-\alpha}}}(\mathrm{Enc}_{k_b^\beta}(k_g^{G_g(\alpha,\beta)}))$	$\mathrm{Enc}_{\mathbf{k_a^{1-\alpha}}}(\mathrm{Enc}_{k_b^\beta}(k_g^0))$
$\mathrm{Enc}_{\mathbf{k_a^{1-\alpha}}}(\mathrm{Enc}_{\mathbf{k_b^{1-\beta}}}(k_g^{G_g(1-\alpha,1-\beta)}))$	$\mathrm{Enc}_{\mathbf{k_a^{1-\alpha}}}(\mathrm{Enc}_{\mathbf{k_b^{1-\beta}}}(k_g^{G_g(\alpha,\beta)}))$	$\mathrm{Enc}_{\mathbf{k_a^{1-\alpha}}}(\mathrm{Enc}_{\mathbf{k_b^{1-\beta}}}(k_g^0))$

Fig. 12.13 Garbling of g as generated by $\mathcal{G}_{\mathsf{Yao}}$, $\mathcal{S}_{\mathsf{Yao}}^{\mathsf{ID}}$ and $\mathcal{S}_{\mathsf{Yao}}$

that we *cannot* reduce the indistinguishability of these two distributions to the CDE-security of the underlying encryption scheme. To understand this, consider a circuit with a single gate g with $A(g) = w_a$ and $B(g) = w_b$. Let $\alpha, \beta \in \{0, 1\}$ be the actual bit values on w_a and w_b respectively. The double-encryptions corresponding to garbling of g as generated by $\mathcal{G}_{\mathsf{Yao}}$, $\mathcal{S}_{\mathsf{Yao}}^{\mathsf{ID}}$ and $\mathcal{S}_{\mathsf{Yao}}$ are shown in the first, second and third column of Fig. 12.13 respectively.[8] The keys k_a^α and k_b^β will be the active keys (available with the evaluator), while the keys $\mathbf{k_a^{1-\alpha}}$ and $\mathbf{k_b^{1-\beta_i}}$ (denoted in bold face) will be the inactive keys (not available with the evaluator).

The indistinguishability of the ciphertexts in the first and second column of Fig. 12.13 *can* be reduced to the CDE-security of the Enc, as done in Claim 7. This is because, the double-encryptions in both the first and second column under the active keys k_a^α and k_b^β encrypt the *same* gate-output key $k_g^{G_g(\alpha,\beta)}$. So the indistinguishability of the remaining three double-encryptions boils down to an instance of $\mathsf{Exp}^{\mathsf{double}}$, where the adversary is challenged to distinguish between an encryption of the 3-tuple $(k_g^{G_g(\alpha,1-\beta)}, k_g^{G_g(1-\alpha,\beta)}, k_g^{G_g(1-\alpha,1-\beta)})$ and $(k_g^{G_g(\alpha,\beta)}, k_g^{G_g(\alpha,\beta)}, k_g^{G_g(\alpha,\beta)})$, given that the adversary knows the keys k_a^α, k_b^β and the message triplets, while the challenger picks the keys $\mathbf{k_a^{1-\alpha}}$ and $\mathbf{k_b^{1-\beta_i}}$ (see Fig. 12.12 for a pictorial illustration).

In contrast, the indistinguishability of the ciphertexts in the first and third column of Fig. 12.13 *cannot* be reduced to the CDE-security of the Enc. This is because, with probability $\frac{1}{2}$, it may happen that $k_g^0 \neq k_g^{G_g(\alpha,\beta)}$. So the double-encryptions in the first and third column under the active keys k_a^α and k_b^β may encrypt *different* gate-output keys. A possible fix could be to define a *variant* of the experiment $\mathsf{Exp}^{\mathsf{double}}$, where instead of distinguishing between triplets of messages, the adversary is challenged to distinguish between an encryption of the 4-tuple $(k_g^{G_g(\alpha,\beta)}, k_g^{G_g(\alpha,1-\beta)}, k_g^{G_g(1-\alpha,\beta)}, k_g^{G_g(1-\alpha,1-\beta)})$ and $(k_g^0, k_g^0, k_g^0, k_g^0)$, where the first ciphertext in the challenge ciphertexts is *always* under the keys k_a^α, k_b^β, available with the attacker. However, it is easy to see that if $G_g(\alpha, \beta) \neq 0$ (for example, if g is an AND gate and $\alpha = \beta = 1$), then clearly $k_g^{G_g(\alpha,\beta)} \neq k_g^0$ and hence adversary on receiving the challenge ciphertext can *always* identify whether it sees an encryption of $(k_g^{G_g(\alpha,\beta)}, k_g^{G_g(\alpha,1-\beta)}, k_g^{G_g(1-\alpha,\beta)}, k_g^{G_g(1-\alpha,1-\beta)})$ or $(k_g^0, k_g^0, k_g^0, k_g^0)$ and win the exper-

---

[8] For the sake of consistency, we denote the simulated keys as k instead of $\widetilde{k}$.

iment.[9] Only if $G_g(\alpha, \beta) = 0$ (which can happen with probability $\frac{1}{2}$), then the indistinguishability between encryptions of $(k_g^{G_g(\alpha,\beta)}, k_g^{G_g(\alpha,1-\beta)}, k_g^{G_g(1-\alpha,\beta)}, k_q^{G_g(1-\alpha,1-\beta)})$ and $(k_g^0, k_g^0, k_g^0, k_g^0)$ can be reduced to the security of an instance of the variant of the CDE experiment.

We stress that the indistinguishability between the double-encryptions in the second and third column of Fig. 12.13 is *perfect* (i.e. they are identically distributed, as proved in Claim 6). This is because both encrypt a single (random) key under all possible combinations of active and inactive keys. So irrespective of what key is available with the evaluator, the double-decryption always result in the same gate-output key (which is either k_g^0 or $k_g^{G_g(\alpha,\beta)}$), which is "programmed" by the underlying simulator to map to the actual gate output bit $G_g(\alpha, \beta)$ (recall that both $\mathcal{S}_{\text{Yao}}$ as well as $\mathcal{S}_{\text{Yao}}^{\text{ID}}$ will be available with the circuit output).

12.3   Yao's Protocol for Secure 2PC

In this section, we discuss how the Yao's garbling scheme $\mathcal{G}_{\text{Yao}}$ can be used to design a secure 2PC protocol in the $\mathcal{F}_{\text{OT}}$-hybrid model. The idea is the following: let $z = f(x, y)$ be the publicly-known Boolean function which parties in $\mathcal{P} = \{P_1, P_2\}$ want to securely compute, with P_1 and P_2 holding private inputs x and y respectively, such that $|x| + |y| = n$. Let cir be the underlying circuit. In the protocol, one of the parties, say P_1, is designated as the *garbler* to garble cir as per Gb_{Yao}, who generates the garbled-circuit GC, the encoding-information e and the decoding-information d. The garbled-circuit GC is handed over to the party P_2, who is designated to play the role of the *evaluator*. For evaluating GC, the evaluator needs to be provided the garbled x and garbled y. The garbled x (namely the keys corresponding to the bits of x) are directly handed over to P_2 and this does not leak any information about the bits of x, as the keys are indistinguishable and their semantics are known only to P_1. To hand over the garbled y (namely the keys corresponding to the bits of y) to P_2 without letting P_1 learn the bits of y, the parties call $\mathcal{F}_{\text{OT}}$, where P_1 plays the role of S with inputs being the keys corresponding to the bits of y and P_2 plays the role of R with the bits of y being its choice-bits. The *receiver's security* of OT guarantees that P_1 does not learn any information about the bits of y, while the *sender's security* guarantees that P_2 learns only the keys corresponding to the bits of y. Once the garbled-circuit and garbled-inputs are available with P_2, it evaluates the circuit and obtains the garbled-output. To let P_2 decode the garbled-output, the decoding-information d is also handed over to P_2 before-hand. Upon decoding the garbled-output, P_2 learns z and if P_1 is also supposed to learn z, it sends z to P_1.

The correctness of the Yao's garbling scheme guarantees that P_2 obtains the correct output, while the privacy follows from the privacy of the garbling scheme and the security

---

[9] For this, the adversary has to decrypt the first ciphertext in the challenge ciphertext using the key-pair (k_a^α, k_b^β) and see if the output is $k_g^{G_g(\alpha,\beta)}$ or k_g^0.

Protocol Π_{Yao}

The public inputs are the circuit cir representing the Boolean function $f : \{0,1\}^n \to \{0,1\}^m$ and the description of the Yao's garbling scheme $\mathcal{G}_{\mathsf{Yao}}$. The private inputs for P_1 and P_2 are $x \in \{0,1\}^{n_1}$ and $y \in \{0,1\}^{n_2}$ respectively, such that $|x| = n_1$ and $|y| = n_2$ and $n_1 + n_2 = n$.

  – *Steps for P_1*: Party P_1 plays the role of the garbler and does the following:
   • Compute $(\mathsf{GC}, e, d) \leftarrow \mathsf{Gb}_{\mathsf{Yao}}(1^\lambda, \mathsf{cir})$, where $e = \{(k_i^0, k_i^1) : i = 1, \dots, n\}$ and $d = \{((k_i^0, 0), (k_i^1, 1)) : i = n + q - m + 1, \dots, n + q\}$.
   • Let $x = (x_1, \dots, x_{n_1})$. Compute $X = (k_1^{x_1}, \dots, k_{n_1}^{x_{n_1}}) = \mathsf{En}_{\mathsf{Yao}}(e, x)$.
   • Send GC, X and d to P_2.
   • Act as S and call $\mathcal{F}_{\mathsf{OT}}$ n_2 number of times, where for $i = 1, \dots, n_2$, the input for the ith call is the message-pair $(k_{n_1+i}^0, k_{n_1+i}^1)$.
   • Upon receiving z from P_2, output z.
  – *Steps for P_2*: Party P_2 plays the role of the evaluator and does the following:
   • Receive GC, X and d from P_1.
   • Let $y = (y_1, \dots, y_{n_2})$. Act as R and call $\mathcal{F}_{\mathsf{OT}}$ n_2 number of times, where for $i = 1, \dots, n_2$, the input choice-bit for the ith call is y_i. Let $k_{n_1+i}^{y_i}$ be the output received from $\mathcal{F}_{\mathsf{OT}}$. Set $Y = (k_{n_1+1}^{y_1}, \dots, k_{n_1+n_2}^{y_{n_2}})$.
   • Compute $Z = (k_{n+q-m+1}^{z_1}, \dots, k_{n+q}^{z_m}) = \mathsf{Ev}_{\mathsf{Yao}}(\mathsf{GC}, X||Y)$
   • Compute $z = (z_1, \dots, z_m) = \mathsf{De}_{\mathsf{Yao}}(Z, d)$
   • Send z to P_1 and output z.

Fig. 12.14 Yao's secure 2PC protocol

of OT. We refer the readers to [22, 116] for the formal proof. The formal steps of the protocol are presented in Fig. 12.14. For a pictorial depiction of the protocol, see Fig. 12.15.

Lemma 12.16 *Let $z = f(x, y)$ be a 2-ary deterministic Boolean function with P_1 holding the private input x and P_2 holding the private input y. Assuming that CDE-secure symmetric-key encryption schemes exist, protocol Π_{Yao} is 1-cryptographically-secure for f in the $\mathcal{F}_{\mathsf{OT}}$-hybrid model.*

The protocol requires $|y|$ number of $\mathcal{F}_{\mathsf{OT}}$ calls. Let cir denote the Boolean circuit representing f. The protocol requires communication of $4|\mathsf{cir}|$ double-encryptions. In the $\mathcal{F}_{\mathsf{OT}}$-hybrid, the protocol requires 2 rounds and in the plain model, the protocol requires 3 rounds.

The sending of the garbled circuit and the calls to $\mathcal{F}_{\mathsf{OT}}$ in parallel take 1 round. The communication of the output takes another round, making Yao's protocol an overall 2-round protocol in the $\mathcal{F}_{\mathsf{OT}}$-hybrid model. It is easy to observe that the protocol requires communicating $4|\mathsf{cir}|$ double-encryptions. Instantiating the calls to $\mathcal{F}_{\mathsf{OT}}$ with any 2-round realization of OT (for instance, the one from the previous chapter based on OWTP), we obtain Yao's protocol in the plain model, where the round complexity becomes 3.

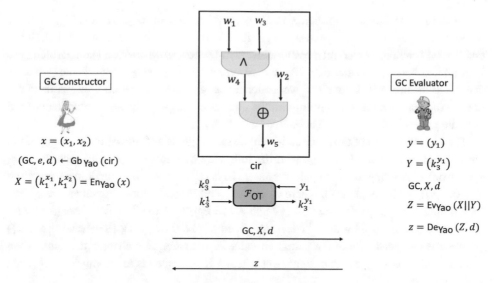

Fig. 12.15 Pictorial depiction of the Yao's secure 2PC protocol

12.4   Optimizations of Yao's Garbling Scheme and Yao's Protocol

In this section, we discuss several optimizations proposed for Yao's garbling scheme which lead to simplifications as well as prominent computation and communication efficiency improvements of the Yao's protocol. We also discuss Yao's protocol in the preprocessing model and it's adaptation in 2 rounds, which is the optimal number of rounds required for *any* passively-secure MPC irrespective of whether one aims for perfect or cryptographic security [87], as elaborated in Sect. 7.4.

12.4.1 The Point-and-Permute Technique or How to Garble from any CPA-secure Encryption Scheme

Recall that the correctness of Yao's garbling scheme depends upon the *special correctness* of the underlying symmetric-key encryption scheme, which induces a negligible (though non-zero) error in the correctness. Moreover, for the evaluation of a garbled-gate, an evaluator may need to decrypt *all* the four double-encryptions associated with the garbled-gate to determine the intended decryption, causing huge slow-down for large circuits. Ideally, to obtain the gate-output key for a garbled-gate, decryption of just *one* double-encryption should be sufficient. To achieve this goal, [126] introduces a mechanism to "signal" the evaluator about the intended decryption (with respect to the pair of gate-input keys available with the evaluator), without revealing any other information. The technique used to realize the "signalling" mechanism is referred as *point-and-permute* and is used in all modern garbling schemes.

We explain the technique in the context of Yao's garbling scheme $\mathcal{G}_{Yao}$. Interestingly, the use of point-and-permute also paves way to get rid of special correctness from the underlying encryption scheme. The correctness property will be now *error-free*, as each garbled gate is evaluated correctly. Hence *any* CPA-secure symmetric-key encryption scheme (which is also CDE-secure) will suffice and we *no* longer require any special correctness from the underlying scheme. Lastly, as promised, the evaluator does *exactly one* double-decryption per gate to obtain the intended gate-output wire key.

The high level idea of the point-and-permute technique is as follows: the garbling of the circuit is almost similar to Gb_{Yao}, with the following additional step. With each wire w_i, apart from associating the usual pair of random keys (k_i^0, k_i^1), a pair of random *permutation bits* $(\pi_i, \overline{\pi_i})$ is also associated, where $\pi_i \in \{0, 1\}$ and $\overline{\pi_i}$ is the bit-complement of π_i. We then define $K_i^0 = k_i^0 || \pi_i$ as the "0-key" and $K_i^1 = k_i^0 || \overline{\pi_i}$ as the "1-key", associated with w_i. Notice that the last bit of K_i^0 (resp. K_i^1) need not be 0 (resp. 1), as π_i (and hence $\overline{\pi_i}$) is selected independently of the actual bit value b_i over w_i. This ensures that later when evaluator obtains $K_i^{b_i}$, it cannot figure out whether it corresponds to bit value 0 or 1, even after seeing the last bit of $K_i^{b_i}$.

The garbling of gates is done by computing the double-encryptions as per Gb_{Yao}. However the double-encryptions are *not* randomly permuted, but instead permuted as per the permutation bits. More specifically, let g be a gate with $A(g) = w_a$ and $B(g) = w_b$. Then the double-encryption under the keys k_a^0 and k_b^0 will constitute the double-encryption c_{π_a, π_b}, the double-encryption under the keys k_a^0 and k_b^1 will constitute the double-encryption $c_{\pi_a, \overline{\pi_b}}$ and so on. In general the encryptions under the key-pair (k_a^0, k_b^0), (k_a^0, k_b^1), (k_a^1, k_b^0) and (k_a^1, k_b^1) will constitute the double-encryptions c_{π_a, π_b}, $c_{\pi_a, \overline{\pi_b}}$, $c_{\overline{\pi_a}, \pi_b}$ and $c_{\overline{\pi_a}, \overline{\pi_b}}$ respectively. Each double-encryption will encrypt either the gate-output wire key K_g^0 and K_g^1, to ensure that the double-encryption under the key-combination (k_a^α, k_b^β) encrypts the key $K_g^{G_g(\alpha, \beta)}$.

Notice that the keys k (*without* the permutation bits) are used for double-encryptions, while the keys K are encrypted in the double-encryptions. It is *essential* to compute the double-encryptions under the keys k instead of K, to reduce the privacy of the point-and-permute based garbling to the CDE-security of the underlying symmetric-key encryption. On the other hand, encrypting the keys K inside the double-encryptions is required to maintain the invariant that the evaluator on seeing the keys K over the gate-input wires can determine which double-decryption amongst the associated four double-decryptions is the intended one, based on the last bit of the available keys K.

The double-encryptions are *always* arranged in the order $(c_{0,0}, c_{0,1}, c_{1,0}, c_{1,1})$. Notice that it is *no* longer the case that $c_{0,0}$ corresponds to the double-encryption under the key-combination k_a^0 and k_b^0. Rather it solely depends upon the value of π_a and π_b. For example, if $\pi_a = 1$ and $\pi_b = 0$ then $c_{0,0}$ corresponds to the double-encryption under key-combination k_a^1 and k_b^0.

The evaluation of a garbled-gate g is done as follows: let $(c_{0,0}, c_{0,1}, c_{1,0}, c_{1,1})$ be the garbling of the gate; moreover let K_a^α and K_b^β be the keys available for the gate-input wires w_a and w_b respectively, where $\alpha, \beta \in \{0, 1\}$ are the actual bits over w_a and w_b (the evaluator will not know α, β). Let $K_a^\alpha = k_a^\alpha || p_a$ and $K_b^\beta = k_b^\beta || p_b$, where $p_a, p_b \in \{0, 1\}$ are called the *signal bits* for the evaluator. As discussed earlier, p_a and p_b do not reveal any information to the evaluator about the semantics of the keys k_a^α and k_b^β (namely the value of α and β). Notice that if $\alpha = 0$, then $p_a = \pi_a$, while $p_a = \overline{\pi_a}$ if $\alpha = 1$. Hence $p_a = \pi_a \oplus \alpha$ holds. Similarly, $p_b = \pi_b \oplus \beta$ holds. Now based on the signal bits p_a, p_b, the evaluator picks the double-encryption c_{p_a, p_b} and decrypts it using the key-pair (k_a^α, k_b^β). By doing so, the evaluator actually decrypts the "correct" double-encryption among $(c_{0,0}, c_{0,1}, c_{1,0}, c_{1,1})$, encrypted under the key-pair (k_a^α, k_b^β). This is because of the invariant $p_a = \pi_a \oplus \alpha$ and $p_b = \pi_b \oplus \beta$. So just based on the signal bits, the evaluator learns which is the intended decryption, without learning anything about α and β.

The formal details of the Yao's garbling scheme, coupled with the point-and-permute technique, is given in Fig. 12.16; the scheme is called $\mathcal{G}_{\text{YaoP\&P}}$.

For a pictorial illustration of the point-and-permute technique, see Fig. 12.17.

We now prove the correctness property of the scheme $\mathcal{G}_{\text{YaoP\&P}}$, for which we prove an analogue of Claim 5, stating that each garbled gate is evaluated correctly in an *error-free* fashion in the point-and-permute technique.

Claim 8 Let g be an arbitrary gate in cir, with gate function $G_g : \{0, 1\}^2 \to \{0, 1\}$, $A(g) = w_a$, $B(g) = w_b$ and gate-output wire w_g. Moreover let c_1^g, c_2^g, c_3^g and c_4^g be the double-encryptions corresponding to the garbled-table of g, computed as per $\text{Gb}_{\text{YaoP\&P}}$. Then for every $\alpha, \beta \in \{0, 1\}$, given keys K_a^α, K_b^β and the garbled-table of g, the evaluation algorithm $\text{Ev}_{\text{YaoP\&P}}$ will always associate the key K_g^γ with w_g where $K_g^\gamma = K_g^{G_g(\alpha, \beta)}$.

Proof Let $(K_a^0, K_a^1) = (k_a^0 || \pi_a, k_a^1 || \overline{\pi_a})$, $(K_b^0, K_b^1) = (k_b^0 || \pi_b, k_b^1 || \overline{\pi_b})$ and $(K_g^0, K_g^1) = (k_g^0 || \pi_g, k_g^1 || \overline{\pi_g})$ be the key-pairs associated with w_a, w_b and w_g respectively by $\text{Gb}_{\text{YaoP\&P}}$. Moreover, let $K_a^\alpha = k_a^\alpha || p_a$ and $K_b^\beta = k_b^\beta || p_b$ be the keys available for w_a and w_b respectively in the evaluation algorithm $\text{Ev}_{\text{YaoP\&P}}$, where $\alpha, \beta \in \{0, 1\}$.

We first claim that $p_a = \pi_a \oplus \alpha$ and $p_b = \pi_b \oplus \beta$ holds. For this, consider the wire w_a. If $\alpha = 0$, then $K_a^\alpha = K_a^0$, which implies that $p_a = \pi_a$. On the other hand, if $\alpha = 1$, then $K_a^\alpha = K_a^1$, implying that $p_a = \overline{\pi_a}$. Hence $p_a = \pi_a \oplus \alpha$ holds. Using a similar argument, it follows that $p_b = \pi_b \oplus \beta$ holds.

Let $(c_1^g, c_2^g, c_3^g, c_4^g)$ be the garbling of g as produced by $\text{Gb}_{\text{YaoP\&P}}$, where c_1^g, c_2^g, c_3^g and c_4^g denotes the double-encryptions $c_{0,0}, c_{0,1}, c_{1,0}$ and $c_{1,1}$ in order. Now in the evaluation algorithm, out of these four double-encryptions, the double-encryption c_{p_a, p_b} is decrypted using the key-pair (k_a^α, k_b^β). This is because the double-encryption c_{p_a, p_b} corresponds to c_ℓ^g in $(c_1^g, c_2^g, c_3^g, c_4^g)$ where $\ell = 2p_a + p_b + 1$; moreover in $\text{Ev}_{\text{YaoP\&P}}$, the double-encryption c_ℓ^g is decrypted by the key-pair (k_a^α, k_b^β). Now to prove the claim, we need to show that the double-encryption c_{p_a, p_b} is indeed produced by $\text{Gb}_{\text{YaoP\&P}}$ using the key-pair (k_a^α, k_b^β); that is $c_{p_a, p_b} = \text{Enc}_{k_a^\alpha}(\text{Enc}_{k_b^\beta}(K_g^{G_g(\alpha, \beta)}))$ holds. We prove this for all values of α and β and use the fact that $c_{p_a, p_b} = c_{\pi_a \oplus \alpha, \pi_b \oplus \beta}$ holds. In Fig. 12.18, we consider all possible values of α

Scheme $\mathcal{G}_{\mathsf{YaoP\&P}}$

$$\mathcal{G}_{\mathsf{YaoP\&P}} = (\mathsf{Gb}_{\mathsf{YaoP\&P}}, \mathsf{En}_{\mathsf{YaoP\&P}}, \mathsf{Ev}_{\mathsf{YaoP\&P}}, \mathsf{De}_{\mathsf{YaoP\&P}})$$

Let $(\mathsf{Gen}, \mathsf{Enc}, \mathsf{Dec})$ be a CPA-secure symmetric-key encryption scheme. Let $\mathsf{cir} = (n, m, q, A, B, G)$ be the given Boolean circuit, with wires $w_1, \ldots, w_{n+q}$, input wires $w_1, \ldots, w_n$, gate-output wires $w_{n+1}, \ldots, w_{n+q}$ and circuit-output wires $w_{n+q-m+1}, \ldots, w_{n+q}$. The set $\mathsf{Gates} = \{n+1, \ldots, n+q\}$ denotes the gates in the circuit, with $G_g : \{0,1\}^2 \to \{0,1\}$ denoting the gate function for each gate $g \in \mathsf{Gates}$. The sets A and B identify the left-input wire and right-input wire respectively for each gate, with $A(g)$ and $B(g)$ denoting the left-input and right-input wires of a gate g respectively.

$$\mathsf{Gb}_{\mathsf{YaoP\&P}}\left(1^\lambda, \mathsf{cir}\right)$$

- For $i = 1, \ldots, n+q$, corresponding to wire w_i, select two random keys $k_i^0 \leftarrow \mathsf{Gen}(1^\lambda), k_i^1 \leftarrow \mathsf{Gen}(1^\lambda)$. In addition, randomly select a permutation bit $\pi_i \in \{0, 1\}$.
- For $i = 1, \ldots, n+q$, define $K_i^0 \stackrel{def}{=} k_i^0 \| \pi_i$ and $K_i^1 \stackrel{def}{=} k_i^1 \| \overline{\pi_i}$, where $\overline{\pi_i} = 1 - \pi_i$. Here K_i^0 and K_i^1 denote the key, corresponding to bit value $b_i = 0$ and $b_i = 1$ respectively over wire w_i.
- For every gate $g \in \mathsf{Gates}$, with gate function G_g, $A(g) = w_a$ and $B(g) = w_b$, do the following:
  - Compute the double-encryptions:

$$c_{\pi_a, \pi_b} \leftarrow \mathsf{Enc}_{k_a^0}(\mathsf{Enc}_{k_b^0}(K_g^{G_g(0,0)})),$$

$$c_{\pi_a, \overline{\pi_b}} \leftarrow \mathsf{Enc}_{k_a^0}(\mathsf{Enc}_{k_b^1}(K_g^{G_g(0,1)})),$$

$$c_{\overline{\pi_a}, \pi_b} \leftarrow \mathsf{Enc}_{k_a^1}(\mathsf{Enc}_{k_b^0}(K_g^{G_g(1,0)})),$$

$$c_{\overline{\pi_a}, \overline{\pi_b}} \leftarrow \mathsf{Enc}_{k_a^1}(\mathsf{Enc}_{k_b^1}(K_g^{G_g(1,1)})).$$

  - Let c_1^g, c_2^g, c_3^g and c_4^g denote the ciphertexts in the order $(c_{0,0}, c_{0,1}, c_{1,0}, c_{1,1})$.
- Set $\mathsf{GC} = \{(c_1^g, c_2^g, c_3^g, c_4^g) : g \in \mathsf{Gates}\}$, $e = \{(K_i^0, K_i^1) : i = 1, \ldots, n\}$ and $d = \{((K_i^0, 0), (K_i^1, 1)) : i = n+q-m+1, \ldots, n+q\}$. Output GC, e and d.

$$\mathsf{En}_{\mathsf{YaoP\&P}}(e, x)$$

Let $e = \{(K_i^0, K_i^1) : i = 1, \ldots, n\}$ and $x = (x_1, \ldots, x_n)$. Output $X = (K_1^{x_1}, \ldots, K_n^{x_n})$.

$$\mathsf{Ev}_{\mathsf{YaoP\&P}}(\mathsf{GC}, X)$$

Let $\mathsf{GC} = \{(c_1^g, c_2^g, c_3^g, c_4^g) : g \in \mathsf{Gates}\}$ and $X = (K_1^{x_1}, \ldots, K_n^{x_n})$.
- For $i = 1, \ldots, n$, associate the key $K_i^{x_i}$ with input wire w_i.
- For every gate $g \in \mathsf{Gates}$, with gate function G_g, $A(g) = w_a$ and $B(g) = w_b$, do the following:
  - Let K_a^α and K_b^β be the keys available, corresponding to the wires w_a and w_b respectively. Parse K_a^α as $k_a^\alpha \| p_a$ and K_b^β as $k_b^\beta \| p_b$.
  - Let $\ell = 2p_a + p_b + 1$. Compute $K_g^\gamma = \mathsf{Dec}_{k_a^\alpha}(\mathsf{Dec}_{k_b^\beta}(c_\ell^g))$ and associate the key K_g^γ with wire w_g.
- Output $Y = (K_{n+q-m+1}^{y_1}, \ldots, K_{n+q}^{y_m})$, namely the keys obtained for the output wires.

$$\mathsf{De}_{\mathsf{YaoP\&P}}(Y, d)$$

Let $Y = (K_{n+q-m+1}^{y_1}, \ldots, K_{n+q}^{y_m})$ and $d = \{((K_i^0, 0), (K_i^1, 1)) : i = n+q-m+1, \ldots, n+q\}$.
- For $i = 1, \ldots, m$, do the following:
  - If $K_{n+q-(m-i)}^{y_i} = K_{n+q-(m-i)}^0$ then set $y_i = 0$.
  - Else if $K_{n+q-(m-i)}^{y_i} = K_{n+q-(m-i)}^1$ then set $y_i = 1$.
- Output $y = (y_1, \ldots, y_m)$.

Fig. 12.16 The Yao's garbling scheme along with the point-and-permute technique

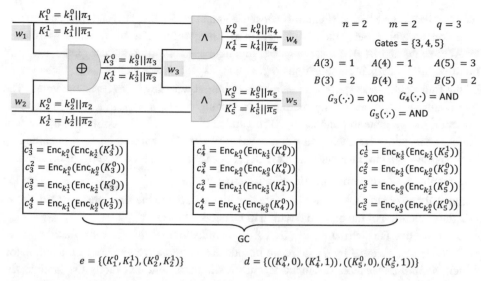

Fig. 12.17 Pictorial depiction of the Yao's garbling scheme with point-and-permute technique. The garbled-gates are computed for the case when $\pi_1 = 0$, $\pi_2 = 1$, $\pi_3 = 1$, $\pi_4 = 0$ and $\pi_5 = 0$

α	β	Position of $\mathrm{Enc}_{k_a^\alpha}(\mathrm{Enc}_{k_b^\beta}(K_g^{G_g(\alpha,\beta)}))$ among $(c_{0,0}, c_{0,1}, c_{1,0}, c_{1,1})$ during $\mathrm{Gb}_{\mathrm{YaoP\&P}}$	Double-encryption $c_{p_a,p_b} = c_{\pi_a \oplus \alpha, \pi_b \oplus \beta}$ among $(c_{0,0}, c_{0,1}, c_{1,0}, c_{1,1})$ decrypted by $\mathrm{Ev}_{\mathrm{YaoP\&P}}$
0	0	c_{π_a, π_b}	$c_{p_a, p_b} = c_{\pi_a, \pi_b}$
0	1	$c_{\pi_a, \overline{\pi_b}}$	$c_{p_a, p_b} = c_{\pi_a, \overline{\pi_b}}$
1	0	$c_{\overline{\pi_a}, \pi_b}$	$c_{p_a, p_b} = c_{\overline{\pi_a}, \pi_b}$
1	1	$c_{\overline{\pi_a}, \overline{\pi_b}}$	$c_{p_a, p_b} = c_{\overline{\pi_a}, \overline{\pi_b}}$

Fig. 12.18 The double-encryption c_{p_a,p_b} is always the intended double-decryption

and β and for each combination of α, β, we show that the double-encryption c_{p_a,p_b} indeed corresponds to the double-encryption under the key-pair (k_a^α, k_b^β). □

The correctness property of $\mathcal{G}_{\mathrm{YaoP\&P}}$ now follows using exactly the same argument as in Theorem 12.13, except that we now use Claim 8 instead of Claim 5. To avoid repetition, we do not give the formal proof.

The privacy of $\mathcal{G}_{\mathrm{YaoP\&P}}$ follows using exactly the same arguments as used for proving the privacy for $\mathcal{G}_{\mathrm{Yao}}$. Again, to avoid repetition, we do not give the complete formal details, but discuss only the high level idea of the proof.

Privacy of $\mathcal{G}_{\mathrm{YaoP\&P}}$: The *input-independent* simulator for proving the privacy works as follows: for every wire w_i, it associates a random key-pair $(\widetilde{K}_i^0, \widetilde{K}_i^1)$, where $\widetilde{K}_i^0 = \widetilde{k}_i^0 || \pi_i$ and

$\widetilde{K}_i^1 = \widetilde{k}_i^1 || \overline{\pi_i}$; here $\widetilde{k}_i^0, \widetilde{k}_i^1$ are randomly chosen keys and $\pi_i \in \{0, 1\}$ is a randomly chosen permutation bit, with $\overline{\pi_i}$ being the complement of π_i. The garbling of a gate g is done as follows: let $A(g) = w_a$ and $B(g) = w_b$. For gate g, four double-encryptions are computed, under all possible input key-pair combinations $(\widetilde{k}_a^0, \widetilde{k}_b^0)$, $(\widetilde{k}_a^0, \widetilde{k}_b^1)$, $(\widetilde{k}_a^1, \widetilde{k}_b^0)$ and $(\widetilde{k}_a^1, \widetilde{k}_b^1)$. However, in all the four double-encryptions, a *common* gate-output wire key, say $\widetilde{K}_g^0$, is encrypted. The four double-encryptions are then permuted and arranged as $\widetilde{c_{0,0}}, \widetilde{c_{0,1}}, \widetilde{c_{1,0}}$ and $\widetilde{c_{1,1}}$, depending upon the permutation bits π_a, π_b. The garbled circuit $\widetilde{\mathsf{GC}}$ is the collection of the four double-encryptions for each gate g computed as above. The garbled input $\widetilde{X}$ is computed by assigning the circuit-input wire keys $\widetilde{K}_1^0, \ldots, \widetilde{K}_n^0$ as $\widetilde{X}$. The decoding information $\widetilde{d}$ is computed by "programming" the circuit-output wire keys $\widetilde{K_{w_{n+q-m+1}}^0}, \ldots, \widetilde{K_{w_{n+q}}^0}$ to the individual bits of $\mathrm{cir}(x)$. It is easy to verify that given $\widetilde{X}, \widetilde{d}$ and the simulated garbled circuit $\widetilde{\mathsf{GC}}$, the evaluation of the garbled circuit will be decoded as $\mathrm{cir}(x)$.

To prove that the distribution of $(\widetilde{GC}, \widetilde{X}, \widetilde{d})$ is indistinguishable from the distribution of (GC, X, d) as generated by $\mathcal{G}_{\mathsf{YaoP\&P}}$, we introduce an alternative version of the simulator, which is *input-dependent*. The input-dependent simulator will be exactly the same as the input-independent simulator, except that in each double-encryption associated with a gate, the *active key* associated with that gate-output wire will be encrypted. Now using exactly the same argument as used for $\mathcal{G}_{\mathsf{Yao}}$, we can first prove that the distribution of (GC, X, d) is indistinguishable from that of $(\widetilde{GC}, \widetilde{X}, \widetilde{d})$ produced by the input-dependent simulator. This is done by a hybrid argument, where the indistinguishability of every two consecutive hybrids is reduced to the CDE-security of the underlying symmetric-key encryption. Next we can show that the distribution of $(\widetilde{GC}, \widetilde{X}, \widetilde{d})$ produced by the input-dependent and input-independent simulator are exactly the same.

12.4.2 The Free-XOR Optimization

In the literature, various optimizations for Yao's garbling scheme has been proposed, with the focus on reducing the size of garbled-gates as well as reducing the computation overhead of computing the garbled-gates. Here the *size* of a garbled-gate refers to the number of double-encryptions, associated with the garbled-gate. In this section, we focus on one such popular optimization called as the *free-XOR* technique [107], which allows the parties to evaluate XOR gates in the circuit "freely". That is, *no* encryption and decryption operation needs to be performed for evaluating the XOR gates.

The main idea here is to choose all wire-keys of the form $(A, A \oplus \Delta)$, where Δ is a random secret (known only to the garbler) and *common* to all the wires, where Δ is also called as the *global offset*. In more detail, the keys for the wires are selected as follows:

– The key k_i^0 corresponding to the bit 0 for all the wires w_i *except* the output-wires of XOR gates are selected *randomly*.

- For every XOR gate g with input wires w_a, w_b and output wire w_g, the key k_g^0 is set to be $k_a^0 \oplus k_b^0$.
- The key k_i^1 corresponding to the bit 1 for every wire w_i (including the output-wire of XOR gates) is set to be $k_i^0 \oplus \Delta$.

If the keys are selected as above then later at the time of evaluating the garbled circuit, the XOR gate can be evaluated by simply taking the XOR of the keys available with the gate-input wires. Namely let k_a^α and k_b^β be the keys corresponding to the gate-input wires of an XOR gate g, where $\alpha, \beta \in \{0, 1\}$ are the bit values over the wires w_a and w_b respectively. Moreover, let $\gamma = \alpha \oplus \beta$. Then it is easy to see that XORing the keys k_a^α and k_b^β will result in the key k_g^γ, corresponding to the wire w_g. More specifically, the following relations hold:

$$k_a^\alpha = k_a^0 \oplus \alpha \cdot \Delta \quad \text{and} \quad k_b^\beta = k_b^0 \oplus \beta \cdot \Delta,$$

where $\alpha \cdot \Delta = 0^{|\Delta|}$ if $\alpha = 0$ and Δ otherwise. This further implies that the following holds:

$$
\begin{aligned}
k_a^\alpha \oplus k_b^\beta &= k_a^0 \oplus \alpha \cdot \Delta \oplus k_b^0 \oplus \beta \cdot \Delta \\
&= (k_a^0 \oplus k_b^0) \oplus (\alpha \oplus \beta) \cdot \Delta \\
&= k_g^0 \oplus \gamma \cdot \Delta \\
&= k_g^\gamma.
\end{aligned}
$$

Hence, garbling and evaluating XOR gates in the circuit will be completely "free". Interestingly, the free-XOR technique is compatible with the point-and-permute technique. For this, the last bit of the pair of keys associated with each wire needs to be compliment of each other. This is ensured by selecting the offset Δ randomly with its last bit being 1. The formal description of the free-XOR technique is given in Fig. 12.19. While presenting the scheme, we assume that keys generated by the key-generation algorithm Gen are of length λ bits.

On the security of the free-XOR technique: We note that unlike the Yao's garbling scheme, the privacy proof of the free-XOR technique *cannot* be reduced to the CDE security of the underlying symmetric-key encryption scheme. This is because the key-pairs over the wires are *no* longer independent, as they are related by the (unknown) global offset Δ. In [107], the authors proposed the following instantiation of the Enc and Dec function to be used in the scheme $\mathcal{G}_{\mathsf{FreeXOR}}$, assuming that the algorithm Gen outputs uniformly random keys of length λ bits: let g be a gate (different from an XOR gate) with input-wires $A(g) = w_a$, $B(g) = w_b$, gate function G_g and output-wire w_g. Moreover, let $(K_a^0 = k_a^0 || \pi_a, K_a^1 = k_a^1 || \bar{\pi}_a)$ and $(K_b^0 = k_b^0 || \pi_b, K_b^1 = k_b^1 || \bar{\pi}_b)$ be the key-pairs corresponding to w_a and w_b respectively. Furthermore, let H be a cryptographic hash function with appropriate domain and co-domain. Then to garble the gate g, the ciphertexts are computed as follows:

Scheme $\mathcal{G}_{\text{FreeXOR}} = (\text{Gb}_{\text{FreeXOR}}, \text{En}_{\text{FreeXOR}}, \text{Ev}_{\text{FreeXOR}}, \text{De}_{\text{FreeXOR}})$

$$\underline{\text{Gb}_{\text{FreeXOR}}\left(1^\lambda, \text{cir}\right)}$$

- Select a uniformly random global offset $\Delta \in \{0,1\}^{\lambda+1}$ with the last bit being 1.
- For $i = 1, \ldots, n$, corresponding to input wire w_i, select a random key $k_i^0 \leftarrow \text{Gen}(1^\lambda)$ and a random permutation bit $\pi_i \in \{0,1\}$. Set $K_i^0 = k_i^0 || \pi_i$ and $K_i^1 = K_i^0 \oplus \Delta$.[a] Here K_i^0 and K_i^1 denote the keys, corresponding to bit value $b_i = 0$ and $b_i = 1$ respectively over wire w_i.
- For every gate $g \in$ Gates, with gate function G_g, left-input wire $A(g) = w_a$, right-input wire $B(g) = w_b$ and output-wire w_g, do the following:
  - If g is an XOR gate, then do the following:
    - Let K_a^0 and K_b^0 be the keys, corresponding to the bit 0 over w_a and w_b respectively.
    - Set $K_g^0 = K_a^0 \oplus K_b^0$.
    - Set $K_g^1 = K_a^0 \oplus \Delta$.
  - If g is different from an XOR gate, then do the following:
    - Let $(K_a^0 = k_a^0 || \pi_a, K_a^1 = k_a^1 || \overline{\pi_a})$ and $(K_b^0 = k_b^0 || \pi_b, K_b^1 = k_b^1 || \overline{\pi_b})$ be the key-pairs corresponding to w_a and w_b respectively.
    - Corresponding to the wire w_g, select a random key $k_g^0 \leftarrow \text{Gen}(1^\lambda)$ and a random permutation bit $\pi_g \in \{0,1\}$. Set $K_g^0 = k_g^0 || \pi_g$.
    - Set $K_g^1 = K_g^0 \oplus \Delta$.
    - Compute the double-encryptions:

$$c_{\pi_a, \pi_b} \leftarrow \text{Enc}_{k_a^0}(\text{Enc}_{k_b^0}(K_g^{G_g(0,0)})),$$

$$c_{\pi_a, \overline{\pi_b}} \leftarrow \text{Enc}_{k_a^0}(\text{Enc}_{k_b^1}(K_g^{G_g(0,1)})),$$

$$c_{\overline{\pi_a}, \pi_b} \leftarrow \text{Enc}_{k_a^1}(\text{Enc}_{k_b^0}(K_g^{G_g(1,0)})),$$

$$c_{\overline{\pi_a}, \overline{\pi_b}} \leftarrow \text{Enc}_{k_a^1}(\text{Enc}_{k_b^1}(K_g^{G_g(1,1)})).$$

    - Let $c_1^g, c_2^g, c_3^g, c_4^g$ denote the ciphertexts in the order $(c_{0,0}, c_{0,1}, c_{1,0}, c_{1,1})$.
- Set $\text{GC} = \{(c_1^g, c_2^g, c_3^g, c_4^g) : g \in \text{Gates and } g \text{ is not an XOR gate}\}$, $e = \{(K_i^0, K_i^1) : i = 1, \ldots, n\}$ and $d = \{((K_i^0, 0), (K_i^1, 1)) : i = n + q - m + 1, \ldots, n + q\}$. Output GC, e and d.

$$\underline{\text{En}_{\text{FreeXOR}}\left(e, x\right)}$$

Let $e = \{(K_i^0, K_i^1) : i = 1, \ldots, n\}$ and $x = (x_1, \ldots, x_n)$. Output $X = (K_1^{x_1}, \ldots, K_n^{x_n})$.

$$\underline{\text{Ev}_{\text{FreeXOR}}\left(\text{GC}, X\right)}$$

Let $\text{GC} = \{(c_1^g, c_2^g, c_3^g, c_4^g) : g \in \text{Gates and } g \text{ is not an XOR gate}\}$ and $X = (K_1^{x_1}, \ldots, K_n^{x_n})$.
- For $i = 1, \ldots, n$, associate the key $K_i^{x_i}$ with input-wire w_i.
- For every gate $g \in$ Gates, do the following:
  - Let G_g be the gate function and let $A(g) = w_a, B(g) = w_b$. Moreover, let $K_a^\alpha = k_a^\alpha || p_a$ and $K_b^\beta = k_a^\beta || p_b$ be the keys available, corresponding to the wires w_a and w_b.
  - If g is an XOR gate, then associate the key $K_g^\gamma = K_a^\alpha \oplus K_b^\beta$ with the wire w_g.
  - If g is a gate different from an XOR gate, then do the following:

    1. Let $\ell = 2p_a + p_b + 1$.
    2. Compute $K_g^\gamma = \text{Dec}_{k_a^\alpha}(\text{Dec}_{k_b^\beta}(c_\ell^g))$ and associate the key K_g^γ with wire w_g.

- Output $Y = (K_{n+q-m+1}^{y_1}, \ldots, K_{n+q}^{y_m})$, namely the keys obtained for the output wires.

$$\underline{\text{De}_{\text{FreeXOR}}\left(Y, d\right)}$$

Let $Y = (K_{n+q-m+1}^{y_1}, \ldots, K_{n+q}^{y_m})$ and $d = \{((K_i^0, 0), (K_i^1, 1)) : i = n + q - m + 1, \ldots, n + q\}$.
- For $i = 1, \ldots, m$, do the following:
  - If $K_{n+q-(m-i)}^{y_i} = K_{n+q-(m-i)}^0$ then set $y_i = 0$.
  - Else if $K_{n+q-(m-i)}^{y_i} = K_{n+q-(m-i)}^1$ then set $y_i = 1$.
- Output $y = (y_1, \ldots, y_m)$.

[a] Since the last bit of Δ is 1, setting K_i^1 like this ensures that the permutation bit in K_i^1 is compliment of π_i.

Fig. 12.19 The Yao's garbling scheme along with the free-XOR technique, coupled with point-and-permute

$$c_{\pi_a, \pi_b} \stackrel{def}{=} H(k_a^0 \| k_b^0 \| g) \oplus K_g^{G_g(0,0)},$$

$$c_{\pi_a, \overline{\pi_b}} \stackrel{def}{=} H(k_a^0 \| k_b^1 \| g) \oplus K_g^{G_g(0,1)},$$

$$c_{\overline{\pi_a}, \pi_b} \stackrel{def}{=} H(k_a^1 \| k_b^0 \| g) \oplus K_g^{G_g(1,0)},$$

$$c_{\overline{\pi_a}, \overline{\pi_b}} \stackrel{def}{=} H(k_a^1 \| k_b^1 \| g) \oplus K_g^{G_g(1,1)}.$$

In the above computations, it is assumed that each gate g has a unique λ bit identifier and for simplicity, we let the identifier to be g itself. Let $c_1^g, c_2^g, c_3^g, c_4^g$ denote the ciphertexts in the order $(c_{0,0}, c_{0,1}, c_{1,0}, c_{1,1})$. Later, given the keys $K_a^\alpha = k_a^\alpha \| p_a$ and $K_b^\beta = k_a^\beta \| p_b$ corresponding to w_a and w_b respectively and the ciphertexts $c_1^g, c_2^g, c_3^g, c_4^g$, the garbled gate g is evaluated as follows: let $\ell = 2p_a + p_b + 1$. Then the key K_g^γ is associated with the wire w_g, which is computed as follows:

$$K_g^\gamma = H(k_a^\alpha \| k_b^\beta \| g) \oplus c_\ell^g$$

Hence, H is used as a keyed pseudorandom one-time pad generator, which generates pseudorandom pads to mask the message to be encrypted. In [107], it is shown that the privacy of the free-XOR technique can be proved in the *random oracle model* (ROM) [102]. Informally, in the ROM, the underlying hash function is modelled as a random function, producing independent random outputs, even if the inputs are related. In practice, H is instantiated with standard cryptographic hash functions, like SHA. ROM being a too strong assumption, there are works that study the possibility of realizing the garbled XOR gate for free, from somewhat standard assumptions [4, 51, 86, 106].

12.4.3 Other Optimizations of Yao's Garbling Scheme

Apart from the free-XOR optimization, there are other optimizations available for the Yao's garbling scheme, in regards to the size of the garbled gates and circuit. Specifically, for non-XOR gates, there are efforts to reduce the number of double-encryptions beyond four. The earliest effort in this line is the *garbled row-deduction* (GRR) optimization of [126] that shows 3 double-encryptions, instead of 4 are sufficient for each garbled-gate. Moreover, the optimization is compatible with both point-and-permute as well as free-XOR techniques. Hence in the resultant garbling scheme, the size of a garbled-XOR gate is *zero* and the size of a garbled non-XOR gate is 3. The work of [131] further brings down the size of each gate to 2 from 4. However, this new GRR optimization is *incompatible* with the free-XOR technique. Hence both XOR, as well as non-XOR gates need to be garbled as per this technique. This loss is regained though a new method called half gates [139] that reduces the size of a garbled-AND gate from 4 to 2, while maintaining compatibility with free XOR (in fact, half gates only work with free XOR). This paper further shows that two encryptions or alternatively 2λ bits for a garbled-AND gate is optimal in a model that captured all known garbling techniques at that time. However, in a recent work [134], this lower bound is bypassed and further improvements are reported for the size of a garbled-AND gate, while being compatible with free-XOR technique.

The full details about the above and other optimizations are out of scope of the current lecture series.

12.4.4 Yao's Protocol in 2 Rounds

From Lemma 12.16, the Yao's protocol requires total 3 rounds in the plain model, where the last round is required by the evaluator to send the function output to the garbler. This last round can be squashed at the expense of running *two* parallel instances of Yao's protocol, where in the first instance P_1 and P_2 plays the role of garbler and evaluator respectively, while in the second instance the roles are reversed. Through the first instance, P_2 will obtain the function output, while the second instance will enable P_1 to obtain the output. Thus, the respective evaluator need not have to send the function output to the corresponding garbler. The resultant protocol will now require only 2 rounds. Recall that 2 rounds are *optimal* for any MPC [87]. The optimal round complexity is a desirable property. A natural question is whether one can obtain this property in the n-party setting, extending the Yao's protocol for n parties. The work of [18] makes the first step towards this by presenting a *constant* round n-party protocol for *any* $n \geq 2$, but the constant is far bigger than 2. After almost three decades, 2-round MPC for any $n \geq 2$, solely relying on OT (and garbled circuits) is shown in [29, 72].

12.4.5 Yao's Protocol in the Pe-processing Model

In this section, we briefly discuss how one can execute the Yao's protocol in the pre-processing model. Recall that in the Yao's protocol, P_1 and P_2 have to engage in $|y|$ number of OT calls to enable P_2 obviously obtain the garbled y. These OTs can be pre-processed in a pre-processing phase on random inputs via instances of *random* OT (ROT) [17] protocol. Informally, an ROT protocol is same as an OT protocol where the inputs of S and R are randomly chosen from the respective domains. The requirements of ROT are formalized through the functionality $\mathcal{F}_{\mathsf{ROT}}$, where:

$$\mathcal{F}_{\mathsf{ROT}} (\bot, \bot) = ((x_0, x_1), (c, x_c)),$$

where x_0, x_1 is a random pair of messages from $\{0, 1\}^\lambda$ and c is a random choice bit. S and R have no input for $\mathcal{F}_{\mathsf{ROT}}$, while $\mathcal{F}_{\mathsf{ROT}}$ outputs (x_0, x_1) and (c, x_c) for S and R respectively.

One can easily show the "equivalence" between $\mathcal{F}_{\mathsf{ROT}}$ and $\mathcal{F}_{\mathsf{OT}}$; i.e. $\mathcal{F}_{\mathsf{ROT}}$ can be securely-computed in the $\mathcal{F}_{\mathsf{OT}}$-hybrid model and vice-versa. For instance, $\mathcal{F}_{\mathsf{ROT}}$ in the $\mathcal{F}_{\mathsf{OT}}$-hybrid model can be computed as follows: S picks a random pair of messages $x_0, x_1 \in \{0, 1\}^\lambda$, while R picks a random bit c. S and R then calls $\mathcal{F}_{\mathsf{OT}}$ with inputs (x_0, x_1) and c respectively. To compute $\mathcal{F}_{\mathsf{OT}}$ in the $\mathcal{F}_{\mathsf{ROT}}$-hybrid model, one can proceed as follows: let $m_0, m_1 \in \{0, 1\}^\lambda$ and $b \in \{0, 1\}$ be the inputs of S and R respectively for $\mathcal{F}_{\mathsf{OT}}$. S and R calls $\mathcal{F}_{\mathsf{ROT}}$ and receives the outputs (x_0, x_1) and (c, x_c) respectively. R then sends an OTP-encryption $d = b \oplus c$ of b to S, who then sends the OTP-encryptions y_0 and y_1 of m_0 and m_1 respectively, where $y_0 = m_0 \oplus x_d$ and $y_1 = m_1 \oplus x_{d \oplus 1}$. R upon receiving (y_0, y_1) outputs $m_b = y_b \oplus x_c$. For a pictorial depiction of the protocol, see Fig. 12.20.

The correctness of the above protocol follows from the fact that $y_b = m_b \oplus x_{d \oplus b}$, since $y_i = m_i \oplus x_{d \oplus i}$ holds for $i \in \{0, 1\}$. And since $d = b \oplus c$, it follows that $y_b = m_b \oplus x_c$. Consequently, $y_b \oplus m_c$ will reveal m_b to R. On the other hand, R does not learn anything about $m_{b \oplus 1}$ from $y_{b \oplus 1}$, since it is encrypted with the pad $x_{c \oplus 1}$, which will be not known to R. Namely, $y_{b \oplus 1} = m_{b \oplus 1} \oplus x_{d \oplus b \oplus 1}$ and hence $y_{b \oplus 1} = m_{b \oplus 1} \oplus x_{c \oplus 1}$. Since $x_{c \oplus 1}$ will be random from the point of view of R, the value $y_{b \oplus 1}$ will be uniformly distributed, independent of $x_{b \oplus 1}$. Notice that the above protocol is *perfectly-secure* in the $\mathcal{F}_{\mathsf{ROT}}$-hybrid.

If the Yao's protocol is executed in a pre-processing model, then P_1 and P_2 plays the role of S and R respectively and invoke the above protocol $|y|$ number of times to enable P_2 obliviously receive the garbled Y. Since the calls to $\mathcal{F}_{\mathsf{ROT}}$ are *independent* of the actual inputs of the parties (namely the bits of y and the keys associated with the bits of y), they can be made during the pre-processing phase. Later, during the circuit-evaluation phase, the parties exchange the corresponding OTP-encryptions, upon having the bits of y and the keys associated with the bits of y (see Fig. 12.20 to see the division of tasks between the pre-

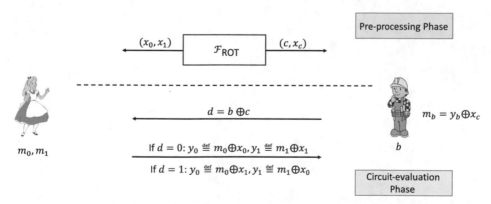

Fig. 12.20 A perfectly-secure protocol for computing $\mathcal{F}_{\mathsf{OT}}$ in the $\mathcal{F}_{\mathsf{ROT}}$-hybrid model. In the context of Yao's protocol, the call to $\mathcal{F}_{\mathsf{ROT}}$ can be made in the pre-processing phase, independent of the inputs (m_0, m_1) and b of the parties. During the circuit-evaluation phase, the parties exchange OTP-encryptions of actual choice-bit b and the actual messages (m_0, m_1)

processing and circuit-evaluation phase). To securely compute the instances of $\mathcal{F}_{ROT}$ in the pre-processing phase (via OT protocols), the parties can use state-of-the-art OT extension protocols.

Finally, if we assume the function f to be known in the pre-processing phase, then we can pre-pone the generation and sending of the garbled circuit to the pre-processing phase. In this case, the circuit-evaluation phase will constitute of just sending the encodings of x and y.

12.5   Tolerating Malicious Adversaries

We conclude this chapter by briefly discussing the challenges for the Yao's protocol in the face of a *malicious* corruption. If the *garbler* is corrupt, then it *may not* construct the garbled-circuit correctly or may participate with incorrect keys in the OT instances while transferring the encoded input to the evaluator. This will lead to an incorrect evaluation by the evaluator. Hence, consistency checks have to be incorporated to check whether a potentially corrupt garbler has prepared the correct garbled circuit and participated with correct inputs in the OT instances. There are various subtleties involved while enforcing these consistency checks and discussing the details is out of scope of the current lecture series. We refer the readers to [88, 113, 115, 117, 118, 136] and their references for complete details.

Cryptographically-Secure 3PC

13

In this chapter, we revisit the *perfectly-secure* 3PC protocols discussed in Chap. 9 and show that one can further improve the communication complexity of these protocols, if instead of perfect security, one settles for *cryptographic security*. Specifically, the pre-processing phase of the protocols are significantly simplified. The setting considered in this chapter is that of 3 mutually-distrusting parties $\mathcal{P} = \{P_1, P_2, P_3\}$, tolerating a *computationally-bounded* adversary who can corrupt at most 1 out of the 3 parties; i.e. $n = 3$ and $t = 1$.

We stress that *none* of the protocols discussed in this chapter offer optimal resilience. This is because in the regime of cryptographic security, one can tolerate a PPT adversary corrupting up to 2 out of the 3 parties. For instance, the parties can run the GMW MPC protocol, which can provide security even if up to 2 parties collude together. The advantage of the cryptographically-secure 3PC protocols is its efficiency (both computational and communication), compared to the GMW protocol being executed between the 3 parties. Specifically, the 3PC protocols *do not* deploy any OT or public-key-based primitives. They deploy only *symmetric-key* cryptographic primitives. This leads to efficiency gains of several orders of magnitude in practice. Hence, we get a tradeoff between optimal resilience and efficiency gain.

13.1 Cryptographically-Secure 3PC Protocol of [9]

Recall the RSS-based secure 3PC protocol presented in Sect. 9.2, where all the computations are performed over a finite ring $\mathbb{R}$. Let $F : \{0, 1\}^\lambda \times \{0, 1\}^\lambda \to \mathbb{R}$ be a PRF, where λ is the security parameter. The idea behind the cryptographically-secure variant of the 3PC protocol is to use the PRF F to generate the correlated randomness required in the protocol. That is, the PRF F is used to design a cryptographically-secure protocol for securely computing the functionality $\mathcal{F}_{\mathsf{Zero}}$.

© The Author(s), under exclusive license to Springer Nature Switzerland AG 2022
A. Choudhury and A. Patra, *Secure Multi-Party Computation Against Passive Adversaries*,
Synthesis Lectures on Distributed Computing Theory,
https://doi.org/10.1007/978-3-031-12164-7_13

We first recall the *perfectly-secure* protocol Π_{Zero} (see Fig. 9.7) for computing $\mathcal{F}_{\mathsf{Zero}}$. In the protocol, each party P_i picks a uniformly random element β_i from $\mathbb{R}$ and sends it to its neighbour P_{i-1}, thus ensuring that *both* P_i and P_{i-1} hold β_i. It then follows that $(\beta_1 - \beta_2) + (\beta_2 - \beta_3) + (\beta_3 - \beta_1) = 0$ holds, where P_1, P_2 and P_3 can locally compute $\alpha_1 \overset{def}{=} (\beta_1 - \beta_2)$, $\alpha_2 \overset{def}{=} (\beta_2 - \beta_3)$ and $\alpha_3 \overset{def}{=} (\beta_3 - \beta_1)$ respectively.

In the cryptographically-secure variant of Π_{Zero}, parties P_i and P_{i-1} jointly and securely generate the value β_i *non-interactively* as follows: imagine that the parties have pair-wise shared PRF-key setup, where there are uniformly random PRF keys, say k_1, k_2 and k_3, held by the pair of parties (P_1, P_3), (P_2, P_1) and (P_3, P_2) respectively. Such a setup can be established by the parties themselves at the beginning of the protocol once for all, where P_i can pick the random key k_i and share it with its neighbour P_{i-1}. Notice that the corrupt party will miss one PRF key in the setup. For instance, if P_1 is *corrupt*, then k_3 will not be known to P_1 and so on.

Given the above setup, to jointly generate β_i, party P_i and P_{i-1} can set β_i to $F_{k_i}(id)$, where $id \in \{0, 1\}^\lambda$ is a *unique* and *publicly-known* identifier. It then follows that $(F_{k_1}(id) - F_{k_2}(id)) + (F_{k_2}(id) - F_{k_3}(id)) + (F_{k_3}(id) - F_{k_2}(id)) = 0$ holds, where P_1, P_2 and P_3 can now locally compute $\alpha_1 \overset{def}{=} (F_{k_1}(id) - F_{k_2}(id))$, $\alpha_2 \overset{def}{=} (F_{k_2}(id) - F_{k_3}(id))$ and $\alpha_3 \overset{def}{=} (F_{k_3}(id) - F_{k_2}(id))$ respectively. Intuitively the protocol is secure as the corrupt party will be missing one PRF-key from the setup and hence the corresponding value generated using the key. For instance, if P_1 is *corrupt*, then it will not know the key k_3 and hence the value $F_{k_3}(id)$, implying that α_2 and α_3 are random for P_1, except that $(\alpha_2 + \alpha_3) = -\alpha_1$ holds.

In practice, the identifier id can be a counter value (initialized to a public value) which all the parties can locally increment after every instance of the protocol. The modified protocol called Π_{CrZero} (the Cr stands for cryptographic) is presented in Fig. 13.2. For a pictorial comparison of the protocol Π_{Zero} and Π_{CrZero}, see Fig. 13.1.

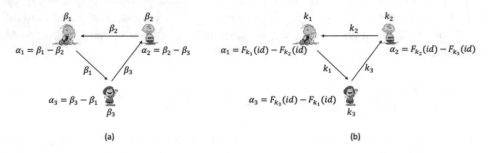

(a)   (b)

Fig. 13.1 Pictorial comparison of the protocol Π_{Zero} and Π_{CrZero}. The first figure illustrates the protocol Π_{Zero} which is perfectly-secure, while the second picture illustrates the protocol Π_{CrZero} which is cryptographically-secure

---

Protocol Π_{CrZero}

Public input: Security parameter λ and the description of a pseudorandom function $F : \{0,1\}^{\lambda} \times \{0,1\}^{\lambda} \rightarrow \mathbb{R}$.
  - **Setup (executed once at the beginning of the 3PC protocol)**:
    - Pick a uniformly random key $k_i \in \{0,1\}^{\lambda}$.
    - Send k_i to P_{i-1}, where $i - 1 \stackrel{def}{=} 3$, if $i = 1$.
  - **Generating randomness**: Upon input $id \in \{0,1\}^{\lambda}$, output $\alpha_i \stackrel{def}{=} F_{k_i}(id) - F_{k_{i+1}}(id)$, where $i + 1 \stackrel{def}{=} 1$, if $i = 3$.

Fig. 13.2 The cryptographically-secure variant of the protocol Π_{Zero}. The above steps are executed by each P_i

One can easily reduce the security of the protocol Π_{CrZero} to the security of the underlying PRF through a standard reduction; we refer the interested readers to [9] for the formal details. Now by plugging in the protocol Π_{CrZero} in the RSS-based 3PC protocol presented in Sect. 9.2, we get a cryptographically-secure variant of the 3PC protocol. For *each* multiplication gate in the circuit, the resultant protocol requires *zero* communication during the pre-processing phase, while during the circuit-evaluation phase, 3 ring elements are communicated, with each party sending 1 ring element to exactly one other party.

13.2   Cryptographically Secure Variant of ASTRA

In this section, we briefly discuss a cryptographically-secure variant of the secure 3PC protocol ASTRA, presented in Fig. 9.3. The idea is to utilize a shared PRF-key setup for generating shared randomness among the parties, thus reducing the interaction among the parties during the pre-processing phase. The setup will be similar to the pair-wise PRF-key setup as used in the previous section. Additionally, an independent PRF-key will be shared among all the 3 parties.

In more detail, let $\{D, E_1, E_2\}$ be the set of 3 parties in the ASTRA 3PC protocol, where D is the *distributor* and E_1, E_2 are the *evaluators*. Then D executes the steps shown in Fig. 13.3 at the beginning of the protocol to generate the shared setup.

Protocol Π_{SetUp}

Public input: Security parameter λ and the description of a pseudorandom function $F : \{0,1\}^{\lambda} \times \{0,1\}^{\lambda} \rightarrow \mathbb{R}$.
  - D executes the following steps:
    - Pick a uniformly random PRF-key $k_{D,E_1} \in \{0,1\}^{\lambda}$ and send it to E_1.
    - Pick a uniformly random PRF-key $k_{D,E_2} \in \{0,1\}^{\lambda}$ and send it to E_2.
    - Pick a uniformly random PRF-key $k_{D,E_1,E_2} \in \{0,1\}^{\lambda}$ and send it to E_1 and E_2.

Fig. 13.3 Steps for generating the PRF-key setup in the cryptographically-secure variant of the ASTRA 3PC protocol

Generating randomness using the PRF-key setup: Using the setup generated through the protocol Π_{SetUp}, the parties can generate shared randomness as follows.

- *Shared randomness between* D *and* E_i: If a random element r from $\mathbb{R}$ is supposed to be picked by D and communicated to *only* E_i, then both D and E_i can *locally* set $r \stackrel{def}{=} F_{k_{\mathsf{D},E_i}}(id)$, where id is a *unique* and *publicly-known* λ-bit identifier. This will ensure that both D and E_i will have the same value r. Moreover, the other evaluator will not know the key k_{D,E_i} and hence the value r will be (pseudo) random from the point of view of the other evaluator.
- *Shared randomness between* D, E_1 *and* E_2: If a random element r from $\mathbb{R}$ is supposed to be picked by D and communicated to *both* E_1 and E_2, then D, E_1 and E_2 can *locally* set $r \stackrel{def}{=} F_{k_{\mathsf{D},E_1,E_2}}(id)$, where id is a *unique* and *publicly-known* λ-bit identifier.

In practice, the identifier id can be a counter value (initialized to a public value) which all the parties can locally increment after every instance of the randomness generation. The above method of generating shared randomness can be used by the parties in the ASTRA 3PC protocol as follows:

- *Shared randomness in the protocol* $\mathsf{Sh}_{\mathsf{MSS}}$: Recall that in the protocol $\mathsf{Sh}_{\mathsf{MSS}}$ for generating a random MSS-sharing of dealer's input (see Fig. 9.9), D randomly selects the OTP-shares $\lambda_{s,1}$ and $\lambda_{s,2}$ and distributes them to the respective evaluators. Now using the key setup, D *need not* have to distribute those values. For instance, if D is the dealer, then D and E_1 can locally sample a (pseudo) random λ_{s_1} using $F_{k_{\mathsf{D},E_1}}(\cdot)$, while D and E_2 can locally sample a (pseudo) random λ_{s_2} using $F_{k_{\mathsf{D},E_2}}(\cdot)$. On the other hand, if E_1 is the dealer, then D and E_1 can locally sample a (pseudo) random λ_{s_1} using $F_{k_{\mathsf{D},E_1}}(\cdot)$, while D, E_1 and E_2 can locally sample a (pseudo) random λ_{s_2} using $F_{k_{\mathsf{D},E_1,E_2}}(\cdot)$. Similar steps are used if E_2 is the dealer. Thus the pre-processing phase of the protocol $\mathsf{Sh}_{\mathsf{MSS}}$ becomes completely *non-interactive*.
- *Shared randomness in the protocol* Π_{MSSMult}: Recall that in the multiplication protocol Π_{MSSMult} (see Fig. 9.12), D selects random OTP-shares $\lambda_{c,1}$ and $\lambda_{c,2}$ and distributes them to E_1 and E_2 respectively. In addition, it also selects random shares $\gamma_{c,1}$ and $\gamma_{c,2}$ for E_1 and E_2 respectively, such that $(\gamma_{c,1} + \gamma_{c,2}) = (\lambda_{a,1} + \lambda_{a,2})(\lambda_{b,1} + \lambda_{b,2})$ holds. Here $(\lambda_{a,1}, \lambda_{a,2})$ and $(\lambda_{b,1}, \lambda_{b,2})$ are the pairs of OTP-shares, corresponding to the inputs of the multiplication gates.

  Now using the shared PRF-key setup, D *need not* have to communicate the OTP-shares $\lambda_{c,1}$ and $\lambda_{c,2}$. Namely, using $F_{k_{\mathsf{D},E_i}}(\cdot)$, parties D and E_i can *locally* sample a (pseudo) random $\lambda_{c,i}$. Moreover, a (pseudo) random $\gamma_{c,1}$ can be *locally* sampled by D and E_1 using $F_{k_{\mathsf{D},E_1}}(\cdot)$. Hence, D now *only* needs to communicate $\gamma_{c,2} \stackrel{def}{=} (\lambda_{a,1} + \lambda_{a,2})(\lambda_{b,1} + \lambda_{b,2}) - \gamma_{c,1}$ to E_2.[1] Thus the pre-processing phase of the protocol Π_{MSSMult} now requires a communication of only 1 ring element.

---

[1] Note that $\gamma_{c,2}$ *cannot* be locally sampled by D and E_2 using $F_{k_{\mathsf{D},E_2}}(\cdot)$, as the sampled $\gamma_{c,2}$ *need not* satisfy the condition $(\gamma_{c,1} + \gamma_{c,2}) = (\lambda_{a,1} + \lambda_{a,2})(\lambda_{b,1} + \lambda_{b,2})$.

One can easily reduce the security of the cryptographically-secure variant of the ASTRA protocol to the security of the underlying PRF through a standard reduction; we refer the interested readers to [47] for the formal details. For *each* multiplication gate in the circuit, the new protocol requires a communication of 1 ring element during the pre-processing phase, while during the circuit-evaluation phase, 2 ring elements are communicated. While the *total* communication cost per-multiplication gate is the same as the cryptographically-secure variant of the RSS-based secure 3PC protocol discussed in the previous section (namely 3 ring elements), the costs are different if we consider only the circuit-evaluation phase. Namely, the ASTRA protocol requires 2 ring elements, while the RSS-based protocol requires 3 ring elements.

13.3 Dealing with Malicious Adversaries

We conclude this chapter by briefly discussing the challenges faced by the cryptographically-secure 3PC protocols in the presence of a *malicious* corruption. For the RSS-based 3PC protocol, the corrupt party can either fail the reconstruction protocol or fail the evaluation of multiplication gates by producing incorrect values.[2] For the MSS-based 3PC protocol, if the distributor is corrupt, then it can distribute inconsistent keys to the evaluators while setting up the PRF keys. For instance, while setting up the key $F_{k_{\mathsf{D},E_1,E_2}}(\cdot)$, a *maliciously-corrupt* D can send *different* copies of $F_{k_{\mathsf{D},E_1,E_2}}(\cdot)$ to E_1 and E_2. Consequently, the inputs of the evaluators will *not* be secret-shared as per the semantics of MSS. On the other hand, the inputs of a corrupt D *may not* be secret-shared as per the semantics of MSS, if it sends different copies of OTP-encryptions of its inputs to the evaluators. Additionally, a corrupt D can distribute inconsistent data corresponding to the multiplication gates during the pre-processing phase. If one of the evaluators is corrupt, then it can send incorrect values to the other evaluator during the evaluation of multiplication gates in circuit-evaluation phase. Additionally, the corrupt party can always fail the reconstruction protocol by providing incorrect shares.

To deal with the above problems, the parties need to incorporate verification mechanisms to ensure the parties follow the protocol instructions, without revealing anything additional about the values of the honest parties. However, the resultant maliciously-secure 3PC protocols have to settle with the notion of security with abort (see [47, 50, 108, 121, 130] for more details). The work of [38] shows how to deal with malicious corruption in the MSS-based protocol and achieve full security.

---

[2] We stress that inputs of the corrupt party *will be* secret-shared as per the semantics of the RSS. For instance, if P_1 is corrupt, then the value s_1 sent by P_1 to P_2, along with the values s_2 and s_3 (generated by the honest parties), define the input of P_1. That is, $s \stackrel{def}{=} s_1 + s_2 + s_3$.

Bibliography

1. Shamir's Secret Sharing. Wikipedia article
2. I. Abraham, G. Asharov, A. Yanai, Efficient perfectly secure computation with optimal resilience, in *TCC*. Lecture Notes in Computer Science, vol. 13043 (Springer, 2021), pp. 66–96
3. A. Appan, A. Chandramouli, A. Choudhury, Perfectly-secure synchronous MPC with asynchronous fallback guarantees, in *IACR Cryptology ePrint Archive* (2022), p. 109
4. B. Applebaum, Garbling XOR gates "for free" in the standard model. J. Cryptol. **29**(3), 552–576 (2016)
5. B. Applebaum, Z. Brakerski, R. Tsabary, Perfect secure computation in two rounds, in *TCC*. Lecture Notes in Computer Science, vol. 11239 (Springer, 2018), pp. 152–174
6. B. Applebaum, Z. Brakerski, R. Tsabary, Perfect secure computation in two rounds. SIAM J. Comput. **50**(1), 68–97 (2021)
7. B. Applebaum, Y. Ishai, E. Kushilevitz, How to garble arithmetic circuits. SIAM J. Comput. **43**(2), 905–929 (2014)
8. B. Applebaum, E. Kachlon, A. Patra, The round complexity of perfect MPC with active security and optimal resiliency, in *FOCS* (IEEE, 2020), pp. 1277–1284
9. T. Araki, J. Furukawa, Y. Lindell, A. Nof, K. Ohara, High-throughput semi-honest secure three-party computation with an honest majority, in *CCS* (ACM, 2016), pp. 805–817
10. G. Asharov, A. Jain, A. López-Alt, E. Tromer, V. Vaikuntanathan, D. Wichs, Multiparty computation with low communication, computation and interaction via threshold FHE, in *EUROCRYPT*. Lecture Notes in Computer Science, vol. 7237 (Springer, 2012), pp. 483–501
11. G. Asharov, Y. Lindell, A full proof of the BGW protocol for perfectly secure multiparty computation. J. Cryptol. **30**(1), 58–151 (2017)
12. M. Ball, T. Malkin, M. Rosulek, Garbling gadgets for boolean and arithmetic circuits, in *CCS* (ACM, 2016), pp. 565–577
13. L. Bangalore, A. Choudhury, A. Patra, The power of shunning: efficient asynchronous byzantine agreement revisited. J. ACM **67**(3), 14:1–14:59 (2020)
14. J. Bar-Ilan, D. Beaver, Non-cryptographic fault-tolerant computing in constant number of rounds of interaction, in *PODC* (ACM, 1989), pp. 201–209

© The Editor(s) (if applicable) and The Author(s), under exclusive license to Springer
Nature Switzerland AG 2022
A. Choudhury and A. Patra, *Secure Multi-Party Computation Against Passive Adversaries*,
Synthesis Lectures on Distributed Computing Theory,
https://doi.org/10.1007/978-3-031-12164-7

15. C. Baum, E. Orsini, P. Scholl, Efficient secure multiparty computation with identifiable abort, in *TCC*. Lecture Notes in Computer Science, vol. 9985 (2016), pp. 461–490

16. D. Beaver, Efficient multiparty protocols using circuit randomization, in *CRYPTO*. Lecture Notes in Computer Science, vol. 576 (Springer, 1991), pp. 420–432

17. D. Beaver, Precomputing oblivious transfer, in *CRYPTO*. Lecture Notes in Computer Science, vol. 963 (Springer, 1995), pp. 97–109

18. D. Beaver, S. Micali, P. Rogaway, The round complexity of secure protocols (Extended Abstract), in *STOC* (ACM, 1990), pp. 503–513

19. Z. Beerliová-Trubíniová, M. Hirt, Efficient multi-party computation with dispute control, in *TCC*. Lecture Notes in Computer Science, vol. 3876 (Springer, 2006), pp 305–328

20. Z. Beerliová-Trubíniová, M. Hirt, Simple and efficient perfectly-secure asynchronous MPC, in *ASIACRYPT*. Lecture Notes in Computer Science, vol. 4833 (Springer, 2007), pp. 376–392

21. Z. Beerliová-Trubíniová, M. Hirt, Perfectly-secure MPC with linear communication complexity, in *TCC*. Lecture Notes in Computer Science, vol. 4948 (Springer, 2008), pp. 213–230

22. M. Bellare, V.T. Hoang, P. Rogaway, Foundations of garbled circuits, in *CCS* (ACM, 2012), pp. 784–796

23. A. Ben-Efraim, Y. Lindell, E. Omri, Optimizing semi-honest secure multiparty computation for the internet, in *CCS* (ACM, 2016), pp. 578–590

24. M. Ben-Or, R. Canetti, O. Goldreich, Asynchronous secure computation, in *STOC* (ACM, 1993), pp. 52–61

25. M. Ben-Or, S. Goldwasser, A. Wigderson, Completeness theorems for non-cryptographic fault-tolerant distributed computation (Extended Abstract), in *STOC* (ACM, 1988), pp. 1–10

26. M. Ben-Or, B. Kelmer, T. Rabin, Asynchronous secure computations with optimal resilience (Extended Abstract), in *PODC* (ACM, 1994), pp. 183–192

27. E. Ben-Sasson, S. Fehr, R. Ostrovsky, Near-linear unconditionally-secure multiparty computation with a dishonest minority, in *CRYPTO*. Lecture Notes in Computer Science, vol. 7417 (Springer, 2012), pp. 663–680

28. R. Bendlin, I. Damgård, C. Orlandi, S. Zakarias, Semi-homomorphic encryption and multiparty computation, in *EUROCRYPT*. Lecture Notes in Computer Science, vol. 6632 (Springer, 2011), pp. 169–188

29. F. Benhamouda, H. Lin, k-round multiparty computation from k-round oblivious transfer via garbled interactive circuits, in *EUROCRYPT*. Lecture Notes in Computer Science, vol. 10821 (Springer, 2018), pp. 500–532

30. N.L. Biggs, *Discrete Mathematics* (Oxford University Press, 2002)

31. G.R. Blakley, Safeguarding cryptographic keys, in *AFIPS National Computer Conference* (IEEE, 1979), pp. 313–317

32. E. Blum, J. Katz, J. Loss, Synchronous consensus with optimal asynchronous fallback guarantees, in *TCC*. Lecture Notes in Computer Science, vol. 11891 (Springer, 2019), pp. 131–150

33. E. Blum, C.L. Zhang, J. Loss, Always have a backup plan: fully secure synchronous MPC with asynchronous fallback, in *CRYPTO*. Lecture Notes in Computer Science, vol. 12171 (Springer, 2020), pp. 707–731

34. D. Bogdanov, S. Laur, J. Willemson, Sharemind: a framework for fast privacy-preserving computations, in *ESORICS*. Lecture Notes in Computer Science, vol. 5283 (Springer, 2008), pp. 192–206

35. D. Bogdanov, R. Talviste, J. Willemson, Deploying secure multi-party computation for financial data analysis—(Short Paper), in *Financial Cryptography and Data Security*. Lecture Notes in Computer Science, vol. 7397 (Springer, 2012), pp. 57–64

36. P. Bogetoft, D.L. Christensen, I. Damgård, M. Geisler, T.P. Jakobsen, M. Krøigaard, J.D. Nielsen, J.B. Nielsen, K. Nielsen, J. Pagter, M.I. Schwartzbach, T. Toft, Secure multiparty

computation goes live, in *Financial Cryptography and Data Security*. Lecture Notes in Computer Science, vol. 5628 (Springer, 2009), pp. 325–343

37. D. Boneh, V. Shoup, *A Graduate Course in Applied Cryptography* (2020)
38. E. Boyle, N. Gilboa, Y. Ishai, A. Nof, Practical fully secure three-party computation via sublinear distributed zero-knowledge proofs, in *CCS* (ACM, 2019), pp. 869–886
39. M. Byali, H. Chaudhari, A. Patra, A. Suresh, FLASH: fast and robust framework for privacy-preserving machine learning. Proc. Priv. Enhancing Technol. **2020**(2), 459–480 (2020)
40. M. Byali, A. Joseph, A. Patra, D. Ravi, Fast secure computation for small population over the internet, in *CCS* (ACM, 2018), pp. 677–694
41. R. Canetti, Security and composition of multiparty cryptographic protocols. J. Cryptol. **13**(1), 143–202 (2000)
42. R. Canetti, Universally composable security. J. ACM 67(5):28:1–28:94 (2020)
43. R. Canetti, U. Feige, O. Goldreich, M. Naor, Adaptively secure multi-party computation, in *STOC* (ACM, 1996), pp. 639–648
44. A. Chandramouli, A. Choudhury, A. Patra, A survey on perfectly-secure verifiable secret-sharing, in *IACR Cryptology ePrint Archive* (2021), p. 445
45. N. Chandran, J.A. Garay, P. Mohassel, S. Vusirikala, Efficient, constant-round and actively secure MPC: beyond the three-party case, in *ACM CCS* (2017)
46. N. Chandran, D. Gupta, A. Rastogi, R. Sharma, S. Tripathi, EzPC: programmable and efficient secure two-party computation for machine learning, in *EuroS&P* (IEEE, 2019), pp. 496–511
47. H. Chaudhari, A. Choudhury, A. Patra, A. Suresh, ASTRA: high throughput 3PC over rings with application to secure prediction, in *CCSW@CCS* (ACM, 2019), pp. 81–92
48. H. Chaudhari, R. Rachuri, A. Suresh, Trident: efficient 4PC framework for privacy preserving machine learning, in *NDSS* (The Internet Society, 2020)
49. D. Chaum, C. Crépeau, I. Damgård, Multiparty unconditionally secure protocols (Extended Abstract), in *STOC* (ACM, 1988), pp. 11–19
50. K. Chida, D. Genkin, K. Hamada, D. Ikarashi, R. Kikuchi, Y. Lindell, A. Nof, Fast large-scale honest-majority MPC for malicious adversaries, in *CRYPTO*. Lecture Notes in Computer Science, vol. 10993 (Springer, 2018), pp. 34–64
51. S.G. Choi, J. Katz, R. Kumaresan, H.S. Zhou, On the Security of the "Free-XOR" technique, in *TCC*. Lecture Notes in Computer Science, vol. 7194 (Springer, 2012), pp. 39–53
52. B. Chor, S. Goldwasser, S. Micali, B. Awerbuch, Verifiable secret sharing and achieving simultaneity in the presence of faults (Extended Abstract), in *FOCS* (IEEE Computer Society, 1985), pp. 383–395
53. A. Choudhury, Protocols for reliable and secure message transmission, in *IACR Cryptology ePrint Archive*, vol. 2010 (2010), p. 281
54. A. Choudhury, A. Patra, An efficient framework for unconditionally secure multiparty computation. IEEE Trans. Inf. Theory **63**(1), 428–468 (2017)
55. G. Couteau, P. Rindal, S. Raghuraman, Silver: silent VOLE and oblivious transfer from hardness of decoding structured LDPC codes, in *CRYPTO*. Lecture Notes in Computer Science, vol. 12827 (Springer, 2021), pp. 502–534
56. R. Cramer, I. Damgård, S. Dziembowski, M. Hirt, T. Rabin, Efficient multiparty computations secure against an adaptive adversary, in *EUROCRYPT*. Lecture Notes in Computer Science, vol. 1592 (Springer, 1999), pp. 311–326
57. R. Cramer, I. Damgård, U.M. Maurer, General secure multi-party computation from any linear secret-sharing scheme, in *EUROCRYPT*. Lecture Notes in Computer Science, vol. 1807 (Springer, 2000), pp. 316–334

58. R. Cramer, I. Damgård, J.B. Nielsen, Multiparty computation from threshold homomorphic encryption, in *EUROCRYPT*. Lecture Notes in Computer Science, vol. 2045 (Springer, 2001), pp. 280–299

59. C. Crépeau, Equivalence between two flavours of oblivious transfers, in *CRYPTO*. Lecture Notes in Computer Science, vol. 293 (Springer, 1987), pp. 350–354

60. I. Damgård, Y. Ishai, M. Krøigaard, Perfectly secure multiparty computation and the computational overhead of cryptography, in *EUROCRYPT*. Lecture Notes in Computer Science, vol. 6110 (Springer, 2010), pp. 445–465

61. I. Damgård, K.G. Larsen, J.B. Nielsen, Communication lower bounds for statistically secure MPC, with or without preprocessing, in *CRYPTO*. Lecture Notes in Computer Science, vol. 11693 (Springer, 2019), pp. 61–84

62. I. Damgård, J.B. Nielsen, Improved non-committing encryption schemes based on a general complexity assumption, in *CRYPTO*. Lecture Notes in Computer Science, vol. 1880 (Springer, 2000), pp. 432–450

63. I. Damgård, J.B. Nielsen, Scalable and unconditionally secure multiparty computation, in *CRYPTO*. Lecture Notes in Computer Science, vol. 4622 (Springer, 2007), pp. 572–590

64. I. Damgård, V. Pastro, N.P. Smart, S. Zakarias, Multiparty computation from somewhat homomorphic encryption, in *CRYPTO*. Lecture Notes in Computer Science, vol. 7417 (Springer, 2012), pp. 643–662

65. G. Deligios, M. Hirt, C. Liu-Zhang, Round-efficient byzantine agreement and multi-party computation with asynchronous fallback, in *TCC*. Lecture Notes in Computer Science, vol. 13042 (Springer, 2021), pp. 623–653

66. D. Demmler, T. Schneider, M. Zohner, ABY—a framework for efficient mixed-protocol secure two-party computation, in *NDSS* (The Internet Society, 2015)

67. D. Dolev, C. Dwork, O. Waarts, M. Yung, Perfectly secure message transmission. J. ACM **40**(1), 17–47 (1993)

68. S. Even, O. Goldreich, A. Lempel, A randomized protocol for signing contracts. Commun. ACM **28**(6), 637–647 (1985)

69. U. Feige, J. Kilian, M. Naor, A minimal model for secure computation (Extended Abstract), in *STOC* (ACM, 1994), pp. 554–563

70. M.K. Franklin, M. Yung, Communication complexity of secure computation (Extended Abstract). *STOC* (1992), pp. 699–710

71. J. Furukawa, Y. Lindell, A. Nof, O. Weinstein, High-throughput secure three-party computation for malicious adversaries and an honest majority, in *EUROCRYPT*. Lecture Notes in Computer Science, vol. 10211 (2017), pp. 225–255

72. S. Garg, A. Srinivasan, Two-round multiparty secure computation from minimal assumptions, in *EUROCRYPT*. Lecture Notes in Computer Science, vol. 10821 (Springer, 2018), pp. 468–499

73. G. Garimella, B. Pinkas, M. Rosulek, N. Trieu, A. Yanai, Oblivious key-value stores and amplification for private set intersection, in *CRYPTO*. Lecture Notes in Computer Science, vol. 12826 (Springer, 2021), pp. 395–425

74. M. Geisler, Viff: virtual ideal functionality framework (2007)

75. R. Gennaro, M.O. Rabin, T. Rabin, Simplified VSS and fast-track multiparty computations with applications to threshold cryptography, in *PODC* (ACM, 1998), pp. 101–111

76. C. Gentry, Fully homomorphic encryption using ideal lattices, in *STOC* (ACM, 2009), pp. 169–178

77. N. Gilboa, Two party RSA key generation, in *CRYPTO*, ed. by M.J. Wiener. Lecture Notes in Computer Science, vol. 1666 (Springer, 1999), pp. 116–129

78. O. Goldreich, *The Foundations of Cryptography—Basic Applications*, vol. 2 (Cambridge University Press, 2004)

79. O. Goldreich, L.A. Levin, A hard-core predicate for all one-way functions, in *STOC* (ACM, 1989), pp. 25–32
80. O. Goldreich, S. Micali, A. Wigderson, How to play any mental game or a completeness theorem for protocols with honest majority, in *STOC* (ACM, 1987), pp. 218–229
81. O. Goldreich, R.D. Rothblum, Enhancements of trapdoor permutations. J. Cryptol. **26**(3), 484–512 (2013)
82. S. Goldwasser, S. Micali, Probabilistic encryption. J. Comput. Syst. Sci. **28**(2), 270–299 (1984)
83. V. Goyal, Y. Liu, Y. Song, Communication-efficient unconditional MPC with guaranteed output delivery, in *CRYPTO*. Lecture Notes in Computer Science, vol. 11693 (Springer, 2019), pp. 85–114
84. V. Goyal, A. O'Neill, V. Rao, Correlated-input secure hash functions, in *TCC*. Lecture Notes in Computer Science, vol. 6597 (Springer, 2011), pp. 182–200
85. V. Goyal, Y. Song, C. Zhu, Guaranteed output delivery comes free in honest majority MPC, in *CRYPTO*. Lecture Notes in Computer Science, vol. 12171 (Springer, 2020), pp. 618–646
86. S. Gueron, Y. Lindell, A. Nof, B. Pinkas, Fast garbling of circuits under standard assumptions, in *CCS* (ACM, 2015)
87. S. Halevi, Y. Lindell, B. Pinkas, Secure computation on the web: computing without simultaneous interaction, in *CRYPTO*. Lecture Notes in Computer Science, vol. 6841 (Springer, 2011), pp. 132–150
88. C. Hazay, Y. Lindell, *Efficient Secure Two-Party Protocols—Techniques and Constructions* Information Security and Cryptography. (Springer, Berlin, 2010)
89. C. Hazay, Y. Lindell, A. Patra, Adaptively secure computation with partial erasures, in *PODC* (ACM, 2015), pp. 291–300
90. B. Hemenway, S. Lu, R. Ostrovsky, W.W. IV, High-precision secure computation of satellite collision probabilities, in *SCN*. Lecture Notes in Computer Science, vol. 9841 (Springer, 2016), pp. 169–187
91. M. Hirt, U.M. Maurer, Complete characterization of adversaries tolerable in secure multi-party computation (Extended Abstract), in *PODC* (ACM, 1997), pp. 25–34
92. M. Hirt, U.M. Maurer, Player simulation and general adversary structures in perfect multiparty computation. J. Cryptol. **13**(1), 31–60 (2000)
93. M. Hirt, D. Tschudi, Efficient general-adversary multi-party computation, in *ASIACRYPT*. Lecture Notes in Computer Science, vol. 8270 (Springer, 2013), pp. 181–200
94. R. Impagliazzo, S. Rudich, Limits on the provable consequences of one-way permutations, in *STOC* (ACM, 1989), pp. 44–61
95. Y. Ishai, J. Kilian, K. Nissim, E. Petrank, Extending oblivious transfers efficiently, in *CRYPTO*. Lecture Notes in Computer Science, vol. 2729 (Springer, 2003), pp. 145–161
96. Y. Ishai, E. Kushilevitz, Randomizing polynomials: a new representation with applications to round-efficient secure computation, in *FOCS* (IEEE Computer Society, 2000), pp. 294–304
97. Y. Ishai, E. Kushilevitz, Perfect constant-round secure computation via perfect randomizing polynomials, in *ICALP*. Lecture Notes in Computer Science, vol. 2380 (Springer, 2002), pp. 244–256
98. M. Ito, A. Saito, T. Nishizeki, Secret sharing schemes realizing general access structures, in *Global Telecommunication Conference, Globecom* (IEEE Computer Society, 1987), pp. 99–102
99. Z. Jafargholi, D. Wichs, Adaptive security of Yao's garbled circuits, in *TCC*. Lecture Notes in Computer Science, vol. 9985 (2016), pp. 433–458
100. L. Kamm, J. Willemson, Secure floating point arithmetic and private satellite collision analysis. Int. J. Inf. Sec. **14**(6), 531–548 (2015)
101. J. Katz, V. Kolesnikov, X. Wang, Improved non-interactive zero knowledge with applications to post-quantum signatures, in *CCS* (ACM, 2018), pp. 525–537

102. J. Katz, Y. Lindell, *Introduction to Modern Cryptography*, 2nd edn (CRC Press, 2014)
103. M. Keller, E. Orsini, P. Scholl, MASCOT: faster malicious arithmetic secure computation with oblivious transfer, in *CCS* (ACM, 2016), pp. 830–842
104. J. Kilian, Founding cryptography on oblivious transfer, in *STOC* (ACM, 1988), pp. 20–31
105. V. Kolesnikov, Gate evaluation secret sharing and secure one-round two-party computation, in *ASIACRYPT*. Lecture Notes in Computer Science, vol. 3788 (Springer, 2005), pp. 136–155
106. V. Kolesnikov, P. Mohassel, M. Rosulek, FleXOR: flexible garbling for XOR gates that beats free-XOR, in *CRYPTO*. Lecture Notes in Computer Science, vol. 8617 (Springer, 2014), pp. 440–457
107. V. Kolesnikov, T. Schneider, Improved garbled circuit: free XOR gates and applications, in *ICALP*. Lecture Notes in Computer Science, vol. 5126 (Springer, 2008), pp. 486–498
108. N. Koti, M. Pancholi, A. Patra, A. Suresh, SWIFT: super-fast and robust privacy-preserving machine learning, in *USENIX Security Symposium* (USENIX Association, 2021), pp. 2651–2668
109. K. Kurosawa, K. Suzuki, Truly efficient 2-round perfectly secure message transmission scheme, in *EUROCRYPT*. Lecture Notes in Computer Science, vol. 4965 (Springer, 2008), pp. 324–340
110. E. Kushilevitz, Y. Lindell, T. Rabin, Information-theoretically secure protocols and security under composition. SIAM J. Comput. **39**(5), 2090–2112 (2010)
111. E. Larraia, E. Orsini, N.P. Smart, Dishonest majority multi-party computation for binary circuits, in *CRYPTO*. Lecture Notes in Computer Science, vol. 8617 (Springer, 2014), pp. 495–512
112. J. Launchbury, D. Archer, T. DuBuisson, E. Mertens, Application-scale secure multiparty computation, in *European Symposium on Programming*. Lecture Notes in Computer Science, vol. 8410 (Springer, 2014), pp. 8–26
113. Y. Lindell, Fast cut-and-choose based protocols for malicious and covert adversaries, in *CRYPTO*. Lecture Notes in Computer Science, vol. 8043 (Springer, 2013), pp. 1–17
114. Y. Lindell, B. Pinkas, *Privacy Preserving Data Mining*, in *CRYPTO*. Lecture Notes in Computer Science, vol. 1880 (Springer, 2000), pp. 36–54
115. Y. Lindell, B. Pinkas, An efficient protocol for secure two-party computation in the presence of malicious adversaries, in *IACR Cryptology ePrint Archive* (2008), p. 49
116. Y. Lindell, B. Pinkas, A proof of security of Yao's protocol for two-party computation. J. Cryptol. **22**(2), 161–188 (2009)
117. Y. Lindell, B. Pinkas, Secure two-party computation via cut-and-choose oblivious transfer, in *TCC*. Lecture Notes in Computer Science, vol. 6597 (Springer, 2011), pp. 329–346
118. Y. Lindell, B. Riva, Cut-and-choose yao-based secure computation in the online/offline and batch settings, in *CRYPTO*. Lecture Notes in Computer Science, vol. 8617 (Springer, 2014), pp. 476–494
119. Y. Lindell, H. Zarosim, On the feasibility of extending oblivious transfer, in *TCC*. Lecture Notes in Computer Science, vol. 7785 (Springer, 2013), pp. 519–538
120. U.M. Maurer, Secure multi-party computation made simple. Discret. Appl. Math. **154**(2), 370–381 (2006)
121. P. Mohassel, P. Rindal, ABY^3: a mixed protocol framework for machine learning, in *CCS* (ACM, 2018), pp. 35–52
122. P. Mohassel, M. Rosulek, Y. Zhang, Fast and secure three-party computation: the garbled circuit approach, in *CCS* (ACM, 2015), pp. 591–602
123. P. Mohassel, Y. Zhang, SecureML: a system for scalable privacy-preserving machine learning, in *IEEE Symposium on Security and Privacy* (IEEE Computer Society, 2017), pp. 19–38
124. A. Momose, L. Ren, Multi-threshold byzantine fault tolerance, in *CCS* (ACM, 2021), pp. 1686–1699

125. M. Naor, B. Pinkas, Oblivious transfer and polynomial evaluation, in *STOC* (ACM, 1999), pp. 245–254

126. M. Naor, B. Pinkas, R. Sumner, Privacy preserving auctions and mechanism design, in *EC* (ACM, 1999), pp. 129–139

127. A. Patra, A. Choudhury, C. Pandu Rangan, Efficient asynchronous verifiable secret sharing and multiparty computation. J. Cryptology **28**(1), 49–109 (2015)

128. A. Patra, D. Ravi, On the power of hybrid networks in multi-party computation. IEEE Trans. Inf. Theory **64**(6), 4207–4227 (2018)

129. A. Patra, T. Schneider, A. Suresh, H. Yalame, ABY2.0: improved mixed-protocol secure two-party computation, in *USENIX Security Symposium* (USENIX Association, 2021), pp. 2165–2182

130. A. Patra, A. Suresh, BLAZE: blazing fast privacy-preserving machine learning, in *NDSS* (The Internet Society, 2020)

131. B. Pinkas, T. Schneider, N.P. Smart, S.C. Williams, Secure two-party computation is practical, in *ASIACRYPT*. Lecture Notes in Computer Science, vol. 5912 (Springer, 2009), pp. 250–267

132. M.O. Rabin, How to exchange secrets with oblivious transfer, in *IACR Cryptology ePrint Archive*, vol. 2005 (2005), p. 187

133. T. Rabin, M. Ben-Or, Verifiable secret sharing and multiparty protocols with honest majority (Extended Abstract), in *STOC* (ACM, 1989), pp. 73–85

134. M. Rosulek, L. Roy, Three halves make a whole? beating the half-gates lower bound for garbled circuits, in *CRYPTO*. Lecture Notes in Computer Science, vol. 12825 (Springer, 2021), pp. 94–124

135. A. Shamir, How to share a secret. Commun. ACM **22**(11), 612–613 (1979)

136. A. Shelat, C. Shen, Fast two-party secure computation with minimal assumptions, in *CCS* (ACM, 2013), pp. 523–534

137. K. Srinathan, A. Narayanan, C. Pandu Rangan, Optimal perfectly secure message transmission, in *CRYPTO*. Lecture Notes in Computer Science, vol. 3152 (Springer, 2004), pp. 545–561

138. A.C. Yao, Protocols for secure computations (Extended Abstract), in *FOCS* (IEEE Computer Society, 1982), pp. 160–164

139. S. Zahur, M. Rosulek, D. Evans, Two halves make a whole—reducing data transfer in garbled circuits using half gates, in *EUROCRYPT*. Lecture Notes in Computer Science, vol. 9057 (Springer, 2015), pp. 220–250

Printed in the United States
by Baker & Taylor Publisher Services